HOPE IN A SCATTERING TIME

Hope in a Scattering Time

A Life of Christopher Lasch

Eric Miller

WILLIAM B. EERDMANS PUBLISHING COMPANY

GRAND RAPIDS, MICHIGAN / CAMBRIDGE, U.K.

Published 2010 by
Wm. B. Eerdmans Publishing Co.
2140 Oak Industrial Drive N.E., Grand Rapids, Michigan 49505 /
P.O. Box 163, Cambridge CB3 9PU U.K.

Printed in the United States of America

16 15 14 13 12 11 10   7 6 5 4 3 2 1

Library of Congress Cataloging-in-Publication Data

Miller, Eric, 1966-
Hope in a scattering time: a life of Christopher Lasch / Eric Miller.
        p.   cm.
ISBN 978-0-8028-1769-3 (cloth: alk. paper)
1. Lasch, Christopher. 2. Christian biography. 3. Christianity and culture
        — United States. 4. United States — Social conditions — 1980-
5. United States — Moral conditions. 6. Social values.   I. Title.

BR1725.L255M55   2010
306.0973 — dc22

2010005622

www.eerdmans.com

For Denise

Contents

Acknowledgments

I f books begin in the hope of conversation, many of my hopes have already been realized. This book itself is testament of a long conversation with Christopher Lasch, one that is far from over. For turning an interest in Lasch toward a book about him, I thank Guy Alchon. He taught me much about Lasch and Lasch's world, and treated me as a graduate student to a rare and fruitful mixture of sympathy and provocation. Also at the University of Delaware, Christine Leigh Heyrman and Gary May joined Guy to provide gracious support, criticism, and encouragement. Sven Dubie, Paul Gottfried, and Eugene McCarraher generously helped me to think about Lasch, and my thinking about Lasch, early on.

Geneva College has furnished me above all with friendships. Ken Carson, Jeffrey Cole, Robert Frazier, David Guthrie, Mark Haas, Suhail Hanna, Shirley Kilpatrick, and Howard Mattson-Boze offered rich discussion and true encouragement along the way. I especially thank Bradshaw Frey for political and intellectual companionship. His own thinking about Lasch, coming to me by way of much splendid conversation, buoyed me time and again. Among the many students who have read Lasch with me and offered keen insight, I'm particularly grateful to Joshua Earl, Matthew Stewart, and Adam Parsons, whose work on Lasch, impressive in its own right, improved mine.

Through its faculty development program Geneva College provided steady financial sustenance for this long endeavor including a timely sabbatical in the fall of 2006. The Charlotte and Walter Kohler Charitable Trust, through the Howard Center for Family, Religion, and Society, awarded me fellowships on two occasions that facilitated the conversion of a dissertation into a book. My thanks especially to Howard Center president Allan C. Carlson for making this support possible. By establishing the Louise S. Walker History Endowment, William, Susan, and Lucas Kriner opened new possibilities for research and writing at Geneva, and helped make my work at the end of this project possible. Their generosity toward me and toward the college has had truly transformative effects.

One of the sources of truest pleasure in the writing of this book came through the exchanges I had with various students, colleagues, and friends of Lasch. For immeasurably advancing my understanding of Lasch through letters, e-mails, conversations, and interviews I thank Gar Alperovitz, Dominic Aquila, Edwin Barber, Robert Bellah, Casey Blake, Scott Caton, David Chappell, Thomas Cole, Jean Bethke Elshtain, Gerald Graff, Bradley Gundlach, Rochelle Gurstein, David Kettler, David Marr, Kevin Mattson, Christopher Shannon, Catherine Tumber, Robert Westbrook, and the late John Updike. Elisabeth Lasch-Quinn also graciously encouraged me to pursue this project at its inception.

For helping me to formulate my thinking in concrete ways, I thank the history departments of Messiah College and Grove City College (and particularly Gillis Harp), which invited me to give lectures on Lasch and then treated me to superb discussion and argument afterward. Don Eberly and Wilfred McClay also asked me to contribute chapters on Lasch to volumes that each edited — a significant aid to my thinking and writing. I happily note, too, that Wilfred McClay has provided a steady stream of ideas, critique, and exhortation related to this book. The 2005 colloquium he organized on *The Culture of Narcissism* proved to be enormously enjoyable and instructive.

The staff of the Department of Rare Books and Special Collections at the University of Rochester ably assisted me in my work at the Lasch Papers; Mary Huth was a particularly helpful and companionable guide through the collection. The McCartney Library staff at Geneva College came often to my aid helping me to secure rare and distant documents.

The late Robert Cummings, a historian at Truman State University, compiled over the course of several years a truly remarkable bibliography of not just Lasch's published writings but also reviews of Lasch's books, writing about Lasch, and Lasch's appearances in the media. He generously has made this bibliography available at the

Lasch Papers website. I cannot begin to estimate the magnitude of my debt to him.

This book is heavily dependent on the good faith of many people, too numerous to list here, who have graciously permitted me to quote from their papers. I wish, though, to direct particular thanks to Mr. and Mrs. Gerald Allen, who made available to me a copy of Zora Schaupp Lasch's autobiography. Robert Westbrook was unfailingly helpful and accommodating in his role as the executor of the Lasch Papers. My deepest thanks go to Nell Lasch for making these papers available for research. They are, quite simply, a treasure.

In a show of outrageous hospitality, Scott and Bonnie Caton, and Scott's parents, Brenon and Bonnie Caton, gave me a home away from home during my research expeditions to Rochester, complete with food, shelter, and friendship.

The William B. Eerdmans Publishing Company took an interest in this book in a way that cheered me and spurred me on. My editor, David Bratt, has been a writer's true friend, offering sage counsel, honest reaction, and, above all, belief.

John Fea and Jay Green, of Messiah College and Covenant College respectively, help me to remember why I in their company started down this path many years ago. Their courage and encouragement, and their dedication to pilgrimage, have led me to a place far better than I would otherwise have known.

The lives of my parents, William and Kathleen Miller, brim with faith, hope, and love: gifts which have made possible, among many other improbable things, the writing of this book. My parents-in-law, Donald and Mary Wagner, have been parents indeed.

The lives of my sons, Ian, Luke, and Christopher, remind me daily why biography matters. And the story Denise has fashioned of our lives has made the world real to me, more real than any book can possibly capture. Still, I offer this one gratefully to her.

Abbreviations

ALS   Autographed Letter Signed
CL   Christopher Lasch
CLP   Christopher Lasch Papers, Department of Rare Books and Special Collections, Rush Rhees Library, University of Rochester, Rochester, New York. Unless otherwise noted, all correspondence cited is from this collection.
NL   Nell Lasch
RL   Robert Lasch
RLP   Robert Lasch Papers, Wisconsin Historical Society, Madison, Wisconsin
TL   Typed Letter
TLS   Typed Letter Signed
ZL   Zora Lasch

Books by Christopher Lasch

AAL   *The Agony of the American Left.* New York: Knopf, 1969.
ALRR   *The American Liberals and the Russian Revolution.* New York: Columbia University Press, 1962.
CON   *The Culture of Narcissism: American Life in an Age of Diminishing Expectations.* New York: Norton, 1979.
HHW   *Haven in a Heartless World: The Family Besieged.* New York: Basic Books, 1977.
MS   *The Minimal Self: Psychic Survival in Troubled Times.* New York: Norton, 1984.

NR   *The New Radicalism in America, 1889-1963: The Intellectual as a Social Type.* New York: Knopf, 1965.

PS   *Plain Style: A Guide to Written English.* Edited and with an Introduction by Stewart Weaver. Philadelphia: University of Pennsylvania Press, 2002.

RE   *The Revolt of the Elites and the Betrayal of Democracy.* New York: Norton, 1994.

STJA *The Social Thought of Jane Addams.* Edited by Christopher Lasch. The American Heritage Series, ed. Leonard W. Levy and Alfred Young. Indianapolis: Bobbs-Merrill, 1965.

TOH   *The True and Only Heaven: Progress and Its Critics.* New York: Norton, 1991.

WCL   *Women and the Common Life: Love, Marriage, and Feminism.* Edited by Elisabeth Lasch-Quinn. New York: Norton, 1997.

WN   *The World of Nations: Reflections on American History, Politics, and Culture.* New York: Knopf, 1973.

Preface

I n his breakthrough book of 1965, Christopher Lasch rendered, in a style stark and subtle at once, "the sickness of American society" and the "general dehumanization of modern life." It was a judgment he could not shake. In the years that followed Lasch became one of the most distinctive voices seeking to illumine the age and seize on a way forward. What he began in *The New Radicalism in America* as a fledgling thirty-two-year-old historian he would continue without halt for three decades: intelligent, insistent probing of the nation's political and cultural terrain, with eyes trained on the unruly thrust of American history and the possibilities of a better way.[1]

By the late 1960s Lasch had embraced the left, a young intellectual calling sharply for a "new culture, absorbing but transcending the old." As the hopes of that moment disintegrated he turned his disappointment into diagnosis, unleashing a spate of essays, books, and lectures that sought to show why such a culture was being thwarted and abandoned. "Undoubtedly Lasch is on to something quite real," wrote *Time*'s reviewer of Lasch's 1979 volume *The Culture of Narcissism: American Life in an Age of Diminishing Expectations.* The review sat oddly next to the books on *Time*'s bestsellers list, itself an unwitting piece of promotion for Lasch's book. *The Complete Book of Running, Jackie Oh!, If Life Is a Bowl of Cherries What Am I Doing in the Pits?:* each confirmed Lasch's thesis and pushed thoughtful readers his way.[2]

---

1. CL, NR, 324.

2. CL, AAL, 212; R. Z. Sheppard, "The Pursuit of Happiness," *Time* (8 January 1979), 78.

But what they found was sure to mystify. Lasch's own bestseller was no jeremiad in the classic American vein, filled with exhortation and prescription, echoing with language descended from the Puritan past, charged with sentimental yearning. But neither was the book, as *Time*'s reviewer pointed out, of the species of "value-neutral history and sociology" that eschewed the kind of "moral conviction" that so decisively shaped Lasch's writing. It was fierce. It was sophisticated. It was secular. It was sharp. It came from a place well above, or below, the usual ideological perches. Those looking for left-center-right pigeonholes looked in vain. "Lasch, so far as I can tell, is a conservative radical," wrote one baffled academic reviewer.[3]

Indeed, throughout his life Lasch was both claimed and dismissed all across the political spectrum, to his mingled dismay and delight. He had little taste for truism but took great delight in creative critical encounter, not for novelty's sake so much as for the sake of history itself. If the past taught anything it was that human societies require all the earnest ingenuity available if satisfactions of a meaningful sort are to be achieved. Convinced that Americans had lost sight of or interest in their touchstone ideals, Lasch sought to move past the mood and measures of the moment to a place of political and spiritual renewal. And as he moved, he moved in the spirit of reckoning, freely casting judgment on all — left, right, and everyone in between.

He was a surveyor, taking the measure of the wilderness. And he was a prophet, showing wilderness-wandering people what was at stake. "A prophet's task is to reveal the fault lines hidden beneath the comfortable surface of the worlds we invent for ourselves," suggests Kathleen Norris, "the national myths as well as the little lies and delusions of control and security that get us through the day." As a critic, Lasch operated at both of these levels, the national and the personal, with preternatural ease, his intellectual virtuosity and versatility leading to essay after essay that might veer from a critique of postmodern theater to a corrective reading of a canonical political thinker to a disputation with psychoanalytic theorists. One editor

3. Sheppard, "The Pursuit of Happiness," 77-78; Michael Kammen, "A Whiplash of Contradictory Expectations," *Reviews in American History* 7:4 (December 1979), 452.

called him "probably the most honest and perceptive critic of his generation."[4]

But none of this was an end in itself. The sense of vast, encompassing catastrophe loomed always, demanding that all forms of delight and longing be experienced in its enlarging shadow. As the discomfiting shape of modern America had begun to reveal itself in the 1860s, Henry Adams later recalled, "Society laughed a vacant and meaningless derision over its own failure" — its failure to realize, so immediately after the overwhelming anguish of civil war, its great ideals and deepest convictions. Adams, a young man seeking a way to tether his hopes and heritage to the American future, laughed along, he admitted. "Yet the spectacle was no laughing matter."[5]

Lasch knew this laughter well, and he, too, might have laughed. But he did not laugh along. As surely as Adams was, in his own words, "struggling to shape himself to his time," Lasch found himself, one hundred years later, struggling to resist that shape and groping for another way.[6]

What Jacques Ellul declared in the aftermath of World War II, Lasch felt instinctually. "It is scarcely necessary to insist on the fact that revolution is needed," Ellul wrote. "Our western civilization has gained control of the whole world from the mechanical and rational point of view, but this has led to a fatal impasse. Disaster, in every possible form, has flooded the world to an extent never known before." In fact, Ellul contended, "the further we go and the more progress we make, the more do we confess that we are incapable of dominating and directing the world which we have made. All of us, in spite of our desire to keep hope alive, are aware that this is true."[7]

Ellul may have claimed too much for this last point, but certainly Lasch was one who shared the depth of Ellul's conviction. Ellul's warning — "This is not the hour for utopias, nor for political realism:

4. Kathleen Norris, *The Cloister Walk* (New York: Riverhead Books, 1996), 34; Paul Piccone, "Introduction," *Telos* 97 (Fall 1993), 5.

5. Henry Adams, *The Education of Henry Adams* (Boston: Massachusetts Historical Society, 1918; reprint, Boston: Houghton Mifflin, 1961), 272, 273 (page references are to reprint edition).

6. Adams, *Education,* 269.

7. Jacques Ellul, *The Presence of the Kingdom,* 2d. ed., expanded; trans. Olive Wyon, with an introduction by Daniel B. Clendenin (Colorado Springs: Helmers & Howard, Publishers, 1989), 21, 22. The book was first published in 1948.

it is the hour for becoming aware" — might have been Lasch's own defining credo, as he from the beginning of his career agitated, often angrily, always earnestly, to convince and persuade Americans of the true nature of their circumstance.[8]

It is now clear that the crisis that so stirred Lasch is bound up in what we call "postmodernity," the vacuity of the name itself an indicator of the nature of the crisis. The historian Eric Hobsbawm describes the last third of the twentieth century as "a new era of decomposition, uncertainty, and crisis," an assessment Lasch's own work certainly supports. Early on Lasch had framed it, simply, as the crisis of "progress," his catchword for the long playing-out of the enlightened, liberal attempt to master the world with the doctrine of universal rights, the application of scientific rationality, and the might of the market. Just out of graduate school, in a 1961 book review published in the *St. Louis Post-Dispatch,* he wondered, "What are we to make of the twentieth century?" "The melancholy history of 'the times,'" he wrote in reply, "suggests a possible connection between social progress and human disintegration." But would Americans accept such a premise, much less act on it? He thought not. Their usual response was to "demand more of what we have already — more health, education, and welfare. But we know by now," he intoned, "that progress is not enough."[9]

"Progress is not enough." Any American writer who would make "decomposition" rather than "progress" his tale is bound for trouble, but this may be especially true for one who would write history. The historian Dorothy Ross notes that American historians of all stripes have tended to meld their researches into the form of the romance, stories that "move forward within history, powered by mythic hope, to a happy ending." It was a form to which Lasch would not submit. By the publication of what the sociologist Robert Bellah later called Lasch's "masterpiece," his 1991 book *The True and Only Heaven: Progress and Its Critics,* Lasch would conclude that "old political ideologies have exhausted their capacity either to explain events or to inspire men and women to constructive action." Despite the recent resur-

8. Ellul, *Presence of the Kingdom,* 101.

9. Eric Hobsbawm, *The Age of Extremes: A History of the World, 1914-1991* (New York: Vintage Books, 1996), 6; CL, "Is Conservatism the Real Enemy?" *St. Louis Post-Dispatch,* 2 August 1961, C2.

gence of the right, he underscored, "Spiritual disrepair, the perception of which furnished much of the popular animus against liberalism, is just as evident today as it was in the seventies."[10]

And yet, his bromides against progress and resistance to romance notwithstanding, Lasch could not — would not — believe that "decomposition" was our inevitable fate, as *The True and Only Heaven* makes clear. This, his longest, most searching book, was not mainly a lament of how we have missed our true end. It was, finally, Lasch's testament of the hope we might yet find.

Hope came with difficulty for Lasch. For much of his life he lived on easier terms with "melancholy," hope's "dark twin," in Andrew Delbanco's formulation. And to some of his critics Lasch was nothing if not hope-less, a sulky naysayer, one who not only understood himself to be living in a time of darkness but who seemed to take a shady delight in describing it.[11]

But as Delbanco's image indicates, melancholy is not despair, though it may quickly enough become a stop along the way. In Lasch's case melancholy became a point along another path, one that led him into a deepening confidence in the persisting reality of the good, the vision of which he fiercely guarded and forcefully pursued. Awaking to a world that had become, in another postwar French writer's phrase, "a vacuum veiled in frivolity" — or what Delbanco five decades later denounced as "a soul-starving present, in which the highest aspiration" had become "to keep the body young forever" — Lasch sought a way out, both for himself and his country. If it is true, as George Packer writes, that although the sixties "changed forever the lives of those who lived through it" it failed to "leave behind a viable worldview," Lasch spent his life in quest of that viability, slowly hammering out a way of seeing and living that could sustain hope amidst the grand fracturing of the age. His discoveries he turned into historical arguments and judgments — and along the way "raised the writing of history to a literary art," in Packer's estimation.[12]

10. Dorothy Ross, "Grand Narrative in American Historical Writing: From Romance to Uncertainty," *American Historical Review* 100 (June 1995), 668; interview with Robert N. Bellah, 16 June 2008; CL, TOH, 21, 22.

11. Andrew Delbanco, *The Real American Dream: A Meditation on Hope* (Cambridge: Harvard University Press, 1999), 2.

12. Jacques Maritain, *The Person and the Common Good,* trans. John J. Fitzger-

His later meditations on the nature of hope retain their force. Hope rises from a profound and tenacious belief in "the goodness of life," Lasch wrote, a belief that also, paradoxically, intensifies awareness of surrounding danger, always present in this world. "The worst is always what the hopeful are prepared for," he sensed — "Their trust in life would not be worth much if it had not survived disappointments in the past." What our situation requires is not "a blind faith that things will somehow work out for the best" but rather hopeful, watchful caretaking: citizenship, neighborliness, stewardship — all time-honored words forged by the overwhelming demands of time, and of goodness itself.[13]

It was this strong and persisting sense of a caretaking obligation that shaped and directed Lasch's most fundamental vocational impulse: to write. If he approached his readers as a prophet, he went after the errors and follies of the age like a novelist, one of his earliest and most enduring ambitions. He sought to connect soul and structure, to interpret through story the passage of time, to render portraits that provoke. It was not mere analysis he wanted. It was *effect*.

The form of response he urged grew more full and convincing as his life passed and deepened, even as the difficulties he decried continued to mount. By the end, his was a pressing, resonant call for a politics of gratitude, a careful, collective arranging of everyday life in such a way that the gifts that make life possible — family, faith, place, work, earth — are honored, celebrated, and preserved. The good for which we long and that is utterly essential to our well-being, he saw with increasing clarity, would come only through a profoundly renewed vision and practice of citizenship: a submission that yields strength, a freeing dependence.

In the years since his death, what has become of Lasch's legacy? "In a period of frantic change," suggests the philosophy Louis Dupré, "no thinkers vanish more rapidly than those of the recent past. Their ideas are not so much refuted as shoved aside for a succession of new ones that address the present more directly. We secretly fear the ideas

---

ald (New York: Charles Scribner's Sons, 1947; reprint, Notre Dame: University of Notre Dame Press, 1966), 45 (page references are to the reprint edition); Delbanco, *Real American Dream*, 111; George Packer, *The Blood of the Liberals* (New York: Farrar, Straus, and Giroux, 1999), 387, 403.

13. CL, TOH, 530, 81.

of the past — not those of the remote past but of the past still remembered. Their growing paleness reminds us uncomfortably of the tran-
siency of our own thought."[14] Perhaps unremarkably, Lasch has if not
vanished, at least grown faint, his significance not now obvious, his
named pinned to another time.

It's striking, though, that in August of 2006 two of our leading political columnists, the liberal E. J. Dionne and the conservative David
Brooks, each turned in the same week to Lasch for ballast, the former
to urge liberals to return to their populist roots, the latter to point to
an exemplar of the lost practice of defining "social problems as matters of intellectual rigor." They each remembered this voice from the
recent past. For those devoted to the dream of progress, this voice may
sound like a nag. But for those whose eyes take in a less cheery scene,
it is a voice of sanity. And hope.[15]

Christopher Lasch embodied the central tensions of twentieth
century American life: the moral ambiguities, the political disarray,
the cultural sea-changes, the intellectual oscillations. He could not
escape these matters, either within himself or his world, and when he
tried to bring them into focus the integrity of his voice, the force of his
vision, and the brilliance of his mind made him difficult to turn aside.
He sought to speak as a citizen to the educated classes — his whole career, in fact, might be understood as an argument with the educated
classes. What he said demands our attention still.

W. H. Auden, the poet Richard Wilbur writes in eulogy, "sustained
the civil tongue/In a scattering time." So, too, did Christopher Lasch,
though his was a tongue that did not mistake civility for servility.
Hope had set his sights far, far higher.[16]

14. Louis Dupré, "Introduction" to Romano Guardini, *Letters from Lake
Como: Explorations in Technology and the Human Race*, trans. Geoffrey W. Bromiley
(Grand Rapids: Eerdmans, 1994), xiii.

15. E. J. Dionne, "A Wrong Turn Led to the 'L-Word,'" *Washington Post*, 22 August 2006, A15; David Brooks, "'Peyton Place' Lives On," *Pittsburgh Post-Gazette*,
25 August 2006, B7.

16. Richard Wilbur, "For W. H. Auden," in Wilbur, *New and Collected Poems*
(New York: Harcourt, 1988), 26.

CHAPTER ONE

Child of a "Brave, Free Land"

Robert C. Lasch, the author, is known to his friends as "Kit." He likes sports. This is his first complete book, though he has started many.

> From the dust jacket of *An Age of Exploration,* a self-published volume by "R. C. Lasch," 1943, 34 pp.[1]

The author apparently intends to keep up his writing career, and several other books are slated.

> From the dust jacket of *Washington to Roosevelt,* a self-published volume by "C. Lasch," 1944, 134 pp.[2]

On March 21, 1937, a brief poem entitled "The Hoover" appeared in the *Omaha World-Herald.* Christopher Lasch was launched.

His mother, upon discovering her four-year-old at work on the family typewriter, offered to take diction. His father, an editor at the *World-Herald,* then foisted his son's work on a colleague. The piece was published under the byline of one "Whitie Polar Bear," a nom de plume the author, according to the newspaper's account, felt conveyed his "real personality for the time being." A grisly tale emerged in metrical form:

1. "An Age of Exploration," 69:8.
2. "Washington to Roosevelt," 69:10.

... And down the little fine dust goes
Into the stomach of the big Hoover
A squealing and a shouting for somebody to come
And let him out.
But nobody comes to pick them out
Squealing with death ...

It was, at the very least, a start, and one his parents witnessed with delight. Amidst the uncertainties of depression and world war they guarded and cultivated their son, impressed by his abilities and pleased by his eagerness to follow their lead.[3]

Given a printing press while still in grade school, Kit, as his family and friends called him, rallied his buddies to help him publish a newspaper for their Omaha neighborhood. By the time he and his family moved to Chicago in 1942 he was already a seasoned newspaperman, appearing in print that summer as the founder of "The Pony Express." "Why not subscribe?" the founder/editor/publisher asked. But Kit Lasch was after far more than circulation. He had a message. "Regardless of any name you give it, stealing's stealing," he charged. "And in back of any reason you can think of is dishonesty." He pounded out his conclusion with force: "It just isn't honest to steal ... you can't escape that."[4]

Kit's creative impulses took him well beyond homemade newspapers. Immersing himself in music as a teenager, he learned to play both the violin and piano, and eventually turned to composition. His accomplishment provided ready copy for his newspapers. "I finish rumpelstiltskin," one of his headlines in 1945 proclaimed, "on which I have been working at one time or another for half a year." That Christmas he gave "Rumpelstiltskin, Opera in D Major" to his parents as a gift, complete with a lengthy score, program, liner notes, and pencil sketches of the opera's soloists. He followed this with "Julius Caesar," a forty-nine page score of "incidental music to Shakespeare's

<hr />

3. "The Hoover, a Poem by Whitie Polar Bear," *Omaha World-Herald*, 21 March 1937, CLP 69:18. Kit's mother writes that "White Polar Bear" was one of Kit's "imaginary friends," in Zora Schaupp Lasch, "The Life and Times of Zora Schaupp Lasch," n.d., unpublished manuscript in the possession of the author, 110.

4. Richard Wightman Fox, "An Interview with Christopher Lasch," *Intellectual History Newsletter* 16 (1994), 3; CL, "Juvenalia," 69:8.

play," which he vividly described in his liner notes: "After a florid passage for the piano, the woods set right out with the development of
theme one. The piano takes up the passionate melody . . . But the orchestra interrupts with a new theme, thundered out fortissimo."[5]

But it was writing that was to be Kit's enduring passion. By age
eleven he boasted of having finished his "first complete book," which
he titled "An Age of Exploration." He had composed biographical essays of several explorers, made careful, credible pencil sketches of
them and their routes, and bound the volume's thirty-four pages with
cardboard and twine. "Robert C. Lasch, the author, is known to his
friends as 'Kit,'" the dust jacket announced. "This is his first complete book, though he has started many."[6]

Lasch's early efforts, as might be expected of the son of a newspaper editor and sometime social worker, sometime professor, often
touched on politics. "Washington to Roosevelt," a 134-page survey of
American presidents (complete with pencil sketches) self-published
at age twelve, made it clear who the heroes of the family were. Thomas
Jefferson, whose portrait graced the volume's cover, was "founder of
the Democratic party and one of the greatest presidents in American
history," the former statement providing much of the justification for
the latter in the Lasch household. Twelve-year-old Kit lauded the most
recently successful of all of Jefferson's progeny, Franklin Delano Roosevelt, for his "remarkable handling of the depression," which had
"restor[ed] the country to normalcy" and led to his re-election "by the
biggest majority in history."[7]

The Democrats, there was no doubt, were the embodiment and
guardians of most of what was good in America — much, in fact, that
made America America. In another hand-made book written in his
early years Kit had created the fictional country of "Vodala," a "brave,
free land," with people "determined to stay the way they are. One nation, indivisible, with liberty, and justice for all." Here, as in so much
else, Kit's ideals mirrored the convictions and sensibilities of his unusually devoted and highly capable parents.[8]

---

5. CL, front page of the "Tower Lake Times," 23 October 1945, 69:8;
"Rumpelstiltskin" and "Julius Caesar" are in 69:8 and 69:15.

6. CL, "Age of Exploration."

7. CL, "Washington to Roosevelt," 9, 124, CLP 69:10.

8. CL, "Vodala," 69:6.

*   *   *

Kit's father, Robert Lasch, was born in 1907 in Lincoln, Nebraska, to Walter and Myrtle Lasch. Much later Robert remembered himself as a "tractable and well-disciplined child, without a trace of rebelliousness" even during his high school years. Throughout his childhood his working-class parents had been plagued by financial hardship; in his unpublished memoirs, written in the 1980s, Robert recalled his father's "bruising encounter with the business cycle": he had lost work in the "panic of 1907, the recession of 1921, and the depression" of 1929. "So far as I was aware," Robert remembered, "we had always been hard up."[9]

The Lasches moved around the Midwest with regularity in the 1910s: from Lincoln to Chicago, then to Springfield, Illinois, finally joining Walter's father, brother, and sister in Kansas City, Missouri, where Walter became a bookkeeper. The family was neither religiously nor politically committed. The parents attended no church, and although his mother at one point enrolled the children in a Presbyterian Sunday school, Robert claimed to have "never experienced religious inspiration, or even curiosity." After a short time, he recalled, "the pretense of piety was gratefully dropped." In terms of political affiliation his father was only "nominally a Democrat," though some political current or another was strong enough to prompt young Robert at the age of nine to write a "blistering letter" to Theodore Roosevelt for being a "bully and a warmonger."[10]

Self-published newspapering, it turns out, became a Lasch tradition during Robert's childhood, when Robert purchased a press and began to publish his own neighborhood newspaper while in high school. Enrolling in 1924 at the University of Nebraska as a philosophy major, he joined the college newspaper staff and the next year accepted a position as a reporter for the *Lincoln Star,* where he often worked the police beat. He found the mix of the earthy and the ethereal stimulating. "There was a refreshing contrast between mornings spent listening to a couple of detectives argue that a woman was no good in bed until she was forty," he recalled, "and afternoons study-

---

9. The following account is taken from Robert Lasch, "What I Remember" (unpublished ms. written 1982-1987, CLP 69:26, 27), 27, 2, 18.

10. Lasch, "What I Remember," 23, 5.

ing the principles of Christian ethics with the very Christian Dr. Patterson."[11]

But his writing was not confined to newspapers during his college years. Besides journalistic pieces, he wrote poetry, penned short stories, and composed philosophic dialogues. He joined various literary clubs on campus, gazing along with his classmates toward a native daughter for inspiration. "Always before us was the illustrious Willa Cather, who had risen from the Nebraska plains to become a leader in American letters," he wrote. "If she could do it, why not we?" During his senior year Robert's hard labors and academic talent were rewarded: he was selected as the university's lone Rhodes scholar, and in 1928 set sail to Oxford, the first time he had ventured more than two hundred miles from home.[12]

His three years at Oxford, he would write with an enthusiasm still palpable many decades later, were "among the best" of his life. Although his studies proved him to be by his own lights less than a "profound scholar," he still considered himself "above average." He was in distinguished company — among the thirty-three in his class was the novelist and future United States Poet Laureate Robert Penn Warren — and he absorbed the atmosphere and moment with the wide-open eyes of an innocent abroad. Having traveled to Paris in 1928, he recalled that it "had even more romantic associations than Oxford. Hemingway, Scott Fitzgerald, Gertrude Stein — they were all there. . . ." After three years at Oxford, he returned to Omaha and took a post at the *World-Herald,* an enviable professional launching point in the midst of the depression.[13]

He did not return to Nebraska alone. Zora Schaupp and Robert were married in 1931 soon upon his return from England. The wedding was the culminating point of a friendship that had begun several years earlier, when Robert had been a student of Zora — a young, zestful professor of philosophy and psychology who had just recently joined the faculty at her alma mater.

In returning to Nebraska she was returning to her native state as well. Born in 1896 in Rockville, Nebraska, to Frederick and Estella Schaupp, Zora too was shaped by a childhood of frequent moves. Her

11. Lasch, "What I Remember," 44.
12. Lasch, "What I Remember," 46-47.
13. Lasch, "What I Remember," 51, 68, 56.

father, the son of committed Lutherans, had graduated from Valparaiso Normal School, moved to Nebraska with his brothers, and eventually became a teacher and principal. In 1894 he married Esta Wilson, whose Catholic parents, natives of Indiana, had achieved success as cattle farmers in Nebraska. Esta's father early on gave Frederick trouble for his "radical politics," as Zora would put it many years later in her unpublished autobiography; in it she proudly noted that her father bore the same stamp as several Valparaiso alums who went on to become distinguished figures in early-twentieth-century America: "They were radicals in politics, iconoclasts in religion, and intensely interested in public affairs."[14]

By age five Zora's parents had carted her along with an older sister and a younger brother off to Oklahoma to try their hand at the hotel business in the recently opened Indian territory. A short time later they moved to "another frontier town full of adventurers looking for a fast dollar," where they lived in a town of houses with "wooden walls and canvas roofs"; she recalled the night "a gang of Indians broke into the house . . . filling the place with shouts and demands for firewater." Finally they returned to Nebraska in 1904, ending what Zora dubbed their "Oklahoma-Texas adventure." Her father took a job managing an elevator for the Wright-Lest Grain Company in Virginia, Nebraska, a town of about two hundred inhabitants, where they would live for the next eight years, and where he would become active in local politics, serving as justice of the peace, on the school board, and eventually in the state legislature. Elected as a Democrat in 1912, Frederick devoted himself to pushing for state aid for road construction, hoping to improve market access for farmers. Despite achieving some success, he finished out his term and took a position with the State Bureau of Weights and Measures in Lincoln.[15]

It was a region that had been energized in the last two decades of the nineteenth century by populism, the political protest of a rural world besieged by the civilization corporate capital was methodically and colossally making. The leading voice of this protest, William Jennings Bryan, was a native Nebraskan, whose ascendancy to the leadership of the Democratic Party around the turn of the twentieth

14. The following account is taken from Schaupp Lasch, "The Life and Times of Zora Schaupp Lasch," 13, 18, 14.

15. Schaupp Lasch, "The Life and Times of Zora Schaupp Lasch," 4, 19.

century was testament to the antagonism multitudes of Americans felt in those decades toward the new order. But the steamroller would not be stopped or slowed, and it touched and remade the lives of everyday people in deeply formative ways.

Zora's family, for instance, was, in this period of rising theological modernism, divided over religion. While her college-educated father was an atheist, her mother was continually active in a series of churches, which Zora from childhood attended with her. In her autobiography, though, she later revealed her own developing irreligion. "By the age of 10 I was questioning the theory of creation, the miracles, Heaven and Hell and even, somewhat fearfully, the existence of God," she remembered. She continued, though, to take part in church activities, teaching Sunday school in Omaha as a teenager and receiving praise from their minister, who "flattered Mother on her brilliant daughter and prophesied a glowing future for me on the 'foreign field'" — this despite the fact that, Zora confessed, she "had not a spark of religious faith."[16]

Her very modern religious skepticism enlarged into a skepticism toward American society itself when she entered the University of Nebraska as a freshman in 1916. Majoring in Latin, she in her second year came upon a book by the pioneering contemporary feminist Charlotte Perkins Gilman; the book, she wrote, "rekindled the smoldering feminist flame" and spurred her to set out on a "program of plain living and high thinking." Convinced that "most, if not all, of the behavioral patterns of the sexes were taught from infancy and that the girlish squeals and giggles, the deceptions and superficiality of my contemporaries were detestable," she distanced herself from the usual habits and styles of her classmates, going so far as to wear "boys' shoes because one couldn't buy girls' without high heels" and to substitute undergarments of her own fashioning for the typical "feminine camisoles and panties." When World War I turned Nebraska's female students to furious knitting in support of the troops, Zora published what she described as a "sardonic article" in protest of such silliness in the student newspaper. This act of defiance ended up winning her fans among the faculty, some of whom began to guide her toward a future in academe.[17]

16. Schaupp Lasch, "The Life and Times of Zora Schaupp Lasch," 62.
17. Schaupp Lasch, "The Life and Times of Zora Schaupp Lasch," 76, 77, 74.

Zora Schaupp in her twenties was edgy, and if not actually on the cultural edge, at least usually near it. Her autobiography reveals a sensible, active woman who was a relentless critic of humans and human behavior. "Merle" was "very fat" and "pasty-faced," a "colorless creature." "Ruby?" A "rather silly, brow-beaten little wife." "Louise," while proving to be not only "pathetically vain and ambitious," also "revealed streaks of dishonesty." Recalling her several suitors years later Zora summed up her opinion of them in one icy judgment: "Each was weak and contemptible in his own way. The better I knew them the more I despised them." Zora was no passive critic, though: from the time of her college awakening on she kept herself continually attuned to the political arena, both local and national, taking left-leaning stances consonant with the evolving shape of post-populist progressivism. She recalled that after World War I, "some of us never returned to our earlier indifference to world events. We railed against the munition [*sic*] makers and war profiteers. We read articles and books about the Russian Revolution and applauded its success. We vowed that if there were ever another war we would go to prison rather than participate in it." In later years she would not only teach philosophy but also do social work, a dynamic which captures well her blending of ideas and activism.[18]

Encouraged by her professors, Zora stayed on at Nebraska following her B.A. to take a masters degree in philosophy. Upon its completion she accepted a scholarship from Bryn Mawr, a women's college in Philadelphia whose students, she noted, were proudly "fed regular statistics on the low proportion of marriages among Bryn Mawr girls and the low fertility rate of those marriages." While working toward a Ph.D. in philosophy she spent her days among the avant-garde and cultural elite, which led to her initial contacts with, among other things, her first cigarette, a lesbian couple, and John Dewey. Attending a philosophy conference shortly after having severely burned her hand, she recalled that Dewey "took charge of me at meals, insisted on sitting at my right hand to cut my meat, and generally babied me as a handicapped child." What she discovered at Bryn Mawr culturally and intellectually she had only dimly experienced in Lincoln; the contrast of the mildly Christian Midwest and the more cos-

18. Schaupp Lasch, "The Life and Times of Zora Schaupp Lasch," 70, 72, 119, 141, 77.

mopolitan East was striking, often stark. One professor, she remembered, was "working on a book which would show the striking resemblance between religious trances, revelations, and visions to drug-induced states of consciousness." At one point, when she expressed alarm to a German professor about a classmate who had committed suicide, she received a reply that left her "aghast": "Suicide should not require justification, he told me; it's the continuation of life that should be justified." He himself, she wrote, later took his own life.[19]

After completing her dissertation on "The Naturalism of Condillac" in 1925 (which, she wryly noted, "set no bells ringing"), she joined the faculty at Nebraska. She was never permitted to teach ethics, due to her department chair's concerns about her "naturalism." Instead she taught courses ranging from the "new realism" to "animal psychology" to the "psychology of advertising." For several years she roomed with a high school teacher named Elsie Cather, a younger sister of Willa Cather. Willa may have been a hero to Robert during those years, but she was certainly not for Zora: "I found her attitude rather patronizing, certainly not conducive to any warm regard on my part."[20]

But Robert, even as an undergraduate, was another story. "He was handsome as few men of that age could possibly be," she wrote — not to mention "extraordinarily intelligent and sensitive." While he was an undergraduate Zora maintained an appropriate distance, but when she won a fellowship through the Social Science Research Council for the 1929-30 academic year to study experimental schools throughout England and Europe they met on several occasions, as he was then in the second year of his Rhodes Scholarship. After one jaunt together around England, Zora, the tough moral critic, concluded that "He was faultless"; she was struck more than ever by "his keenness of intelligence, his innate honesty and his wholly natural kindness and consideration toward others." She had begun the trip "prepared to be disillusioned," but by the end discovered that she had become "completely and irrevocably in love."

19. Schaupp Lasch, "The Life and Times of Zora Schaupp Lasch," 90, 89, 96, 98.

20. Schaupp Lasch, "The Life and Times of Zora Schaupp Lasch," 105, 146, 144, 138.

Before she left for Nebraska at the end of the year they had gotten engaged.[21]

For much of the year she had served as the "visiting psychologist" at Bertrand Russell's Beacon Hill School in England, where "Bertie" and his wife Dora lived and taught. Small and highly experimental, the school was a vessel for the most progressive educational theory of the day; by the end of the year Zora seemed to have become disillusioned with the school, and perhaps with some of the philosophic assumptions that lay beneath it. "Certainly no one could say that the children's sex education had been neglected," she dryly noted. "Dora instructed them *ad nauseam,* until one requested that she and Mr. Russell give them a demonstration so they could understand it better." Yet in the course of the year the Russells' moral progressivism would be challenged by the open presence of Dora's lover at the school. Professedly approving of the relationship, Russell grumbled his disapproval to Zora, and soon after asked her to marry him. Zora, stunned, recalled that she felt "nothing remotely resembling sexual attraction," nor had she an appetite for "waiting through notorious divorce proceedings for an equally publicized marriage."[22]

She later concluded that not only did Russell "never really understand women," he also failed to understand children. It was "uninhibited individualism," she later noted with disdain, to which this school and a few others she studied were devoted. She returned to Nebraska, resumed her teaching duties, and awaited Robert's return. They were married in the summer of 1931; she continued to teach at Nebraska while Robert began his work at the *Omaha World-Herald.* When Zora discovered that fall that she was pregnant they were both shocked: she had believed that due to a childhood illness she was infertile. When Robert Christopher Lasch was born on June 1, 1932, Zora switched from teaching to social work, where she waged battles in behalf of the poor under the auspices of the Family Welfare Association, and later the Child Welfare Association. Unable to have more children of their own, they adopted a daughter, Kate, in 1937.[23]

Robert and Zora left Kit in the hands of various housekeepers during the days, who assisted with his care and education. His "precoc-

21. Schaupp Lasch, "The Life and Times of Zora Schaupp Lasch," 142, 182.
22. Schaupp Lasch, "The Life and Times of Zora Schaupp Lasch," 162, 169.
23. Schaupp Lasch, "The Life and Times of Zora Schaupp Lasch," 170, 171.

ity," as Zora termed it, was impressive; "Kit," she wrote, "developed at an astounding rate." Among his earliest playmates were some neighborhood girls who, he one day reported to his mother, had been "teaching him things." Zora, a bit nervous, prodded him to disclose the nature of the lessons. "Well, it was all about someone called Jesus Christ," replied young Kit, "but what I want to know is if he is the guy that makes the Chrysler cars."[24]

Although in the course of their careers neither Robert nor Zora attained the heights of Willa Cather, they were, in a less glamorous way, members of the same storied generation of American intellectuals. A young Alfred Kazin, writing just after this era in 1941, rhapsodized of a time "twenty or thirty years ago, when the birds began to sing . . . almost, as it seemed in chorus." Indeed, the bright, academically gifted students of the 1920s had a host of reasons for excitement. Despite the fashionable despair of those intellectuals enduring self-imposed exile in Europe, the pervading sense was that American letters and learning were, finally, "coming of age," as Kazin put it. Not only were authors such as Hemingway and Sinclair Lewis making serious strides in fortifying a genuinely American literature, but the strongholds of "tradition" and "prejudice" seemed everywhere to be yielding to the confident prescriptions of the modern mind and its cool, confident rationality. Kazin described American letters as emerging from a "period of dark ignorance and repressive victorian gentility," and college students by the thousands gloried, albeit at times uneasily, in the visions of this bright new world that lay before them.[25]

24. Schaupp Lasch, "The Life and Times of Zora Schaupp Lasch," 212, 210.

25. Alfred Kazin, *On Native Grounds: An Interpretation of Modern American Prose Literature* (New York: Harcourt, Brace and Company, 1942, 3rd Harvest edition, 1995), xxi.

George M. Marsden, in his study of Protestant fundamentalism, paints a compelling picture of the sea change that occurred in the 1920s: "In some respects America after 1918 was a new world as compared with America at the end of the nineteenth century. People who had retained the dominant beliefs of the culture in which they were raised now found themselves living in a society where those same beliefs were widely considered out-dated, or even bizarre." *Fundamentalism and American Culture: The Shaping of American Evangelicalism, 1870-1925* (New York: Oxford University Press, 1980), 204. Warren I. Susman depicts the view from the other side of the cultural divide, writing that many of the era's intellectuals "thought of the New Era as a New Enlightenment." *Culture as History: The Transformation of American Society in the Twentieth Century* (New York: Pantheon Books, 1984), 107.

It was a world that was theirs for the taking. These students, schooled in the scientistic language and methodology that promised deliverance from a way of life both outmoded and undesirable, were the latest exponents of the self-consciously "modern" ideas and sensibilities that were transforming America. New or refurbished institutions were arising, staffed by these proficient agents of the liberating modern creed. Robert and Zora's generation of college-trained experts, what some have termed the "new class," was ascendant, transforming the worlds of business, government, and civil society, and providing a world of economic opportunity that many, such as Robert Lasch, had not previously known.[26]

For Robert and Zora Lasch these were heady times, and their carefully cultivated skills, their youthful energies, and their progressive ideas found easy expression in politics. Robert, who described himself as "relatively apolitical at Oxford," became "rapidly politicized in Omaha." The *World-Herald* preserved what Robert termed the "tradition of populist-radicalism," having been edited by William Jennings Bryan himself less than forty years before Robert joined the staff, and Robert quickly fell under its sway. Along with Zora, he voted for the socialist candidate, Norman Thomas, in 1932. "I wanted social change," he recalled, "but I wanted it through democratic socialism," as opposed to revolutionary communism. As the depression continued he edged toward the political center, holding to a more pragmatic, still idealistic, liberalism: "In the end, as the hope of socialism faded, I settled for liberal reform and a mixed economy," and, as he put it, "attached myself emotionally to the New Deal." While Kit later speculated that his mother ended up the more radical of the two, throughout their lives their politics continued to bear the unmistakable imprint of the economic populism of the Progressive era Democrats,

---

26. For this general perspective on the "New Class," see Barbara and John Ehrenreich, "The Professional-Managerial Class," in Pat Walker, ed., *Between Labor and Capital* (Boston: South End Press, 1979), 5-45; Barbara Ehrenreich, *Fear of Falling: The Inner Life of the Middle Class* (New York: Pantheon, 1989; New York: HarperPerennial, 1990); Alvin W. Gouldner, *The Future of Intellectuals and the Rise of the New Class* (New York: The Seabury Press, 1979); Guy Alchon, "Managerialism," in Richard Wightman Fox and James Kloppenberg, eds., *A Companion to American Thought* (Malden, Mass.: Blackwell Publishers, 1995), 427-28; and Eugene B. McCarraher, *Christian Critics: Religion and the Impasse in Modern American Social Thought* (Ithaca: Cornell University Press, 2000).

over against what the historian Alan Brinkley has termed the "consumer-oriented" liberalism of the postwar era. Despite the increasing dissonance with the direction of American liberalism, they made the Democratic Party their home, and devoted much of their lives to its success.[27]

In 1942 Robert Lasch took a position as an editorial writer for Marshall Field's new journalistic venture, the *Chicago Sun*. By then the *World-Herald* had, in Robert's view, taken a conservative turn, leaving him to hope that in Chicago he could earn a living "as a working liberal." Soon after arriving he began to seek outlets beyond the *Sun* for his writing, "in quest of," he later confessed, "a national reputation." He partly succeeded, his sane tone and clear style proving to be an efficient vehicle for his progressive convictions. He published several articles in the *Atlantic Monthly* in the 1940s, including a contest-winning essay of 1944, "For a Free Press," which won a $1000 prize as the jury's unanimous choice out of more than 700 entries. Newspaper publishers, Robert warned, had become an oligarchy, representing the interests of business rather than the interests of "the people." In an egregious abuse of their power, publishers had ceased viewing themselves as "trustees of constitutional liberty" and had instead become "the beneficiaries of a special privilege"; newspapers, "as part of business," now "helped to run politics." Lasch urged journalists to stay true to their "professional conscience," guided by the "love of truth combined with zeal for the people's cause." Newspapers should

27. Lasch, "What I Remember," 76, 77. Casey Blake and Christopher Phelps, "History as Social Criticism: Conversations with Christopher Lasch," *Journal of American History* 80:4 (March 1994), 1311.
While the older progressives had taken aim at the structural inadequacies of corporate capitalism, which they believed to be at the root of contemporary social discord, the liberals who gained ascendance during the New Deal's later years espoused a program that left the corporate capitalist structure intact, while using the federal government to counter, via public spending, the inevitable downturns that accompanied the capitalist system. Prosperity through mass consumption, not freedom through small-scale production, became the new guiding premise. See Alan Brinkley, *The End of Reform: New Deal Liberalism in Recession and War* (New York: Knopf, 1995), 4, 224. I follow Brinkley for much of this general argument, found also in many of the essays in his *Liberalism and Its Discontents* (Cambridge: Harvard University Press, 1998,). See especially chapter five, "The Two World Wars and American Liberalism," 79-93, and chapter six, "Legacies of World War II," 94-110.

above all "fight the people's battles against special interests" rather than "fight the people for the interests."[28]

The one book Robert would publish in his lifetime was aimed at the crisis in housing that analysts were predicting for postwar America, and it underscored the extent to which he, as the postwar world was taking shape, was still committed to the left-leaning social vision of the early New Deal. Robert was certainly right to call attention to the housing crisis — in 1945 housing shortages plagued ninety-eight percent of all American cities — but *Breaking the Building Blockade,* published in 1946 by the University of Chicago Press, represented a politics going quietly out of fashion. Lasch's call to arms, though peppered with all the key words of political progressives of the first third of the century — "interests," "the people," "democratic faith," "private profit" versus the "public good," "commonweal," "community" — fell on ears rapidly becoming attuned to different frequencies. While many critics welcomed his call for a "crusade" that "must enlist neighborhood groups, citizens' committees, city councils and planning boards, state legislatures, the congress, and the federal administration in a coordinated drive to stamp out bad housing," it was suburbia that emerged to meet the vast housing need, rather than the politically enlivened neighborhoods and villages that Robert had in mind.[29]

Robert and Zora Lasch were far from relics, however, and if they sensed that they were falling out of step with current liberal politics

28. Robert Lasch, "What I Remember," 94, 103; Robert Lasch, "For a Free Press," *Atlantic Monthly* 174:1 (July 1944), 40, 41, 43, 44.

29. The statistic on the housing shortage is found in Elaine Tyler May, *Homeward Bound: American Families in the Cold War Era* (New York: Basic Books, 1988), 168; Tyler May writes that in 1947 six million families across the nation were living with other family members or friends. Robert Lasch, *Breaking the Building Blockade* (Chicago: University of Chicago Press, 1946), 143. On the critical reception of the book, see especially Catherine Bauer's review, where she called it "lively and readable," a "layman's handbook," and noted that "it comes out at the exact moment when it can do the most good." She concluded with this glowing commendation: "Here's hoping that all the millions who have devoured Dream Home literature during the past few years will now read the Lasch book too . . . and let their Congressmen know how they feel as the result." See "Housing Expert Praises Housing Book," *Boston Morning Globe,* 24 April 1946, n.p., in RLP, box one, folder entitled "Magazine Articles Written by Lasch, 1942-1947." For a reviewer who took issue with Lasch's faith in government to provide solutions to such problems, see Miles Colean, "Housing Bottlenecks," *Progressive,* 20 May 1946, 10.

they did not let that dissuade them from civic activism or professional advance. Zora in these years was involved in the leadership of the League of Women Voters and supported Henry Wallace and his left-liberal Progressive Party in the presidential election of 1948. With the war's end Robert began to write most of the lead editorials at the *Sun*, his professional clout growing — more and more business lunches with Marshall Field, meetings with Walter Lippmann and other leading journalists, and dinner parties with the Chicago elite. The *Sun's* editorials still bubbled with progressive faith. After Truman's stunning victory in 1948 the lead editorial jubilantly declared that "One historic byproduct of the election is that the Democratic Party has become, genuinely, and we hope for all time, the party of undiluted American liberalism." As the midcentury mark neared, the Lasches, along with America itself, seemed to be hitting their stride.[30]

*   *   *

At Barrington High School, in Chicago's northwest suburbs, Kit too continued to distinguish himself in any number of ways. Baseball, despite his earnest efforts, was not among them; he was, he recalled, "all field and no hit, and not such a hot fielder either." He joined the drama club, writing the scripts for some of its productions, and also took part in the high school orchestra and string ensembles. As a senior he entered the "1950 Piano Playing Auditions, U.S.A.," conducted by the American College of Musicians, and performed notably. One judge glowingly commended him for his "definite creative ability" and "exceptional musical feeling." He perceived in Kit an "excellent mind" and sensed that he might be "good concert material." Kit's level of involvement and investment in the world of his high school was high by any standard. One friend, departed to college before he, wondered how his high school would "survive after the loss of its charter member." She referred to him as "my little genius friend."[31]

For all his remarkable talents and interests, Kit was drawn increasingly to writing, and his confidence in his abilities grew. "I have

30. Editorial, *Chicago Sun-Times*, 4 November 1948, 35.
31. Fox, "Interview," 4; comments on his piano performance are in 69:19; his friend's comments: Patricia Jane Miller to Christopher Lasch, TLS, 10 March 1950 and 8 October 1948, 0:24.

attempted to cover the entire history of English poetry down to the present day," the twelve-year-old explained in the preface of a school project he titled "Chief English Poets," going on to convey grand intentions for the piece: "I hope only to kindle some enthusiasm for British poetry through my effort. Having accomplished that, I will feel that I have succeeded." Years later, while corresponding with his daughter Elisabeth during her freshman year of college, Lasch remembered the sense of relief he had felt upon entering college, giving a revealing glimpse of his teenage years:

> To me the most exciting thing about going to college, initially, at least, was meeting people as smart as myself; it was gratifying, and completely unexpected, to meet people who had also been editors of their school paper, who had been as contemptuous of the high school social scene as I had been, and who had been thinking about a lot of the same things.[32]

This contempt of "the high school social scene" was also reflective of the mores and habit of his class, particularly the intellectually engaged wing of it. Their efforts to achieve distance from the ways of their more "Victorian" counterparts took them, and their children, to very different places and postures. For many new-class denizens, to take one example, the arts came to fill part of the spiritual vacancy left by organized religion, emerging as a preeminent pathway to meaningful human experience.

For Kit, the arts became a quasi-religious integration point for his assorted interests and quests. He disclosed hints of this in a novel, never completed, that he began while in college, in which he etched the stumbling efforts of a small violin ensemble of teenagers to attain meaning through their music. Music, in this story, is clearly the central medium for a delicate intimacy with others and with the world itself.[33]

---

32. CL, "Chief English Poets," 69:8; CL to Elisabeth Lasch, TL, 29 August 1977, 4:3.

33. Lawrence W. Levine etches the emergence of aesthetics as a quasi-religion for American elites in *Highbrow/Lowbrow: The Emergence of Cultural Hierarchy in America* (Cambridge: Harvard University Press, 1988). Quips Levine: "Some of those who helped to build the impressive array of artistic and musical institutions in late nineteenth-century America may have come initially to play but many of them stayed to pray," 228.

Such intimacy certainly could not be achieved through the normal folkways of Cherokee (a fictitious village he located in northern Illinois) — at least according to the mother of one "Madison," a member of the ensemble. "Cherokee is a very dull, provincial little town," she reminds Madison in one scene. "The people who live in Cherokee are ignorant of all the finer things in life, the things you and I respect and try to live by." Unlike most of Cherokee's natives, Madison has "talent," his mother reminds him, exhorting him always to remember "the things that give life its meaning." "Life without these things is no better than death, because art and music are the only things that are permanent. All the rest withers away." She concludes her homily with a bitter judgment: "Living in Cherokee is more like death than life"; better to leave home than to wither in the desert of the rural Midwest. Although the characters in the novel finally fail to achieve the ideals of harmony and authenticity that inspire the narrator, the narrator never signals disillusion with the point of view expressed by the mother: the arts lead to life; the arts, indeed, are the best — perhaps the only — hope for life.[34]

This quest for meaning through art — and politics — helps to illumine the broad turn progressives were taking as they moved further away from western religious traditions, and sheds light on some of the political and cultural tensions they left in their wake. True to form, the Lasches, though clearly understanding themselves as working in behalf of "the people," had little time for their religion-suffused modes of thinking and living. Toward the end of his life Kit went so far as to describe his parents as "militant secularists." In his retirement years Robert wrote that while many had over the years adjudged him an "unbeliever," he saw the matter quite differently. "I do hold beliefs," he averred, and in Painean cadence he recited them: "I believe that no divine power intervenes in human affairs; that death is the end of life and not a gateway to immortality; that the true, the good, and the beautiful should be pursued not for rewards in heaven but for their own sake." These tenets, he explained, he had "thought through to my own satisfaction while in college." Not surprisingly, when he argued for a free press in 1944 he grounded his understanding of freedom in the pragmatist philosophy of his day. "The value of personal

---

34. Christopher Lasch, "This Is the Way to Grandmother's House," unpublished ms. (1954), 92, in 58:13.

liberty," he wrote, "rests not upon any putative divinity, nor upon the naturalness of 'natural rights,' but upon the plain fact of its social usefulness and, indeed, its indispensability in a democracy."[35]

"The people," then, were benighted not only due to the banality of their aesthetic experience but also due to their misguided, medieval conceptions of the ultimate and the real. When Robert at some later point was giving counsel to Kit on parenting, he reminded Kit that he had been raised by "two extreme rationalists." Small wonder, then, that when the recently installed Harvard president Nathan Pusey threatened compulsory chapel attendance, Kit, then a senior in Cambridge, scoffingly tagged him "a Midwestern puritan of the worst kind." Kit had hoped that by heading east to Harvard he could escape provincial superstition. Apparently he shared such hopes with the Harvard faculty — according to Kit, most of them seemed "very riled by [Pusey's] pronouncement on religion." "Against the people, for the people" might well have been the rallying cry of this and the previous generation of university-educated professionals, modernity's missionaries, as disruptive of "native traditions" in America as the Christian missionaries to foreign lands whom they so deplored. Lasch later waged war against this variety of "progressivism," understanding it, by the late 1980s, as contributing mightily to the culture wars of late-twentieth-century American life.[36]

But this was not the Kit Lasch of the 1940s and 1950s. As a youth Kit embodied the outlook and sensibilities of his parents and their class. At age sixteen he won first prize (out of 5,362 contestants) in the Illinois division of a national essay contest with a piece entitled "Human Rights: The Key to World Peace." That fall he made "impassioned speeches" for Progressive party candidate Henry Wallace in school assemblies — an activity which, in his own words, did not

35. Blake and Phelps, "History as Social Criticism," 1313; Lasch, "What I Remember," 23; Lasch, "For a Free Press," 40. Gouldner notes that the language of the "new class" is "relatively more situation-free" than more tradition-bound language, discounting the authority of region and local custom and making dialectical rationality the universal judge over all particulars. Gouldner, *The Future of Intellectuals,* 28.

36. RL to CL, TLS, 31 March 1970, 2:21; CL to RL and ZL, TLS, 7 October 1953, 0:10; CL, *The Revolt of the Elites and the Betrayal of Democracy* (New York: Norton, 1994), 20-21. Levine writes that "Although the stated intention of the arbiters of culture was to proselytize and convert, to lift the masses up to their level, in fact their attitudes often had the opposite effect." *Highbrow/Lowbrow,* 235.

"make me popular with my classmates," residents of the overwhelmingly Republican suburb of Barrington. On a more philosophic level, he remembered "flaunting" his atheism, and poking fun at his classmates' "religiosity." One of his high school girlfriends, a Wellesley student with Quaker leanings, debated the merits of pacifism with Kit by letter, and pleaded with him to reconsider his fundamental beliefs: "But you — you do not believe in God, and I know it! I wish you could understand that God exists. Maybe you will when you begin to love someone, or an idea, or a creative medium within yourself." Earlier he had taunted her for her religious questing, and she furiously defended herself: "I am not participating in a search for religion just because it is done and that is an unfair thing for you to say to me." The next fall, Kit's senior year of high school, she confessed to having "become morbidly religious," regularly going to the chapel and singing in the choir — activities she knew he did not "sanction."[37]

His contempt for high school notwithstanding, during his senior year he edited the school newspaper, wrote a play for performance at commencement, and won a statewide Latin contest, for which he was awarded a scholarship at the University of Chicago. He continued to pour most of his literary efforts into fiction, and by the time of his graduation from high school in the spring of 1950 he had submitted his work for publication to many elite magazines, including *The New Yorker, The Atlantic Monthly,* and *Harper's.* They each rejected his submissions, but an editor of the *Saturday Evening Post* took care to commend him for his "free-ranging inventiveness." As graduation neared, despite the scholarship offer at Chicago, he had his eyes trained on one school only: venerable Harvard College.[38]

---

37. The newspaper article, "His Birthday Present: First Prize For Essay," is from the *Tower Lakes in Barrington,* in 69:8; Blake and Phelps, "History as Social Criticism," 1311-1313; Patricia Miller to CL, ALS, 4 November 1948 and 31 October 1949, 0:24. Gouldner describes accurately the child-rearing approach of the Lasches: "An older generation of the New Class . . . typically imparted concern for autonomy and a skepticism of traditional authority"; not surprisingly, many sixties radicals "had often learned the rudiments of the culture of critical discourse from their parents *long before they went to college*" (italics his). Gouldner describes the new class as both "emancipatory *and* elitist" (italics his). Gouldner, *The Future of Intellectuals,* 70, 84.

38. Fox, "An Interview with Christopher Lasch," 4; the rejection notes are in 58:6.

CHAPTER TWO

A Part of America Whatever That Means

It is at these times, when I realize I am not alone (but a part of America whatever that means, except that the one thing it means is that wherever I go I can not not be a part of it) — that I feel most alone.
                Christopher Lasch to Naomi Dagen, 22 January 1954[1]

T he state of the world in which Christopher Lasch made his fledgling steps as a young adult proved to be utterly decisive in the formation of his settled political orientation and his mature moral sensibilities. It was a world for which his parents' upbeat progressivism had ill prepared him. Dachau and Hiroshima now stood alongside the likes of Paris and Vienna on the grand international landscape, as the crises of the 1930s and 1940s continued to batter progressive notions of identity and hope. Visions of fluid and steady uplift were slipping away.

Kit enrolled in Harvard in the fall of 1950, returning to the place where his family had lived during the 1940-41 academic year, when Robert had been a Nieman fellow at the university. His father later credited that year in Cambridge with nurturing within Kit "a passionate interest in history," and suspected that it had "strongly motivated him to attend Harvard." Robert's own influence also seemed to weigh heavily in Kit's decision. When a friend pressed Kit during his junior year of high school on his motive for attending Harvard, she pointed

---

1. CL to Naomi Dagen, ALS, 22 January 1954, 0:34.

toward Robert: "Why are you going to Harvard? Because your father expects it or because it has something you want or because it is the thing to do?"[2]

Whatever his motivations, Lasch boarded a train to Boston in the fall of 1950 and quickly found himself delighting in his new world. Red Sox baseball, new friendships, and vigorous intellectual challenge helped him endure the usual bouts of homesickness. His roommate was also planning a future in writing, though Kit was not impressed, at least initially. After a week in Cambridge he described John Updike as "a very intelligent kid . . . more industrious than I, but I think his stuff lacks perception and doesn't go very deep. He is primarily a humorist. As he himself admits, he is probably a hack. At least he has more of a hack in him than a profound artist." Updike and Lasch would engage in a friendly writer's competition over the next few years, one that Lasch gradually began to sense he was losing. But it was not for not trying: one week following his arrival at Harvard he complained to his parents that he had "started to write a story" but only "managed to get three lines down before the thundering herd descended." Freshmen roommates, not surprisingly, cramped this aspiring writer's style.[3]

The cultural meaning of his move east was not lost on Kit. Keenly and uneasily aware of his Midwestern roots as he ventured into the Ivy League, he would in his junior year decry to his parents the "insecurity" that is "often found in people who are from the Midwest but seem ashamed to admit it" — an insecurity he himself reflected. The lingering memory of Wisconsin's Frederick Jackson Turner and the presence of the Ohioan Schlesingers on the history faculty proved that Harvard was willing to graft in outsiders who were of suitable stock, but overall the aged Bostonian trunk was still strong. James Bryant Conant, president since 1933, was in 1950 busily expanding graduate

2. Robert Lasch, "What I Remember" (unpublished ms. written 1982-1987, CLP 69:26, 27), 90; Patricia Jane Miller to CL, ALS, 6 December 1948, 0:24.

3. CL to ZL & RL, TLS, 26 September 1950, 0:2. Lasch later recalled that he and Updike "were both equally conscious of wanting to be fiction writers." Lasch remembered "reading everything he wrote almost, for the *Advocate* and the *Lampoon,* and I think it must have been getting through to me that he was a lot better at this than I was, which may have had something to do with the fact that I didn't pursue it." Richard Wightman Fox, "An Interview with Christopher Lasch," *Intellectual History Newsletter* 16 (1994), 5. Lasch did "pursue" fiction writing in a more serious way than he lets on in this interview.

programs, promoting research, and raising academic standards. Harvard still stood proudly at the pinnacle of elite Eastern culture, although the removal of anti-Jewish quotas and the passing of the GI Bill had begun to alter its complexion.[4]

Like the rest of America, Harvard was forced to confront and adapt to the cultural and geopolitical realities of the early cold war, and its means of doing so is worth noting. Indeed, it is plausible that Lasch's eventual rejection of elite progressive culture had its roots in just such maneuvering. Former Harvard professor Sigmund Diamond's study of midcentury Harvard, for instance, reveals a pattern of covert cooperation with Washington's official and unofficial waging of the cold war; in Diamond's words, Harvard in the 1950s was characterized by a sharp "contrast between official statements and offstage acts." Diamond, himself a victim of Harvard's red purge, discovered that university officials had requested that the Federal Bureau of Investigation probe its faculty, and had gone so far as to call upon faculty members to investigate one another; professor of government Henry Kissinger, in cooperation with the bureau, notoriously tampered with the mail of his colleagues. "Harvard had not always required informing as the price of continued association with the university," Diamond wryly notes. Meanwhile, the eminent Harvard sociologist Talcott Parsons — who in the 1970s would become one of Lasch's primary targets in a set of more theoretical controversies — approved for cold war purposes the covert importation into the university community of German scientists who had collaborated with the Nazi regime. Robert Lasch, a vocal critic of the red scare, was not unaware of at least the tip of this iceberg, making mention to Kit in the fall of 1950 that a Harvard geology professor, Kirtley F. Mather, "has now had the honor of being McCarthyized."[5]

Kit's parents continued nurturing his political convictions in a nat-

4. CL to ZL & RL, TLS, 27 March 1953, 0:10. Significantly, an important part of Conant's mission was, in his words, to make Harvard "more representative in terms of both geography and family income," not just a school for young Brahmins. Quoted in Richard M. Freeland, *Academia's Golden Age: Universities in Massachusetts, 1945-1970* (New York: Oxford University Press, 1992), 128.

5. Sigmund Diamond, *Compromised Campus: The Collaboration of Universities with the Intelligence Community, 1945-1955* (New York: Oxford University Press, 1992), 123, 34, 18. On Kissinger, see 138-10; on Parsons, 88-95; RL to CL, TL, 31 October 1950, 0:1.

ural if protective way during his Harvard years, even as they themselves were navigating the rapidly changing times. How they, as Midwestern progressives of working-class origins, conceived of and responded to Harvard is itself a study in middle-class tensions. Zora, at least in one mood, viewed Harvard's elitist ethos with distaste. She scoffed to Kit about those who "believed that 'social contacts' are the chief value in a place like Harvard," and took issue with the notion that "future advancement is largely a matter of knowing the right people." But aside from such criticism of class dynamics, Harvard, to Robert and Zora, still represented that to which Robert had directed his own creedal reverence, "the true, the good, and the beautiful." The reach for a higher plane was justified so long as it was directed toward the service of the common good. Harvard was to be admired only insofar as it advanced the broader hope for a more democratic, liberally cultivated, world.[6]

What Harvard alum Roger Rosenblatt has called the "genteel Harvard of the 1950s" turned out to be politely hospitable to this variety of progressivism. Rosenblatt, a graduate student and faculty member in English throughout the 1960s, recalls that before the events of the late sixties nothing mattered more at Harvard "than the mutual reassurance that everybody shared the same liberal beliefs about everything, even if that were not the case, and as long as those opinions did not put the believers in any real jeopardy." So Kit felt quite free to fly the family flag. In the fall of 1950, while his father was speaking out against the McCarran Act and loyalty tests at an Omaha teachers convention, and as his mother was becoming a central figure in the League of Women Voters chapter in St. Louis, where the Lasches had moved when Robert was appointed editor of the editorial page at the *St. Louis Post-Dispatch,* Kit was enduring his first Thanksgiving away from home with friends of the family, whom he derided as "typical Indiana reactionaries." Reflecting on the visit in a letter to his parents, he reported that when the host had dared to make "an attack on British socialism," he had "sat nervously" but, he assured his parents, managed to keep quiet. Although other interests frequently diverted his attention from the political scene during his college years — especially his constant fiction writing — his political convictions did not suffer. After reading Alistair Cooke's *A Generation on Trial* as a junior, he made it clear that in this cold war cause célèbre, in which the ex-

6. ZL to CL, TL, 22 September 1950, 0:1.

communist Whittaker Chambers accused FDR aide Alger Hiss of espionage, he knew where he stood: "Chambers is so clearly a degenerate, and Hiss represents everything we like to think of as admirable; and he was a New Dealer, an idealist."[7]

The campaign of Democrat and former Illinois governor Adlai Stevenson in 1952 drew Kit's full attention. In mid-October he reported to his parents that "Everybody here is getting more and more pessimistic about Stevenson's chances." Perry Miller, his generation's leading historian of Puritan New England, "seemed quite concerned," and Kit's tutor, Donald B. Meyer, went so far as to send off "a memorandum to Springfield urging them to get tough." Despite the portent of imminent disaster, Kit maintained hope: "I would like to feel that the election will be decided on issues, and there it seems to me Stevenson has an obvious advantage." On election day he worked for Volunteers for Stevenson, marching at the polls with a placard, and, "sensing the closeness of the contest," he made a "modest donation" the day before the election.[8]

On November 5, the morning after the election, a heartbroken and shocked Kit Lasch commiserated with his parents in a lengthy letter. He had never before seen a Republican president. He wrote his parents,

7. Roger Rosenblatt, *Coming Apart: A Memoir of the Harvard Wars of 1969* (Boston: Little, Brown and Company, 1997), 13, 29, 30; RL to CL, TL, 31 October 1950, 0:1; CL to RL and ZL, TLS, 21 November 1950, 0:2; CL to ZL & RL, TLS, 24 October 1952, 0:8. The McCarran Act made it a crime (in its own language) to "agree with any other person to engage in any overt act which would substantially contribute to the establishment within the United States of a totalitarian dictatorship." See Geoffrey Perrett, *A Dream of Greatness: The American People, 1945-1963* (New York: Coward, McCann & Geoghegan, 1979), 222-28.

On his constant writing: Zora encouraged Kit to engage in some "frivolous activity" during the inter-semester break of his junior year, but suspected that he would instead be "working at the novel." Later that year Kit described his summer plans to his parents: "I have a great many novels and plays and stories I would like to write this summer if I have time. I would also like to write a movie script on Benedict Arnold . . . One of the novels would be an epic and slightly beyond me at this stage." ZL to CL, TL, 21 January 1953, 0:9; CL to ZL & RL, TLS, 11 May 1953, 0:10.

8. CL to ZL & RL, TLS, 15 October 1952, 0:8. After watching Richard Nixon's famed "Checkers Speech" in September of 1952, he wryly noted that he found it "interesting that the Republicans, who harp on Stevenson's degrading the campaign with humor, seemed to have no qualms about employing the cheapest kind of melodrama." CL to ZL & RL, TLS, 27 September 1952, 0:8.

For me the hardest thing to realize is that the Democrats will no longer be in the White House, that the long journey is at last finished, that the last of the New Dealers are passing from the scene. It was inevitable that it should end; but it seems impossible.

Lasch doubted that the Republican would make the "bold and imaginative steps toward peace" that Stevenson might have made. He hoped that things weren't "too depressed at home."[9]

His engagement with American political history deepened during his final two years at Harvard, and his family continued to share a political world. In the spring of 1953, while Robert was writing for Robert La Follette's old organ, the *Progressive,* and Zora was beginning her stint as first vice-president of the Missouri League of Women Voters, Kit was declaring, in an essay on R. H. Tawney, that it was liberalism that had "brought capitalism within control and thereby saved it from destroying itself and everything we value." "Liberalism," he concluded, "in spite of continuous clamorings to the contrary, is not yet dead."[10]

Far from it. It in fact represented the very best hope for democracy, as he explained to his parents in the fall of his junior year. "I show all this concern for the Democratic Party," he explained, "because I still believe that, at this time at any rate, it alone can reflect the people." But Lasch was just getting started on his peripatetic way, and his experience at Harvard, what he later remembered as an "exciting intellectual life," unveiled possibilities disturbing and alluring at once.[11]

*   *   *

Lasch's four years at Harvard coincided with the college's most intensive period of experimentation with a new, liberal arts–driven curriculum, a weaker version of the one introduced at the University of Chicago in those same years by Robert Maynard Hutchins. Hutchins, who

---

9. CL to ZL & RL, TLS, 5 November 1952, 0:8.

10. RL to CL, TL, 11 March 1953, 0:9; ZL to CL, TL, 15 May 1953, 0:9; "Religion versus Capitalism," unpublished paper by Christopher Lasch, in CLP, 58:8.

11. CL to ZL & RL, TLS, 5 November 1952, 0:8; Fox, "An Interview with Christopher Lasch," 7.

had become president at only thirty years of age, hoped to arrest the drift toward curricular fragmentation and what he and others feared was an amoral scientism, tendencies that seemed especially troubling in the aftermath of the world wars. Canonical texts in western civilization, especially those that focused on moral and political philosophy, were especially central to Hutchins's vision. The historian James Sloan Allen calls this movement "a revival of traditional humanism," and the fact that it could be so classified is itself telling, the elasticity of the term reflecting well the philosophical ambivalence and political impotence of the movement. But it did powerfully reflect, as Allen puts it, "a hunger for certainty, unity, and metaphysical and moral truth," fomented by the vast moral and political crises of the 1930s and 1940s.[12]

Influenced by this reform movement, Harvard in 1949 adopted a core curriculum that limited freshmen and sophomores to twelve basic courses within the subdivisions of the humanities, social sciences, and science and mathematics. In 1955, the year following Lasch's graduation, these requirements were relaxed, as the insularity of academic disciplines, along with a general lack of philosophic consensus, began to erode the postwar hopes. The period of experimentation came to a quick end, but not before a cohort of students had been guided toward an encounter with and reconsideration of old texts and older understandings of the world.[13]

12. James Sloan Allen, *The Romance of Commerce and Culture: Capitalism, Modernism, and the Chicago-Aspen Crusade for Cultural Reform* (Chicago: University of Chicago Press, 1983), 79, 91.

13. See Thomas Bender, "Politics, Intellect, and the American University, 1945-1995," *Daedalus* 126:1 (Winter 1997), 5-18. See also Christopher J. Lucas, *American Higher Education: A History* (New York: St. Martin's Press, 1994), 247-55. For Paul A. Carter's gloss on this period, see *Another Part of the Fifties* (New York: Columbia University Press, 1983), especially chapter six, "History, Mystery, and the Modern World," 141-67, and chapter seven, "The Inmates of the Academy: The World of Worthal and Snarf," 168-97. Writes Carter: "To listen to commencement speeches, Phi Beta Kappa luncheon addresses, or inspirational talks to incoming freshmen in those years one would have imagined that all the professors were holding up against the onslaught of barbarism the standards of the Good, the Beautiful, and the True. Probably some of them were," 179. Thomas Bender notes the paradoxical relationship between the consumerist order gaining strength in the postwar world and the conservative drift of the academy: "Even as Americans embraced a bright and shiny world of consumer products, American

Kit, despite chronic self-doubts about his intellectual abilities and the usual misgivings about the demands of the courses, found himself thriving in this altered climate. His first semester featured a humanities course that began with the Old Testament book of Job. With surprise he reported to his parents in early October of his first semester that "The Job business turned out to be fairly fascinating going." At the same time he was studying the intellectual history of the late Roman Empire. Again, the young freshman unexpectedly found himself drawn to theology, this time through the writings of Augustine:

> I must confess that I got to like St. Augustine. I don't know how this happened. I can't stomach his theology, and I certainly could not lead what he calls the good life; in fact, there are very few ideas of his I do like. . . . What is compelling about him, I guess, is the sheer weight of his personality and intellect projected with great force into every line.[14]

Lasch's early forays into the Old Testament and Christian theology certainly would have pleased the likes of Conant and Hutchins, stressing as they had the importance of religion, or at least religious inquiry, for their broader cultural vision. The sense that the religious heritage of the West should not be neglected and could actually be appropriated for salutary ends pervaded their thinking. Democracy, these educators thought, would only be strengthened by a collective immersion into the intellectual traditions they understood to have produced it. Religion, though, was always in service of democracy, and theology could entertain no hopes of rising above handmaiden status. The familiar lines of subordination were never seriously questioned.[15]

---

intellectuals became more sensitive to the problem of evil than at any time since the seventeenth century," 10.

14. CL to ZL & RL, TLS, 5 October 1950, 0:2; CL to ZL & RL, TLS, 29 October 1950, 0:2.

15. The Harvard commission, recognizing the delicacy of this issue, had written that "the goal of education is not in conflict with but largely includes the goal of religious education, education in the western tradition, and education in modern democracy." *General Education in a Free Society: Report of the Harvard Committee* (Cambridge: Harvard University Press, 1945), 46. Tellingly, Hutchins himself had no truck with organized religion, and was boosting religion-in-general rather than

Still, this revival of respect for what became known as the nation's "Judeo-Christian heritage" touched Kit at some level, and since his parents were decidedly less than enthusiastic about such developments, Kit's nascent interest in theology became a recurring point of tension. He was encountering religion as if for the first time, both academically and personally; besides reading St. Augustine for class, he was living with students who seemed to be believers of various sorts. After making his confession about Augustine to his parents he reported that a friend had actually undertaken a fast. He hastened to assure them, though, and perhaps himself, that he was

> not getting converted . . . although if I escape it will be remarkable, because I am daily subjected to a steady bombardment of religious ideas I had never thought about much before. What's more, with all the fasts, etc., going on . . . it is hard to maintain one's intellectual integrity.[16]

Zora was especially quick to respond to Kit's plight, knowledgeable as she was about the "physical ailments and religious manias" that beset so many freshmen. "I hope you won't be infected with French's religious fanaticism," she wrote; she claimed not to be "seriously worried about it," but warned that such experience could "seriously affect your thinking." A "religious flare-up," she noted, could require consultation with a "psychiatric advisor," and suggested that the dean's

---

the necessity of membership in particular communions. George M. Marsden argues that these educators "were affirming, as liberal Protestantism had done, the religious value of the best of Western culture itself. . . . If religion was valued primarily for its civilizing moral ideals, then one could identify those moral ideals and determine how to promote them without directly resorting to Christianity." Marsden, *The Soul of the American University: From Protestant Establishment to Established Nonbelief* (New York: Oxford University Press, 1994), 377, 389. On the curricular appropriation of religion, see also George M. Marsden and Bradley J. Longfield, eds., *The Secularization of the Academy* (New York: Oxford University Press, 1992), as well as David Hollinger, *Science, Jews, and Secular Culture: Studies in Mid-Twentieth-Century American Intellectual History* (Princeton: Princeton University Press, 1996). D. G. Hart sets this selective appropriation of religion in the context of the longer development of academic religious studies in *The University Gets Religion: Religious Studies in American Higher Education since 1870* (Baltimore: Johns Hopkins University Press, 1999).

16. CL to ZL & RL, TLS, 29 October 1950, 0:2.

office should be more closely monitoring residence life at Harvard. At the mid-semester point of his first semester Kit reassured his parents again. Worried about his grades, he declared that "I have not become converted yet, else I would pray for divine assistance. Only hard work, I fear, will see me through this ordeal."[17]

Divine assistance or no, Kit worked hard, and excelled. He gradually became more committed to the field of history, winning the history department's William Scott Ferguson Prize for an essay on Thucydides at the end of his sophomore year. He also continued to enjoy the broad humanistic orientation of the curriculum, and, despite the warnings of his parents, persisted in nurturing an interest in theology, influenced by the broad effect neo-orthodox theologians, especially the Lutheran Reinhold Niebuhr, were having on American intellectuals of all sorts in these years. In a time when both Catholic and Protestant seminaries had by 1950 doubled their prewar enrollments, and when, in the 1959 declaration of the philosopher Hans Meyerhoff, "Christian interpretations of history, in the Augustinian tradition, have reasserted themselves strongly after a lapse of a few hundred years," Niebuhr's elaboration of the doctrine of original sin, delivered in the pointed language of social criticism, had won him a wide audience. "The culture craved a spokesman for the tragic sense of life," Niebuhr's biographer Richard Wightman Fox has noted. "Niebuhr had the intellectual skill, religious credentials and personal charisma to step forward and seize the day."[18]

It's neither surprising, then, nor perhaps atypical, that in the spring of his sophomore year Lasch wrote that "the everlasting St. Augustine" was "coming to symbolize Harvard" for him. He was far from embracing the Christian faith, however. In the fall of his junior year he commended his formerly fasting friend Ed French for having "chosen to build his ideas around the figure of Socrates and the serene idealism of Plato, rather than the twisted, tortured framework of Christian theology."[19]

---

17. ZL to CL, TL, 7 November 1950, 0:1; CL to ZL & RL, TLS, 6 November 1950, 0:2.

18. Mark A. Noll, *A History of Christianity in the United States and Canada* (Grand Rapids: Eerdmans, 1992), 437; Hans Meyerhoff, ed., *The Philosophy of History in Our Time* (Garden City, N.Y.: Doubleday Anchor Books, 1959), 23; Richard Wightman Fox, *Reinhold Niebuhr: A Biography* (New York: Pantheon, 1985), 234.

19. CL to ZL & RL, TLS, 5 March 1952, 0:8; CL to ZL & RL, TLS, 20 October 1952, 0:8.

Still, the religious flavor of the era pervaded his coursework, sometimes by his own choice, other times not. In the fall of his senior year he enrolled in a course taught by Sydney Ahlstrom on Pauline theology and Western history. And while considering the possibility of taking a class in systematic theology his final semester, he confided to his girlfriend, a student at Oberlin, that he had been reading modern theological luminaries Albert Schweitzer, Karl Barth, Søren Kierkegaard, and the ubiquitous Niebuhr. Even as a senior Kit felt the need to apologize to his parents for these interests. The course on St. Paul "may seem like a peculiar thing to take," he cautiously wrote — adding that "indeed it is." When he later mentioned to his parents the course he was considering in systematic theology (he found it, he admitted, "pretty tempting") his defense was that he had "discovered that theology — or at least some theologians — are very enjoyable to read if you have a sloppy mind like mine. You don't have to worry about defining things the way you do in philosophy."[20]

The letter he received from his father in response signaled that his patience with his son's wandering had come to an end: "I am bound to say that this seems to me about the dopiest subject a practicing atheist could take. . . . As you can deduce, if there were 200 courses in the catalogue I would count 199 of them as preferable to theology." In the end, Kit chose not to take the course, and shortly thereafter confirmed his allegiance to the generation of Darrow when, after reading about William Jennings Bryan's later years, he denounced Bryan's "shameful conduct at the Scopes Trial," scorning such "smug bigotry" and the "narrow-mindedness of organized religion." If by his graduation he was no longer a "practicing atheist," he kept the news to himself. Years later he admitted, in a letter to the social critic Barbara Ehrenreich, that he had "flirted with existential-

20. CL to ZL & RL, TL, 7 October 1953, 0:10; CL to Naomi Dagen, TLS, 8 January 1954, 0:34; CL to ZL & RL, TLS, 15 January 1954, 0:12. In the October 7, 1953, letter Lasch admitted to having to purchase a Bible for the Ahlstrom course, and then gave another glimpse of the midcentury religious ferment at Harvard: "I am sure this will make [the recently installed] President Pusey very happy, as he seems to feel there is not enough religion at Harvard and stated that if the chapel were big enough to hold everyone he would institute compulsory chapel. Mr. Pusey seems to be a Midwestern puritan of the worst kind. Most of the professors seem very riled by his pronouncement on religion."

ism by way of relief" from what he described as his parents' "optimistic rationalism."[21]

For the time being his parents' basic moral and intellectual deposit was safe with their son, but his exposure to the postwar burst of European humanism and the general revival of interest in religion helped to place a wedge between the world of his childhood and his own emerging adulthood. Of the many short stories he wrote during college, one in particular captures his internal wrangling. In "Christmas 1853," published in the *Harvard Advocate* in the spring of his senior year — the only piece of fiction he would ever publish — he depicted a thirteen-year-old girl's secret efforts to come to terms with her own beliefs about God. Her father was the bold, quietly audacious village atheist who, despite the warnings of the townspeople, "would not go to church." He was rational and confident in his heterodoxy and she quietly admired him; like him, she "knew that God was not there." Yet the girl remained perplexed by her father and his ways, and, despite her assurances to herself, her questions about God remained. Prone to wonder and brood, she sensed, in her words, "how the world was deep and dark." Despite her father's powerful example, or perhaps because of it, God, for her, was more than a memory.[22]

*   *   *

Deep and dark: an apt description of Lasch's own interior life. If in his correspondence with his parents he tended to mimic somewhat woodenly their rational progressive outlook, his own writing and his correspondence with friends reveal another Christopher Lasch: introspective, moody, passionate, fierce. Politicking for Stevenson and defending liberalism in class papers begin to look rehearsed; some-

---

21. Robert Lasch's comments are quoted by Lasch in CL to Naomi Dagen, TLS, 1 February 1954, 0:34; CL to ZL & RL, TLS, 5 March 1954, 0:12; CL to Barbara Ehrenreich, TLS, n.d., 7b:9 (this letter was written sometime after Ehrenreich's *Fear of Falling* was published in 1989). For an illuminating autobiographical take on religion and academe in this era, see Henry F. May, "Religion and American Intellectual History, 1945-1985: Reflections on an Uneasy Relationship," in *Religion and Twentieth Century American Intellectual Life,* ed. Michael J. Lacey, Woodrow Wilson Center Series (New York: Cambridge University Press, 1989): 12-22.

22. Christopher Lasch, "Christmas 1853," *Harvard Advocate* 137:4 (March 1954), 6.

where beneath the surface, as his encounter with religion at Harvard hints, he was beginning what would become a lifelong reckoning with his parents' legacy and identity, a burden he did not bear lightly.

His college fiction (most of which he turned in as assignments for writing classes) surfaced that which elsewhere tended to lie submerged. His narratives flowed with strong currents of adolescent yearning and disappointment, pulsing with a steady, somber undertow. He had imbibed his mother's relentless intolerance of banality, and ultimately he, in a time-honored pattern, turned the sharpness of her perspective back upon his own received way of life. And like many literarily-inclined youth, he turned to writing fiction in a quest for self-understanding.

Although Kit's prose was lithe and tight (his teachers cheered on his attempts to find publishers for his work), the stories themselves tended to be lugubrious and doleful; he remembered years later writing "in the Hemingway manner." Updike, in a 1964 short story rooted in his college experience and set at Harvard in 1950, created a Laschian character, "Dawson," the roommate of one "Kern." Both were freshmen and "wanted to be writers"; Dawson, "a disciple of Sherwood Anderson and Ernest Hemingway," wrote in a "stern, plain style." Lasch later blessed Updike's description of his writing when he, by then chair of the graduate studies program at Rochester, titled the writing primer he developed for the students "Plain Style," published in-house at the University of Rochester and later posthumously by the University of Pennsylvania Press. But for now, Lasch's stylistic energies were absorbed in other, more acutely personal preoccupations.[23]

If midcentury middle-class American life represented The American Way of Life, young Lasch seemed to experience more than a mild generational discontent with it. Often his stories, usually written in a form he described to his parents as "semi-autobiographical," featured characters at odds with the culture of the upper-middle class, despising its inanities and beleaguered at the prospect of trying to find fulfillment within it. In "Home Is the Sailor" he told the story of a

---

23. Fox, "Interview with Christopher Lasch," 4; John Updike, "The Christian Roomates," in *The Early Stories, 1953-1975* (New York: Knopf, 2003), 167; CL, *Plain Style: A Guide to Written English,* ed. Stewart Weaver (Philadelphia: University of Pennsylvania Press, 2002).

college student who while home in St. Louis throws a party for her old friends. She knows that in coming home she had felt a measure of peace, understanding, finally, that the one who leaves home "has traveled only when he returns." Yet she also knows that "home" cannot bear the weight of her expectations, of her hopes, of her newfound wisdom; "The parties, the pretense of gaiety, would go on and on." At the story's end she feels trapped. Despite her new knowledge and learning, "She was as weak and empty as they. She knew things they did not know and yet would continue to live with them." Home in middle-class America was where she belonged — she had no other true place — but this quiet epiphany, far from boosting her spirits, only adds to her burden.[24]

Hovering, critical parents at odds with their older, self-absorbed teenagers figure prominently in several of Lasch's stories, including one about a nineteen-year-old boy (a story he wrote at the same age), "Honor Thy Father and Mother." Is "happiness," the boy wonders, "a highway stretching endlessly into the past, a road dusty and monotonous under the feet of the traveler, but to his backward gaze a path sparkling amid green hills, tinged with magic?" This pervading melancholic sense, perhaps the dominant quality of Lasch's college fiction, reveals a young man wrestling with a den of fierce, if familiar, adolescent demons while struggling mightily to envision a satisfying future for himself. "Spring Song," a *Wasteland*-inspired series of fictional vignettes, describes a man who "had played and loved once," but then had allowed himself to drift into "a lifetime of passivity," never having fulfilled his dream of becoming a writer, turning away even from marriage due to his mother's interfering, pressuring presence. The man, he writes, "lived acted upon, but never acting; observing, unseen," an isolating passivity that Lasch seemed to know and fear. In "Narcissus" he tells the story of a self-obsessed woman. The story features no action — just the girl reflecting from within the shelter of her own imagination, isolated by her own will yet unable to break beyond the borders of self. "Nothing Elizabeth remembers seems real. The only thing that seems to exist is what is in her room at this moment. She knows only herself and what belongs to her." This mood and stance would in later years tinge and shape much of

24. CL to ZL & RL, 19 January 1953, TLS, 0:10; CL, "Home Is the Sailor," unpublished ms. in 58:1.

Lasch's mature cultural criticism. But even in college his writing took the shape of a stern, even severe form of criticism, not focused on the possible so much as the writer's perception of the actual.[25]

Wrestling with his parents' political legacy figured deeply in Lasch's struggle to imagine a future. While many college students of his generation were confronting, in sometimes terrifying ways, their received religious beliefs, Lasch's variety of self-encounter took on a more political and philosophic cast — while still carrying the religious charge. The fundamental assumptions Robert and Zora Lasch had as college students seized upon in replacing religious categories and experience were the ones Lasch was forced to grapple with most intensively.

In a letter during his senior year to Naomi Dagen, a junior at Oberlin College whom he was then dating, he poured out his discontent with his parents, and with life itself, in a bitter sarcastic stream. Imagining their parents meeting at a party (both sets lived in St. Louis), he granted that "maybe they would stop to acknowledge that they had a son and daughter," but then they "would be on to politics in no time at all." If he announced to his parents that he and Naomi had gotten engaged, his parents would "probably say That's fine, Dear, and return to their respective newspapers or copies of the Reporter." Despite their intense political engagement and their cultural and intellectual sophistication, in his eyes they tended to skate along in the same surfacy way that made the American middle class so deplorable. They seemed to him unable or unwilling to fathom his dark world. For his part, Kit seemed unable to conceive of a way to bring them into it — much easier to maintain the peace. But beneath the surface turmoil held sway.[26]

In a letter to Dagen written the next day he ruminated on his upbringing, unveiling its profoundly political quality in a deluge of retrospection brought on by the prospect of the draft. After an evening listening to a former classmate describe his recent experience in the service, Kit admitted to being "awfully scared" — but not of the rigors of military life. Rather, it was the new America that he feared, the

25. CL, "Honor Thy Father and Mother," 10 April 1952, unpublished ms. in 58:3; CL, "Spring Song," unpublished ms. dated 29 April 1952 in 58:1; CL, "Narcissus," unpublished ms. in 58:3.

26. CL to Naomi Dagen, ALS, 21 January 1954, 0:34.

America of Eisenhower and McCarthy, a country that "claims to be a democracy and yet has this hideous fascist monster in its insides." Yet he could not deny that he was intricately, ineluctably connected to this America, whatever its awful shape, and so obligated to take action on its behalf. He knew that "somehow something must be saved out of the wreckage of whatever hopes were entertained by the eminently sensible people who managed to send this country into the world with a sensible birthright." The ideals of his childhood he still held tightly, recognizing that they were "buried in me," linked inextricably to the "unforgettable heritage of a liberal upbringing." He recalled

> the voice of Roosevelt which made you not afraid, and you never really believed that he could hardly walk; and the death of Roosevelt with the radio commentator having to stop and you realized suddenly that he could not go on because he was crying, and knew that even radio announcers cried when a Man died, and you were crying too, for a man you didn't even know, whom you had never met and whose hand you had never shaken — although your father had shaken his hand and would tell you about it if you asked him. . . .

He remembered how his "mother always said They, the unknown forces which were trying to drag the whole world to rack and ruin and must somehow be resisted and fought and beaten so the world would be a place you could fall in love in." But now, he could see, the unknown forces were within the beloved nation, threatening the hopeful future he had innocently imagined.

One basic, bedrock fact he knew: he was "a part of America whatever that means, except that the one thing it means is that wherever I go I can not not be a part of it." Yet this sense of membership seemed to only deepen his sense of alienation: "It is at these times, when I realize I am not alone . . . that I feel most alone." Even then, Lasch's sense of personal well-being commingled with his perception of the condition of the nation, and in 1954 this left him little reason for hope. Dissatisfied with the world his parents had embraced and made, he had failed to strike out on an alternative path that was satisfying, one that might restore his youthful hopes for a decent world.[27]

27. Quotations from this and the previous paragraph are from CL to Naomi Dagen, ALS, 22 January 1954, 0:34.

But it was not just the contours of national politics that had led Lasch to a sense of despair and alienation during his Harvard years. Unusually self-aware, he acknowledged to his parents his own introspective bent and called it "a curse." He knew that he was often cynical, tended to agree with a roommate who had called him a "chronic malcontent," yet admitted to his parents, that this persisting bitterness was "based on fundamental sentimentalism." Naomi Dagen too puzzled at what she called his "strange mixture of pessimism and idealism," unsure how to explain it or even understand it. Updike, Lasch's roommate for three years, later remembered Lasch as "a sensitive, intelligent, and even loving guy with a disconcerting way of throwing sulks." He sensed that as the years passed this "sulkiness kept getting in the way of the considerable wisdom and erudition he brought to the matter of America." Shaking off gloom did not come easily for the young Kit, or the aging Kit for that matter, but neither could he retreat from idealism into a hardened "realism." In his magnum opus, *The True and Only Heaven: Progress and Its Critics* (1991), he playfully titled one section of an autobiographical chapter "The Making of a Malcontent." Beneath the title he placed an epigraph from Randolph Bourne, one that he hoped, in the end, told his own story: "Malcontentedness may be the beginning of promise."[28]

If Lasch was sulky and sometimes cynical, he also managed to retain an enviable sense of proportion; in his case it led to a sardonic self-knowledge, a wistful ability to laugh at himself, albeit with a bitter edge. Writing as a senior to Dagen about the less-than-exciting routines of his college life, he reported that he had the day before done the usual: read two books, gone out for a beer with some friends, and then "came home and tried to Think. I had sort of resolved to Think for an hour or so before going to bed but it did not work very well. I am not going to assign any more Thinking periods." Yet his sense of struggle was real, rooted in more than personal idiosyncrasy or adolescent moodiness. Just months before graduation he expressed to Dagen, in the existential argot of the day, his sense that apart from intimacy "the world which I can touch and feel is yet with-

---

28. CL to ZL & RL, TLS, 19 January 1953, 0:10; CL to ZL & RL, TLS, 13 October 1953, 0:10; Naomi Dagen to CL, ALS, 22 February 1954, 0:30; John Updike, TLS to author, 3 March 1999; CL, TOH, 25.

out meaning, yet insists on confronting you as though it did." This, he complained, "is what is so tiring."[29]

* * *

Lasch's academic performance at Harvard was outstanding through and through. Not only did he graduate summa cum laude, the history department awarded his honors thesis, "Imperialism and the Independents: A Conflict of Allegiance," the prize for the best thesis of the year. Lasch, who had been aiming all along for a career as a writer, confessed to his parents that he had "enjoyed writing this thesis more than I can remember ever having enjoyed writing fiction." His commitment to history had grown steadily during his final years at Harvard. Although he had often expressed doubts that he would ever become "a scholar," historical writing, at least of a certain sort, could enfold both his artistic inclinations and his knack for political and cultural critique.[30]

His interest in history was from the beginning spurred by a presentist urgency, a legacy of both his father's editorial work and the progressive historiography of his youthful studies. As Lasch later put it, he had grown up understanding history to have "an inescapable element of the current in it." He displayed from the outset an interest in recent history, despite his often expressed distaste for the modern era, or perhaps because of it. As a sophomore he had begun to sense that "the closer you get to the present the more depressing history becomes." During his senior year he described late-nineteenth-century

29. CL to Naomi Dagen, TLS, 11 February 1954, 0:34; CL to Naomi Dagen, TLS, 28 January 1954, 0:34.

30. CL to ZL & RL, TLS, 20 March 1954, 0:12. In a typical pre-exams panic, Kit had written to his parents as a sophomore that "I really am not a scholar, I feel I must warn you." Sounding very scholarly the following year, he expressed concern that he had "lived a rather narrow life, scholastically," having "tried to learn well the few things I've read, instead of reading widely. . . . This constant re-reading and note-taking, and making little information cards, has not been too successful." He made a new pledge: "In short, I propose to enjoy myself, to indulge myself. . . . The main difference will be that I will not be staring at the same books all the time and trying to memorize things I will soon forget. . . . I will have only another year here to make up for the various intellectual opportunities wasted." Still, he concluded the letter doubting that he would ever become "a scholar." CL to RZ, TLS, 20 April 1952, 0:8; CL to ZL & RL, TLS, 20 May 1953, 0:10.

politics as "meaningless." There was "no purpose at all" in the constant "rushing about" of the various political leaders and movements: "'Progressives,' 'reformers,' the phrases are meaningless. All are conservatives. . . . all are men of the eighteenth century lost in the twentieth. And there is not one sane voice in the whole uproar." To become a sane voice at least in the field of history seemed a manageable goal to him as he began to walk, almost against his will, a more narrow vocational path.[31]

His honors thesis detailed the cause of the "anti-imperialists" who had opposed the United States' foreign policy at the turn of the twentieth century. Denouncing the "industrial despotism" that characterized the Republican party in the last half of the nineteenth century, he also railed against the "mad and uncontrollable longing after identity and adventure and power and glory" that characterized Teddy Roosevelt and his gang. The liberals, of course, were the heroes of this story, but he now depicted them, significantly, as flawed, having failed to bring "their issue before the country as the issue which outranked all others." Lasch's critical engagement with liberalism, still largely as affirmation, had begun in earnest.[32]

Writing, as he had mentioned to his parents, was a big factor in his decision to pursue a career as a historian. After three and a half years of studying history at Harvard, he had reported to Naomi Dagen that "The best writing encountered in history books would never stand up to a third rate novel." He had made it a point to rewrite his thesis so as to "eliminate the rather stuffy academic quality which seemed to have crept in to it"; he also vowed that if he ever did go into teaching, he would forbid students "to use any academic jargon whatsoever," or to ever use words "such as 'thus' and 'inasmuch'" (a commitment born out in *Plain Style*, where he denounced "the dull,

31. Blake and Phelps, "History as Social Criticism," 1313, 1319; CL to ZL & RL, TLS, 24 February 1952, 0:8; CL to Naomi Dagen, TLS, 8 February 1954, 0:34. On "progressive historiography" and its presentism, as well as its passageway into the postwar era, see Richard Hofstadter, *The Progressive Historians: Turner, Beard, Parrington* (New York: Knopf, 1969); Peter Novick, *That Noble Dream: The "Objectivity Question" and the American Historical Profession* (New York: Cambridge, 1988), Part II, "Objectivity Besieged," 111-278, and Part III, "Objectivity Reconstructed," 281-411.

32. CL, "Imperialism and the Independents: A Conflict of Allegiance," senior honors thesis, Harvard College, 31 March 1954, 7, 53, 108; in CLP 58:30.

noun-heavy, Germanic prose churned out in such abundance by the academy"). On the eve of his graduation he mentioned to Dagen that he had just read "two good books in American history," which had taken him by surprise since he "did not think there even were two good books in the whole field." The books, W. J. Cash's *The Mind of the South* and Arthur Schlesinger Jr.'s *The Age of Jackson,* were both classics in political and intellectual history, the fields that Lasch would bring together with considerable literary and historiographical verve in his later writing.[33]

As he prepared to leave Harvard, Lasch's professional future looked bright. His tutor Donald B. Meyer later recalled that "finding the young Christopher Lasch in class forty years ago was something like Leo Durocher's first sight of Willie Mays: What was there to teach? He could do it all." As Lasch made preparations to begin graduate studies in history at Columbia University in the fall of 1954, he took with him what Meyer described as "wonderful promise."[34]

Personally, Lasch was unsettled. He was writing a lot of fiction, and he was wrestling — with himself and with his future. "I can't seem to want what other people want," he had earlier in the year confided to Dagen. He confessed that he saw himself as distastefully "egocentric," someone who is "quite sure he is better than almost anyone else, who is desperately determined to get somewhere even if he doesn't know where." Torturing himself for his own faults, he warned her of the heated comment one of his roommates had once hurled at him: "I pity the girl who marries him thinking she'll save him." He did not disagree; he was "awfully afraid" that this observation had "a great deal of truth in it."[35]

His honest self-assessment was matched by a youthful, earnest belief in some final cosmic goodness, however inchoately defined. His comments for a Harvard class on Norman Mailer's postwar novel of World War II, *The Naked and the Dead,* which moved him deeply, reveal both the point of his internal battle and the hope he continued to

33. CL to Naomi Dagen, TLS, 14 January 1954, 0:34; CL to ZL & RL, TLS, 22 February 1954, 0:12; CL to Naomi Dagen, TLS, 27 January 1954, 0:34; CL, PS, 75; CL to Naomi Dagen, TLS, 2 May 1954, 0:35.

34. Donald B. Meyer, in "A Tribute to Christopher Lasch," bound edition of comments presented at the annual meeting of the Association of American Historians, 8 January 1994; in CLP 68:14.

35. CL to Naomi Dagen, TLS, 14 January 1954, 0:34.

guard. "Through their toil and suffering," he wrote of the beleaguered soldiers, "the men know not only themselves, but life. They learn the bitterness of failure; there is hardly a man who does not wonder if life is, after all, meaningless. They doubt God." But by the story's end, despite their failure and distress, "they grasp certain truths." They learn that "men are weak and helpless when removed from the considerations they have invented to shelter themselves." They discover that "one of the hardest things to do is to be true to themselves." Lasch applauded the book, in the end, for giving testament to "the remarkable endurance and recuperative powers of man." Struggling to keep the faith he had always known but also to move beyond it, Kit uneasily headed south to New York.[36]

36. CL, "Norman Mailer: *The Naked and the Dead,*" unpublished ms. in 58:4.

CHAPTER THREE

The Important Thing Is This Skepticism

The important thing is this skepticism: the refusal to be taken in by the slogans with which societies try to beguile us into thinking that they are transacting important business; the refusal to stop making distinctions; the refusal to stop writing poems and start building bomb shelters; the refusal to do one's part, to do something socially useful, to be "of service." If this attitude seems negative, a negative attitude is just what is called for.

Christopher Lasch to Walt Davis, July 1960[1]

C hristopher Lasch learned one thing quickly: Columbia University was not Harvard College, nor was New York City Cambridge. Discouragement pervaded his graduate school experience from the outset. On the verge of his first major academic appointment several years later he, in a candid letter to his dissertation mentor, William Leuchtenburg, described the period between 1954 and 1959 as "those dark years," a "very trying period." He had, he could see now, arrived at Columbia with an "exaggerated sense of my own accomplishments," which had "complicated" the ordinary difficulties of adjusting to a new city, a new school, and a new level of academic engagement. So deep was his discouragement that by the end of his first year he was considering graduate studies elsewhere.[2]

1. CL to Walt Davis, TL, 14 July 1960, 1:3.
2. CL to William Leuchtenburg, TL, 24 May 1961, 1:5.

Dissatisfaction had mounted on all sides. Living with a fellow Harvard alum on 114th Street, Lasch found Manhattan's vaunted midcentury cosmopolitanism less than alluring. During his first semester at Columbia he wrote to Naomi Dagen, "In spite of your high recommendation of New York, I am bound to say I dislike the place more and more. Detest would not be too strong a word." "Any hick college has more culture than New York," he stormed. He loathed the fact that "you can go there and not look up anybody you know, can stay within two or three blocks of them without looking them up." Strangely, this urban isolation seemed to be exactly what New Yorkers preferred:

> Everybody has a furtive look as if he were likely at any moment to run smack into a friend. The man without friends is lucky. He just has to avoid strangers. But woe to the man with friends! He can never be sure that some of his friends, instead of avoiding him, may actually be looking for him. He must be always on the alert, must develop a cat's watchfulness and agility; He must be light of foot and quick of eye . . . more animal than human.

Life in suburban Omaha and Chicago, not to mention Cambridge, had done little to prepare him for upper Manhattan.[3]

Having to cook for himself, of course, only added to the disorientation. Zora aided the cause by supplying cookbooks and recipes, along with socks and cookies. "There are many simple dishes you can prepare besides hot dogs and hamburgers," she lightly scolded. "Meat balls, for instance, or stews, or casserole dishes." Keeping body and soul together was a continual feat. Tucked into notes on his reading assignments was a card titled "Recipes Which Everyone Should Know," including *"Chicken Which You Will Love"* and *"Mom's Old Fashioned Beef Stew."* For his part, Robert continued to feed his son's political appetite, offering to send tapes of the McCarthy hearings during Lasch's first semester.[4]

The politics of the present, though, were far from Lasch's mind

3. CL to Naomi Dagen, TLS, 20 November 1954, 0:35; CL to Naomi Dagen, TLS, 28 January 1955, 0:36.

4. ZL to CL, n.d. (Fall 1954), TL, 0:11; "Recipes Which Everyone Should Know," by "Mrs. Austin Briggs," n.d., 59:4; RL to CL, TL, 30 September 1954, 0:11.

as he struggled to apprehend a past, a profession, and a discipline with which he had, he discovered, mistakenly presumed himself to be on easy terms. Early on he ranted to Dagen, in only a semi-playful tone, "Not only am I utterly incapable of understanding what in hell the New Deal is all about — it seems, as far as I can make out, to be some kind of elaborate game where everything has a name composed of a set of initials. . . . I am working on a theory (the only real idea I have come up with yet) by which the entire history of the period could be written only with initials." His sarcasm, though, was only the flipside of his heightened sense of failure. "It *has* been a great misfortune to discover that I am no longer capable of thought; that I read without comprehension and write in an equally unconscious state; that I pass through life in a kind of intellectual mist in which not only the real objects before me are indistinct but the sound of my own mental footsteps is muffled. A poor metaphor," he concluded in a cloud.[5]

Trying to diminish Kit's early sense of failure, Robert assured him that "your teachers are hazing you a bit in the old game of spurring the mule on to do his best. . . . They want to touch you up to make sure you don't coast on your *summa*." Despite these paternal gestures, Kit struggled to reconcile himself to his decision to attend Columbia. He began to investigate other graduate programs, including Harvard and Michigan State, and later admitted to Leuchtenburg that he had considered giving up entirely. He continued to take refuge in writing fiction, inciting at one point a gentle reprimand from Robert to "put aside the novel and TV plays until you get this more urgent work out of the way." To no avail. In the course of his first year at Columbia he entered negotiations with Little, Brown, and Company over a novel he was hoping to complete during the course of his graduate studies. In the fall of his second year Lasch reported to an editor, in what was by then a recurring refrain, that he had "written more than a hundred pages" of the novel; unfortunately, he continued, it "appears to be no nearer completion than it was in June." He was stubbornly reluctant to let go of the project, though. "I have more interest in writing now than I ever had before, and I have a number of ideas I am beginning to work on," he told the editor.[6]

5. CL to Naomi Dagen, TLS, 20 November 1954, 0:35.
6. RL to CL, TL, 26 October 1954, 0:11; CL to Alexander W. Williams, TL, 13

The bohemian life of a writer was far from the disciplined life of a scholar, not to mention the parochial life of the graduate student — at least a graduate student in the 1950s. At the end of his first year he complained to Dagen that he had not "been bombed, stoned, potted, pickled, stewed, tipsy, blotto, or even high in a long time." Of more consequence, Lasch later recalled having had no "conversation with anybody at Columbia during all this time about politics and international affairs." With a lively disdain he remembered, some forty years later, his training as "rigorously professional," all available energies consumed with tedious preparation for qualifying exams. Despite the presence of bona fide "New York Intellectuals" such as Richard Hofstadter and Lionel Trilling, as well as the legendary leftist sociologist C. Wright Mills, to Lasch graduate studies at Columbia were sterile, at a far remove from the "exciting intellectual life" he remembered at Harvard. Just a year after completing the Ph.D. he would urge a Columbia graduate student to "try not to get discouraged by the callousness of the system and the surprising lack of intellectual content." Grappling with ideas was what he desired; training for life in a guild was what he got.[7]

Despite his forays into fiction and his looming sense of failure, within his first year the history faculty at Columbia had singled Lasch out. In the spring of 1955 Robert Lasch met Leuchtenburg at a history convention in Chicago, and the professor allayed any doubts that Robert might have developed about Kit's future: Kit, according to Leuchtenburg, was "the most competent student they had ever had at Columbia," and "had a wonderful gift for writing." With delight Zora passed along to Kit this sorely needed encouragement, and added some more. "He said," wrote Zora, that "if a professor made a suggestion with reference to something you were working on you went away and came back with the idea developed far beyond what they had anticipated or sometimes beyond what he would have been able to do himself." After comparing notes on Lasch, the faculty had determined

February 1955, 1:5; CL to Alexander W. Williams, draft of a letter, 23 September 1955, 1:5.

7. CL to Naomi Dagen, TLS, 20 May 1955, 0:36; Casey Blake and Christopher Phelps, "History as Social Criticism: Conversations with Christopher Lasch," *Journal of American History* 80:4 (March 1994), 1315; Richard Wightman Fox, "An Interview with Christopher Lasch," *Intellectual History Newsletter* 16 (1994), 7; CL to Loren Farmer, TL, 7 May 1962, 1:9.

to keep him at Columbia "at all costs," sensing that Harvard might try to lure him back. "All of this was music to Daddy's ears — and naturally, to mine, too," wrote the reassured Zora.[8]

Leuchtenburg proved to be an anchor for Lasch during these early years. He had joined the faculty only two years prior to Lasch's first semester, having already piled up impressive academic and political achievements; during his career as a graduate student alone, Leuchtenburg had served as State Director of the Liberal Party, a field representative for a civil rights organization, and an organizer for Americans for Democratic Action. His own work in recent American history, tied explicitly to his political concerns, meshed well with Lasch's own personal history and presentist instincts (and also cast in doubt Lasch's later blanket denunciation of his strictly professional graduate training); Lasch enrolled early on in Leuchtenburg's classes, quickly winning the admiration of his instructor, who took to Lasch's style and verve. "A most discerning, non-grad-student essay" was a typical Leuchtenburg reaction to Lasch's work.[9]

A "non-grad-student essay": already Lasch's distaste for the orthodoxies that bound scholarly writing was becoming entrenched, which helps to shed light on his distaste for Columbia. It also helps to explain why of all the stars on Columbia's history faculty Richard Hofstadter, rather than Leuchtenburg, would come to exert the most profound and sustained influence on Lasch's thinking and approach to history. A Columbia Ph.D. and a member of its faculty since 1946, Hofstadter by the mid-1950s had emerged as one of the nation's prominent American historians. Particularly influential for Lasch was Hofstadter's 1948 *The American Political Tradition,* a book that attempted to recast American political history in a single stroke, erasing the old progressive vision of an America riven by class division and etching a distinctly midcentury vision of Americans united by liberal capitalism (a form of unity Hofstadter, in no uncertain terms, deplored). Hofstadter conceived of *The American Political Tradition* as an attempt to speak to the current "cultural crisis," and both the sophis-

8. ZL to CL, n.d. (Spring 1955), TL, 0:13.
9. William E. Leuchtenburg, "The Historian and the Public Realm," in *The Liberal Persuasion: Arthur Schlesinger, Jr., and the Challenge of the American Past,* ed. John Patrick Diggins (Princeton: Princeton University Press, 1997), 22-26; CL, "Two Views of Henry Cabot Lodge," unpublished ms. in 43:5.

tication of his thought and brilliance of his writing ensured that he would not be dismissed as a mere publicist. Hofstadter was living evidence for Lasch that historians could bring both the historical and the literary imagination to bear on the present with a force that demanded response. They could shape opinion. They could be intellectuals.[10]

It was a vision Lasch was groping toward. Remarkably, in part due to a curriculum centered on lecture classes rather than seminars and in part due to his early decision to study with Leuchtenburg, Lasch never ended up taking a single course from Hofstadter. He did serve as Hofstadter's research assistant during the summer of 1955, writing introductions to a collection of documents Hofstadter was editing. But Hofstadter's influence on Lasch would grow as his thinking matured. Late in his life Lasch reflected that Hofstadter had been "In many ways . . . the dominant figure on my intellectual horizon." "It took me a whole lifetime to come to term with this guy's work," he admitted, after decades of seeking himself to understand and illumine the American political tradition.[11]

At the time, though, Lasch's sense of the contours of American intellectual and political life was only beginning to form, and during his years at Columbia Lasch found himself for the most part simply trying to survive. "We were so loaded with work, staggering work, that it didn't leave much time for anything else," he recalled. After two years he was eager to get away from New York to begin teaching, though "the authorities," he wrote Donald Meyer, had advised him to stay on as a full-time student. He told Meyer that he wished to begin to teach "not because I know enough to pass on to anybody, but because I might learn more that way than I am currently learning in graduate school." Besides, he added, teaching "could scarcely be more hectic than this."[12]

---

10. *The American Political Tradition and the Men Who Made It*, Twenty-fifth Anniversary Edition, Foreword by Christopher Lasch (New York: Knopf, 1973), xxx, xxxii. Daniel Walker Howe and Peter Elliott Finn capture well Hofstadter's approach, so influential on Lasch: "Hofstadter thought of himself as both scholar and social critic. For him the categories were complementary, the function of the intellectual in modern society being that of critic." "Richard Hofstadter: The Ironies of an American Historian," *Pacific Historical Review* 43:1 (February 1974), 11.

11. Blake and Phelps, "History as Social Criticism," 1317; Fox, "Interview," 6.

12. Fox, "Interview," 7; CL to Donald B. Meyer, TLS, 7 February 1956, 1:6.

Teaching also provided a means of making more money than the fellowships at Columbia could provide, especially important due to his engagement in the spring of 1956 to Nell Commager, daughter of the eminent Columbia historian Henry Steele Commager. They were married that summer, and in November of 1956 Lasch accepted a three-year appointment at Williams College, in Williamstown, Massachusetts, with a salary of $2,100 for the spring semester. Robert wrote that he and Zora had been "glowing with pleasure" since hearing the news of his Williams appointment. "I'm sure Williams will be a fine place to start teaching and that you won't delay your thesis too long," he added.[13]

In December of 1956, though, calamity struck when he took his qualifying examinations, required for passage to the dissertation stage of the Ph.D. program. Lasch had already passed the first portion of these examinations in January of that year and had scheduled the final part, the "comprehensive subject orals," for the end of the fall term just before his departure to Williams. Forced to answer questions before a faculty committee, Lasch remembered that he "simply froze." "Everything seemed more complex than it had before," and he found himself going "out of my way to avoid stating the obvious, for fear that I would reveal myself as some kind of superficial person: 'Everybody knows that!'"[14]

Zora especially was shocked by his failure: "Nothing in your history prepared me for this," she wrote, confessing to being "so incredulous" that she "returned from time to time to read the letter." Robert, predictably, was more sanguine: "I would feel worse if I weren't perfectly confident that you will pass them when you put your mind to it and get it done." For Lasch, though, failing the exams was a severe blow. In a letter to his father-in-law more than five years later he professed to being "amazed" that David Donald, then at Johns Hopkins, had recently offered him a one-year appointment. Donald, he reminded Commager, had been on the committee that had failed him, "the memory of which is still so humiliating." His two and a half years

---

Lasch recalled of his years at Columbia: "I remember attending a couple of Lionel Trilling's lectures, but I didn't understand who Trilling was or who Reinhold Niebuhr was or even who Hofstadter was [in the wider intellectual community]. I didn't grasp the significance of that intellectual moment." Fox, "Interview," 7.

13. RL to CL, TL, 19 November 1956, 0:14.
14. Blake and Phelps, "History as Social Criticism," 1316.

in New York City ended with the sting of unprecedented academic failure, making his move to Williams feel more like retreat than advance. "Dark years" indeed.[15]

*   *   *

The marriage of Christopher Lasch and Nell Commager in 1956 placed them squarely amidst what a later generation of historians dubbed the "retreat to domesticity," a formulation that Lasch, looking back in the 1990s, considered "glib." Coming from a family that had nurtured him not only in progressive politics but also in a moderately conventional form of family life, Lasch tended to see the traditional home not as an incubator of pathology but rather, at its best, as a vital and nourishing place, unsurpassed in its potential for personal and political formation.[16]

To be sure, a host of factors converged in the postwar era to make traditional domestic ideals unusually alluring, to the Lasches and many others: peace and prosperity after years of war and dearth — in disquieting juxtaposition to the prospect of nuclear catastrophe; a culture-wide inward turn in reaction to the globe's shrinking size; and the ongoing development of a national consumer culture aimed at promoting such domesticity. Yet the very fact that domestic life received such an enthusiastic and familiar embrace in those years only underscores its central place in American life in previous eras. Lasch looked back on their early years and their relationships with other families not as a form of "emotional retreat" but as reflective of a common yearning "to re-create in the circle of our friends the intensity of a common purpose, which could no longer be found in politics or the workplace." Theirs was not a retreat so much as a reflexive effort to strengthen something vital that seemed to be eroding: a more fluid, organic experience of the most basic human relations, and a common moral framework in which they might flourish.[17]

15. ZL to CL and NL, TL, n.d., 0:14; RL to CL, TL, 12 December 1956, 0:14; CL to Henry Steele Commager, TL, 12 February 1963, 1:11.

16. CL, TOH, 31

17. CL, TOH, 32. For an interpretation in the "retreat to domesticity" vein, see Elaine Tyler May's *Homeward Bound: American Families in the Cold War Era* (New York: Basic Books, 1988). For a recent anthology that complicates this perspective on postwar social history, see *Not June Cleaver: Women and Gender in Postwar*

After their wedding in the summer of 1956, Nell and Kit lived in Brooklyn until they moved to Williamstown the next January, when Kit began to teach at Williams College. "I love to think of Nell scouring pots and pans and Kit building shelves," wrote Zora shortly after their move. "It seems so *basic.* I think I must make you a sampler saying 'God Bless Our Home,'" she joked. Throughout the early years of their marriage, and long after, Zora and Robert remained involved in their lives in immediate, practical ways. Kit and Nell's first child, Robert, was born in 1958, and from then on Robert and Zora became a steady source of clothing, various and sundry household staples, and the occasional loan. Zora made dresses and other outfits for the family over the years; Robert built a crib and shipped it to New England in preparation for the imminent arrival of Elisabeth. The distance between them was a nuisance, but never more than that. Their ties, though sometimes strained, remained strong.[18]

Looking back on his years as a graduate student Lasch recalled being "very much in the process of formation. I didn't have settled views on anything." But it was not for not trying. Coming to a political stance that he could truly own absorbed much of his intellectual energy. He remained loyally liberal through the 1950s, criticizing from within and never seriously considering other ideological possibilities, limited as they were in the midst of the cold war. He ridiculed the emergent "new conservatism" during these years, for instance, although it is possible that his scorn was fueled by some latent sense of self-recognition. Much of the energy behind the new conservatism of the 1950s was hardly anti-progressive and sharply reflective of the recent recovery of belief in the doctrine of original sin — orientations not without a certain appeal to Lasch. Catholics such as William F. Buckley Jr., who in 1955 launched the movement's flagship journal the *National Review,* supported capitalism, to be sure, but only, in Patrick Allitt's words, "as a means to preserve and nurture families," which they believed were under direct threat from intrusions of the state into the realm of economics. More broadly, the new conservatives were convinced that contemporary liberalism lacked the resources of mind and spirit to halt the degradation of the traditional

---

America, 1945-1960, ed. Joanne Meyerowitz (Philadelphia: Temple University Press, 1994).

18. ZL to CL, ALS, 22 January 1957, 0:15.

communal and familial norms they believed to be essential for the future of the West.[19]

Writing for a general audience became one way Lasch found to help himself respond alertly to developments such as these. Even before Kit had graduated from Harvard, Robert had helped establish a connection to the *St. Louis Post-Dispatch*'s book review editor, and the paper proved to be a fine training ground for Lasch for this kind of writing. His style — smart, cocky, snappy — made for good reading, especially when he was pronouncing judgment upon the new conservatives. He dismissed George N. Crocker, in *Roosevelt's Road to Russia,* as a "California lawyer, amateur historian and professional Roosevelt hater"; his book should be "classified not as history but as folklore." Lasch razed William F. Buckley in *Up from Liberalism* for his haphazard use of the term "liberalism." What is liberalism for Buckley? Lasch asked. "One thing, at least, is clear: Liberalism is socialism. But then, what isn't, from Mr. Buckley's point of view?"[20]

It was not that Lasch did not recognize merit in conservatism, or even a need for it. "In the terrifying, collectivized, bureaucratized modern world," he wrote in a review of Morton Keller's *In Defense of Yesterday,* "conservatives are needed more than ever." But the recent "conservative" incarnation was not worthy of the name, judged Lasch, in a review full of portent of his own emerging political vision. Self-proclaimed conservatives promote business at all possible expense, he charged, failing "to protect the country from unwise innovation." They made conservatism "synonymous with dogmatism, with opposition . . . to any changes at all," opposing child labor laws, for instance, while blessing and boosting the rise of exploitative corporations. All of this, for Lasch, was damning evidence of the new conservatism's "intellectual bankruptcy." Liberal means must be used to advance conservative ends, he seemed to suggest.[21]

Lasch's tone became less vituperative, though still critical, when assessing writers who hewed more closely to the familiar terrain of

---

19. Fox, "Interview," 7; Patrick Allitt, *Catholic Intellectuals and Conservative Politics in America, 1950-1985* (Ithaca: Cornell University Press, 1993), 2.

20. CL, review of George N. Crocker, *Roosevelt's Road to Russia, St. Louis Post-Dispatch,* 2 February 1960, 2C; CL, review of William F. Buckley, Jr., *Up from Liberalism, St. Louis Post-Dispatch,* November 1959, in 9:9.

21. CL, review of Morton Keller, *In Defense of Yesterday: James M. Beck and the Politics of Conservatism, 1861-1936, St. Louis Post-Dispatch,* 16 July 1959, in 9:9.

midcentury centrist thought and politics. He reflected the chastened mood of leading midcentury liberals, such as Schlesinger, Niebuhr, and Harvard sociologist Daniel Bell, who were, at least by their own reckoning, no longer naively optimistic about the realities of history and the limits of politics. While the new conservatives were attacking liberalism's progressive hopefulness from without, liberal intellectuals such as these were doing the same from within, leavening their continued belief in the ongoing need for social action with, as Richard Pells puts it, the foreboding knowledge that "the attempt to alter society might well unleash man's not-so-latent capacity for brutality and fanaticism." The recent global cataclysms had forced a reckoning with their earlier hopes and visions, and this palpably altered world left liberals looking for a way to preserve their ideological identity while adjusting to realities that seemed to threaten it.[22]

Harvard economist and former New Dealer John Kenneth Galbraith was one of the most influential of these intellectuals, and his 1958 volume *The Affluent Society* Lasch deemed "a masterpiece." Galbraith's depiction of America's commercially dominated, culturally impoverished public life resonated deeply with Lasch, as did his notion that "The solution, at the outset, at least, lies not so much in concrete programs as in new habits of thought." At the same time he scored Mario Einaudi for his complacent paean to FDR, whose "leadership," according to Einaudi, "was an unqualified blessing," since he had enabled the United States to steer clear of both fascism and communism. Lasch took this stance as representative of a rather stolid but sizable group of cold war centrists who seemed to assume that "anything at all is better than communism." This feeble assumption, he observed, had become "the cornerstone of their defense of freedom," leading him to pose a probing question, one that, it turns out, would have considerable staying power: "Has freedom no more positive meaning than this?"[23]

Just what it was that American liberals like the Lasches were fighting to preserve became the question that slowly began to absorb him. "Liberalism" remained his social ideal, but just what liberalism as a

22. Richard Pells, *The Liberal Mind in a Conservative Age: American Intellectuals in the 1940s and 1950s* (New York: Harper & Row, 1985), 138.

23. CL, "Prediction Is Not the Key," *St. Louis Post-Dispatch*, 15 June 1958, 4C; CL, "Brief for the New Deal," *St. Louis Post-Dispatch*, 9 August 1959, 4E.

social ideal meant became more and more misty, ill-defined, and un-satisfying. Did liberalism as an *ideal* adequately define all that needed to be achieved and preserved if America was to regain a measure of strength and health? He was uncertain, and his confusion manifested itself as opacity. He weakly warned his Williams students in one lecture that even though FDR had managed to align the southern Democrats with his New Deal agenda, the Democratic party was still not necessarily "a liberal coalition." Why? "Yesterday's liberalism is the conservatism of today. We are living in a Democratic era . . . but we are not necessarily living in a liberal era."[24]

If not "liberal," then what sort of era was it? This line of questioning began to take him down other intellectual paths, away from political history and toward the social sciences — especially sociology and psychology — for insight into the nature of his own time, including its politics. An unpublished essay submitted to the *Reporter* in 1958 displayed more than anything he wrote in the 1950s the gelling of the concerns, questions, and convictions that would emerge more fully in his work over the next two decades. Troubled by the shift in ethos that the New Deal's "consumer-oriented economy" had fostered, Lasch charged that "American 'civilization' has become dangerously frivolous and banal just at the time when its very survival is in question." Indeed, a new and pernicious form of education was undermining both the social status and civic efficacy of public schooling: "Advertising in the last fifteen years has usurped the place of education, for incomparably more time, money, energy, and imagination are spent in educating Americans to the advantages of particular commodities than in educating them to English, Arithmetic, Physics, and History."

Lasch sensed that most liberals, mysteriously, had not seemed to notice the harm that was being done — which made sense, given the fact that it was the liberally enlarged federal government itself that had sponsored the new consumer culture. While there had always been a tension between the world of business and the sphere of education, now "for the first time in history it has become a national policy to encourage the former over the latter. The omnipotent consumer has become the heart of our economic life." America had devolved into a place in which "the greatest rewards will fall to those whose job

24. CL, lecture, "The President and His Party: The Purge," 43:12.

it is to keep consumers consuming." For those who believed, as did the Lasches, that civic virtues were dependent on sound educational institutions, this broad social and cultural turn was, to say the least, a disturbing sign of the times.

As the implications of his growing sense that it was actually the liberals who had presided over this social slippage became clear to him, a more radical, yet also recognizably conservative political vision began to take root. Crucially, it was not the classical concerns of the left — justice, equality, freedom — that were shaping his emerging stance, but rather cultural concerns of a more traditional variety. The interests of "professional molders of mass taste and opinion," he declared in the essay, "are incompatible with the national interest." But he was not troubled by the public's poor judgment or taste so much as the more fundamental problem that the public's "capacity for resisting the brain-washing techniques of mass advertising is so low." The government, he concluded, has the responsibility to act to preserve more enriching civic habits and ideals, the demands of the consumer economy be damned. He went so far as to suggest that the appropriate economic framework "may more nearly resemble the pattern of wartime planning." He was convinced, in the end, that should "price controls and wage controls prove unacceptable some more palatable alternatives will have to be devised."[25]

This new liberal-sponsored consumerist direction was culturally and politically barren, he knew; by deduction, the liberal politics that had broadcast it as a solution were too. Lasch proved to be acutely attuned to what Michael Sandel has called "the demise of the republican strand in American politics and the rise of contemporary liberalism," when in the midcentury years the "political economy of growth and distributive justice displaced the political economy of citizenship." Working through the argument in his essay seemed to quicken a resolve to urge a better way, an older way, upon the rapidly transforming American citizenry. But what, precisely, did this stance make him? If he was neither cold war liberal nor new conservative, what was he?[26]

*   *   *

25. CL, "Inflation and Education," unpublished ms. in 8:13.
26. Michael Sandel, *Democracy's Discontent: America in Search of a Public Philosophy* (Cambridge: Harvard University Press, 1996), 262, 250.

In 1959, five years after beginning at Columbia, Lasch finally settled on the dissertation topic that would become his first book, an examination of the response of American liberals to the Russian Revolution. By July of 1960, only seventeen months after Lasch and Leuchtenburg had agreed on the general contours of the project, Lasch delivered to Leuchtenburg a complete draft of the dissertation. Necessity had spawned his haste; Williams had informed him at the end of 1958 that his appointment would end following the spring semester. The Lasches opted to move to Washington, D.C., that June, where Kit completed his research. By this time they were a young family. Robert Evans had been born in January of 1958 and Elisabeth Dan followed less than two years later, sparking the urgency to finish the degree and secure a teaching position. With some help from Richard Hofstadter, Lasch received in the spring of 1960 a six-month, $2500 fellowship from the Social Science Research Council that enabled him to finish the dissertation. Hofstadter's sparkling estimation of Lasch no doubt lifted his spirits at a crucial moment. "I just wrote SSRC, told them I haven't seen a better PhD prospect in a dozen yrs at Columbia, which is true," he wrote to Lasch.[27]

For his part Lasch was delighted to be leaving Williams, despite the added familial pressures. Just prior to his graduation from Columbia in 1961 he confided to Leuchtenburg that "Williamstown was terrible for me"; he had not been given the opportunity to "do any but the most menial work, thereby reinforcing my sense of failure." "[T]he thesis itself was the least of my ordeals," he reflected, "and by the time we arrived in Washington I was on the road to some sort of recovery, I think."[28]

By 1960 a shift in the postwar ethos was also under way. Eisenhower's warning in his farewell address of a vast "military industrial complex" was just one of the signs of wide and general loosening that was fostering more critical perspectives on postwar American politics and culture. Early 1960s films such as the darkly comic *Dr. Strangelove* or the merely dark *Fail-Safe,* both nuclear doomsday fare, reflected an enlarging discontent with America's conduct of the cold war, and indicated an increasing willingness to assign guilt to the western side of

27. Richard Hofstadter to CL, TLS, n.d.; 1:4; internal evidence suggests that this letter was written in early January 1960.
28. CL to William Leuchtenburg, TL, 24 May 1961, 1:5.

the iron curtain as well as the eastern. Within five short years of Eisenhower's address both President Kennedy and Malcolm X would be assassinated, Lyndon Johnson would be routing thousands of young Americans to southeast Asia, the Civil Rights Act would be passed, and a sweeping uprising against the enlarging presence of the global capitalist order would be under way. A major shift indeed, though in 1960 even the most prescient could not have begun to fathom what the decade would hold.

Alert to these shifts — or openings — as he was writing his dissertation, Lasch became more probing and pointed in his questioning. If his sense that America was in cultural decline was pushing him leftward in terms of political economy, his evolving take on the cold war revealed a similar willingness to question liberal foreign policy and, at bottom, the liberal tradition itself. His critical head of steam was building, which helps to account for the remarkable speed at which he completed his dissertation.

In it he concluded, after surveying the varying responses of American liberals to the Bolshevik Revolution, that in the end it was the American liberals' millennial confidence in their own eventual global triumph that had led to their failure at the most crucial moment to apprehend the true nature of the Bolshevik regime — a failure with many disturbing, deviant consequences now playing out daily before America's eyes. The "tidy dualism," as he put it, with which World War I liberals viewed the world, picturing themselves as the avatars of the Good and the non-democratic nations as the embodiment of evil, had led them at first to see the fledgling Soviet Union as noble and democratic, and later to swing to the other extreme, demonizing it after World War II. Neither response made for wise politics, much less the kind of inspired leadership the moment demanded. From 1917 to the present American liberals had been unable "to admit the necessity of living with an unregenerate Russia." Their inability to apprehend the ways in which good and evil mixed in this world had made them political incompetents, even though they remained powerful.[29]

29. Quotations from this study are taken from the substantially unrevised published version of his dissertation, *The American Liberals and the Russian Revolution* (New York: Columbia University Press, 1962, McGraw-Hill paperback edition, 1972; hereafter ALRR), 109, 217.

Importantly, by this time "liberalism" had come to represent more than a political proclivity for Lasch. Liberal politics were, in fact, just one expression of what was for him an encompassing way of life, one for which his distaste was steadily building. When he spoke of liberalism in his dissertation, published with few significant alterations in 1962 as *American Liberals and the Russian Revolution,* he was referring to a worldview that he contended, following in the traces of Hofstadter and political scientist Louis Hartz, most Americans had always shared. Liberalism was a "set of assumptions about human affairs" that had in the twentieth century's first two decades morphed into "progressivism" (though in the study Lasch opted to use the term "liberal" rather than "progressive" in order "to emphasize the continuity between the liberalism of 1917 and that of 1962," the term "progressive" having since fallen out of favor). Americans, born with a liberal birthright, had been "brought up in the benevolent assumptions of the eighteenth-century Enlightenment," he wrote, believing that "human reason could ultimately order the world so as to eliminate poverty, disease, discomfort and war." Lasch was taking aim not simply at politicians but at their underlying political and intellectual tradition — and in the background, America itself.[30]

By the time Lasch completed the dissertation, his days of cheering the Democratic party — and "liberalism" — were over. If his fiction writing and theological exploring at Harvard were expressions of his early dissatisfaction with the progressive tradition, his dissertation only extended and deepened it. As a matter of course, liberals sentimentally believed in "the inevitable spread of democracy throughout the world, by orderly change or by revolution, as circumstances might dictate." While the events surrounding the Russian Revolution should have signaled that the ascendance of the Bolsheviks was not "simply another stage in the long struggle against tyranny," American liberals instead could only evade the obvious conclusion. They were psychologically and intellectually unprepared "to live in a world half of which is dominated by one's enemies." America's demonizing approach to the Soviet Union in subsequent years pro-

---

30. CL, ALRR, vii, xvi, vii. See Louis Hartz, *The Liberal Tradition in America: An Interpretation of American Political Thought Since the Revolution* (New York: Harcourt, Brace, and World, 1955); Hofstadter, *The American Political Tradition* (New York: Knopf, 1948).

vided abundant evidence that this Manichean worldview was still firmly intact.[31]

Lasch's perspective on American liberalism and World War I was of a piece with the resurging appreciation of tragedy and irony in the postwar years, as writers and thinkers sought adequate expression of their collapsing confidence. In his acknowledgements Lasch disclosed his obligation to an intellectual and statesman whose thinking profoundly reflected, and indeed helped to shape, this turn, the American diplomat and historian George F. Kennan. Kennan, a Democrat, had served with the State Department in the Soviet Union, and in the early years of the cold war became the architect of the United States' containment policy (though by the mid-1950s he had become a critic of the way it was being carried out). Crucially, it was Kennan's searching critique of the optimistic assumptions that had underpinned progressive policy both domestically and internationally that had the most immediate impact on Lasch. Over against the Wilsonian internationalism that had shaped Democratic foreign policy since the progressive era (what Kennan deemed the "legalistic-moralistic approach to international problems"), Kennan offered a softened realpolitik for the atomic age: rather than developing a foreign policy founded upon abstractions like equality and justice, Americans must, he argued, accept the unhappy necessity of putting "the national interest" first — a particularly bitter pill for liberals to swallow. Indeed, he suggested that the United States must "have the modesty to admit that our own national interest is all that we are really capable of knowing and understanding," and went so far as to express doubts that "state behavior is a fit subject for moral judgment." A devout Presbyterian, Kennan managed to sound high-minded and benevolent even as he gutted the very moral center of the American liberal tradition.[32]

It was a stark ideological departure, at least for liberals, but one that Lasch, in full self-conscious revolt by now against liberal optimism, welcomed. Later Lasch recalled that after he had completed

31. CL, ALRR, xiv, xvi.

32. The article is reprinted in George F. Kennan, *American Diplomacy* (Chicago: University of Chicago Press, 1951, expanded edition, 1984), "The Sources of Soviet Conduct"; Kennan, "Diplomacy in the Modern World," chapter in *American Diplomacy*, 95, 103, 100.

much of the research for the dissertation in the fall of 1959, he was still searching for an argument that might pull the material together. "It was at that point," recalled Lasch, "that I went to Kennan and sort of inflicted myself on him." Lasch ended up grounding much of his argument in Kennan's thinking, and Kennan's "new realism" furnished some of the dynamite for his break from his parents' progressivism. In his first article in a national journal of opinion, a 1962 essay in the *Nation,* Lasch recounted his own "relief and gratitude" upon his discovery of Kennan's thoughtful realism.[33]

But if in *American Liberals* his general vantage reflected Kennan's, his argument was not mere mimicry. Most notably, where Kennan exuded the reformer's loyal and confident belief in the basic integrity of the American political structure, Lasch had by 1960 become more distant and skeptical. In his opening chapter he linked progressive-era liberalism to the all-encompassing hubris of most westerners of the period, "who took it as a matter of course that they lived in a civilization surpassing any which history had been able to record," naively believing that "their own particular customs, institutions, and ideas had universal validity." Although he did not hesitate to deem the Soviet Union "evil" and the Bolsheviks "ruthless and desperate," he did not elevate the United States by comparison, much less the liberalism in which he understood the nation itself to be rooted. To the contrary, he suggested that the USSR and the USA had in common at least one overarching dream: the fantasy of ideological conquest. "For liberalism in America, no less than communism in Russia, has always been a messianic creed, which staked everything on the ultimate triumph of liberalism throughout the world. What else did progress mean?" Lasch, coming of age during the cold war, wrote not in chastened hope but scornful lament, profoundly disturbed by the geopolitical morass and poisoned political culture his generation had inherited.[34]

If Lasch's bitterly critical depiction of American triumphalism at home and abroad was a foretaste of a broad body of historical writing that would eventually mature into, as Peter Novick has put it, a "new, left historiography" intent on "challenging fundamental assumptions of existing mainstream historiography on a variety of fronts," in

33. Fox, "Interview," 8; CL, "The Historian as Diplomat," *Nation,* 24 November 1962, 348.
34. CL, ALRR, 1, 118, xvi.

Lasch's case this response was emerging most deeply from his own autobiography — it was this dynamic that gave *American Liberals and the Russian Revolution* its heat. The "unforgettable heritage of a liberal upbringing" that had gripped him as a senior at Harvard was still priming his thinking and sharpening his ideological senses. He dedicated *American Liberals* to his mother and father, but it seems more accurate to say it was aimed at them, or at least at their way of viewing the world. When he referred to liberal confidence in rationality and to the "moral progress of the human spirit," he was rehearsing the catchphrases of his own childhood. He was the American "brought up in the benevolent assumptions of the eighteenth-century Enlightenment," raised by parents who were by their own admission "extreme rationalists." And it was this dynamic that, in Lasch's case at least, was helping open up the possibility of a vital, viable political left once more.[35]

At the same time Lasch's narrative in key respects continued to reflect his parents' overall secularist outlook. Nowhere in his study, for instance, did he consider the cultural shifts that had given the sunny progressivism of the early twentieth century its own distinctive, sentimental shape. Enlightenment liberalism had emerged in uneasy, often antagonistic tension with the more harsh and sober Christian anthropologies stemming from Augustine, Luther, and Calvin. But the weakening of Christian orthodoxy throughout the nineteenth century, in both America and western Europe, had distanced the enlightenment tradition from its more dour Protestant counterweight, helping to make possible the construction of the optimistic "empires of the imagination" with which liberals, Lasch charged, had deluded themselves. Lasch's collegiate explorations in Barthian neo-orthodoxy no doubt helped to render Kennan attractive to him in the 1950s, but his nascent theological sensibilities had not altered his historiographical framework, which failed to account for the theological currents that had helped give shape to early-twentieth-century American political culture.[36]

35. Peter Novick, *That Noble Dream: The "Objectivity Question" and the American Historical Profession* (New York: Cambridge University Press, 1988), 218, 242; CL to Naomi Dagen, ALS, 22 January 1954, 0:34; CL, ALRR, vii, xvi; RL to CL, TLS, 31 March 1970, 2:21.

36. CL, ALRR, 220. On liberalism's relationship with Christian theology, see

In retrospect, it was Lasch's testy reaction to liberalism — as a cultural as well as a political phenomenon — that was the most striking dimension of *American Liberals and the Russian Revolution*. His embrace of the new realism turned out to be only a stopgap measure. When he began to reconsider Kennan and the "new realism" even as he was completing his dissertation in 1960, his movement into the unknown began in earnest.

*   *   *

Leuchtenburg could hardly have been more effusive in response to the draft of the dissertation he received in July of 1960. "I am simply overwhelmed," he confessed. "I don't know how to say strongly enough how superb I think it is. No one reading it would suppose for a minute that it is a doctoral dissertation. It reads like the work of a finished scholar. You are in command every inch of the way." The rapidity with which Lasch had completed it may have contributed to Leuchtenburg's amazement: he had written the entire manuscript of 400 pages in little more than six months.[37]

Lasch had little interest in revising it prior to publication; he admitted later to being "tired of it" and "impatient to publish." After a rejection by the University of Chicago Press, it was accepted in the fall of 1961 by Columbia University Press. He jotted off the news to a friend: "They expect it to be a best seller, and they are already dickering with Hollywood over the movie rights. Don't worry, success has not gone to my head. I'll always be the modest, self-effacing down to earth Real Joe that all my friends know and admire." Monetary success certainly was not in the offing. Columbia ordered a 1500-copy first run of the book; after one year it had sold only 318. By the end of

---

especially James Kloppenberg, "The Virtues of Liberalism: Christianity, Republicanism, and Ethics in Early American Political Discourse," *Journal of American History* 74 (June 1987), 9-33. See also James Turner, *Without God, without Creed: The Origins of Unbelief in America* (Baltimore: Johns Hopkins University Press, 1985); T. J. Jackson Lears, *No Place of Grace: Antimodernism and the Transformation of American Culture, 1880-1920* (New York: Pantheon, 1981). For a nineteenth-century strike against the softening of the older republican-Calvinist culture, see Herman Melville, *The Confidence-Man: His Masquerade,* Norton Critical Edition, ed. Hershel Parker (New York: Norton, 1971).

37. William Leuchtenburg to CL, TLS, 17 July 1960, 1:5.

1964 the total had reached 807 and his sole royalty check was made out for $23.73.[38]

Neither did the book make much of an academic splash, though reviews were generally positive. Selig Adler, at the State University of New York at Buffalo, lauded Lasch for helping to shed light on the cold war. A. E. Campbell, of Oxford University, called it "an admirable book" of "illuminating analysis," though he charged Lasch, in what was in the mid-1960s becoming a historiographical truism, with failing to see that most Americans in 1917 could be seen as "conservatives" as well as "liberals," since they were not interested mainly in changing their own country but rather in seeing "the rest of the world becoming more like America." This dominant conservative tendency, he thought, had led liberals to misunderstand the Soviet Union: political inertia at home put blinders on American eyes as they tried to interpret international events.[39]

It did not take long for Lasch to distance himself from the general outlook (or what he came to see as the lack of a general outlook) that had guided *American Liberals.* He knew why liberalism must be rejected, but he foundered in trying to replace it. Staughton Lynd, a young historian Lasch had recently befriended who was a professor at Spellman College and the son of eminent American sociologists Robert and Helen Lynd, noted upon reading the book, "I think the reader is left unsure of your own evaluation." "Your mind is so subtle and your manner so ironic that we move through a hall of receding mirrors in which each exaggeration sets the stage for a corresponding distortion in the other direction. Were there no Western liberals who made a judicious evaluation of the Russian Revolution?" he wondered.[40]

Lasch, cornered by Lynd's judgment, acknowledged that "What is missing, I suppose, is some indication of my general point of view. The reason why it is missing is that I don't have one." As much as he admired the pre–World War I pacifists, he knew he was no pacifist.

38. CL to Staughton Lynd, TL, 25 January 1964, 1:15; CL to John Clive, TL, 31 October 1961, 1:2; Columbia University Press to Christopher Lasch, TD, 1 April 1965, 8:10. Royalties began only after 750 were sold. In 1972 McGraw-Hill published a paperback edition of the book.

39. Selig Adler, review of ALRR, *Canadian Historical Review* 45:1 (March 1964), 65; A. E. Campbell, review of ALRR, *English Historical Review* 81 (April 1966), 431, 432.

40. Staughton Lynd to CL, TLS, 26 November 1962, 1:10.

But "Neither am I an anarchist," he wrote. "I think I thought I was, however, that year in Washington when I was writing this." He solicited more comments from Lynd on the book, which he supposed might put him "in a position to write another book explaining what I meant in this one" — a publishing pattern that would actually take hold in the following years.[41]

It was the U-2 incident of May 1960, and the subsequent collapse of what was to have been the first summit of the cold war, that sparked Lasch's final rejection of cold war liberalism, including its embrace of realism as a guide for international policy; his movement away from it, tellingly, was rooted in a fundamental sense of moral outrage. "The U-2 affair abounded in revelations," he wrote in his 1962 *Nation* essay on Kennan and the new realism (a publishing opportunity made possible through Lynd's connections at that magazine). He had found himself most incensed that Kennan and the realists of the Eisenhower administration had not even bothered to condemn on pragmatic grounds the risky practice of conducting espionage flights right up to the eve of the summit, let alone call the general practice of this sort of spying into question. Worse, in response to the crisis Kennan drew "only the familiar lesson about the futility of summit diplomacy." Rather than backing the hopeful pursuit of a thaw in the cold war, Lasch could now see that the realists, along with the Republicans, had "embraced the cold war as a way of life." This was repugnant to him, a politics of hopelessness and an abdication of moral responsibility, a posture that was in effect providing cover for great moral malignity. The "realism" of many leading intellectuals had, as he would put it in a withering exchange with the sociologist Daniel Bell many years later, "congealed into a passive political dogma supportive of many of the worst tendencies in American life." He concluded his *Nation* essay with a seething question that revealed both the depth of his disaffection with cold war liberalism and the degree to which his received vision of America had been punctured: "Can the national interest" — so important in Kennan's outlook — "be disentangled from the arrogance and hostility and delusions of superiority that seem to have characterized the behavior of nations at all times?"[42]

41. CL to Staughton Lynd, TL, 28 November 1962, 1:10.
42. CL, "The Historian as Diplomat," 351; CL to Daniel Bell, TL, 12 November 1978, 4:17; CL, "The Historian as Diplomat," 353.

Lasch, like so many coming of age in the postwar years, felt an increasing burden to articulate a more bracing moral vision. He no longer knew where he fit on the political spectrum, as he confided to Lynd in 1962, but he knew where he did not. Liberalism's inability to lead the nation toward the fulfillment of axiomatic American ideals was now painfully apparent. "No other incident has demonstrated so clearly," he wrote in a letter on the U-2 incident printed in the *New Republic,* "the utter incapacity of the American people to perform the responsibilities which history has ironically thrust upon them." "The new realism can be useful in discouraging easy solutions," he jotted down on a sheet of paper around 1962, "but it too easily leads to our present intransigence. It fails to distinguish the main trouble, which is not popular utopianism but fatalism." Another way of achieving America needed to be discovered.[43]

If anything, Lasch's read of the contemporary moment became even more harsh after his turn from realism. The general ethical questions that galvanized liberals were the right ones, so far as they went. But it was their particular answers, rooted in their shallow rationalism, that had led to social and political despair. Lasch's increasingly settled sense, as he put in a *Post-Dispatch* book review published in August 1961, was that "the melancholy history of 'the times' suggests a possible connection between social progress and human disintegration." Did the liberal tradition make possible an intelligent apprehension of this paradox? No. "Liberalism, committed to progress and confident of man's essential reasonableness, has no way of dealing with this fact. It can only demand more of what we have already — more health, education, and welfare. But we know by now that progress is not enough."[44]

By the early 1960s, as he was turning thirty, Lasch had transformed himself, after a period of hazy confusion, back into the sort of political idealist he had been raised to be: uncompromising in his belief in the reality of moral ideals, hopeful that these ideals — for citizenship, for equality, for peace — were within reach, and above all

43. Lasch, "Our Spy," *New Republic,* 30 May 1960, 24; the note on "the new realism" is written in Lasch's hand, with ink, on a sheet with no title or date, in 8:5 (folder title: "Kennan and the New Realism — Nation").

44. CL, "Is Conservatism the Enemy?" *St. Louis Post-Dispatch,* 2 August 1961, 2C.

convinced that human beings were in some fashion obligated not only to pursue these ideals but to achieve them. But he was also certain of the need to root his politics in more fertile soil. And so Lasch began his intensive search for an intellectual tradition capable of yielding a moral vision more capacious and discerning than enlightened progressivism.

In the end, it was to the left that he headed for hope: hope in the form of bigger ideas, deeper perspectives, greater intellectual power, a broader interpretive range, and most importantly, a truer moral framework. Somehow, the possibility of a better end for humanity must be held in tension with the impossible-to-deny malignancy the midcentury generation could so well see. The teleological instincts of progressivism must not be rejected but rather corrected by the understandings of human history that neo-orthodox sensibilities had so perceptively intuited. Above all, despair must not become the outcome of this moment of crisis, as it had for the "realists." Hope must be reclaimed — but by taking a radical, not a "progressive," route.[45]

Throughout the year in Washington, Lasch, with the help of some well-placed boosters, had worked on landing a teaching position for the 1960-61 academic year while awaiting his dissertation defense. By May he received word that he had been offered a position at Roosevelt University in Chicago, which he accepted. He would stay there just a year. By December of 1960 Allan Bogue of the University of Iowa informed Lasch that "a number of historians have suggested your name to us" in their search to fill the opening in recent American history vacated by Samuel Hays. "[T]he members of our department," he wrote,

---

45. He later recalled that as he began to distance himself from liberalism he began to sense that more democracy, rather than less, was the general need (the realists, as he later put it, seemed to think of democracy "as part of the problem" rather than as a "part of the solution"). Anarchism, for instance, was a tradition he lauded because of the clear vision it made possible: it was "perhaps the only point of view from which one can look at the modern society, the only moral position, the only position which does not concede everything at the outset," he wrote in the summer of 1960. And it was, in turn, the tradition, along with the pacifism, that had best discerned modern political and ethical complexities. Anarchists and pacifists "were the only people, except for the reactionaries, who remained skeptical about Russia during the Second World War, to cite only one instance." Blake and Phelps, "History as Social Criticism," 1314-15; CL to Walt Davis, TL, 14 July 1960, 1:3.

"are impressed by your credentials." He arranged to meet with Lasch at the upcoming meeting of the American Historian Association. By early January of 1961 Bogue confirmed to Lasch that he was "the outstanding man in our field of candidates." At the end of the month Lasch accepted an appointment as assistant professor, at a salary of $7200 per year. During his first year he would teach six hours per semester; in his second year he would add a seminar to that load.[46]

While finishing up his year at Roosevelt and preparing to graduate from Columbia, Lasch paused to thank Leuchtenburg for his considerable part in making his personal progression possible. "Looking back," Lasch recalled, poignantly,

> I am struck by the many times I must have tried your patience sorely, and I am amazed that you never lost it. To have confidence in somebody who has no confidence in himself must be the most difficult of achievements. I can't say how grateful I am for that continuing confidence. . . . It is especially the earlier period, those dark years, when your help was indispensable, and all the more dear to me at that time because of my sense that it was undeserved — a true gift of grace.[47]

Leuchtenburg responded gently: "I felt very warmly about what you said in your letter to me." Trying to soften Lasch's harsh self-evaluation, he suggested that "you often were too hard on yourself . . . too ready to see shortcomings and too unwilling to accept your accomplishments." It had been "exciting," he wished Lasch to understand, "to have a student and friend who was genuinely excited by ideas and dedicated to his craft."[48]

Lasch moved to Iowa invigorated by his new setting and prospects. Shortly after arriving he reported to Leuchtenburg his intention to write "a short book, a mere interpretive essay, on the American intellectual from 1900 to c. 1930" that would show that the "progressive movement" was "a stage of the acclimation of the intellectuals."[49]

---

46. Allan G. Bogue to CL, TLS, 9 December 1960, 1:1; Allan G. Bogue to CL, TLS, 5 January 1961, 1:1; Allan G. Bogue to CL, TLS, 23 January 1961, 1:1.

47. CL to William Leuchtenburg, TL, 24 May 1961, 1:5.

48. William Leuchtenburg to CL, ALS, 26 July 1961, 1:5.

49. CL to William Leuchtenburg, TL, 22 August 1961, 1:5.

He was himself about to emerge as an intellectual, and in working on this volume, which became his breakthrough book, *The New Radicalism in America,* he would unleash a sharp critique of the leftist political tradition he was beginning to embrace. Lasch was becoming one of the numerous new radicals — almost in spite of himself.

CHAPTER FOUR

At Odds with My Country

My life in England is not quite bleak, and my spirits aren't low.
It's . . . given me respite from the grinding business of being at
odds with my country.

Christopher Lasch to William R. Taylor, January 1964[1]

We can't become believers. Our job, as Lincoln Steffens once
said, is to doubt.

Christopher Lasch speaking at the 1966 meeting of the
Organization of American Historians, Cincinnati, Ohio[2]

"A teacher at Roosevelt has no sense of living in a distinct community," replied Lasch when a Roosevelt University official
asked why he was leaving after just one year. He had found Roosevelt
all too similar to Columbia; at each the faculty tended to live far from
both the university and one another. He was searching for something
else, he wrote: "a real university community."[3]

The University of Iowa and Iowa City certainly offered a contrast
to Roosevelt University as well as Chicago, a city Lasch thought "dirty,

1. CL to William R. Taylor, TL, 3 January 1964, 7d:8.
2. The quotation is in an unpublished ms. in 9:30 (folder titled "New Radicalism — Cincinnati Session"). Lasch was responding to comments on *The New Radicalism* made by Samuel Haber, Ihab Hassan, and David Noble. The meeting was
held April 28-30, 1966.
3. CL to Jack Roth, TL, 7 February 1961, 1:6.

unbeautiful, and hard to get around in." Although not altogether sure Iowa approximated his ideal either, other considerations drew him to Iowa, not the least of which was its relative stature. Iowa was a respected research university, and Lasch would be one of four Americanists on an accomplished history faculty. He would teach both graduate and undergraduate students, with ample space for research and writing. "This is a wonderful place," Lasch wrote to the Commagers in the fall of his first semester:

> I'm expected to spend all my time writing. . . . I have been given a research assistant; I have been offered graders, typists, everything conceivable which might facilitate my getting into print. As a result of all these attentions, I do nothing from sun-up to sundown except lecture to my docile students. I say I am writing a book, but it is just a front.

It was his self-deprecating irony, of course, that was the front. Iowa was the big leagues, and he was eager to step up to the plate.[4]

Into his second semester, in the midst of a long Midwestern winter, he professed to William Leuchtenburg that he was "still terribly pleased with Iowa, more and more, in fact." He was discovering that teaching in the graduate program was a boon to his research and writing. He described the undergraduates as "pretty eager to learn, even if they don't start out with the best equipment." Life at Iowa, in short, seemed to promise a healthy measure of satisfaction. When at the end of his first year his father-in-law urged him to consider a post at Carleton College, Lasch felt little temptation. He enjoyed working with graduate students, he replied, and could not abide the thought of an increased teaching load. "I like to teach very much," he explained, "but I hate to have to do nothing else."[5]

He admitted to his Harvard tutor Donald B. Meyer that he preferred "cities and urban types to teach," but he had hopes that Iowa City would be more than just a temporary stopover, since he and Nell had "moved around too much." The Lasches, at the moment a family

4. CL to Jack Roth, TL, 7 February 1961, 1:6; CL to Henry Steele and Evan Commager, TL, 22 October 1961, 1:3.

5. CL to William Leuchtenburg, TL, 13 February 1962, 1:10; CL to Henry Steele Commager, TL, 4 April 1962, 1:9.

of four, were finding Midwestern life pleasing. During their first spring Lasch reported to his parents that he was "growing tomato plants indoors, to be transplanted if it ever warms up," while Nell was busying herself planting trees.[6]

*   *   *

Lasch's yearnings for community were both sated and fueled in the early sixties by his ties to a circle of friends within the historical profession. His scholarly ambitions and political concerns, already developing into a distinct and original form, took the shape they did due in part to strong, if volatile, friendships.

William R. Taylor, a Harvard Ph.D. who was completing his graduate studies at the time Lasch was an undergraduate, became one of Lasch's first friends in the profession. Ten years older than Lasch, Taylor became acquainted with him while they were researching at the Library of Congress during the 1959-60 academic year. Taylor was then finishing work on an exploration of Southern identity published in 1961 as *Cavalier and Yankee,* a book that would make him a leading voice in the nascent field of American cultural history. Lasch and Taylor quickly discovered an area of mutual interest in a broad, still largely unexplored area: the history of women. They began to plan a collaborative effort, and eventually won advances from George Braziller for their proposed book, *The Opposite Sex: The American Woman in Historical Perspective,* targeted for publication in June 1965. Lasch later fondly remembered his and Taylor's attempts at collaborative scholarship: "We had endless meetings in the early 1960s," he recalled. "I would drive back and forth from Iowa City to Madison [where Taylor was teaching]. We would have conversations long into the night which struck us as extraordinarily brilliant. You know he's a brilliant conversationalist, just swept me off my feet, ideas popping around." This was a combination Lasch would persistently covet: fraternally spawned intellectual vitality.[7]

6. CL to Donald B. Meyer, TL, 4 January 1962, 1:11; CL to ZL & RL, TL, 12 April 1962, 1:10.

7. William R. Taylor, *Cavalier and Yankee: The Old South and American National Character* (New York: George Braziller, 1961); "Prospectus for Book on American Women, by William R. Taylor and Christopher Lasch," in 7d:7. Fox, "In-

Lasch's turn so early in his career from political and intellectual history to social history underscores the extent to which he was temperamentally drawn to explore human experience in broad compass — the same impulse that lay behind his yearning to write fiction. "Social history," devoted to telling the stories of human communities, was in this sense a far better fit for him than political history. But what had driven him toward the history of women in particular, well before the cultural upheaval of the 1960s turned gender studies into a historiographical hotbed?

He later explained this turn in the light of his own coming of age in postwar America. "Something in the atmosphere of the late fifties," he recalled in an interview, "made it seem important to come to terms with the 'woman question.'" Contrary to the common depiction of the midcentury years as a time of placid traditionalism in gender relations and sexuality, Lasch remembered it as a time of much "sexual experimentation," including "'open marriages' and other unconventional arrangements." "Women were becoming more assertive," he recalled, and "men often wore a defensive expression, an expression of apology." In *Haven in a Heartless World: The Family Beseiged,* published in 1977, he contended that "the fifties did not even fully repudiate feminism." Some college-educated women had "renounced careers" but had at the same time "asserted their sexual rights without reserve, and refused to consider themselves bound by older canons of respectability. They no more wished to revive the nineteenth-century ideal of the lady than their husbands wished to pose as patriarchs." The sorts of profound cultural shifts that such changes in gender relations reflected had made work in the history of women seem increasingly necessary, emerging from profound social shifts that defied existing conventions of historical inquiry.[8]

Trying to push past these conventions, Taylor and Lasch reflected what the historian Patrick Joyce sums up as "the desire to transcend the narrowness of an older political history." In this revamped historiographical framework, "society," rather than the nation-state,

---

terview," 10. Lasch noted that "Specifically, it was what [Taylor] wrote about Harriet Stowe that suggested to both of us that it was a marvelous subject."

8. Blake and Phelps, "History as Social Criticism," 1326; CL, HHW, 106. Lasch's interviewer pointed out that Lasch had been part of a small group of men, including Taylor, Carl Degler, and William O'Neill, who prior to the 1960s reawakening of feminism began to explore the history of women.

would become the starting point from which the past might most fruitfully be explored. Lasch and Taylor began to immerse themselves in the enormous literature emerging at midcentury from the social sciences, seeking to build a new framework for their research. For his part, Lasch, by the time he began teaching at Iowa in 1961, was defining himself as a "social historian."[9]

Lasch's early explorations at the intersection of sociology and history provided theoretical ballast for his ongoing, ever-enlarging revolt against the culture of enlightened liberalism. Early-twentieth-century progressives, such as his parents, had tended to understand humans as essentially seekers of "freedom," never doubting, in the words of Joyce Appleby, Margaret Jacob, and Lynn Hunt, "that aspirations for personal freedom and economic opportunity represented core human drives." Seen through these enlightened eyes, the old repressive social webs (church, state, family) were no match for the strength of the human being who had been made to see his or her true destiny: "freedom." Native traditions and medieval community structures would yield easily to the liberated individual, rational and self-aware, and the enlightened would, as the story went, go on to forge wholesome democratic states.[10]

---

9. Patrick Joyce, "The End of Social History?" *Social History* 20:1 (January 1995), 75. CL to Morris H. Rubin, TL, 22 November 1961, 1:6. Among the notes Lasch gathered for *The New Radicalism in America* is one of his early-sixties attempts to work out his understanding of social history. Social history, wrote Lasch, is "a cooperative undertaking, involving not only history but literature, sociology, psychology and anthropology, and economics and political science as well." He defined it as not "a collection of details about 'social life.'" Rather, it was the "study of the social order." A letter to one of his Roosevelt students who had complained about a low grade on a paper underscores not only his understanding of social history but the degree to which it was a part of his teaching of history. The paper, he wrote, "remains a study in political science, not of the social conditions which lie behind such a piece of legislation, as the one you deal with." CL, "New Radicalism: Notes," 9:25; CL to Arthur Gillis, TL, 3 June 1961, 1:4.

10. Appleby, Hunt, and Jacob, *Telling the Truth about History* (New York: Norton, 1994), 141. They note that beginning in the postwar era, though, these progressive notions faced an increasing challenge: "The undersocialized concept of man that we identified as characteristic of earlier national histories ran headlong into the oversocialized concept of men and women that emerged from work in the social sciences. That old, familiar tale of the pioneer alone with his family on the frontier, or the Protestant alone with his God, or the rights-bearing man alone with his conscience, only made sense within a frame of reference celebrating the individual over the group" (152).

Instead, in the fifties and sixties Lasch was drawn to those voices in the American academic community and beyond who, in the aftermath of catastrophic depression and war, were decisively rejecting such visions. By the middle of the century the anthropological conception of "culture" and the sociological notion of "structure" had emerged as commandeering constructs within the social sciences, reducing the individual from an enlightened position of strength to mere creaturedom — a creature not of divine origin but of the thick web of values, beliefs, symbols, and practices social scientists now believed gave individuals their "identity." This confidence in the shaping power of structure and culture, rather than nation or nature, became a critical starting point for most of the newer forms of histories then emerging in opposition to the older "progressive" historiography. And the heroic, independent individual tended to be reduced to a malleable, indistinct, essentially shapeless entity, with little history-shaping possibility. On this new view, no destiny for the human being could be expected except the destiny demanded by the particular structure which had bound, even created, the individual; not the individual but the structure was larger than life. This was a dagger in the heart of the older progressive historiography of Lasch's childhood, and at least a stab at the soul of the larger liberal culture that it reflected.[11]

Not that the newer historiographical approaches parted ways entirely with the tradition of Enlightenment rationality, of course. In fact they gained their plausibility only within what sociologist Alvin Gouldner has termed the "culture of critical discourse," or the "New Class." If, to put it simply, these historians rejected the narrative of the freedom-destined individual, they continued to embrace the overarching, persisting aim of liberating the individual from all manner of structural and cultural oppression: the fundamental new class project, which, as Gouldner notes, "desacralizes authority-claims and fa-

11. Joyce Appleby traces the emergence of "structure" as the subject of historical inquiry in "A Different Kind of Independence: The Postwar Restructuring of the Historical Study of Early America," *William and Mary Quarterly*, 3rd ser., 50:2 (April 1993), 245-67. See also Dorothy Ross, "The New and Newer Histories: Social Theory and Historiography in an American Key," *Rethinking History* 1:2 (1997), who notes that "American historians finally turned to analytic, structural history and a full alliance with the social sciences in the decade after World War II," 126.

cilitates challenges to definitions of social reality made by traditional authorities linked to the church." The ongoing efforts of new class intellectuals were aimed at forging a more democratic, communitarian polity by rooting all human relationships in, as the historian Christopher Shannon puts it, "choice and consent" rather than traditional authority structures. But with its rendering of human community and activity as the product of various "forces," "structures," and "conditions," the unintended effect of this way of seeing was on the one hand to diminish the individual's sense of agency while on the other to empower the individual to think of herself as subject to no authority beyond the particular, socially constructed, historically contingent institutions of her own circumstance. In the end, social-science-inspired historiography only buttressed a vision of the world in which humans, while shaped by powerful social structures, were morally on their own and finally responsible to no authority higher than their own. The atomizing, antinomian tendencies latent in this individualistic ideology did not bode well for communitarian political hopes — such as those that were fueling Lasch's nascent historical work and political vision.[12]

12. Alvin Gouldner, *The Future of Intellectuals and the Rise of the New Class* (New York: Seabury Press, 1979), 1; Christopher Shannon, *Conspicuous Criticism: Tradition, the Individual, and Culture in American Social Thought, from Veblen to Mills,* New Studies in American Intellectual and Cultural History Series, ed. Dorothy Ross and Kenneth Cmiel (Baltimore: Johns Hopkins University Press, 1996), 84. See also Christopher Shannon, *A World Made Safe for Differences: Postwar Intellectuals and the Politics of Identity* (Lanham, Md.: Rowman and Littlefield, 2001).

Gouldner is more sanguine than Shannon about the "culture of critical discourse," but he notes that "Secularization was decisive in the formation of the New Class." Gouldner also emphasizes the claim of the New Class to "moral superiority" over older ways due to its "objective" pursuit of knowledge; the New Class, accordingly, had tended to understand itself as "emancipatory." Gouldner, *The Future of Intellectuals,* 1, 19, 48.

In his study of the political thought of the postwar era, Robert Booth Fowler comments incisively on the ideological commitments inherent in secularization. He concludes that "American political intellectuals did not see themselves objecting to other ideologies in the name of their own, but rather objecting to all ideologies in the name of empirical science, which reported a complex and intricate social reality." This ideology of rationality eventually collapsed beneath the weight of its own contradictions. Fowler, for instance, notes the contradiction inherent in Richard Hofstadter's defense of academic "freedom." Hofstadter had declared that "since ultimate truths were absent, freedom was crucial for human develop-

These varied but strong political and historiographical tendencies manifested themselves in the only piece of scholarship the Taylor-Lasch collaboration actually yielded, a *New England Quarterly* article from 1963 entitled "Two 'Kindred Spirits': Sorority and Family in New England, 1839-1846." Writing self-consciously as "social historians," Taylor and Lasch used the record of a literary friendship between two nondescript women writers to unpack the social dynamics of antebellum New England, aiming to explain the "general cultural phenomenon" of "the longing of women for literary careers" in the 1830s and 1840s. The innovative dimension of their argument lay precisely in the way in which structure, rather than ideas or innate longings, dominated their explanation. Although the friendship under investigation ostensibly centered on a mutual interest in social reform through literary endeavor, Taylor and Lasch contended, that activity merely "furnished the setting for a friendship," one that "had very little to do with reform" but had everything to do with "the social conditions which drove women into such relationships."[13]

What were these "social conditions"? Lasch and Taylor sketched out a time in which family and church were no longer "a source of affection and understanding, of meaningful contact with other people," since "migration and dispersal" had "eroded all agencies of social cohesion — not merely the family but church, state, and social

---

ment, and therefore fanaticism must be soundly defeated wherever it appears." Hofstadter failed to recognize, argues Fowler, that "these premises were themselves a powerful orthodoxy whose application in universities and elsewhere had an inevitably discouraging effect on those who did not believe them." *Believing Skeptics: American Political Intellectuals, 1945-1964* (Westport, Conn.: Greenwood Press, 1978), 15, 228.

13. William R. Taylor and Christopher Lasch, "Two 'Kindred Spirits': Sorority and Family in New England, 1839-1846," *New England Quarterly* 36 (March 1963), 24, 32, 33. This essay was drafted by Lasch; Taylor's contribution, apparently, was mainly in the form of a mutual conceiving of it. (See CL to William R. Taylor, TL, 3 January 1964, 7d:8.) Ten years after its original publication Lasch included it in WN, and in his bibliographic commentary on the piece criticized it severely. "Searching too eagerly for evidences of institutional decay," he wrote, "I took for granted in this essay the validity of clichés about the decline of the extended family and the loss of the family's functions, which have so long prevented scholars from seeing that the modern family represented not a decline from some hypothetical extended family (which tends to recede the more we pursue it backward in time) but a reorientation of domestic life around the ideal of privacy," 318.

classes." In a foreshadowing of Lasch's argument fourteen years later in *Haven in a Heartless World,* and one that the sociologist David Riesman had made in his 1950 book, *The Lonely Crowd,* they argued that in the antebellum period "The family lost its economic and even its educational functions; extended kin-groups broke down; and as a result the family was driven in upon itself: man, wife, and children held together not by mutual dependence, as formerly, but by affection." This one remaining bond was, alas, a weak one: "affection was not enough to hold either the family — even this remnant that remained — or society together."[14]

This picture of modernizing nineteenth-century America was, to say the least, bleak. To be living in America was to be a "victim of the relentless American environment, which ripped men and women from the safety of a predefined social context and cast them out into a world where a man was defined only by his own efforts — where every man and woman was obliged to become, in a sense more profound than those who coined the phrase may have intended, 'self-made.'" In this anarchic climate Lasch and Taylor saw in the "myth of the purity of women" a desperate attempt to achieve a point of cohesion for a society cut adrift from sturdy moorings, a society that was "a 'frontier' in the broadest sense of the term." "Women came to represent cohesion, decency, and self-restraint; and the cult of the Home, over which they presided, became the national religion."[15]

Lasch and Taylor, with many others, were probing the past with something less than a triumphal spirit. Seen through the eyes of a generation whose childhood was framed by depression and war and that lived with the memory of one Holocaust and the daily prospect of another, the progressive boast of liberation and hope seemed gauche at best. Modern Americans, far from having achieved freedom and democracy, seemed to Lasch a people without a polis, citizens of neither the city of God nor man. Unusually driven from early on to unearth the roots of this modern American condition, he had, like others of the day, little to offer by way of a counter-vision; in its place he could only

14. Taylor and Lasch, "Two 'Kindred Spirits,'" 33. For Riesman's argument on the evolving relations between parents and children, see *The Lonely Crowd,* chapter two, "From Morality to Morale: Change in the Agents of Character Formation" (New Haven: Yale University Press, 2001, abridged version), 37-65.

15. Taylor and Lasch, "Two 'Kindred Spirits,'" 41, 35.

deliver a relentless debunking and complicating of the received progressive story line. Truth-telling, made possible by the social sciences, was the main aim, the necessary first stage toward some future hope. American society and its history must be depicted for what it was, and this more complex, more dour, but, he was sure, more accurate understanding must be the new starting point for any way forward.

Richard Hofstadter, the historiographical embodiment of this postwar turn, cogently described it in 1968: "If there is a single way of characterizing what has happened in historical writing since the 1950s, it must be, I believe, the rediscovery of complexity in American history: an engaging and moving simplicity, accessible to the casual reader of history, has given way to a new awareness of the multiplicity of forces." Later, the historian Daniel Joseph Singal would term Hofstadter's vision an example of the "mature American modernist sensibility," seen also in writers such as John Dos Passos and William Faulkner and theologians Reinhold Niebuhr and Paul Tillich. Singal called this overarching shift "an attempt to restore a sense of order to human experience under the often chaotic conditions of twentieth-century existence," yet without reverting to a "fixed and absolute system of morality." Experimental living, guided by scientific inquiry, promised to deliver whatever stability was possible.[16]

As he was launching his career, Lasch devoted himself to understanding the past through these darkened midcentury lenses, and he sought out colleagues who seemed to be of like mind. Taylor was his most kindred spirit, but Staughton Lynd was also an early ally, and following a weekend with the Lasches in the summer of 1962 he agreed to embark upon a textbook project Lasch and Taylor had conceived, a

16. Richard Hofstadter, *The Progressive Historians: Turner, Beard, Parrington* (New York: Knopf, 1968), 442; Daniel Joseph Singal, "Towards a Definition of American Modernism," *American Quarterly* 39 (Spring 1987), 20, 8, 15. Richard Hofstadter's efforts to deepen the methodological apparatus of historians can be seen in a volume he co-edited with Seymour Martin Lipset: *Sociology and History: Methods* (New York: Basic Books, 1968). On Hofstadter's use of the social sciences see Daniel Joseph Singal, "Beyond Consensus: Richard Hofstadter and American Historiography," *American Historical Review* 89 (October 1984), 976-1004; Alan Brinkley, "In Retrospect: Richard Hofstadter's *The Age of Reform:* A Reconsideration," *Reviews in American History* 13 (September 1985), 462-80; Robert M. Collins, "The Originality Trap: Richard Hofstadter on Populism," *Journal of American History* 76 (June 1989), 150-67; and David S. Brown, *Richard Hofstadter: An Intellectual Biography* (Chicago: University of Chicago Press, 2006).

series of volumes covering the entire span of American history, which Wadsworth Publishing eventually took an interest in. They planned boldly and grandly. It was an attempt, Lasch wrote Lynd, "on a broad scale to integrate social with political and intellectual history," in the hope of reorienting the professional practice of history itself. The title Lasch gave to his own projected volume in the series — *The Price of Progress,* slated to explore the years 1877-1914 — underscored the direction in which his thinking was heading. In a 1964 review of a recent book on American populism he suggested that the late-nineteenth-century agrarian revolt may have been "one of the last expressions of what once had been a flourishing provincial culture," and it was this he intended to explore in his volume. Writing a prospectus for the book in the spring of 1963 he highlighted not only the paradox of Gilded Age wealth and poverty but also the era's most striking fear: "the lurking suspicion that 'progress' might undermine old values and create a nightmarish mechanized world of depersonalized efficiency — the anti-utopia that lurked in the utopian vision of the better world to which the period was committed." As in his "Two 'Kindred Spirits'" article, modern "structure" dominated his historical vision, in a malevolent, alienating fashion.[17]

In the end, the series with Wadsworth never materialized. Taylor struggled to get his volume off the ground, and the other historians they had sought to attract, Donald B. Meyer and Winthrop Jordan, never made firm commitments. Lasch's disappointment was extreme, revealing the extent to which deep collegial connections grounded his early professional hopes. In a particularly frank letter to Lynd in December of 1963 he wrote that he had had "some half-formed conviction that there really was a New History coming into being," and he had felt acutely "a desire to be a part of it." He now was seized by "a fear of being isolated professionally." "I don't think my own work will ever command any widespread support in the profession," he wrote, "and I suppose it would be nice to have some sort of buffer, in the form of friends and collaborators, between me and what

17. CL to Staughton Lynd, draft of a TL, 31 July 1962, 7d:8; CL, "Prospectus for Volume IV, 1877-1914," April 1963, 7d:8; CL, review of *The Populist Response to Industrial America: Midwestern Populist Thought* by Norman Pollack, and *The Tolerant Populists: Kansas Populism and Nativism,* by Walter T. K. Nungent, *Pacific Historical Review* 33 (1964), 72.

I sense to be a more or less hostile or indifferent professional readership."[18]

His disappointment, though, did not stop there. Lasch also confided to Lynd his sense that his and Taylor's projected volume on the history of women "will never get written." Less than a month later he confronted Taylor. "I have had for some time the feeling that the collaboration has yielded about all it is going to yield . . . and that from here on we would probably do best to follow our own work." Disillusioned by personal difficulties that had arisen between them, Lasch suggested that "cessation of collaboration" might be the best way to "clear away some of the accumulated debris under which, for both of us, both work and friendship currently labor." Taylor, sadly, agreed. The breakup of the collaboration was painful for both; Lasch told Taylor that he was "the one friend I have in the profession," a sentiment Taylor reciprocated. But their once-promising efforts had failed.[19]

Almost three decades later, after years of drift in their friendship, Lasch expressed his gratitude to Taylor for his companionship during those years. His words afford a revealing glimpse of the ideals and hopes that had fired his imagination in his early years of teaching and writing:

> I was lucky, at an impressionable stage of my intellectual life, to stumble into the company of a gifted conversationalist, from whom I learned, among other things, that the written word is a poor substitute for the spoken word. . . . I somehow had the expectation, when I started out in this line of work, that academic life would be an endless conversation of the kind you taught me to relish. It wasn't, of course, as almost anyone could have told me; all the more reason to thank my lucky stars that I had the chance to go to school with you.

In the course of their collaboration Lasch had been candid about the shortcomings that made him a difficult partner, admitting to Taylor on one occasion that "I am afraid I probably do need praise, constant

18. CL to Staughton Lynd, TL, 11 December 1963, 1:12.

19. CL to Staughton Lynd, TL, 11 December 1963, 1:12; CL to William R. Taylor, TL, 3 January 1964, 7d:8; CL to William R. Taylor, TL, 4 September 1964, 7d:9; William R. Taylor to CL, ALS, 9 September 1964, 7d:9.

praise, plaudits, acclaim, recognition, especially when I'm not very sure of what I've done." But in Lasch, the sense of personal vulnerability propelled him toward, rather than away from, close communal ties. His longstanding looming sense of alienation, so vividly projected in his historical writing, compelled him to seek to eliminate it in any arena possible — whether personal, vocational, or political.[20]

*   *   *

This sense of estrangement was also fueling the leftward turn he had begun to take. Intrigued and repelled at once by national and international politics, he continued to search for a more sure place to stand, a quest closely connected to his efforts to stake out his own ground in the historical profession. Indeed, his historiographical and political concerns continually played off of one another: the aggressiveness with which he attacked progressive understandings of history was matched by the fury with which he assaulted cold war liberals, the erstwhile "progressives." If his march left had moments of hesitancy and drift, it was in large part because by moving in that direction he had entered the cold war's badlands, where few inhabitants and fewer still redoubts existed to shelter the odd wanderer. To call oneself a radical in the age of what Arthur Schlesinger Jr. had proclaimed "the vital center" had little concrete meaning. Even the small number of the most committed leftists, such as those writing for the fledgling magazine *Dissent* (launched in 1954), "felt deeply the loss of innocence and good hope," writes John Patrick Diggins, and struggled to spawn a political vision that could adequately address itself to "the moral complexities of political action and the structural complexities of political power." *Dissent*'s founding editor, Irving Howe, captured poignantly the depths of the disorientation when, describing the postwar period, he recalled that "the mounting reports of the Holocaust evoked not just horror but a new and unspoken bewilderment as to the possibilities of the human creature — possibilities, after all, upon which the hope for socialism must ultimately rest."[21]

20. CL to William R. Taylor, TLS, 9 October 1992, 7c:2; CL to William R. Taylor, TL, 15 March 1962, 7d:7.
21. Arthur Schlesinger Jr., *The Vital Center: The Politics of Freedom* (Boston: Houghton Mifflin, 1949); John Patrick Diggins, *The Rise and Fall of the American*

Lasch's efforts to write publicly in the early sixties reflected this sense of resigned, confused quiescence. He conferred often with his usually sympathetic parents — whom he once described as "anti-cold war liberals" — about recent events in the ongoing international imbroglio, and admitted shortly after moving to Iowa that there were "times when it hardly seems worth the trouble" to stay in the "debate." When Jules Chametzky, editor of the recently launched journal of opinion the *Massachusetts Review,* urged him to contribute a book review, Lasch replied, months later, that he had been "alternately too busy and too apathetic about the plight of the world to write anything for you of any current significance."[22]

He was spurred toward some response, though, by Herman Kahn's widely debated *On Thermonuclear War,* and his 1962 discussion of it in the *Massachusetts Review* brought to light the distance that had opened by then between his own thinking and mainstream liberal opinion. Kahn, a realist proponent of nuclear deterrence, had argued that not only did the United States lack an adequate nuclear arsenal, it was also unprepared to engage in nuclear war because of its almost complete failure to prepare, both psychologically and materially, for atomic attack. In view of this deficit, he urged the government to begin a massive campaign to ready the nation for nuclear assault by convincing Americans that survival would be possible if the right precautions were taken, including the construction of bomb shelters, distribution of radiation meters, and development of evacuation plans. He went so far as to suggest that this sort of hardy preparation might actually leave rejuvenated and renewed those Americans who survived.[23]

Lasch, granting that Kahn's argument was "plausible, even powerful, as long as one accepts his assumptions," proceeded to attack them. "The book," he wrote, "has a certain dreamlike quality — great lucidity superimposed on fundamental confusion." A sterling example of "realism" turned surreal, Kahn's book was for him the *reductio ad absurdum* of the liberal consensus, which was growing increasingly

---

Left (New York: Norton, 1992), 216, 217; Irving Howe, *A Margin of Hope: An Intellectual Autobiography* (San Diego: Harcourt Brace Jovanovich, 1982), 106.

22. CL to Linda Smithson, TL, 4 December 1974, 3:19; CL to ZL & RL, TL, 14 August 1961, 1:5; CL to Jules Chametzky, TL, 18 February 1961, 1:2.

23. Herman Kahn, *On Thermonuclear War* (Princeton, N.J.: Princeton University Press, 1960).

more abstract and bizarre. His own proposal, just as dramatic as Kahn's but its mirror opposite, was for unilateral disarmament, which, he contended, was far more "realistic" than deterrence. The very suggestion of the need for "civil defense" was proof, Lasch charged, that deterrence was not such a sure way to avoid nuclear confrontation; in fact, it had not even managed to stop Russia from conventional military advance, as the recent construction of the Berlin Wall had proven. More hopefully, he suspected that if the United States took the initiative to disarm, the Soviet Union might well do the same, if for no other reason than to take advantage of the opportunity to reallocate its limited resources. Most provocatively, he expressed doubts that living in a Soviet-occupied America would be worse than trying to recover from the nuclear war both he and Kahn agreed was "imminent, if not inevitable, if things continue as they are." "How much freedom would there be in Kahn's reconstructed society?" he asked. "How much 'individualism'? How many of those intangibles of the American way of life . . . ?" Kahn's greatest error was taking "for granted the desirability of 'survival' without ever asking what it is that we wish to see survive."[24]

To argue publicly for unilateral disarmament did not make one a folk hero in cold war America, and to suggest the superiority of any Soviet regime over any American government made one a traitor. Lasch's willingness to suggest such a view signaled the depth of his sense of alienation from his country, which he saw wandering in a trance toward its own destruction, led by men whose hubris, foolhardiness, and naiveté were not only shameful but precipitous. (His disdain of cold war liberals was by now a given. Upon learning that Kennedy's National Security Advisor McGeorge Bundy — a former Harvard dean — was the son-in-law of Dean Acheson, Truman's secretary of state, he exclaimed to his parents: "What a pair of unspeakable

24. CL, "Herman Kahn on Thermonuclear War: What Price Survival," *Massachusetts Review* 2;3 (Spring 1962), 575, 578, 580. Lasch especially disputed Kahn's contention that a vibrant citizenry might emerge in the aftermath of a nuclear assault that had taken millions of lives: "I have my own idea about the reactions of Americans, who haven't been invaded by an enemy for a long time, and who now enjoy the 'highest standard of living in the world,'" 577. Closer to the heart of the matter, Kahn's proposed campaign for nuclear war preparedness would actually increase the likelihood of war by inducing both a fatalistic spirit and, ironically, a dangerous confidence that nuclear war might be worth the risk.

asses"!) Americans, in accord with their historically entrenched "messianic ideology," were deluded, even in the midst of the cold war, by their conviction that their "institutions and habits of mind" were "destined to spread over large areas of the world's habitable surface," he scoffed bitterly in the *Nation* the next year. In trying to combat cold war liberals, he and others of like mind were, he warned, "dealing with a state of mind to which the ordinary rules of logic do not necessarily apply."[25]

Upon arriving at Iowa he began to make dealing with this state of mind a part of his own educational mission. If by the early 1960s he had come to see Americans as handicapped by an inability to comprehend, discern, weigh, and evaluate their true situation, he reacted to it with a zeal and scorn bred in him by parents who made confronting such ills their civic duty. But much to his surprise, Lasch discovered at Iowa a certain amount of interest, even support, for his increasingly radical views. The day after he denounced bomb shelters at a party during his first semester at Iowa in 1961, he wrote his parents, "delegations from all the radical student organizations — socialists, pacifists — came to me wanting me to sponsor them." He decided to stand with the pacifists, although in a letter to a former Harvard classmate he made light of his emerging reputation, conveying the sense of ambivalence he felt toward the American left, or at least its public image:

> I will shortly, no doubt, be presiding over little meetings of anarchists, pacifists, and other desperate people. I plan to grow a goatee, and if you know where I can get a pince-nez, do let me know. I also am planning a seminar on Free Love, and would appreciate suggestions. There is clearly nothing for me to do but to live up to the part in which I have been cast.

His sense of discomfort notwithstanding, he found himself vigorously defending left-leaning positions as the sixties slowly began to heat up.[26]

25. CL to RL & ZL, TL, 13 December 1962, 1:10; CL, "America's Place in the Sun," *Nation,* 22 June 1963, 531, 532.

26. CL to ZL & RL, TL, 22 October 1961, 1:5; CL to Austin and Margaret Briggs, TL, 4 October 1961, 1:2.

One Iowa alum remembers well the effect of Lasch on the university in those years. David Marr, who would go on to become a professor of American Studies at Evergreen State College, recalls that Lasch did not hesitate to register his own political judgments in the midst of his "carefully crafted" lectures, and students responded to his style and views with energy. "If you went to see him in his office on certain days," remembers Marr, "there would be a stream of students outside waiting to talk to him — anywhere from ten to twenty people lined up. . . . I never saw this connection with *any* other teacher there." Lasch had "an edge to him that others didn't — and it wasn't just personality. It was an intellectual power that he had." This appeal, he notes, registered prior to the politicization of the student body, "just on the eve of these developments." He recalls that at one of the early public political meetings at Iowa, centered on American foreign policy, Lasch was present "with his yellow pad and pencil, taking notes." Lasch's characteristic response to one speaker's endorsement of the government's official position has, more than forty years later, stuck fast in Marr's mind. Said Lasch, simply, "You don't have to go along with that."[27]

He himself was not about to, and his bleak estimate of the cold war circumstance was confirmed for him in the Cuban Missile Crisis of October 1962, when President Kennedy demanded that the Soviets remove recently installed missiles on Cuba or else face American invasion of the island. In a letter to his parents, Lasch gave Cuba the benefit of the doubt. Given the Kennedy-instigated attempt to overthrow Castro's government the previous year — the notorious Bay of Pigs fiasco — Cuba had had no choice but to seek more potent weapons for self-defense. For their part, "the Russians were simply deceived by the sense of their own righteousness, as we are consistently by ours. Because it was obvious to them that this was a defensive move, they assumed it would be equally obvious to everybody." Moreover, in light of the presence of American nuclear armaments in Turkey, the Soviet Union might have felt pressured to reciprocate in kind by installing missiles close to American shores.[28]

Robert disagreed with Kit's take on Soviet motives, viewing the missile installation as "an enormous power play" by the Kremlin, a

27. Interview with David Marr, 15 November 2006.
28. CL to ZL & RL, TL, 25 October 1962, 1:10.

brazen attempt to alter the balance of power; Kit later conceded that this may have been the case. Still, as he wrote to another correspondent, Kennedy had foolishly preferred to make a public ultimatum to the Soviet Union rather than privately confer with the Russian leaders first — or, as his father would have liked, cooperate more closely with the United Nations during the crisis. "We are very lucky that this ultimatum did not lead to war," wrote Lasch, "and I hope that we don't forget . . . that we owe the happy outcome more to Russian restraint than to American forcefulness."[29]

This embittered, soured tone toward cold war America came out in almost everything he wrote. In the introduction he published in 1961 to a new edition of Dickens's *American Notes* (an opportunity he received through Commager), he used his few pages to relate what Dickens had wanted to say about his 1842 visit but due to marketing considerations could not. By the end of his visit, Lasch wrote, Dickens was "heartily sick of America," going so far as to write one friend, "'I would not condemn you to a year's residence on this side of the Atlantic for any money.'" "'This is not the republic I came to see,'" he sadly admitted. Dickens had despised, Lasch noted, "the meanness of the press, the low tone of public discussion, the tyranny of public opinion"; America, per Dickens, was "utterly lacking either in taste or in imagination." In sum, wrote Lasch, to Dickens "America is disgusting, but what is worse, it is dull." He was all too willing to sum up these nineteenth-century perceptions in the present tense.[30]

*   *   *

"It was with a tremendous sense of relief" that Dickens and his wife had finally left America, Lasch wrote. Little more than a century later Lasch followed him back across the Atlantic with a similar sense of anticipation. He had received word in December 1962 that the Social Science Research Council had awarded him a research fellowship of $6000 for the 1963-64 academic year, which he would spend writing a book on progressive-era intellectuals. Never having been abroad, and

29. RL to CL, TL, 29 October 1962, 1:10; CL to ZL & RL, TL, 11 November 1962, 1:10; CL to H. R. Amidon, TL, 11 November 1962, 1:9.

30. CL, "Introduction," in Charles Dickens, *American Notes* (Greenwich, Conn.: Fawcett, 1961; reprint, Glouscester, Mass.: Peter Smith, 1968), x, xi.

having received an invitation to stay in a house the Commagers owned in Cambridgeshire, he and Nell decided to sail to England during the summer of 1963 and spend the academic year there.[31]

Catherine Thomas, born in May of 1963, had brought the number of little Lasches to three, making traveling more than a little challenging. Lasch explained to friends soon after their arrival that "It turns out that three children really do slow you down. In fact they paralyze you altogether. You don't somehow pick up and go gaily down to London, as I imagined you did . . . you spend them where you always spend them."[32]

The bookstores, too, were a disappointment. He reported to Taylor that they were "only fair," and certainly not useful for his concerns:

> They run heavily to literature and literary "classics" and old-fashioned history, and the English paperbacks run to the same. No sociology, no social history, no social psychology. . . . Cambridge, in short, is not, I am afraid, the world center of the social sciences.

Midway through their year he described their stay to Taylor as "a hell of a time": "five-and-a-half months of sustained and unmitigated hard labor, and no relief in sight; domestic turmoil, financial insolvency . . . discouraging." Five weeks later he confessed to Taylor that he was "tired, tired of England, tired of writing this damned book. I hope the book isn't beginning to show it."[33]

If anything, the assassination of John F. Kennedy that November only intensified his efforts to define more incisively the American circumstance and his own relationship to it. "Kennedy's death filled me with a grief I do not understand," he wrote Lynd from England. His frequent letters to his parents touched often on the subject. While Zora immediately suspected that it had been "instigated by the J. Birchers and the Goldwater fanatics" ("For pure hatred they surpass anyone I ever knew"), Robert's first inclination, she wrote, was to blame the "crackpot segregationists." Kit agreed that conspiracy the-

31. CL, "Introduction," x; CL to John C. Weaver, TL, 18 December 1962, 1:11; CL to ZL & RL, TL, 12 January 1963, 1:12. Lasch's salary from Iowa for the 1963-1964 year was $8600. Virgil M. Hancher to CL, TLS, n.d., 1:12.

32. CL to Diane and Larry Barett, TL, 20 November 1963, 1:11.

33. CL to William R. Taylor, 17 October 1963, TL, 7d:8; CL to William R. Taylor, TL, 15 February 1964, 7d:9; CL to William R. Taylor, TL, 26 March 1964, 7d:9.

ories were appealing, offering "the comfort of a rational motive," but concluded, initially, that "we are left with pure madness." Oswald's act expressed, he wrote, in a characteristic socio-psychological riff, "the alienation which is so pronounced and characteristic of American political life." People like Oswald, sadly, had little connection to "the common life around them." Oswald was the "totally politicized man, the man whose mind has been given over wholly to ideology, to the point where no other claims of any kind make any impression whatsoever."[34]

But after Robert made a visit that winter to the site from which Oswald had fired the shots and concluded that the chances were nil that he could have succeeded alone, Kit began to reconsider. He revisited the assassination in a letter to his parents in the spring of 1964. "I know one American who still thinks the Oswald case is not yet closed: me." His suspicion of government machinations had been heightened due to its strenuous "efforts to suppress everything connected to the case." He sensed the government "had something to hide."[35]

Despite the disappointment and disarray, Lasch's year in England was far from squandered; indeed, he seemed to emerge from it with a sense of deliverance. He tried to explain his experience to Lynd. "The effect of removal from America," he sensed, "and on top of it this isolation here, partly enforced, partly self-imposed, has thrown me back on myself in a way that takes me back to adolescence." Far from negative, though, this cloistering had helped him become "free from a lot of old and previously unacknowledged academic ambitions," a theme he expanded on to Taylor. By removing to England he had gained the distance necessary to discern more clearly "the pressures on a young historian, even when he thinks he is resisting them, to be brilliant and original and epater the old guard; all of which, it seems to me now, had seeped into everything I wrote." Fortunately, he had ended up "weeding out" of his writing "all of the academic crap and the futile, sterile academic controversies of no interest to anyone who is not neurotically enmeshed in them." This process had been "trying," to be sure, but it had also been deeply "liberating," in both academic

34. CL to Staughton Lynd, TL, 11 December 1963, 1:12; ZL to CL & NL, TL, 23 November 1963, 1:12; CL to ZL & RL, TL, 9 December 1963, 1:12.
35. CL to ZL & RL, TL, 20 January 1964, 1:15; CL to ZL & RL, TL, 13 April 1964, 1:15.

and political ways. Being in England had given him "respite from the grinding business of being at odds with my country. . . . Sometimes it seems to me now that one's whole life is poisoned in America by the friction of being continually at war with one's surroundings. Everything you write becomes subtly, and often not subtly at all, colored by polemic and controversy" and shaped by "the political despair one continually feels in America."[36]

All of these tensions, from the political to the personal, came together to help create an ideal moment to write a book, and Lasch's sense of upheaval fueled his efforts rather than choked them. In the midst of writing, he told Taylor, he had begun finally to sense that "the real stuff of history" was beginning "at last feebly to struggle to light." Once, in the course of a conversation over a holiday weekend, he recalled, he and Taylor had speculated that perhaps "the way to write" history "wasn't to argue it and 'interpret' it," but rather allow it "to *emerge*"; this, Lasch sensed, was finally happening. On May 6 he wrote to his parents in tired triumph: "I finished my book last night, nine chapters, 556 pages. I am exhausted."[37]

It was largely the descriptive and interpretive flair of the book, written in the self-consciously dramatic and sharply interpretive narrative style of Lasch's early heroes Hofstadter and Schlesinger, that made *The New Radicalism in America* stand out. Not surprisingly, Lasch admitted to both Lynd and Taylor that as he was writing he was battling his old yearning to write fiction. To Taylor he spoke of a "terrific struggle": for about a month he had been seized with "the feeling that I really ought to be writing fiction, that it was weakness not to do so, that I was playing it safe, etc." He had succeeded, with much effort, in overcoming these impulses, convinced that they were rooted in an "old set of preoccupations" that stemmed from his involuted adolescence and that had recently resurfaced in England. He considered his desire to write fiction a "fatal urge." "I do think that if I let myself waver at this point I'll never be any good at anything," he wrote Taylor. The highly pressured atmospherics of Lasch's internal world, coupled with the wandering, ruminating, reconfiguring eye of the novelist,

36. CL to Staughton Lynd, TL, 11 December 1963, 1:12; CL to William R. Taylor, TL, 3 January 1964, 7d:8; CL to William R. Taylor, TL, 3 January 1964, 7d:8.

37. CL to William R. Taylor, TL, 3 January 1964, 7d:8; CL to ZL & RL, TL, 6 May 1964, 1:15.

yielded the creative energy that in the end brought *The New Radicalism* to life.[38]

Richard Hofstadter, who had recently become a trade book advisor with Knopf and had followed Lasch's progress attentively since his Columbia years, had begun in the fall of 1962 to try to attract Lasch to Knopf. "I have a feeling that anything you turned your hand to would be worth having a closer look at," he wrote. Lasch demurred, due to his contract with Braziller for the book on the history of women. Only at the last minute had he decided to spend his leave working instead on what became *The New Radicalism*. In July of 1963, in the midst of financial distress, he ended up broaching Hofstadter with his prospectus (the same day on which he had written to Taylor, "I've got to dig up some money somewhere quick"). The book, he explained to Hofstadter, would be "designed to document the thesis that progressivism can best be understood as the manifestation of a deep and growing dissatisfaction, on the part of middle-class intellectuals, with middle-class life and culture (and not as a 'response to industrialism')," as the title of a recent survey updating the old progressive thesis had put it. He appealed to Hofstadter as a historiographical ally. The book, he wrote, would be "designed also to show that it is possible to 'psychologize' about history without psychologizing your subjects away." By mid-September Hofstadter had read a draft of the opening chapter of the book, and responded approvingly. Later that fall Lasch sent Hofstadter his working title: "Sources of the New Radicalism: Studies in the Social History of the American Intellectual." To publisher Alfred A. Knopf he explained that the subtitle "shows where my real interest lies: there, more than in progressivism or radicalism itself." His eye was trained on the subterranean context he perceived to be history's true shaper.[39]

38. CL to William R. Taylor, TL, 3 January 1964, 7d:8; CL to Staughton Lynd, TL, 11 December 1963, 1:12. In his review, Daniel Aaron remarked on Lasch's literary style: "What is most striking about this intelligent and sophisticated book, however, are the insights, casually dropped and often brilliantly phrased, that illuminate a person or a period, and the almost novelistic way in which Mr. Lasch makes use of published and unpublished material." Daniel Aaron, "Parallel Lines Met in the New Frontier," *New York Times Book Review*, 13 June 1965, 38.

39. Richard Hofstadter to CL, TLS, 20 September 1962, 1:10; CL to William R. Taylor, TL, 24 July 1963, 7d:8; CL to Richard Hofstadter, TL, 24 July 1963, 1:12; Richard Hofstadter to CL, TLS, 11 September 1963, 1:12; CL to Richard

Knopf was pleased with Lasch's rapid progress and after reading 47,000 words of the text in December 1963 offered him a $1000 advance, as well as a word of encouragement: "From what Dick Hofstadter tells me . . . I know we are adding something very distinguished to our list."[40]

*   *   *

The New Radicalism in America, 1889-1963: The Intellectual as a Social Type turned a promising young historian into a star. In the space of a few weeks in the spring of 1965 Christopher Lasch went from being a slightly heterodox, little-known academic to a literary commodity — and a beacon to many both in his generation and the one that followed. The writer who since childhood had dreamed of great achievement, had, to his own surprise, delivered.[41]

The New Radicalism hit with the force of a shotgun shell, at once complex, entertaining, analytic, sexed, and ambivalent. Cooly modernist, bearing a sophistication and sheen that recalls the Kennedy years ("learned, crisp, cocksure," in the *New Yorker*'s description), it was in reality the anti-Camelot protest of a young intellectual who had distanced himself from that realm, repelled by its easy belief in its own inherent goodness. With well-heeled confidence, Lasch had written what would be his most ironic, wistful, and conflicted meditation on the plight of the newly secular, finally homeless modern intellectual, struggling for vitality and identity in a profoundly fractured world. The book presaged the ideological and philosophical course he would chart in the years following its publication, revealing him to be cautiously but intensely in search of some pathway that might lead to true cultural renewal. But also palpable throughout was Lasch's abiding sense of confusion and despair. When he wrote of the "rich-

---

Hofstadter, TL, 7 November 1963, 1:12; CL to Alfred A. Knopf, TL, 12 November 1963, 1:12; Alfred A. Knopf to CL, TLS, 18 December 1963, 1:12. See Samuel Hays, *The Response to Industrialism* (Chicago: University of Chicago Press, 1959). Hays was Lasch's predecessor at Iowa.

40. Alfred A. Knopf to CL, TLS, 18 December 1963, 1:12.

41. In 1993 Lasch recalled, "I didn't want to write a merely academic book but I don't think I had any great expectations for it. What I remember is thinking that whatever reception it was going to have, [it would be] a considerable advance beyond what I had done before." Fox, "Interview," 9.

ness of the larger social and public life which had disappeared for good," he was registering a sense of loss that would shadow him thereafter.[42]

It is impossible to grasp the enthusiastic reception and potent effect of *The New Radicalism* without first taking into account the power of Lasch's writing. Lasch had long since embraced and ingested the rhetorical assumptions described pointedly by writer and editor Betsy Lerner in a shrewd piece of advice to writers:

> Everything you put on the page is a deliberate manipulation of what happened, written to keep the reader entertained, moved, sympathetic, horrified, scared, whatever. You are never writing what *really* happened. Instead, you are choosing words, building images, creating a sense of rhythm, sense, and structure through which to move your characters and unfold your story. You are making a thousand miniscule choices that you hope will add up in such a way that your readers believe what they're reading is real. And this is why, when the writer is successful, the best fiction reads like nonfiction and the best nonfiction like a novel.

Lasch's long labor at writing fiction had clearly not been in vain. His chapter on the memoirist and Greenwich Village salon hostess Mabel Dodge Luhan was just one among many that pulsed with discriminating judgment, psychological perception, and descriptive flair. "The houses of the rich," wrote Lasch,

> had become fortresses against intrusion. Even the architecture of the period reflected the tendency of each family to withdraw into a world of its own making. To the outsider these edifices presented a massive wall of impenetrable stone, into which doors and windows were deeply set, mere slits, like those of the medieval castles to which the buildings of Richardson and his imitators obscurely alluded. The effect of the heavy doors and ponderous draperies was not only to shut out intruders but to stifle the human sounds within. A pervasive silence descended. Life came to be lived behind locked doors.

42. Brief review of *The New Radicalism in America*, *The New Yorker*, 31 July 1965, 80; CL, NR, 102.

Such passages are, of course, impervious to strict empirical standards of evidence. But these were never the standards that counted to Lasch — the past was too important for so much bean-counting. People would only come to care about the past if it were somehow resurrected before their eyes, brought to life in the present in such a way as to make the present *more* present. This was in sum a literary endeavor, of course, and it required far more than accuracy. It required the kind of vision, sensibilities, and style honed and sharpened by poets, novelists, and other agents of the imagination.[43]

But *The New Radicalism* was not simply a good story, as Lasch's fiercely iconoclastic intent made clear. Taking the pioneering generation of modern American intellectuals as his subject, he proceeded, through a series of interpretive biographical portraits, to mercilessly deconstruct their identity and ambitions — in form and spirit (if not in message) very much in the mode of Hofstadter's *The American Political Tradition*. His charge: American intellectuals, called above all to be critics of and for their nation, had from the outset abdicated this most basic responsibility. The untoward effects of their failure were now legion, the most obvious sign the thoroughly complicit involvement of their progeny, the contemporary "liberals," in the governance and maintenance of cold war America. His verdict: American intellectuals must recover a truer understanding of how to carry out what he termed their "vocation" if the follies of contemporary liberalism were to be corrected and the nation's course righted.[44]

This vision obviously placed a great burden on and trust in intellectuals to be the guides of society, a sort of latter-day clergy fanning out to provide instruction for all, at all social levels. Building on a rationalist epistemology — what he at one point in the book termed "the rock of rationalism" — intellectuals, as thoughtful, educated analysts, carried the civic responsibility of pointing the way toward a more satisfying realization of the nation's most fundamental social and political ideals. And it was in this, their most basic charge, that they had utterly failed.[45]

---

43. Betsy Lerner, *The Forest for the Trees: An Editor's Guide to Writers* (New York: Riverhead Books, 2000), 67; CL, NR, 113-14.

44. CL, NR, ix.

45. CL, NR, 11. Lasch's colleague Robert B. Westbrook notes that *The New Radicalism* "seems to have been grounded in a universalism and rationalism (even

Crucially, the defect Lasch aimed to expose in the new radicals was not at root intellectual; they already possessed the proper epistemological and educational starting point for their mission. What Lasch was seeking to do, through story, was to illumine their failure to achieve a proper *social* understanding of their condition and plight. As historically situated human beings, they had failed to perceive clearly where they were in the American circumstance, and how this location had deleteriously affected their ability to steer modern America toward its highest ends and noblest ideals. They, as moderns, had the proper training and tradition. What they lacked was perception.

Above all, Lasch thought, an intellectual needs to achieve critical distance in order to provide this badly needed social and political commentary — "the value of his criticism," as he put it, "is presumed to rest on a measure of detachment from the current scene." The new radicals' perennial need for critical detachment and their continual failure to achieve it made his story a tragedy, one that he narrated harshly; indeed, his severe tone led Daniel Aaron in the *New York Times Book Review* to call the book "a low-pitched homily." Jane Addams, Randolph Bourne, Lincoln Steffens, Walter Lippmann, John Dewey, Dwight Macdonald: these supposed giants (and many more) of the American left had abandoned critical detachment and succumbed in varying ways to the false "religion of experience," a misguided, self-satisfied hope "to live fully, directly, spontaneously; to live to the outer limits of one's capacities; to immerse oneself in the stream of experience," and so diminish their ability to *see*. This betrayal of the life of reason Lasch bitterly christened "the anti-intellectualism of the intellectuals" (the title of his closing chapter) — an obvious counter to the brighter rendering of American intellectuals Hofstadter had sketched in his 1964 Pulitzer Prize–winning volume, *Anti-Intellectualism and American Life,* where he had blamed not the intellectuals but the backward masses for the absence of a more vibrant and salutary intellectual dimension in contemporary American society.[46]

Platonism) of the sort we have come to call 'foundationalist' in that it sought to provide intellectuals with a transcendent standpoint outside of the contingencies of history and culture." See Westbrook, "Christopher Lasch, *The New Radicalism,* and the Vocation of Intellectuals," *Reviews in American History* 23 (1995), 188.

46. CL, NR, ix, 63, 64; Daniel Aaron, "Parallel Lines," 2; Richard Hofstadter, *Anti-Intellectualism and American Life* (New York: Knopf, 1964).

What had made the "religion of experience" so tempting to intellectuals, averred Lasch, was their "alienage." Emerging as a distinct social class at the end of the nineteenth century, they were forced to find their own way just as the old cultural consensus, rooted in allegiance to capitalism and the tradition of patriarchal authority, was crumbling. "The mass society," Lasch explained, "lacking the cohesive influences that make a society into a community, tends to break up into smaller communities, autonomous, self-contained, and having no viable connection to the whole." This fracturing left the intellectuals culturally homeless and prone to dysfunctional reactions to mainstream middle-class American life, itself in a state of fissure. At the precise moment that America, for its own well-being, most needed intellectual leadership, they offered an odd, conceited, convoluted cacophony of voices and ideas.[47]

It is surprising, perhaps, given their exceedingly grim prospects for achieving cohesion, that Lasch examined his subjects with such small doses of sympathy and high levels of chagrin. "Seeking experience," he charged, "they rejected a culture which seemed to them increasingly artificial, increasingly cut off from life; yet, having broken away from the middle class, intellectuals often found themselves no nearer to 'life' than before." Lasch found them, one after another, in the smog of compromise, ennui, or folly. Jane Addams, in settling for a "god . . . of doing rather than of knowing," had engaged in a "renunciation of culture, of the past, of history itself." Edward A. Ross came to have "confidence . . . 'only in that philosophy which begins by renouncing philosophy.' What counted was not thought but feeling." On the decision of the *New Republic* to reverse its pacifist stance and support American involvement in World War I, Lasch bitingly wrote:

> Logic may have dictated nonintervention, but something deeper than logic dictated war. The thirst for action, the craving for involvement, the longing to commit themselves to the onward march of events — these things dictated war. The realists feared isolation not only for America but for themselves. Accordingly, they went to war and invented the reasons for it afterward.[48]

47. CL, NR, 62, 69.
48. CL, NR, 101, 29, 28, 172, 223.

Lasch's new radicals were victims of the modern world, to be sure, but victims with a taste for self-destruction. And without the moral and critical fortitude only a true "community" could provide, the intellectuals had suffered their malformation in the hostile sea of twentieth-century American life. Crucially, it was their allowing this fate to befall them, despite its seeming inevitability, that had been their Adamic sin, and this fall had in turn damned their children: Lasch's contemporaries, and Lasch himself.

What sort of "community" might have enabled these intellectuals to succeed? As would become even more the case in his later work, Lasch's unrelenting critical style left it up to the reader to tease out his positive ideal, which was itself buried in paradox. On the one hand his narrative sounded a lament for a pre-modern, closely connected world that had irretrievably passed; on the other, his vision was not only resolutely secular in framework but also almost entirely centered on the quintessentially modern virtues of "disinterested inquiry and speculation." These dueling impulses amounted to a plea for a kind of rationalist, monastic asceticism, a "community" that would be modern and anti-modern at once — mysterious, high-minded, and severe.[49]

It's hard to imagine many of his radicals having the ability, let alone the desire, to embrace it. Committed to a way of understanding the world that in effect (as well as in theory) divorced affection from knowing, and isolated in an epistemic world shaped by a strict subject-object dichotomy, Lasch's new radicals were bound to find their way into some "religion of experience" or another. The example of sociologist Edward Ross provides a striking example of this bipolar movement between reason and experience to which moderns were so prone. Lasch noted that in 1889 Ross "announced his discovery that a person 'who plants himself on the shore of some remote idea,' in order to get a more panoramic view of the world, 'is sure to be overwhelmed by an awful feeling of loneliness.'" It was, tragically and tellingly, "the philosopher" who ended up, per Ross, "'dying of loneliness and purposelessness,'" and who in turn "envied 'the heats of passion, intensity of desire, energy of will, warmth of life and fierceness of hate felt by those struggling and shouting amid the multitude.'" Ross, sensing an expanding spiritual void, had put his finger

49. CL, NR, 64.

directly on the essential modernist dialectic, in which a strict secularity of "detached" and "critical" vision of the world turns out to propel the individual back into the world in an unbounded, autonomous (but still "scientific") way.[50]

Whatever its logic, this tendency led to a manner of comportment Lasch could not abide. The "new radicals" tended to give themselves over to sexual and political adventures with not just a sense excitement but relief — glad to escape the chilly laboratory for a time, and happy to be free of the old, discredited creeds. They thought of such experience as the very definition of freedom, but Lasch could not reconcile himself to this troubling definitional evolution. He seemed bound early on by the ascetic's intuition that some vital dimension of reality is unknowable apart from the practice of self-denial, an intuition that, growing in strength, would contribute to his eventual split with the left.

Accordingly, Lasch defiantly attacked the cultural modernism — its spirit, if not its form — that had helped to call this "social type," the intellectual, into existence. "The new radicalism differed from the old in its interest in questions which lay outside the realm of conventional politics," he contended. "What characterized the person of advanced opinions in the first two decades of the twentieth century — and what by and large continues to characterize him at the present time — was his position with regard to such issues as childhood, education, and sex; sex, above all." Lasch discerned sinister machinations in the new radicals' desire to make what he considered to be cultural matters the object of politics. Estranged from mainstream America, the new radicals sought, with a "manipulative mind," to transform the bourgeoisie not by cultural means, which would of necessity be more democratic and reliant on persuasion, but rather by strokes of coercive power. Lasch found this morally repugnant — not so much because he opposed cultural modernism (though one senses a vague and indefinite discomfort with it), but because the new radicals' methods were an arrogant assault on fellow citizens and were a further manifestation of their own self-congratulating conceit, which, he believed, deserved more suspicion.[51]

50. CL, NR, 172.
51. CL, NR, 90, 163. Lasch cited several of philosopher Benjamin Ginzburg's articles from the 1930s as he was establishing his thesis about the necessity of

To make matters worse, the new radicals sought to deal with problems that were properly "political" by confronting them in the sphere of culture, thus losing sight of the web of power structures that their own convictions required them to confront. "They proposed to attack such public problems as the conflict between capital and labor by eliminating the psychological sources of conflict, by 'educating' capitalists and laborers to a more altruistic and social point of view — in other words," he acidly wrote, "by improving the quality of men's private lives." Due to this confusion between culture and politics — "the essence of the new radicalism" — he saw little hope that either these intellectuals or their progeny would ever lead America in more fruitful directions, whether culturally or politically. Their "liberal values of wholesomeness and adjustment" could never effect the structural changes their political vision required, and their willingness to archly impose this new culture was itself a disquieting sign of a morally corrupting hubris. Rather than positioning themselves as enemies of unbounded power, the intellectuals were actually vying for it.[52]

Lasch's analysis of the new radicalism's revolutionary cultural agenda — its determination to change Americans' conception of "childhood, education, and sex" — pointed to one of the mysterious shortcomings of the book: its almost complete failure to connect the emergence of these intellectuals to the European intellectual and cultural movements of which the new radicals themselves were self-consciously a part. Instead, he depicted the American class structure and social conditions as the creator of this welter of threatening new ideas and activities, leaving his book without the textual richness that

---

"detachment" and the priority of criticism for intellectuals. See Benjamin Ginzburg, "Against Messianism," *New Republic,* 18 February 1931, 15-17; *Rededication to Freedom* (New York: Simon and Schuster, 1959). In a 1962 review of Daniel Aaron's *Writers on the Left: Episodes in American Literary Communism,* Lasch had referenced approvingly Ginzburg's understanding of the proper role of intellectuals, and then sketched briefly what would become a key theme in NR: intellectuals of the 1930s had been bedeviled not by communism but by "pragmatism," which he regarded as "a symptom of an underlying self-contempt." Trying desperately to "escape the responsibility of being intellectuals," they had undertaken a "retreat which in our own day, far from being arrested, threatens to become a route." CL, "Radicals of the Thirties," *St. Louis Post-Dispatch,* 11 February 1962, 4C.

52. CL, NR, 163, 158.

intellectual historians such as Perry Miller and Henry F. May had recently brought to the study of American intellectual life. The *New Yorker* succinctly noted the effect of his approach: "Too often, he gives the impression that he is disposing of, rather than understanding, his subjects."[53]

But while Lasch's resolute turn from intellectual history to social history no doubt affected his method, he was also governed by political intent. He perceived no need for yet another exploration and defense of the rationalist or modernist traditions in the form of historical genealogy; American intellectuals were already well-versed in it. Instead, the more urgent need of the day was for American intellectuals to respond adequately to what they already knew to be true. Once the corrosive effects of the modern social condition were more fully understood, Lasch hoped, truly rational thinkers would repent of their ways and begin once more to move in constructive directions.

He had little sense, at this point, that the rationalist assumptions of modern intellectuals might themselves be contributing to the morass he was trying to expunge, convinced as he was, to use John Ralston Saul's pithy phrase, that "reason was a moral force." As Lasch wrote in his introduction, his book was intended to suggest — and exemplify — "what it means to pursue the life of reason in a world in which the irrational has come to appear not the exception but the

---

53. CL, NR, 90; brief review of *The New Radicalism in America, New Yorker,* 31 July 1965, 80. Alfred Kazin, in an otherwise flattering review, noted that Lasch "does not admit the past as an historical dimension, an objective presence: He is too intent on showing the comparative shallowness and abstractness of the intellectuals' revolt against it." In his review Norman Birnbaum, who would later become an ally of Lasch's, noted that "History is here recounted like a late bourgeois novel, a serious *Bildungsroman* whose hero — the American intellectual — seems unable ever to reach maturity, compelled indefinitely to repeat the follies of his youth. Lasch maintains the unity of his own critical thought by insisting upon the traits common to his subjects. A fully achieved portrait is the result, but the era's inner movement comes rather short. In the end, he has very little to say about the changes in our circumstances; living history turns out to be, disappointingly, not entirely alive and moving." Kazin, "Radicals and Intellectuals," *New York Review of Books* 4:8 (20 May 1965), 3; Birnbaum, "The Radical Circle," *Partisan Review* 33:3 (Summer 1966), 463.

Interestingly, writing a *Bildungsroman* had been Lasch's perennial quest; he himself described the novel he had been trying to write during graduate school in these terms in an interview with Richard Fox. See Fox, "Interview," 6.

rule." Employing a Weberian (and something of a soft Nietzschean) line of argument to unmask the corruptions of power and strength in the modern West, he did not see enlightened rationality as itself a regime that, unable in its self-isolated classification as "intellect" to establish a political or moral *telos,* ended up being complicit in the very moral and communal fracturing that so disturbed him.[54]

Instead, as a thoroughgoing modern, liberal intellectual himself, Lasch continued to see the present as a period of promise, of hope — at least ideally. Through his portrait of the new radicals Lasch was seeking to capture with both analysis and story the turn-of-the-century conditions in which a truly post-Christian culture became possible in the United States, the age when for varying, complex reasons the myth of secularity became believable, and thus when the possibility of a truly "rational" society appeared within reach. And he was attempting to make sense of this circumstance in a way that might lead to salutary political prescription. In this early effort he came off as the knowing grandchild of the awful, wondrous enlightenment that had so confused and liberated this earlier generation, a deeply restless young man in search of decency and hope. He was betting all on the belief that the great iron cage was the product not of scientific rationality but malignant social conditions and collective folly, and that social-scientific inquiry might yet awaken Americans, now more sharply attuned to themselves and their world, to a more satisfying end. By prophetically illuminating the spiritual, intellectual, and political predicament of his own "social type," he both disturbed the peace and gestured toward a better way — but one that nonetheless still lay within their received secularity, built squarely upon the "rock of rationalism."

Did Lasch point readers in any particular political directions? The anger and disappointment that suffused his story betrayed him as an acutely frustrated new radical himself, hoping against hope for some alternative to emerge, trying to find some pathway between alienation and acquiescence. He dimly suggested (again echoing Hofstadter) that a heavily chastened, decidedly non-celebratory pluralist conception of the political sphere was the best available structural option: a mere

54. John Ralston Saul, *Voltaire's Bastards* (New York: Vintage Books, 1993), 16; CL, NR, xvii, 11. On the myth of secularity, see John Milbank, *Theology and Social Theory: Beyond Secular Reason* (Cambridge: Blackwell, 1990).

politics, as it were, politics as "a forum for the resolution of competing interests" rather than the medium of cosmic translation to another plane. He saw nothing but disaster in what he called "total politics, in which men turn to the realm of power in search of satisfactions that once belonged to the realm of love and beauty." This was "the confusion of ultimate and immediate ends" that had so ensnared the new radicals, and he had no inclination to even hint at a grand architectonic counter-vision. In fact, in a 1964 letter to Hofstadter, Lasch confessed his inability to "associate myself with 'radical' causes, led by 'radicals' whose thinking has stopped dead at the political ideology of a generation ago — *two* generations ago. I find it hard to be anything but skeptical about politics these days," he admitted. He was harsh in criticism, modest in hope, but also strangely insistent — and ambiguous — on vision. It was a stance and mien that would shape all of his writing to come.[55]

As it turned out, the ambiguous nature of both his argument and his politics probably worked to his advantage: he came across as a genuine seeker, which in turn made it easy for the reader to press him into any number of molds. His greatest intellectual debt for a theory of modern society was certainly to Weber (as he himself put it in a letter to the communist historian Herbert Aptheker), yet he criticized Jane Addams for not seeing that capitalism "values individuals only for their labor power," for "asking, in effect, that young people be adjusted to a social order which by her own admission was cynically indifferent to their welfare." The honesty of his quest was palpable. But however much his entire argument was premised on his sense that some ideal American society was yet possible, he held out little actual hope for it, and even less affection for the entire trajectory of modern America. If, as he wrote, the premodern world of tightly-knit communities had held "little opportunity for the naked embrace of the spirit which the modern world has since learned to understand as the essence of love and friendship, the essence of life itself," the reader was left with the sense that to Lasch the world so singularly characterized by this "naked embrace" was entirely too chilly.[56]

55. CL, NR, 227, 228; CL to Richard Hofstadter, TL, 3 October 1964, 9:26.
56. CL, NR, 156, 157, 110. "I feel myself rather closer to Weber than to Marx," he told Aptheker while writing the book. Indeed, one of the more striking aspects of *The New Radicalism*'s critical framework is its only faint political-economic di-

Given the relentlessly gray cast of the book, it's not surprising that in the otherwise enthusiastic review Lasch later said "launched the thing," Alfred Kazin in the *New York Review of Books* described his stance as "pretty hopeless." John Roche, less sympathetically, proclaimed it "a message of nihilism," while Leuchtenburg, in a private letter, referred to *The New Radicalism* as "one of the most deeply pessimistic" books he had ever read. In Lasch's world, even the most wise, knowing modern seers were abjectly powerless to combat the "relentless American environment," much less construct a decent society upon it.[57]

Of course, in failing to present a concrete, positive counter-vision Lasch was certainly not alone. As the popularity of nuclear doomsday films and books in the mid-sixties suggests, strong pessimism about American prospects resonated, the fruit of decades of world war and cold war, and behind them the looming crisis of confidence in America's manifest destiny. If Lasch wrote with what Christopher Shannon terms "the ironic self-consciousness fostered by intellectual elites of the consensus era," he also wrote with a subtle yet palpable sense of desperation, quietly achieving a personal vulnerability that never surfaced to such an extent in the writings of historians such as Hofstadter, C. Vann Woodward, and others who conceived of history as social criticism. His readers discovered that they were being led along by a young author who was bold enough to take on established ideologies and ideologues, which perhaps predisposed them to give consideration to his admonitions. When Lasch charged that "The liberalism of the fifties and sixties, with its unconcealed elitism and its adulation of wealth, power, and 'style,'" was evidence of "the rise of the intellectuals to the status of a privileged class, fully integrated into the social organism," Kazin responded in a chastened yet affirmative tone: "It was about time that someone made a categorical definition of the stake that so many intellectuals now have in the inequalities of our society, in the perpetuation of the cold war. . . ." Lasch's courage of conviction was magnetic.[58]

---

mension, a shortfall for which he would more than compensate in the next two decades. CL to Herbert Aptheker, TL, 16 February 1964, 1:14.

57. Kazin, "Radicals and Intellectuals," 3; John Roche, "Profiles in 'Tsoores,'" *New Leader* 48:16 (16 August 1965), 16; William Leuchtenburg to CL, TLS, 5 July 1965, 1:18; Taylor and Lasch, "Two 'Kindred Spirits,'" 41; Lasch's comment on Kazin's review is in Fox, "Interview," 10.

58. Christopher Shannon, *Conspicuous Criticism,* 176; CL, NR, 316; Kazin, "Radicals and Intellectuals," 3.

What some saw as courageous intelligence, though, others saw as conceited ineptitude. In what would become a pattern over the course of his career, those who found the general direction of his social criticism compelling tended to embrace the contours of his historical arguments, pardoning his unproven generalizations and routine rhetorical overkill, while those who disagreed dismissed his work due to its lack of empirical evidence and his pull-no-punches political intent. Arthur Mann, in the *Journal of American History,* called the book "almost flawless in its failure." Marcus Cunliffe, in *Encounter,* wrote that "Instead of being original, his approach turns out to be merely eccentric: so eccentric that it is hard to be sure what he is getting at or whom." In the *New Leader* Roche termed it "Dada historicism with a vengeance," "a gospel of rejection and despair." All of these reviewers made telling points, especially regarding his method. None of them expressed sympathy for Lasch's primary political concerns.[59]

Arthur Schlesinger Jr., fresh from service in Camelot as house intellectual, found Lasch's book particularly damnable. "You will be interested to know," he wrote in a letter to the political writer Richard Rovere, "that a smart aleck kid named Christopher Lasch (son of Bob Lasch of the *Post Dispatch*) exposes us both in a new book called *The New Radicalism in America.*" "I wish you would review it," he urged. Schlesinger took out his own cudgels in the *Sunday Times* of London. Admitting to being one of the "attendant minor villains" in the book, he conceded that Lasch's "psychological speculations are occasionally perceptive and often entertaining," and that Lasch was "probably a talented writer." But the book itself was "poor and pretentious." "With imperturbable skill," wrote Schlesinger, "he draws from the evidence whatever conclusion his thesis needs. An intellectual who rejects society has surrendered to one form of neurosis, one who takes part, another." He perceived the book to be, in the end, a brief against "liberalism which is critical of communism," and dismissed Lasch as himself a wistful radical: "For all the author's dogged insistence on his own contemporaneity, *The New Radicalism in America* is really a last dying flicker of the thirties."[60]

59. Arthur Mann, review of *The New Radicalism in America, Journal of American History* 53:4 (March 1967), 872; Marcus Cunliffe, "Goulasch," *Encounter* 27:3 (September 1966), 76; Roche, "Profiles in 'Tsoores,'" 14.

60. Arthur Schlesinger Jr. to Richard Rovere, TL, 10 April 1965, in the Arthur

Others, though, saw it as a flame to be fanned — and a flame that did indeed help reignite radical political visions dominant in the 1930s. Robert Westbrook's sense that the *New Radicalism* "made Lasch a figure of commanding importance for the generation of historians that followed his" is born out by the evidence. Many of the leading historians of the last third of the century regarded the book as pivotal in their own professional and personal trajectories. Richard Wightman Fox recalled that it was reading *The New Radicalism,* and the subsequent essays that Lasch published in the sixties, that prodded him "to become an historian, not the journalist I was thinking about being." Lasch's "prose in the whole book sounded like music and felt like revelation. I wanted to know what he knew, and write as he wrote." Jackson Lears, in a retrospective essay after Lasch's death, recalled that "*The New Radicalism* held up a demanding and exhilarating ideal of mental independence. Lasch was an inspiring model of critical engagement, proof that you did not have to lose your mind or your soul to pursue an intellectual career." Joan Wallach Scott, then a graduate student at Wisconsin, testified of its immediate effect — "the smiles which marveled at your insight haven't yet worn off," she wrote in a letter to Lasch. Laurence Veysey, who in the same year published his first book, *The Emergence of the American University,* deemed it, "frankly," the "most important book in American intellectual history of at least the past decade or so." "Over and over again," he wrote, the book had given him "a sense of exhilaration that was purely intellectual."[61]

But it was not just to the younger scholars that the book appealed. The letters Lasch received showed he had reached across generational lines. While offering many searching criticisms, Leuchtenburg joined in the chorus of praise and tried to get at its appeal. "*The New Radicalism* is really a brilliant book," he wrote to Lasch, "a book of such importance that people will be talking about it as long as they are talking about 20th Century history. It is an unconventional book,

---

Schlesinger Jr. Papers, Box P-38, Harvard University; Arthur Schlesinger, Jr., "Intellectuals under Fire," *Sunday Times,* 27 February 1966, 30. Thanks to Sven Dubie for procuring this letter for me.

61. Westbrook, "Christopher Lasch," 176; Fox, quoted in Westbrook, "Christopher Lasch," 177; Jackson Lears, "The Man Who Knew Too Much," *New Republic,* 2 October 1995, 45; Joan W. Scott to CL, TLS, 10 July 1965, 2:1; Laurence R. Veysey to CL, TLS, 13 May 1965, 2:2.

because it is based not on massing evidence but on *thinking* about history, an endeavor that has largely gone out of fashion." Stanley Elkins, the author of a recent study of slavery that had stirred the profession, complimented Lasch on a "shrewd, imaginative, and very perceptive book." Lasch's old graduate school teacher (and sometime nemesis) David Donald rang in with one of the most glowing estimates of all: it was, he wrote, "truly a brilliant performance, one which surely ought to win a Pulitzer prize next spring." Randolph Bourne's example, as he made his case against American intervention in World War I, had clearly been a good one for Lasch. Bourne, Lasch wrote, hoped that "a lonely protest which carried the ring of truth might in the long run count for more than the self-justification of men who were determined at all costs to hold on to their influence."[62]

Richard Hofstadter, of course, had shepherded the undertaking along, and knew as much about its evolution as any of Lasch's colleagues. Despite Lasch's not-so-veiled attack on Hofstadter's own *Anti-Intellectualism and American Life,* he was likewise pleased and impressed. Upon reading the manuscript in the fall of 1964 he called it "a remarkable book, and a delight to read," "a first-rate and truly original study of the intellectual, vocational, and spiritual problems of the turn-of-the-century generation" of intellectuals. The book, wrote Hofstadter, "strengthens my belief, based on your first book, that you write better than most of the top-ranking historians in the country today, whether of your generation or any other." While he found "the greater part of your general argument . . . valid, or persuasive at least," he perceived that "the most valuable thing" about it was the "steady flow of marginal insight, about the people you've chosen, the intellectual life as a vocation, and the development of our culture." Alluding to Isaiah Berlin's famous division of scholars between those who like the fox, know many things, and those who, taking after the hedgehog, know one big thing, he deemed Lasch "much more a fox than a hedgehog" (which he considered himself to be as well). "This is why," he proposed, "the book can be read with great pleasure and profit by someone who happens not to agree with your central point, and why I think you will still find people reading it when you are an old man."[63]

62. William Leuchtenburg to CL, TLS, 5 July 1965, 1:18; Stanley Elkins to CL, TLS, 27 May 1965, 1:17; David Donald to CL, TLS, 4 June 1965, 1:17; CL, NR, 208.
63. Richard Hofstadter to CL, TLS, 27 September 1964.

Lasch received Hofstadter's blessing with relief, for he was aware that though he was intellectually and professionally in Hofstadter's debt, the more politically radical force of his argument was at odds with Hofstadter's own politics, which by the mid-sixties were supportive though not celebratory of America's liberal pluralistic achievement. (In the words of Hofstadter's biographer David S. Brown, Hofstadter's "distinctive brand of pluralism encouraged a cosmopolitan consensus, with New York standing as the supreme achievement, a Hapsburg-like enclave sustaining intellectual and cultural openness.") Lasch had expressed his fear to Hofstadter that his "conclusions" would "probably strike you as quite unwarranted." Hofstadter was generous in his reply. "I can't conceive that I wouldn't 'like' it, regardless of how much disagreement I might have," he wrote, "simply because I like so much the way you go about things and the way you write."[64]

In the years between 1964 and Hofstadter's premature death in 1973, Lasch wrestled more intensely with Hofstadter's legacy and politics, yet the two remained on good terms. By December 1965, more than half a year after the book's publication, Lasch wrote Hofstadter that he had had the "satisfaction . . . of having been attacked from every possible point of view, left, right, and center." Hofstadter shared with Lasch his own weathered approach to the storm. "I must confess that over the years I have developed a rather crass viewpoint about these matters," he wrote. "I pay a great more attention to sales than to reviews or attacks. . . . I hope you will forgive this bourgeois reaction, but it is really mostly a comment on the fact that the level of our criticism isn't very high."[65]

Within the profession and within the publishing world Lasch had become a phenomenon. In the spring of 1966 the Organization of American Historians, together with the American Studies Association, featured a panel discussion on the *The New Radicalism.* After listening to the criticisms of the book, Lasch responded to the audience by filling out his definition of intellectuals. He considered them "people who think about contemporary society from the perspective of

64. Brown, *Richard Hofstadter,* 91; CL to Richard Hofstadter, TL, 6 July 1964, 1:14; Richard Hofstadter to CL, TLS, 10 July 1964, 1:14.

65. CL to Richard Hofstadter, TL, 8 December 1965, 1:17; Richard Hofstadter to CL, TLS, n.d., 1:17.

general ideas, people whose claim to be heard derives not from the material power they command but from whatever wisdom comes from a continuing preoccupation with values." They were "in short, wise men."[66]

For many of his auditors Lasch had, meteorically, become just that: a scholar and writer whose ethical barometer could be trusted. Scholarship of the free and edgy sort reflected in *The New Radicalism* may well have turned out to be his means of at least partial escape from what the philosopher Charles Taylor has termed "the inexhaustible inner domain" and the pathway to a more solid and satisfying connection to the world beyond the self. If so, Lasch's nagging sense that his desire to write fiction was a "fatal urge" may have been altogether perceptive and in the end liberating, alerting him to a profound need to pursue a form of writing and public engagement more suited to his psychological needs. The rock-solid nature of modern scholarship, with its unceasing attempt to take the measure of the world itself, forced the intensely introspective Lasch into constant disciplined contact with it — a connection that helped keep aflame, among other things, his deep political instincts.[67]

But amidst the quickly shifting world of the mid-1960s he offered no easily accessible, programmatic solutions. He warned the audience at that OAH session instead that "The world is full of instant ideologies and ready-made radicalisms. As scholars, as radicals if you like, we can have nothing to do with them. We can't become believers. Our job, as Lincoln Steffens once said, is to doubt."[68]

---

66. All information and quotations from box nine, folder 30, "New Radicalism — Cincinnati Session," CLP. The respondents were Samuel Haber, Ihab Hassan, and David Noble. The meeting was held April 28-30, 1966.

67. Charles Taylor, *Sources of the Self: The Making of Modern Identity* (Cambridge: Harvard University Press, 1989), 390.

68. CL, "New Radicalism — Cincinnati Session."

CHAPTER FIVE

A New Culture

The United States is a society in which capitalism itself, by solving the problem of capital accumulation, has created the material conditions for a humane and democratic socialism, but in which the consciousness of alternatives to capitalism, once so pervasive, has almost faded from memory. This contradiction will not disappear in the course of struggle against capitalism, unless the struggle is carried into the realm of ideology and becomes a demand not merely for equality and justice but for a new culture, absorbing but transcending the old.

Christopher Lasch, in
The Agony of the American Left, 1969[1]

"Your book is already becoming a classic," William Leuchtenburg raved to Christopher Lasch in January of 1966. "The current crop of graduate students discusses it avidly, and I got a good response when I assigned a big chunk of it in my large lecture course this spring." Indeed, letters of commendation and invitations to write and speak arrived at a steady clip throughout the year following *The New Radicalism*'s publication. By summer of 1966 sales of the clothbound edition had hit 6000, and a paperback issue was scheduled for 1967. "Book Find Club, Inc." featured *The New Radicalism* as a main selection, with a black-and-white picture of a youthful, seri-

1. CL, AAL, 212.

ous Lasch gracing its brochure, his foreboding face set against a wintry landscape.[2]

Along with the blurbed superlatives on the book club's brochure were lengthy excerpts from the effusive review of Amherst College critic Benjamin DeMott, who in *Book Week* seized on the leftward drift of Lasch's argument. "Much of it points the way, indirect but legible, toward an adequate radical politics," enthused DeMott, "in which 'social awareness' nourishes the sense of intellectual responsibility instead of canceling it." He then fingered Lasch for an office beyond the professorial: "It would be neither surprising, nor unhelpful to those whose political choices are still to be made, nor unlucky for the country as a whole, if, as a result of the response to this book, Christopher Lasch awoke one morning this summer to find himself accepted as a spokesman." DeMott had foresight. A year after its publication William Stanton, a historian at the University of Pittsburgh, wrote to Lasch, "Your manifesto — for it is being accepted as just that and will be more and more — lays down some lines that will be battle lines among intellectuals in this country, and now having read it, I put myself down as a Lasch man."[3]

Lasch accepted the wide acclaim with a sense of uneasy satisfaction. After Schlesinger's derisive review in the *Sunday Times* of London he conceded in a letter to his parents that "the book has been praised beyond its merits," but added, "I can't pretend I'd rather have it otherwise." A few years later, while catching up with a childhood friend who had noticed his name in a newspaper article, he recounted that *The New Radicalism* "won me a limited reputation, not entirely undeserved, as a smart-alecky social critic, and a still more limited reputation, in other circles . . . as a thoughtful observer of the political-cultural scene." From the outset, though, Lasch himself was far from content with his achievement in *The New Radicalism*. Six months after its appearance he remarked to a colleague that "so far the book has been mostly overpraised or very stupidly condemned, and even many of the reviewers who like it convey the impression . . . that it's some sort of tract. I still cling to the idea that it has something to do with history."[4]

2. William Leuchtenburg to CL, TLS, 29 January 1966, 2:5; "Book Find Club" material in 9:27.

3. Folder 9:27: "Sources: Correspondence"; William Stanton to CL, TLS, 19 July 1966, 2:5.

4. CL to ZL & RL, TL, 15 March 1966, 2:4; CL to Patsy Rein, TL, 12 May 1969, 2:16; CL to Robert Burby, TL, 21 November 1965, 1:16.

Lasch knew that "history" is always mediated through the historian's own theoretical and ideological assumptions, and it was at this level that he felt most vulnerable. He readily admitted to Leuchtenburg that "the underlying theory which supports the argument" was its "weakest point." The connections he had tried to make between what he understood to be "the breakdown of cohesion" in American society, the "gradual decline of paternalism in Western history," and the demise of "small town" life were all "too vague." But his analytic confusion was not causing him to back away from his dark view of modern civilization. "Who can be very optimistic about a century that has seen such horrors as our own," he asked. "The modern age has a certain implacable grimness," he suspected, precisely because of the West's spectacular failure to remedy the social and cultural ills that plague advanced societies. To him, this was poignant irony: "Our incredible skill at understanding certain features of our plight is exceeded only by our inability to do anything about them." It was this paradox that kept him searching for truer understanding, political and otherwise. His starting point was the conviction that "the modern world," while not "an unmitigated disaster," was not the profoundly progressive civilization its boosters believed it to be. "We still imagine ourselves to be in the vanguard of progress," he wrote in exasperation to his father in the summer of 1962.[5]

By the mid-1960s Lasch's pursuit of a mastery of twentieth-century European and American social thought and cultural criticism had become intense, even fierce. Those authors he found most persuasive tended to come from the left. Since the late fifties he had been absorbing various strains of contemporary leftist criticism, ranging from the highly independent, self-described anarchist cultural critic Dwight MacDonald to the proto–New Left sociologist C. Wright Mills to the work of the Frankfurt School, the loosely aligned German intellectuals who were attempting in the aftermath of the Holocaust to renew and recast a Marxian vision adequate to the historical realities they had recently witnessed. Lasch regularly assigned the counterculture icon Paul Goodman in classes in the early sixties, and when he taught the "Social History of the 'Gilded Age'" in September of 1962 the class read not standard textbooks but social theory: *The Commu-*

5. CL to William Leuchtenburg, TL, 17 July 1965, 1:18; CL to RL & ZL, TL, 17 July 1962, 1:10.

nist Manifesto, Weber's *Class, Status, Party,* and Mills's *White Collar.* His course "Twentieth Century Social Theory in the United States" in the fall of 1964 featured Mills's *The Power Elite,* Michael Harrington's *The Other America,* and Herbert Marcuse's *One-Dimensional Man.* In 1962 he favorably reviewed Marcuse's *Eros and Civilization* in the *Daily Iowan.* All of this was evidence of both deep thinking and deep change. As he later put it, "The reading I was doing in the early sixties influenced me more directly than any political movement."[6]

If his maturing political stance was rooted in his rejection of what he termed in a 1966 book review "the liberal, enlightened, 'progressive' position," his confidence in what he described to Leuchtenburg as "the language of criticism, the Western tradition of rational discourse" was itself unshaken. Indeed, it was responsible, he told Leuchtenburg, for all that was "intellectually liberating" about the modern world. He mined it for a better accounting of the cultural and political realities he found so perplexing.

He gradually discovered an ideological stopping place by tunneling beneath the twentieth century to Marx himself. Lasch's enlarging sense in the early sixties of the overawing presence of "structure" in the shaping of human life certainly contributed to the growing plausibility of Marxian theory for him by the mid-sixties; of course, Marx's own *oeuvre* was itself one of the intellectual forces behind the more diffuse "structural turn" that had earlier begun to influence Lasch. He also found himself attracted to the fiercely rationalistic tenor of recent Marxian writing, with its strident confidence in the capacity of human reason to unpack reality itself. In the words of Peter Novick, the "epistemological posture" of the young Marxist historians was "overwhelmingly objectivist," brooking no doubt about the possibility of historians discovering "objective truth."[7]

6. "History 105: American Character," 44:50; "History 253, September 1960" list of "suggested readings," in "Miscellaneous Course Outlines," 45:18; "History 16:273, Social History of the 'Gilded Age,'" September 1962, in 43:28; "History 16-273, 20th Century Social Theory in the United States," September 1964, in 44:1; CL, "New Book Analyzed Freud's Theories of Man and Society," *Daily Iowan,* 26 October 1962, 3; Casey Blake and Christopher Phelps, "History as Social Criticism: Conversations with Christopher Lasch," *Journal of American History* 80:4 (March 1994), 1321.

7. CL, "A Profusion of Information," *Nation,* 4 April 1966, 398; CL to William Leuchtenburg, TL, 17 July 1965, 1:18; Peter Novick, *That Noble Dream: The "Objec-*

The unifying elements Lasch later detected in the books he was then reading — in his words, "the pathology of domination, the growing influence of organizations (economic as well as military) that operate without regard to any rational objectives except their own aggrandizement; the powerlessness of individuals in the face of these gigantic agglomerations and the arrogance of those ostensibly in charge of them" — were staples of mid-twentieth-century social thought in various quarters, Marxist and otherwise, a perhaps inevitable response to the harshly catastrophic turn western history had taken. But the tensions within this discourse were considerable, though still largely latent (in the United States, at least), as the Enlightenment intellectual project moved briskly toward the fissure that would become widely known in the last quarter of the century as "postmodernism," when hallmark philosophic assumptions of all kinds would implode. For now, though, a broad confidence in the possibility of a unifying, knowledge-yielding rationality existed uneasily with an emerging Nietzschean sensibility that called into question such conceptions of rationality. For those orienting themselves toward this latter stance, "criticism" became above all the necessary effort to expose, as Alasdair MacIntyre puts it, "those social and psychological formations in which the will to power is distorted into and concealed by the will to the truth." Its understanding of the world required a bottomless skepticism toward any claims to knowledge — but especially of those avowing "enlightenment" through rationality.[8]

The tension between these jostling epistemologies was certainly alive in Lasch's mind, though in a very submerged way. The appeal of each was obvious, and for the moment he, in the company of a whole generation of American academics, had the luxury of allowing the tension to remain latent — and thus, paradoxically, highly productive. At this pivotal moment in his own political development Lasch, like other intellectuals of the left, had found resources that enabled him to wed an uncompromising critical rationality to a radically suspicious, deconstructive sensibility, which was slowly giving birth to a

---

tivity Question" and the American Historical Profession (New York: Cambridge University Press, 1988), 422.

8. CL, TOH, 26; Alasdair MacIntyre, *Three Rival Versions of Moral Inquiry: Encyclopedia, Genealogy, and Tradition* (Notre Dame: University of Notre Dame Press, 1990), 39.

new vision of history. The marriage was bound to fracture, but while it lasted its union bore considerable fruit. Lasch read and read. Theory illumined experience. The appeal of the radical left deepened.

On a more personal level, Lasch found Marxism alluring in ways that reflect both his temperament and his upbringing. Prone to dark discouragement yet nurtured on political hope, Lasch recognized a familiar shape in Marxist eschatology. Marxists knew the present to be dark, yet they also understood it to be preparing the way, in subterranean fashion, for a triumphal, resplendent future.

This eschatology was of course not original with Marx. When in 1954 Naomi Dagen described Lasch's "strange mixture of pessimism and idealism" she unwittingly underscored two central pillars not just of his personality, or of Marxism, but of most modern western political visions, two poles that for centuries have shaped western thought. At the one pole ancient Greek and Hebrew visions of the world understood it to be fundamentally corrupted, and this perspective has yielded a variety of "realist" ideologies that stress the limits of politics. At the other pole the Hebrew and Christian belief in a millennial destiny for humankind has contributed to a collective longing for and pursuit of justice, peace, and prosperity. Centuries of living between these poles has created a powerful undertow that continues to shape western politics; westerners, ever torn between the now and not yet, have tended to approach politics with a restless hope, sensing the evil of this present age even as they catch the occasional foretaste of the good to come. In Karl Löwith's formulation, westerners have tended to imagine the realization of "human essence as a common sociopolitical existence," and thus live uneasily with the "tension of a transcendent faith over against the existing world."[9]

The most successful ideologies have managed to account for each of these poles, and Marxism at various times in the twentieth century seemed particularly convincing to many. Its brilliantly negative view of the present pulsed with transcendent hope, creating visions of a more exalted way of life that to many westerners rang true. Irving Howe, in his memoir *A Margin of Hope,* underlines Marxism's "profoundly dramatic view of human experience" as central to its allure for his youthful circle of companions in the 1930s. "Its stress upon in-

9. Naomi Dagen to CL, ALS, 22 February 1954, 0:30; Karl Löwith, *Meaning in History* (Chicago: University of Chicago Press, 1949), 50, 51.

evitable conflicts, apocalyptic climaxes, inevitable doom, and glorious futures gripped our imagination," he recalls. For Lasch — considerably less prone to visions of glory than Howe and his generation had been — Marxism comported well with his tendency to find hope not in the present but rather just beyond it, either in a locked-away past or an unrealized future. While his ironic disposition led often to a certain urbane levity, the ever-present, enervating weight he bore was not easily relieved. He had trouble tasting hope in his current existence. But Marxism kept alive for him, at least for a time, the promise of a way out.[10]

In the middle third of the twentieth century the intellectuals attached to the Institute for Social Research of the University of Frankfurt (or "the Frankfurt School," now centered in New York City), refashioned the Marxist worldview in a way that held particular promise for Lasch precisely because its analysis and prescription began at the intersection of personality and culture. Seeking a means to explain both the failure of socialism in interwar Germany and the horrors that followed, they turned to Freud for insight into the connections between personality, character, and history. Russell Jacoby, in a book building on the work of the Frankfurt School (and which began as a dissertation that Lasch supervised), stresses how "The subterranean explorations of Freud cast doubt on the autonomous subject" so fundamental to liberal American assumptions. They "revealed an individual shot through with sedimented layers of history," layers that provided startling archaeological evidence of the true nature of the society in which the individual was formed — in the western case, a society with significant delusions about human freedom and autonomy. The dialectical relationship between individual and society was thus inescapable for these Marxists, and any attempts to radically alter the condition of the one depended on the other. As Marcuse had put it in *Eros and Civilization,* "Freud's individual psychology is in its very essence social psychology." The political implications were obvious: acute and penetrating historical diagnosis might lead to constructive political vision, which might in turn transform the human condition itself. The faith of an earlier generation of Marxists in a mechanistic historical process was replaced by a highly analytic

10. Irving Howe, *A Margin of Hope: An Intellectual Autobiography* (San Diego: Harcourt Brace Jovanovich, 1982), 53.

search for ways to alter both the economic and psychic conditions of society, and thus make possible the long-anticipated revolution. Maintaining a vision of profound historical fluidity, they kept alive political possibility, seeing truth itself as having a "temporal core," in Horkheimer and Adorno's words, in contrast to the older notion of truth as "something invariable to the movement of history." And this movement was above all what they were seeking to understand and shape. "What is at stake," they wrote, "is not conservation of the past but the fulfillment of past hopes."[11]

As Lasch later recalled, he greeted these thinkers with enthusiasm, believing they "were providing Marxism for the first time with a serious theory of culture," one that more fully rendered the human person — utterly central to twentieth-century thinkers — in the midst of the overweening social and political realities of modern history. Horkheimer and Adorno, crucially, placed the Enlightenment in the center of the modern devastation, and their critique of it, so resonant with Lasch, anticipated the mood and measure of many of the postmodern ideas that were to divide the academy and dominate academic discourse at the end of the century. The major effect of enlightened freedom, they contended, had been to give human beings an unprecedented sense of mastery, so that "the wholly enlightened earth" was now "radiant with triumphant calamity." The abstracting nature of scientific thought had transmuted to all of reality its own abstract properties, and so had made everything — and everyone — eminently susceptible to the destructive powers of the liberated. Strangely but predictably, the result of all this power was, once more, historical and political stasis, as the enlightened now proved unable to see beyond the dreary (and deadly) mathematical calculus when encountering the world — what Lasch, glossing the argument of *Dialectic* in his 1991 book *The True and Only Heaven,* would call a "dangerous fantasy" still very much alive.[12]

---

11. Russell Jacoby, *Social Amnesia* (Boston: Beacon Press, 1976), 46; Herbert Marcuse, *Eros and Civilization: A Philosophical Inquiry into Freud* (New York: Vintage Books Edition, 1962), 15; Max Horkheimer and Theodor W. Adorno, *Dialectic of Enlightenment: Philosophical Fragments,* ed. Gunzelin Schmid Noerr, trans. Edmund Jephcott, Cultural Memory in the Present Series, ed. Mieke Bal, Hent de Vries (Stanford: Stanford University Press, 2002), xi, xvii.

12. Lasch, TOH, 29; Horkheimer and Adorno, *Dialectic of Enlightenment,* 1, 4; Lasch, TOH, 446.

But Lasch's Marxist turn was not simply a pivot toward the Frankfurt School. The intricate, abstruse, and liberationist tenor of its vision was counterbalanced by the huge influence of another center of thought and politics in the midcentury revival of the Left, what Lasch called "the tradition of English Marxism." It had recently been invigorated by, among others, the historian E. P. Thompson and the literary critic and all-purpose theorist Raymond Williams, whose books and lives reflected a form of earthy historical connectedness that Lasch prized just as deeply as the more abstract formulations of the Frankfurt School. Indeed, *The True and Only Heaven* was written in the mold and under the inspiration of Williams's classic of 1958, *Culture and Society, 1780-1950.* In it Williams had argued (more as a self-consciously English leftist than as an out-and-out Marxist) not simply for the merits but rather for the necessity of fusing the variegated radical, liberal, and conservative critiques of industrial civilization in the attempt to develop "a new general theory of culture" and thus an adequate political and intellectual response to the times. Williams masterfully brought together unsuspecting pairs — Cobbett and Burke, Coleridge and Mill — and sought the place of wisdom in a sharply discerning synthesis of their views. His aim was both to discover and forge a tradition, a way of life that guarded and advanced the great humanist achievements and sensibilities that had flowered in the modern West but which were also under siege by industrial capitalism. He approvingly quoted the British historian R. H. Tawney's 1931 summation of what he referred to simply as "the tradition":

> What matters to a society is less what it owns than what it is and how it uses its possessions. It is civilized in so far as its conduct is guided by a just appreciation of spiritual ends, in so far as it uses its material resources to promote the dignity and refinement of the individual human beings who compose it.

Clearly the "free market," with its underpinnings in liberal political theory, was not able to advance western nations in this direction. What was needed was a gathering together of all of those streams of thought and practice that honored and elevated the organic ideal, the bedrock conviction, as he emphatically put it, that "life is whole and continuous — it is the whole complex that matters." Discussing John Ruskin, Williams noted that

One kind of conservative thinker, and one kind of socialist thinker, seemed thus to use the same terms, not only for criticizing a *laissez-faire* society, but also for expressing the idea of a superior society. This situation has persisted, in that "organic" is now a central term both in this kind of conservative thinking and in Marxist thinking. The common enemy . . . is Liberalism.[13]

When Lasch recalled in 1991 his early attraction to English Marxism he specially underscored the centrality of "tradition" in Thompson and Williams's political vision. These thinkers had shown him

> how Marxism could absorb the insights of cultural conservatives and provide a sympathetic account, not just of the economic hardships imposed by capitalism, but of the way in which capitalism thwarted the need for joy in work, stable connections, family life, a sense of place, and a sense of historical continuity.

In the sixties, though, this sort of self-conscious appreciation of cultural conservatism tended to be only latent in Lasch's writing, not a primary plank of his program. Despite his own conservative instincts, he certainly felt no desire to side ideologically with what in 1966 he derided as "common-sense conservatism," with its belief in an intransigent, natural set of human limitations that could never be overcome, including the assumption that there will always exist "the ingrained and unchangeable lust for power, which assures that some people will always prey on others." In this he followed the lead of thinkers like Williams, who (rejecting the more Augustinian beliefs of some members of "the tradition," such as T. S. Eliot) had closed his book with the insistent claim that "The human crisis is always a crisis of understanding: what we genuinely understand we can do." Lasch was finding that in their historical materialism neo-Marxists offered explanations of history and the human condition that could secure aspects of the conservative vision he prized without giving up hope for more complete social transformations. (In the thinking of Marx, Williams had concluded, "The materials for restoring a whole and adequate consciousness of our common life were given into our hands.")

13. Raymond Williams, *Culture and Society, 1780-1950* (Garden City, N.Y.: Anchor Books, 1960), vi, 239, 278, 151.

Once a social ill was understood to be "historically determined — the sum of innumerable individual and collective choices, conscious or otherwise," there was hope, in other words, that future historical actions, guided by more historical insight, might yield radical change. Lasch lauded *The Psychology of Power,* by English radical R. V. Sampson, for exploring potential sources of inequality in the history of the sexes, and he tried to use Sampson's insights to advance his own efforts to understand the history of American women in the nineteenth century. Proper historical diagnosis would provide the understanding required for a society to move toward the requisite political and social change.[14]

From these and other theorists Lasch absorbed a Marxism that was supple and pliant, a departure from late-nineteenth- and early-twentieth-century Marxist thinking. He placed this newer understanding of Marx, or "neo-Marxism," in opposition to what in a 1966 essay he called "Vulgar Marxism." "Marx did not say," he lectured his readers, that "economic levels determine human consciousness. He said: social existence determines human consciousness. Between the first and second of these statements there is the difference between vulgarity and insight." After a few more years of steady reading he could articulate a cryptic definition of neo-Marxism to Knopf editor Andre Schiffrin. Neo-Marxism was the "rediscovery of the early Marx, renewed emphasis on voluntarism, attack on economic determinism, attempt to absorb Freud, Sorel, Nietzsche, et. al, Hegelianized Marxism." This "re-discovery" — and his own first-time discovery — began to nurture a kind of hope not evident in his earlier writing. And it began, finally, to manifest itself in something like a program.[15]

As he moved in this direction Lasch's historical thinking became sharper, but the literary spirit that had animated *The New Radicalism* ebbed. William O'Neill had provided a particularly arresting testimonial to Lasch's artistic skill. He had been visiting former Greenwich Village radical Max Eastman while Eastman was reading *The New Radicalism,* and O'Neill told Lasch that "After reading your analysis of Lincoln Steffens and Ella Winter, Eastman said that you wrote as if you'd

14. CL, TOH, 29; CL, "What Shall a Moral Man Do?" *Nation,* 28 November 1966, 584; Williams, *Culture and Society,* 357, 299.

15. CL, "What about the Intellectuals?" *New York Times Book Review,* 16 October 1966, 58; CL to Andre Schiffrin, TL, 24 November 1971, 3:5.

known them." Significantly, this vision of his subjects — or, rather, this interest in making particular human beings his subject — largely disappeared from Lasch's work after 1965, not to reappear until the mid-1980s. It was a course, in fact, that his earlier turn toward the social sciences had presaged; as he continued his ambitious quest for historical understanding via the social sciences and Marxist theory, humans went from being subservient to structure in Lasch's thinking to being eclipsed by it. "How to try to learn several new countries, at this point, quite apart from having to learn sociology, psychology, and anthropology is something for which nothing in my training has prepared me," he lamented to social historian Lawrence Stone as he prepared in 1966 to again embark on his study of women and the family, calling the pursuit "presumptuous" but necessary. The past for him had gone from being fodder for literary pursuit to being a social-scientific laboratory where he could search for a way out of the reigning political and moral chaos. His quest for a "theory of society," in the end, left little room for a study of the human face; indeed, his subjects increasingly became faceless.[16]

With review requests tumbling in by the week Lasch had unprecedented opportunity to try out his emerging Marxian framework on a host of books related to his ever-widening areas of research interest and political concern. Many of his most ambitious essays appeared in what had rapidly become the most sophisticatedly edgy journal of them all, the *New York Review of Books.* Launched in 1963 in the midst of a newspaper strike in New York City, it was, at the time Lasch began to write for it, "the most prestigious outlet in America for serious social criticism," as James Miller puts it, intent on "linking the New Left to a large audience of academic readers." Lasch was particularly gratified by the interest the *New York Review* took in his work, but his reach extended well beyond it. He wrote about political theory in the *Nation,* about cold war history in the *New York Times Magazine,* about the new realism in the *Progressive.* Book reviewing became a sort of epistemological exercise for him; he seemed to understand his own thinking best through the sort of forced encounter book-reviewing requires. His slashing style, honed in the pages of the *St. Louis Post-Dispatch* from the mid-fifties to the

16. William O'Neill to CL, TLS, 11 August 1965, 2:1; CL to Lawrence Stone, TL, 1 March 1966, 2:5 (this letter was never sent).

mid-sixties, could make any author's efforts seem utterly worthless or highly significant.[17]

Those he liked he showered with respect. He lauded Elsa V. Goveia for not depicting slavery in the Caribbean as "a faithful reflection" of the "economic interests" of the slave-owners, as progressive historians and "vulgar Marxists" had done; she understood, rather, that slavery was "a distinctively colonial phenomenon," one that was "embedded in and dependent upon the speculative capitalism of the mercantile age." Sampson's *The Psychology of Power* was "a compelling statement of the pacifist position," "a powerful assault on the moral sensibilities of the reader." A reading of a collection of socialist Irving Howe's essays from the 1950s convinced him that it was "too bad" that "some of us — members of my generation in particular — did not get around to reading Irving Howe a little sooner."[18]

But usually the works under review fell short, and often he exposed flaws and failures with a biting style, touched by youthful conceit, that was sure to alienate many and enrage some. Playing tit-for-tat with John Roche, who had written one of the most negative reviews of *The New Radicalism,* he derided the "vulgarity and sentimentality" in Roche's defense of the Kennedy years; his "piece reads like a parody of contemporary liberalism," scorned Lasch. Several of historian Frank A. Warren's subjects in his history of the cold war possessed "a political awareness considerably more complex than anything Warren's account even hints at," while Earl Latham's book on the same topic "brims over with unexamined assumption, innuendo substituting for argument, and mindless anti-Communist rhetoric." In Robert Bruce Flanders's scholarly account of the nineteenth-century Mormon settlement in Illinois Lasch expected to find attempts to connect the early days of that religion to its "historical context," but Flanders fell pathetically short: "In the history of Anglo-American society, the Mormons are so clearly a pathological symptom that a historian could not address himself to the Mormons, it would seem, without asking

17. James Miller, *Democracy Is in the Streets: From Port Huron to the Siege of Chicago* (New York: Simon and Schuster, 1987), 275.

18. CL, review of *Slave Society in the British Leeward Islands at the End of the Eighteenth Century,* by Elsa V. Goveia, *William and Mary Quarterly* 24:1 (January 1967), 143, 144; CL, "What Shall a Moral Man Do?" *Nation,* 28 November 1966, 586, 581; CL, "What about the Intellectuals?" *New York Times Book Review,* 16 October 1966, 58.

himself what kind of society could have produced them." The glistening edge knifed onward: "The same uncertainty of judgment and the same ineptitude in handling political material can be seen in two new books on Victoria Woodhull. . . ."[19]

Many of Lasch's readers, of course, found his critical performances to be unusually stimulating, even exciting, as indeed they often were. But his demonizing rhetoric limited the breadth of his appeal. He relentlessly emptied the unworthy book or opponent of any substantial virtue, countering always with a suggestive alternative that was more rich, more intelligent, more weighty. His own high standards and his grand mission to elevate the critical standards of the intelligentsia often led to a harshness that may have militated against his own hopes for intellectual and political influence.

But Lasch's mind was on fire in the 1960s, and burning of all sorts was perhaps the inevitable result. He was feverishly trying to out-think everyone. Whatever conceit he had was certainly not founded on any abiding and deep sense of confidence; what confidence he possessed flickered in darkened and lonely inner passageways, from whence came the striking "sulks" John Updike later recalled. If his overstated critical style reflected his sustained sense (and fear) of isolation, his criticism itself was the flip side of his earnest struggle for knowledge, for a foundation capable of anchoring the moral vision driving his political quest. Simply put, Lasch made his entry into the politically enlivened world of the 1960s with much at stake. And as he immersed himself in Marxist thought and politics he wanted desperately to prove the new object of his hope sure.

Moving into avowedly leftist regions, while exhilarating, meant in Lasch's case being an outsider. Challenged by a reader of *The New Radicalism* in 1965 for his failure to include any discussion of intellectuals involved in organizations such as the Student Nonviolent Coordinating Committee or the Students for a Democratic Society, Lasch conceded that "One reason I didn't deal with the civil rights movement or SDS is that I hadn't been exposed to any of these movements when I wrote *The New Radicalism*." In an interview years later, the

---

19. CL, "Democratic Vistas," *New York Review of Books,* 30 September 1965, 4; CL, "UnAmerican Activities," *New York Review of Books,* 6 October 1966, 18; CL, "Burned Over Utopia," *New York Review of Books,* 26 January 1967, 16; CL, "Emancipated Women," *New York Review of Books,* 13 July 1967, 28-29.

memory of his discomfort seemed fresh. "I had no left-wing background or credentials, and I was acutely aware of this," he recalled. "I felt I had come out of a quite different tradition. It was somewhat disconcerting to find myself consorting with people who spoke Marxism as an original language and were steeped in the lore of the Left."[20]

Among the locals was Eugene D. Genovese. A young historian about the same age as Lasch, Genovese stepped forward at a ripe moment to became both mentor and comrade to Lasch, helping Lasch solidify his theoretical base and enlarge his circle of friends. Genovese was a committed, controversial socialist who had grown up in Brooklyn and joined the Communist Party as a teenager (though he was kicked out in short time). After attending City College as an undergraduate he earned a Ph.D. in history at Columbia (graduating in 1959, though Lasch and he did not know one another there); his dissertation had just been published as *The Political Economy of Slavery.* He enthusiastically welcomed Lasch into his orbit, commending him on his accomplishment in *The New Radicalism* — he went so far as to tell Lasch that it deserved to win the Pulitzer — and began guiding him through the expanding world of 1960s American socialism.[21]

Genovese had little use for most existing American socialisms, as Lasch soon discovered. When Lasch asked him about the present crop of self-consciously left-wing historians, Genovese dismissed them as "a sorry collection of radical moralists, economic determinists, and true believers." He himself, he explained, was a student of the twentieth-century Italian theorist Antonio Gramsci, whose influential interpretation of Marx had softened the deterministic edges of much early-twentieth-century Marxist thought and had stressed the strategic importance of intellectuals in fostering a broad socialist consciousness. Genovese recognized in Lasch a potential ally in his mission to assemble a more sophisticated and savvy cohort of Marxist intellectuals who might engender social and political change through their writing and activism. "The intellectuals will avoid Marxism as long as it commits them to a simple view of the world and to a mecha-

20. CL to Arthur I. Waskow, TL, 12 October 1965, 2:2; Blake and Phelps, "History as Social Criticism," 1323.

21. Biographical information on Genovese is in Novick, *That Noble Dream; The Political Economy of Slavery: Studies in the Economy and Society of the Slave South* was published by Pantheon in 1965. Genovese's quip about the Pulitzer is in Eugene D. Genovese to CL, TLS, 22 January 1966, 2:3.

nistic philosophy," wrote Genovese to Lasch in one of their early exchanges. He followed Gramsci in contending that "no serious radical politics is possible without the defection of a significant section of the intelligentsia to socialism."[22]

Genovese was only too willing to enlist Lasch in his cause; he blew into Lasch's confusing but energized post–*New Radicalism* world like a storm. The more dynamic Marxism Genovese professed, with its stress on the role of intellectuals, ended up filling some of the gaps and eliminating some of the conceptual problems Lasch continued to find troubling in *The New Radicalism.* By January 1966 Genovese was urging Lasch to write "a serious article on Marxist historiography in America." Lasch desisted. "I'd love to write something on Marxist historiography, but I don't know enough to do it. I hope to learn," he added. They made plans to meet at the 1966 meeting of the Organization of American Historians in Cincinnati, where Lasch and *The New Radicalism* would be among the attractions. But throughout the 1960s Lasch continued to feel that he lagged behind Genovese and others in their circle in his grasp of and participation in the Marxist tradition. In the fall of 1968, a few days after he received a letter from a reader requesting "a reading list for a socialist America," Lasch urged Genovese to begin work on a neo-Marxist reader. "I am too ignorant myself, too new to any serious systematic radical thinking, to put together such a list," he had told his correspondent, and he repeated the same to Genovese.[23]

Not that this lack of confidence caused him to refrain from vociferous participation in the debates swirling around him. He was already a player in this conversation that seemed of world-historical moment, and gradually he made a home in this new land, trying hard to lose his accent. In the *New York Times Book Review* in September 1967 he sounded a sure note when he lauded the Marxist theorist George Lichteim for his "indispensable contribution to the revival of historical materialism." Lichteim, though, had failed to address the question of whether "modern society" could be "understood in class terms," which was "precisely the question that anyone defending the

22. Eugene D. Genovese to CL, TLS, 22 January 1966, 2:3.

23. Eugene D. Genovese to CL, TLS, 22 January 1966, 2:3; CL to Eugene D. Genovese, TL, 12 February 1966, 2:3; CL to Peter Israel, TL, 2 October 1968, 2:11; CL to Eugene D. Genovese, TL, 9 October 1968, 2:10.

relevance of Marx has to try to resolve." That same month in the *New York Review* he scored social critic David Bazelon for misunderstanding the nature of social classes and revolutionary change in his *Power in America: The Politics of the New Class.* Bazelon saw the intellectuals and managers as a potentially revolutionary "new class," but to Lasch they were no class at all, since there was little reason to believe they were "active agents of long-run historical change." Lasch saw Bazelon's "new class," rather, as bound to economic and governmental bureaucracies, which were taking history in unsavory, unrevolutionary directions.[24]

By 1968 Lasch's whole understanding of America — its meaning, its direction — had taken a strong, distinctly Marxian turn. Political economy, largely absent in his historical vision prior to 1966, had moved to center stage. In his review of Bazelon's book he etched his re-visioned portrait of the American past with stark, angular lines. The war in Vietnam had shown America to be just one of the "Western empires" that were now shown to be "helpless" in "the face of revolutionary resistance." Contrary to Bazelon's view, the "class struggle" had "not subsided" but had "been renewed with terrible intensity on an international scale." The "major defeats" suffered by the "Western empires" proved that "The era of Western colonialism, at least in its liberal-democratic form," was ending. "America's impending defeat in the international class war" could very well trigger a horrific reaction, perhaps a new era of fascism, unless the "underlying decency of liberal societies" was ignited and they were pushed to consider radical restructuring as a means of salvation. *The New Radicalism's* cool, ambivalent critic of modern America had become an earnest, outraged opponent of imperial America, while still advocating boldly what his former Iowa student David Marr referred to in a 1968 letter as "a politics of reason" — a politics, as Marr later put it, "conditioned by rational political argument." His long developing "theory of society," seen in mid-passage in *The New Radicalism,* was now largely in place.[25]

24. CL, "A Definite Set of Principles," *New York Times Book Review,* 24 September 1967, 44; CL, "Same Old New Class," 28 September 1967, 12.

25. CL, "Same Old New Class," 14; David Marr to CL, TLS, 12 July 1968, 2:12; David Marr to author, 10 July 2008.

*   *   *

For all of his commitment to "detachment," Lasch was no distanced observer of the melee that convulsed American campuses from the emergence of the Free Speech Movement at Berkeley in 1964 through the waning days of the Vietnam War in the early seventies. If *The New Radicalism* exploded on the scene in the spring of 1965 it was in part due to the volatile atmosphere into which it, and Lasch along with it, fell. President Lyndon Johnson had in March initiated Operation Rolling Thunder, routing the first 3500 ground troops to Vietnam; by the end of that year 180,000 more would land in southeast Asia. Rhetoric like "escalation" took euphemism to new heights. That same month faculty and students at the University of Michigan conducted the first "teach-in," a dramatic attempt to foster a different kind of understanding and response to American politics at home and abroad. In April the first major protest of the war attracted 20,000 in Washington, D.C., the largest peace rally in American history and perhaps the most important trigger of the mushrooming student movement. Its foremost national political organization would quickly become the Students for a Democratic Society (known universally as "SDS"). Its roots were in the old left, but it had recently been reinvented and reinvigorated through the leadership of Tom Hayden and the adopting of the Port Huron Statement in 1962, which called for "participatory democracy." Advancing what Lasch would later appreciatively call a "populist strategy of political action," it initially sought, in Lasch's words, to "build a broad coalition of groups effectively dispossessed by the growth of irresponsible bureaucratic organizations like the corporation, the multiversity, and the Pentagon." Its membership would top out around 100,000 by the decade's end, with its influence extending to tens of thousands more. By 1966 the liberal consensus that had appeared secure with LBJ's resounding victory in 1964 was rapidly disintegrating. Cold war critics like Lasch now seemed prescient and worthy of attention to an increasing number of people. The timing of *The New Radicalism* could hardly have been better.[26]

Lasch had been agitating for broader resistance to the cold war

---

26. CL, "The Conservative 'Backlash' and the Cultural Civil War," in *Neo-Conservatism: Social and Religious Phenomenon*, ed. Gregory Baum (New York: Seabury Press, 1981), 8.

consensus for several years, denouncing, to take one example, Michigan State University in the *Iowa Defender* (a student newspaper) for its dismissal of professor Samuel Shapiro, who had been charged with insufficient scholarly production. Shapiro, a historian, had dared to criticize Kennedy's actions in Cuba, but the real crime, wrote Lasch, was that Shapiro had "taken the position that history has something to do with contemporary events, and vice versa"; it was Shapiro's "refusal to see history as conveniently ending at some point before any of us were born" that had led to his demise. The university's explanation — that he had failed to publish in scholarly journals ("journals that is, which nobody really reads," quipped Lasch) — was an obvious screen.[27]

Most striking, perhaps, was Lasch's continued confidence that intellectuals — operating as intellectuals and not political power-brokers — truly could affect events. On the night the U.S. Congress passed the Gulf of Tonkin resolution in 1964, effectively giving Lyndon Johnson the powers of a wartime president, Lasch took to the typewriter, where he wrote a terse letter to Johnson himself. "Our continuing presence in Vietnam is productive of nothing but trouble," he warned. "The real task of American statesmanship is as gracefully as possible to liquidate our commitments in that area."[28]

As Johnson proceeded directly in the opposite direction, the mood of at least part of the nation began to shift quickly — a repositioning Lasch's father was helping to steer. Robert Lasch was in the midst of the assault, tempered yet critical, on Johnson's war efforts that would lead to his winning the Pulitzer Prize for editorial writing in 1966. In the editorial the Pulitzer committee signaled out as particularly decisive in their decision "The Containment of Ideas," published in the *Post-Dispatch* on January 17, 1965, Robert had denounced Johnson's militaristic turn. "After World War Two the Soviet Union sought to expand its power wherever possible," he granted. But since coercion was no match for freedom, the United States must not respond in kind. "Aspirations for independence, self-respect, and self-government are too universal and too powerful to be subdued by any ideology," he wrote with Wilsonian echoes. The appro-

27. CL, "AAUP Reports Are Contradictory on Shapiro," *Iowa Defender,* 21 February 1963, 3.

28. CL to Lyndon Baines Johnson, TL, 7 August 1964, 1:15.

priate response for Americans would be to recognize that the battle against communism should be pitched not at the level of the "national power struggle" but rather at the level of ideas. "It is not the American function to combat revolution everywhere — to stand as the universal, all-embracing guardian of the status quo," he insisted; "the C.I.A. is not enfranchised to swagger around the world setting up governments and knocking them down." Rather, the United States must show the world that "we have enough faith in the ideas of freedom to entrust to them, rather than arms, the task of containing the ideas of communism."[29]

Kit, nominated for a Pulitzer as well but in the history category (it ended up going to Perry Miller for his posthumously published *The Life of the Mind in America, from the Revolution to the Civil War*), embraced the general drift of his father's protest, if not his liberal premises. "Your editorials on Vietnam continue to be a source of comfort," he wrote to his father in March of 1965. "Something of a reaction seems to setting in," both nationally and close to home. "The 'teach-in' at Michigan is being widely imitated elsewhere. We had a Vietnam weekend here a couple of weeks ago, in which we gave an officer of the State Department a hard time."[30]

The following fall he helped lead a committee of faculty and students that was attempting to organize "Colloquia on the Cold War" as part of a "university within a university," a form of extracurricular education faculty and students at other universities were pioneering. The committee produced a prospectus that called for "the reintroducing in academic life of the speculative concerns, philosophical and political, which have been crowded out by increasing emphasis on specialized 'services to community.'" Students and faculty would meet every two weeks to discuss writings from a reading list; all participants would "consider themselves students," involving themselves in discussions rather than listening to lectures. In seeking to examine the assumptions and history of the cold war, they would try to "overcome some of the deficiencies of conventional academic practice." It

29. RL, "The Containment of Ideas," *St. Louis Post-Dispatch,* 17 January 1965, in 2:4. In a letter to his parents written on August 12, 1964, Lasch remarked on "Johnson's nicely manufactured crisis in Vietnam" and mentioned that he had written "a polite letter to him on Vietnam," adding, "in future communications I may not be so polite." TL, 1:15.

30. CL to ZL & RL, TL, 30 March 1965, 1:18.

was very much of a piece with what was going on at the same time at Wisconsin. In the summer of 1965 Joan W. Scott and Donald M. Scott, graduate students at Wisconsin, sent Lasch a copy of their proposal on "Protest and Education," in which Donald Scott spoke forcefully of "an increasingly strident demand that moral vision replace techno-logical vision." This cohort wished to close the divide "between thought and action, between values and knowledge, between the indi-vidual and the common life."[31]

This was a vision Lasch could get behind — but not without sharply critical cautions, as he made clear in a lead article in the *Na-tion* in the fall of 1965. Lasch had agreed to cover a teach-in for the *Nation* at the University of Michigan on the Vietnam War. Too often, he wrote, the discussions at the teach-in "degenerated into quibbles among experts about the facts of the situation in Vietnam, thereby blunting the moral issue raised by American involvement." Instead of trying to use rationalistic methods to persuade the government to abandon its Vietnam policy, he urged activists to center their efforts on two other means of protesting the war. One was "mass civil dis-obedience," the other "effective opposition along traditional lines — a body of opinion, translatable into votes, which will be resistant to cold-war clichés and skeptical of anti-Communist crusades." In urg-ing the latter he was trying to call out a group of intellectuals to match wits with the compromised "anti-Communist Left," who in failing "to function as an opposition" since the 1940s had made "possible the emergence of the 'bipartisan' foreign policy from which we still suffer."[32]

Indeed, much of Lasch's locutionary thrust in the mid-1960s was aimed at smashing the "new realism" of these cold war intellectuals, which he now targeted as the theoretical foundation of the shaken lib-eral consensus. He wrote not to inform but to alter, as if words them-selves had the power both to crush and reconstruct at this crossroads moment. The true face of realism, Lasch charged, was masked by the celebratory haze of the liberal consensus and the style of politics it boasted. It was a politics of "ritual," designed to evade and enchant

31. "Student-Faculty Committee on Public Affairs, Prospectus: Colloquia on the Cold War," in 12:38; Joan W. Scott to CL, TLS, 10 July 1965, 2:1; Donald M. Scott, "Protest and Education: A Proposal," unpublished mss., in 2:1.

32. CL, "New Curriculum for Teach-Ins," *Nation,* 18 October 1965, 239, 241.

rather than address and resolve. When the consensus liberal "talks about the democratic process," Lasch warned, "what he really means is that when you talk about politics you must observe a particular ritual," which he went on to spoof:

> You must first of all admit that political issues are complicated. You must talk about "alternatives"; if you make a suggestion, it has to be "constructive." (Just being against something is not enough. What are you *for?*) You must remember to say that disagreements in a democracy involve means, not ends. (We all agree about ends.) You must weigh every course of action against the "national interest." Above all, never raise a moral issue. (Political questions are complex. Moral questions are simple or "simplistic.") People who talk about moral questions . . . are likely to become "wildly emotional."

"Any deviation from this routine," concluded Lasch, "is by definition undemocratic and 'anti-political.'"[33]

Lasch himself offered little instruction as to how "morality" might properly be apprehended and plied into politics; he was content, for the time being, to insist only that it should. He understood realism to be corrupted by its rooting in "moral empiricism," as he put it, and this "definition of reality as empirical objectivity" had made moral judgment problematic, to say the least. His own morality still emanated from the liberal tradition itself (and, more distantly, the republican tradition that historians were just then beginning to rediscover) — a debt that helps to illumine his ongoing pique. David Marr recalls Lasch's "lifelong bitter argument with American liberalism" as already being on full display in these years. It "clearly was a passion," Marr stresses. "He just would not let up." Liberals were, in the name of "realism," not true to their own professed standards and ideals. This was conduct unfitting for a member of their clan. Lasch, as something of a post-liberal, was reading them out.[34]

He unflinchingly undertook this responsibility in public. Amidst a welter of articles in various journals of opinion in 1966 and 1967 came what was perhaps Lasch's most widely regarded strike against

33. CL, "Politics as Ritual," *Progressive* 31:11 (November 1967), 45.
34. CL, "What Shall a Moral Man Do?" 582; interview with David Marr, 15 November 2006.

the new realism and the cold war consensus itself. It was a historical essay entitled "The Cultural Cold War," which appeared in the *Nation* in September 1967, and which, remembers his colleague Gerald Graff, "everyone was talking about." Fifteen pages in length and featuring some of the most bruising polemical punches of his career, it was a sort of coda to *The New Radicalism,* another chapter in the tragicomic saga of intellectuals who should have known better. As debates intensified about the federal government's involvement in and sustenance of vital "free" American institutions, including the university, Lasch, in this essay, told a story filled with villains and stooges — and no heroes.[35]

This time the setting was not Greenwich Village but Paris, where the Congress for Cultural Freedom had been based since its founding in 1950. The congress, funded generously by prominent foundations, conducted regular conferences and produced, among other journals, *Encounter,* edited originally by leading midcentury intellectuals Stephen Spender and Irving Kristol. Above all, though, it was brought into being to unmask through its own example the Soviet Union's faux state-sponsored artistic and intellectual freedom. Its overarching aim, as Richard Pells puts it, was to display "the militant unity of Western intellectuals" in the midst of the cold war, but it turned into yet one more site wherein "scholarly initiatives and ideological preferences converged as the liberal moment aspired to orthodoxy," in David S. Brown's sharp summary.[36]

Lasch's charge against the congress was stark. Set up to be the exemplar of intellectual freedom — including the virtue of detached criticism — the Congress for Cultural Freedom had in practice defined freedom not as unrestricted intellectual and political activity but rather as that intellectual activity that reflected the policies, activities, and ethos of the American state. Spender and Kristol were only two of the leaders of a large cadre of writers and thinkers, including Arthur Schlesinger, Reinhold Niebuhr, Sidney Hook, John Kenneth Galbraith, and many more, whom Lasch, with searing rhetoric,

35. Interview with Gerald Graff, 2 August 2001.
36. Richard Pells, *The Liberal Mind in a Conservative Age: American Intellectuals in the 1940s and 1950s* (New York: Harper & Row, 1985), 129; David S. Brown, *Richard Hofstadter: An Intellectual Biography* (Chicago: University of Chicago Press, 2006), 95.

claimed had "consistently approved the broad lines and even the details of American policy, until the war in Vietnam shattered the cold-war coalition and introduced a new phase of American politics."[37]

What evidence did Lasch offer? That some of these "cold-war intellectuals" had "revealed themselves to be servants of bureaucratic power" was literally true because, as he showed in a rhetorical flourish at the end of the article, the congress had from its origins been secretly propped up by the CIA; indeed, the CIA had gone so far as to supply an editor for *Encounter* in the early fifties. This was no revelation, though; the *New York Times* had broken the story more than a year before, in April 1966, causing some defensive embarrassment but little outrage among those affiliated with the congress. More salient was Lasch's deeper argument, rooted in his evolving hermeneutic of suspicion. What the history of the congress most convincingly revealed, he contended, was that American intellectuals as a whole were trapped in a compromising state of "self-censorship" that virtually guaranteed their compliance with the aims and ends of the government. Having achieved professional independence only due to the sponsorship of the corporate state, the intellectuals, "unusually sensitive to their interests as a group," had over time "defined those interests in such a way as to make them fully compatible with the interests of the state." They had thus achieved "semiofficial status," Lasch wrote, and were utterly committed to maintaining it — and thus utterly useless as intellectuals.[38]

But were they so overtly crass in their desire to keep this status intact? No. Rather, to Lasch, they were predictably but disturbingly naïve. Religiously adhering by the late nineteenth century to the scientific ideal of "pure" objective science and research (which in turn became the justification for governmental, educational, and corporate bureaucracies to support their activities), the intellectuals believed the "knowledge" they provided for the public to be free of political assumption or implication, not perceiving that the very questions they asked and the projects they undertook were forcefully shaped, or delimited, by the overweening political and economic ap-

37. CL, "The Cultural Cold War," *Nation,* 11 September 1967, 201.
38. CL, "Cultural Cold War," 206, 208; the quotations in the last two sentences of this paragraph are found in the version of the article published in AAL, 94.

paratus that sustained their work. The intellectuals, owing their "autonomy and affluence" to the state, were not inclined to protest, for both political and epistemic reasons, which of course made possible a subtle form of co-optation.[39]

In short, Lasch contended that American scholars and intellectuals were as far from the exercise of true freedom as their opposites in the Soviet Union. Seeing themselves as neutral and free, they unwittingly became the apologists of governments all too eager to sustain the illusion of the intellectuals' autonomous position. Most of those associated with the congress and *Encounter,* of course, had denied all along that the government had done any meddling whatsoever with organizational policy and operations. Lasch pointed to the record and argued the opposite. "Whatever the intellectuals may have thought of the relationship, the CIA regarded them exactly as the Communist party regarded its fronts in the thirties and forties — as instruments of its own purpose." The history of the congress, which had demonstrably not "defended cultural freedom in the United States with the same consistency and vigor with which they defended it in Russia," had evidenced not freedom but servility. "We have heard a great deal about the 'credibility gap' that is supposed to have been created by the Johnson administration," Lasch wrote, "but what about the credibility of our most eminent intellectuals?"[40]

Readers responded in high volume. The following month the *Nation* featured a special "representative sample" of responses, including a letter from the Trappist monk and bestselling author Thomas Merton; Lasch's article, Merton wrote, had made his "blood run cold." While lauding Lasch, he suggested that the liberals' "identification with what seems to be an established disorder" made the triumph of "lucid reason" seem dubitable. Of the ten letters printed in the *Nation,* nine were favorable.[41]

The lone dissenter pointed to the near complete absence of a pragmatic turn in Lasch's thought. "It is better that there should be some intellectual prostitution with a possibility of influencing the war machine," countered one Donald E. Drake of Illinois, "rather than intellectual purity for all and a government which would 'judge

39. CL, "Cultural Cold War," 206-7.
40. CL, "Cultural Cold War," 211, 206, 210.
41. "The Cultural Cold War: Comments," *Nation,* 9 October 1967, 340.

the validity of ideas by the requirements of national power and other entrenched interests.'" This response previewed the criticism the American philosopher Richard Rorty would level at this same piece thirty years later in his Massey Lectures in the History of American Civilization at Harvard University, where he faulted Lasch for needlessly dismissing the "old left" for its inability to achieve what Lasch perceived as ideological purity.[42]

But Lasch was no pragmatist. He was a prophetic idealist animated by a vision of a higher form that must be glimpsed and emulated if the corrosion was to be halted. Indeed, most striking about the "Cultural Cold War" essay was Lasch's fierce, persisting belief that knowledge gained through scientific critical encounter can and must lead to culture-transforming illumination — or, to put it differently, that the public square, and American democracy itself, were in fact finally amenable to reason. Lasch had little tolerance for compromises of this ideal made in the name of prudential politics. The course of twentieth-century history demanded a higher form of prudence. And so he, a native son taking in the desolation of his homeland, relentlessly assailed the liberals and prodded the radicals, leaving an emotionally charged record along the way.

They were in the main negative emotions. His tone usually varied between lament and rage, and more and more he seemed to understand history itself as one long moment of overarching devastation. His tendency to present this devastation without a human face only added to the harshness of his "rational," "objective" renderings. Working from a distant observation deck, he ended up evading an intimate study of the humans who actually comprised the story. Had he dared to move closer, to place himself eye-to-eye with his subjects, he might have seen more ambiguity and been more forgiving of error. But instead of particular humans he found only containers of "consciousness" and banal compromise.

There was one human who was quite present in this narrative of destruction, of course: Christopher Lasch. He was the one with the ability to see through the haze and spy the desolation and speak in a salvific voice. But this at times unseemly interpretive confidence was a reflection not so much of his sense of the power of his own criticism

42. "The Cultural Cold War: Comments," 341; Richard Rorty, *Achieving Our Country* (Cambridge: Harvard University Press, 1998), 64-66.

as of his faith in the ability of those like him — the intellectuals — to move history itself. Their access to knowledge, their ability to perceive its relevance for the nation, their skill in bringing that knowledge before the public with authority: these factors made intellectuals of paramount importance, utterly central to his hope for something like a beloved community of national dimensions to emerge. If his criticism was often overweening, it was sustained and motivated by his conviction that as a public intellectual he held a civic office, one he sought to honor with wise and timely judgment. In his own mind, he was upholding ideals that, if understood and embraced, would lead to cultural and political renewal.

As the sixties moved toward their denouement, Lasch's investment in the movement for radical political change deepened. When in 1969 he titled a collection of his essays *The Agony of the American Left* he gave testimony to his own psychological state. Comprised of slightly re-worked review essays reflecting on and evaluating American radical movements from the populists through the recent eruptions of the black power movement and the new left (including the "Cultural Cold War" essay), the book called on American radicals to intensively probe their history with an eye on the present. "All that we find in the past of American radicalism," he wrote in the preface,

> are ordinary men and women struggling with questions which the best of them realized were too difficult to resolve but which nevertheless seemed to demand a continuing effort to resolve them. Radicalism in the United States has no great triumphs to record; but the sooner we begin to understand why this should be so, the sooner we will be able to change it.

Highly analytic, the book was more than a *cri de coeur;* indeed, Lasch intended to incite reaction and help build a movement.[43]

But it was more than a movement that he was after: an entire *new culture,* as he put it in the concluding paragraph of the book, had become his aim and hope: he envisioned a "struggle . . . not merely for equality and justice but for a new culture, absorbing but transcending the old," yielding, finally, "a humane and democratic socialism." In view of the debased condition of American life, forging a new culture

43. CL, AAL, viii-ix.

was the only remaining hope. This was not, in other words, simply a platitude tacked on to the end of a book. It permeated his whole vision and underscored the way his native "Middle Western progressivism," as he years later described it, continued to powerfully direct his hope, shaping his appropriation of Marx. He recognized this hope as far beyond the pale of what most Americans now knew, yet he glimpsed instances of it in the present. He wrote sympathetically of the advance of the civil rights movement in the South in the 1950s and early 1960s, made possible, he argued, by the emergence of an "American Negro culture" that had been established due to strong families and churches with "strict standards of sexual morality." These institutions fostered the "accumulation of talents, skills and leadership" that had made the civil rights movement successful in the south. A healthy culture, he underscored, had taken root among African Americans, one whose commitment to community basics — solid families and religious institutions — enabled it to move in salutary political directions.[44]

These were only pockets of hope, he knew. America as a whole was far from achieving this sort of community, and its existing power structures — sanctioned by the soulless liberal-capitalist ideology — ensured that the malignant status quo would be maintained. The triumph of corporate capitalism, he contended, "has created a society characterized by a high degree of uniformity, which nevertheless lacks the cohesiveness and sense of shared experience that distinguish a truly integrated community from an atomistic society. . . . the United States of the mid-twentieth century might better be described as an empire than as a community." He was reaching for something beyond, for this "new culture," while trying to quicken a reckoning in the present.[45]

"Liberals and/or Radicals, and Where They Went Wrong?" This, said Otis L. Graham Jr. in the title of his review of *The Agony of the American Left,* is the book Lasch had been writing and rewriting "for several years," featuring the "vintage Lasch blend of lucidity and obscurity, oversimplification, and brilliance — with a good amount of the latter." Graham, largely sympathetic, judged this latest version of the story Lasch's best effort yet. Minor blights aside, Lasch, with an

44. CL, AAL, 212, 122
45. CL, AAL, 27.

"admirable combination of moral passion and unflagging rationality," had delivered another book that was highly "perceptive about the
American Left." P. P. Ardery Jr., writing in the conservative flagship the
National Review, agreed. When Lasch moved away from "partisan writing for fellow partisans," he was, Ardery remarked, "a near-pure analyst, the best the New Left has produced to date." Ardery urged his fellow conservatives to take heed: "The New Left can become a serious
revolutionary movement if it follows the course that Lasch is beginning to chart. Conservatives should read his book to learn where the
Left may be headed, thus to head it off."[46]

The Agony of the American Left was a work in progress, a message
from and to the front. He released it well aware of its flaws, less than
satisfied, again, with his performance, as he explained in a letter to
one of the book's reviewers: "In general, the book suffers from the fact
that my ideas were changing very rapidly in the period during which
these essays were written, and the result is not always coherent." But
the point for Lasch was never to keep hushed until his thinking was
settled and all tensions were resolved. Rather, it was to keep moving
toward that ideal while conversing with friends — and arguing with
enemies — along the way. Michael Harrington, a leading socialist activist and intellectual whom Lasch criticized in the book for his efforts
to work within the Democratic party rather than build a third party,
recognized Lasch's intent. "Lasch is committed to rational dialogue
on the Left," he wrote, "and is as critical of his friends as of his enemies . . . he raises most of the crucial problems and that is a gain even
when one does not accept his answers; this is his real contribution to
these times of rhetorical overkill on the Left."[47]

Teach-ins, blasts at the liberal consensus, articles addressed to
the left: Lasch was moving at a feverish pace, coming into his own as
an intellectual and gaining a solidifying sense of his own deepest political hopes and beliefs. As the sixties turned combustive, his commitment level was high — he even considered leaving the academy to
devote more time to political activity. "The question is what practical

46. Otis L. Graham Jr., "Failure on the Left," *Progressive* 33:8 (August 1969),
29, 30; P. P. Ardery Jr., review of *The Agony of the American Left,* by Christopher
Lasch, in "Books in Brief," *National Review,* 20 May 1969, 501.
    47. CL to Martin Duberman, TL, 20 May 1969, 2:14; Michael Harrington,
"Who Are the True Redeemers?" *New Republic,* 12 April 1969, 25.

arrangements to make so that I can devote myself more effectively to political work," he wrote to Gar Alperovitz in the spring of 1969; his "Yours in haste" at the close of the letter captures well his late-sixties clip. In one letter to his parents in December 1967 he recounted a teach-in he had conducted with Staughton Lynd, his recent efforts at "gathering signatures" to place Eugene McCarthy's name on the presidential ballot, and his participation in a "town committee on race relations." His style and message always drew fire. Indeed, Lasch provoked reactions that most other writers could only dream of, some of it sophisticated and fair, some of it not. After reading *Agony* Warren Susman, a historian at Rutgers, effusively called it "a *thrilling* experience, intellectually *and* emotionally." One Manhattan attorney was just as impassioned: "Why don't you shut your emotional and bigoted mouth? God save us from the day when you and the Carmichael's, Rap Brown's, Cleaver's, and other assorted 'intellectuals' run this country." His advice? "Shut up, nut."[48]

But Lasch could no more "shut up" than he could vote for the establishment. He, pen in hand, was at war. Or was at least looking for one.

---

48. CL to Gar Alperovitz, TL, 7 April 1969, 2:14; CL to ZL & RL, TL, 10 December 1967, 2:7; Warren I. Susman to CL, ALS, n.d., 2:17; Daniel G. Buckley to CL, TLS, 30 December 1968, 2:9.

CHAPTER SIX

To Build a Movement

I am not at all convinced that the student "revolutionaries" are going to be around for very long; many of the most militant will have no difficulty adjusting themselves to the "capitalist system" in future years; many of them, indeed, would probably have no difficulty adjusting themselves to fascism. . . . To build a socialist movement on the student movement is to build on sand.

Christopher Lasch to Gar Alperovitz, 15 February 1969[1]

Following the publication of *The New Radicalism* Lasch became a coveted figure in departments of history around the country. This was of course gratifying, especially since after returning from England he and Nell were hoping to explore possibilities at other universities. In 1965 they was given every opportunity to do so, receiving serious inquiries from, among other schools, the University of Massachusetts, the University of Washington, SUNY-Buffalo, Northwestern University, and the University of Wisconsin. Wisconsin's offer was particularly alluring; it included a $2000 increase over his current salary of $14,000 and membership in a storied left-leaning department that included the likes of the iconoclastic diplomatic historian William Appleman Williams and the dean of contemporary intellectual historians, Merle Curti. Iowa matched the offer, though, and suggested switching Lasch's teaching responsibilities from recent American history to so-

1. CL to Gar Alperovitz, TL, 15 February 1969, 2:14.

cial history. Lasch subsequently rejected the Wisconsin offer. For the moment, he and Nell were content with their decision: "Having decided not to go [to Wisconsin], for eminently sensible reasons, conveyable to anyone but the most convinced believers in academic prestige, we don't seem to be worried about whether or not we're staying here."[2]

Their contentment with Iowa was not strong enough to withstand the next offer, though, which came from Northwestern University. By December Lasch was interviewing there, and before the end of the year had accepted their offer of a full professorship and a $20,000 salary. He had gone through, he told his parents, several weeks of "painful consideration during which I changed my mind repeatedly." But he was eager to live in Chicago again; they had decided on a house on Lake Michigan, five blocks from downtown and nine from the university. "With the absurd salary they're paying me solvency appears to be a real possibility," he wrote. "So we are delighted from every point of view, even though we find ourselves more attached to Iowa City . . . than either of us suspected."[3]

To Genovese he explained his decision as rooted in displeasure with Iowa's history department, which he ridiculed as "terribly 'professional,'" one that "goes in for 'solid' work, which means that there isn't much to talk about." He hoped to convince Northwestern to consider hiring Genovese as well, anticipating, no doubt, the same collegial vacuum there that he had found at Iowa. Genovese was never hired, and, predictably, by the first semester Lasch was writing in frustration to his parents, "I find it difficult to get very excited about departmental affairs."[4]

He found himself dismayed too by the political apathy of Northwestern students, especially compared to what he had known at Iowa and Wisconsin. "Northwestern is not a bad place, but the students seem to be somewhat quiescent," he drily wrote to his Iowa colleague Frank Burdick in November 1966. "They don't think of themselves as victims of bureaucracy and the multiversity. . . . It's hard to convince the students that they're being victimized. That makes things a bit

2. CL to ZL & RL, TL, 2 November 1965; 1:18.

3. CL to Simeon E. Leland, TL, 22 December 1965, 1:18; CL to ZL & RL, TL, 1 January 1966, 2:4.

4. CL to Eugene D. Genovese, TL, 12 February 1966, 2:3; CL to ZL & RL, TL, 15 October 1966, 2:4.

dull, extracurricularly." But it was not just the students that fell short; it was the institution as a whole. "Northwestern has no political life at all," he complained to his parents — while also admitting that "from a purely selfish point of view" this mixture of dedication and somnolence was "not necessarily a bad thing, since it gives me time to do some other things."[5]

With spring came not only signs of life among the students, but also the beginning of Lasch's cleavage from the student movement and his subsequent journey down a path that would, by its end, turn lonely and narrow. The particular form the burgeoning student movement took, with its revolutionary enthusiasms and anti-intellectual tendencies, only convinced Lasch that its very ascendance might destroy whatever radical possibilities existed, which on his view could only be realized through long-term persistence in institution-building and intellectual influence.

The students' apocalyptic style bothered him from the outset. In 1967 he groused to his parents that students observe that "something is wrong with America," and then "immediately jump to the conclusion that nothing short of full-scale revolution will correct it." They should focus on reforming the university "before reforming the rest of the world," he wrote. In the fall of 1966 he had in the *New York Times Book Review* urged readers to be patient with the student movement, arguing that, contra Irving Howe, "attacks on the new radicalism may be premature," but by spring his own general reaction against it was beginning to harden. Still, he continued to make common cause with students, hoping that more sensible and intelligent leadership might emerge. After conducting a teach-in with Staughton Lynd in the autumn of 1967 he told his parents that "some semblance of rationality may be returning to those on the Left who have been talking of resistance, revolution, etc."[6]

But his hope ebbed quickly, and his teach-in partner and erstwhile friend Staughton Lynd ended up becoming one of the targets of his intensifying attacks against the new left. Early on in their friendship

5. CL to Frank Burdick, TL, 8 November 1966, 2:3; CL to ZL & RL, TL, 5 November 1966, 2:4.
6. CL to ZL & RL, TL, 18 April 1967, 2:7; CL, "What About the Intellectuals?" *New York Times Books Review,* 16 October 1966, 58; CL to ZL & RL, TL, 10 December 1967, 2:7.

Lasch had bristled at Lynd's pious progressivism. "If progressives really did locate the source of the sickness of American society," he wrote in a 1962 letter following the appearance of Lynd's neo-progressive defense of Jane Addams in *Commentary,* "why is American society still so sick, even after the adoption of most of the measures championed by the progressives?" When in 1964 Lynd in turn criticized Lasch's chapter on Jane Addams in an early draft of *The New Radicalism,* Lasch responded indignantly in what became a longstanding accusation: "To you the radical tradition is sacred and must not be analyzed, except to murmur approvingly." In his correspondence later that year with self-identified radical N. Gordon Levin, then a Harvard Ph.D. candidate, he underscored the need for more honesty and sophistication: "You can glorify radicalism all you want, Lynd-like and Pollack-like, but all that glorification . . . strikes me as leaving us as historians absolutely nowhere." Of course for Lasch, that which left historians nowhere left those seeking political change in the same place, since one's vision of the past and one's politics were inseparably entwined.[7]

As the student movement gained strength so did Lynd's connection to it. From teaching with fellow radical historian Howard Zinn at historically black Spelman College in Atlanta to writing curricula for Freedom Schools in Mississippi to making an unauthorized trip to North Vietnam with SDS leader Tom Hayden and historian Herbert Aptheker, Lynd in no uncertain terms pledged his allegiance to the student wing of the broader leftist movement. His rhetoric often had a lyrical lift, as when he recalled the first peace rally in Washington, D.C. "It was unbearably moving," he wrote just after the event,

> to watch the sea of banners and signs move out from the Sylvan Theater toward the Capitol as Joan Baez, Judy Collins and others sang "We Shall Overcome." . . . it seemed that the great mass of people would simply flow on through and over the marble buildings, that our forward movement was irresistibly strong, that even had some been shot or arrested nothing could have stopped that crowd from taking possession of its government.[8]

7. CL to Staughton Lynd, TL, 8 September 1962, 1:10; CL to Staughton Lynd, TL, 16 June 1964, 1:15; CL to N. Gordon Levin, TL, 26 January 1963, 1:12.

8. Lynd quoted in James Miller, *Democracy Is in the Streets: From Port Huron to the Siege of Chicago* (New York: Simon and Schuster, 1987), 233, 234.

If Lasch had had little tolerance for Lynd's romantic radicalism in the quieter early sixties, as the stakes grew higher his tolerance diminished yet more. Privately he excoriated Lynd in a letter to William Taylor; Lynd, he wrote in March 1967, epitomized for him "the special blend of simple-minded sentimentality and real ruthlessness . . . that is emerging as the chief characteristic of the 'new' Left." But when he reviewed Lynd and Hayden's account of their recent trip to North Vietnam in the *New York Times Book Review* that spring, he was still guarded in his criticism. He granted that their visit had an "honorable objective," to show the northern Vietnamese that the official activities of the Vietnamese government did not reflect the will of all Americans, and to help themselves come to see their official enemies as no less than human. But their actual description of their experience (which included teaching the Vietnamese, in the authors' words, to "make a human circle and sing 'We Shall Overcome'") led Lasch to tag it a "sentimental journey," disabled by an unctuous posture that made serious observation and true encounter impossible. "Justly revolted by the propagandistic picture of Communists as monsters, Lynd and Hayden have turned them into equally lifeless symbols of international brotherhood." Their book was merely an "ideological document," not different in function or pitch from the sort of materials being made available to the public by the State Department.[9]

Although Lasch and Lynd managed to maintain a relationship of sorts throughout the sixties (Lasch worked publicly on Lynd's behalf to try to keep secure his teaching positions when various academic institutions tried to oust him), their differences were emblematic of larger divisions that were roiling the left as it lurched and surged after 1964. Eventually these differences hardened into factions of the most fractious sort, a recurring pattern on the American left. The students, of course, were in the late sixties the largest of these factions, and the most important prudential question radical intellectuals faced centered on how to regard them. Having just come out of an era in which radicals of any sort had been scarce, no sane leftist could gainsay the sheer value of numbers. Should they embrace the students as the agents of a new revolutionary movement? This was the position for

9. CL to William R. Taylor, TL, 11 March 1967, 2:8; CL, "Journey to Hanoi," *New York Times Book Review,* 23 April 1967, 16, 18. The quotation from the book is on p. 16.

which Lynd opted, casting his lot with them and defending them as one of their elder spokespersons and defenders. On the other side stood a cohort of intellectuals that included Genovese and Lasch, for whom Lasch spoke when at the end of 1967 he wrote that "the new left, in its infatuation with revolution, resistance, and other catchwords, is destined to go from one absurdity to another." "I'm all for revolution," Lasch wrote to Mary Leve, an activist, in January 1968. "But I don't see any possibility of a revolution in this country right now, and unfortunately the crisis is right now, not fifty years from now." In view of this, "radicals have to redouble their efforts to *convince* people that the war is wrong, to show people there is connection between Vietnam and Detroit, to support McCarthy in the absence of a better candidate, . . . to try to begin very patiently to build a movement" centered on the conviction that "long-range social change will only come through a radical movement based not on alienation or wild gestures of rebellion but on wide popular support, a constituency. . . ."[10]

This reading of the moment did not leave much space for co-belligerence with those who embraced the student movement; as Peter Novick notes, the "political and strategic evaluations" of these two groups were "diametrically opposed." Lasch's evolving perspective on the students and the larger circumstance also underscored the tensions in his own politics. His conviction that profound, radical change was necessary was matched by his equally strong presumption, rooted in his anti-progressive instinct that *any* far-reaching radical change was bound to be difficult, that noble aspirations would be invariably endangered by any number of threats — including threats sourced in the structure of reality itself. Whether the former conviction could survive the latter was the intellectual tension that spurred some of his most perceptive observation and analysis. But it certainly did not predispose a certain kind of sixties radical to align with him.[11]

And yet for all his realist sensibilities, by the volatile spring of 1968 — a season of mounting chaos bookended by the assassinations of Martin Luther King Jr. and Robert Kennedy — Lasch and others perceived that hopes for substantive change of any sort must begin to take

10. CL to Robin Brooks, TL, 12 October 1967, 2:6; CL to Mary Leve, TL, 16 January 1968, 2:7.

11. Peter Novick, *That Noble Dream: The "Objectivity Question" and the American Historical Profession* (New York: Cambridge University Press, 1988), 432.

flesh, must rapidly mature into a solid program, or risk being lost for good. Lasch thus began his most intense activist period. Writing to Genovese in May 1968, during the cataclysmic student revolt at Columbia University that included a dean being taken hostage and the student occupation of several buildings, Lasch sounded an urgent note: "Judging from yesterday's events at Columbia (insofar as one can understand them filtered through the smog disseminated by the local media), the time for picking up the pieces may be approaching (like everything else) more rapidly than anyone might have supposed." Using the same "picking up the pieces" metaphor in a letter to Irving Howe a few days later, he confessed that the previous weeks had left him wondering "whether we are not living through a kind of 1848, a series of unplanned, uncoordinate [*sic*], more or less spontaneous eruptions throughout the West which will be followed by a general reaction so severe that even moderates will find themselves subject not only to the unofficial harassment of a McCarthy but to official repression."[12]

Salvaging and strategizing were the obvious needs. In March of 1968, the young Harvard historian and political economist Gar Alperovitz had invited Lasch to meet with a small group of intellectuals in Cambridge, including sociologist and former *New Republic* editor Christopher Jencks and the literary scholar and civil rights activist Paul Lauter. They were attempting to discern, he told Lasch, "how we may begin to transcend the despairing militancy and negativism of the left through the development of a positive radical perspective, strategy, and concrete program." Lasch, enticed by the prospect, addressed the group in April 1968, just after the assassination of King, but left disappointed with the level of critical engagement he found there. He would not participate further until Lauter, the ringleader, invited "a few more people who can *think*."[13]

Alperovitz remained a political companion of Lasch's for many years, their shared Midwestern roots and orientation toward a decentralist yet socialist political economy binding them together well past the 1960s. Alperovitz and Jencks were by 1968 in the midst of launching a small think tank called the Cambridge Institute — an at-

12. CL to Eugene Genovse, TL, 23 May 1968, 2:10; CL to Irving Howe, TL, 28 May 1968, 2:11.

13. Gar Alperovitz to CL, TLS, 11 March 1968, 2:9; CL to Gar Alperovitz, TL, 30 April 1968, 2:9.

tempt, as Alperovitz puts it, "to avoid the outrageous kind of enormous rhetoric that was bouncing around the left in those days" and propound a leftist vision that was "actually meaningful and practical in American communities." Alperovitz, who by this time already had considerable experience in politics (he had served as an aide on Capitol Hill) as well as academe, sought to connect both Lasch and Genovese to the effort. Lasch was, he recalls, "a hot left intellectual" whose appeal was considerable, given the institute's efforts to "put together a serious intellectual base for long-term political change." The left, by then, "took his writing and thought very seriously," Alperovitz remembers, a perspective that echoes that of Lasch's Northwestern colleague and friend Gerald Graff, who pithily sums up Lasch's presence on the left in those years: Lasch "modeled 'intellectual' for everybody," generating a "kind of intellectual magnetism that I think all his friends will attest to."[14]

Not surprisingly, then, at this same moment another group in the early stages of formation sought Lasch's allegiance. Led by the historian and future founder of the socialist newspaper *In These Times,* James Weinstein, it was the vanguard effort of a group of intellectuals working toward what they hoped might be the launching of a socialist party. The group included Genovese and William Appleman Williams; several current or former Wisconsin students, including Mari-Jo Buhle, Paul Buhle, Martin J. Sklar, Ronald Radosh, and James Gilbert; two other historians, Jesse Lemisch and David Horowitz; and such emerging intellectuals as Barbara Ehrenreich, John Ehrenreich, Naomi Weisstein, and Saul Landau. The document they were trying to pull together was ambitious: it intended to present an accessible critique of American society, a rationale for the development of a new party, and a statement of its mission. Since the participants were spread around the country (indeed, around the continent — Genovese was then teaching at Sir George Williams University in Montreal), cooperative efforts were cumbersome. Writing by committee entailed sending drafts to centrally located points (there was, for instance, a "Chicago group"), where committee members would work on the document, revise it, and send it back to Weinstein, who was in San Francisco.[15]

14. Interview with Gar Alperovitz, 18 December 2006; interview with Gerald Graff, 2 August 2001.
15. CL to Gar Alperovitz, TL, 23 May 1968, 2:9; "Pre-Party Papers, Draft III," unpublished ms. in 13:19.

Upon his first examination of the document in May 1968 Lasch decided to join the group, and over the next ten months heavily devoted himself to their immediate agenda, which centered on the call for a new party, planning a journal, and elaborating its ideas in public forums. Indeed, he ended up using much of his sabbatical during the 1968-69 academic year for this political work rather than for the continued work on the history of women for which the American Council of Learned Societies had awarded him a fellowship.[16]

The theory that underlay this document (which went by the working title "Pre-Party Papers") was self-consciously Gramscian, yet the writing was aimed, as one might expect from a group dominated by historians, at addressing the contemporary moment with concrete, particular diagnoses. Forty-seven pages in length (in its fifth draft), it distilled with clarity and conviction the neo-Marxist consensus shared by many leftist intellectuals by the late sixties. Contending that due to capitalism's ability to generate wealth what was once "a utopian vision" was now a "historical possibility," they heralded a society in which all citizens would have opportunity to not only "devote themselves to creative self-development and meaningful work" but also "to explore the degree to which human society can be organized around as yet unliberated capacities for love, joy, cooperation, and trust." But if capitalism had made such a world possible, what was blocking its emergence? The keyword they used to describe this process was *hegemony,* a concept developed by Gramsci to help explain the inability of those under the sway of capitalism to recognize both the irrationality of their political-economic circumstance and the possibility of realizing something more. Most Americans, the document explained, "find it necessary to spend their lives preparing and offering themselves for sale in a self-defeating search for economic security, status, and the sterile satisfactions of compulsive consumption." They were stuck in capitalism's shadow lands. "The system's oppressiveness . . . is experienced not as social oppression but as personal maladjustment, or again as institutional malfunctioning, or corruption." Blind eyes needed to see.[17]

16. CL to Gar Alperovitz, TL, 23 May 1968, 2:9. Wrote Lasch to Alperovitz in the spring of 1969: "It is no longer a question with me as to whether to sacrifice a certain portion of my scholarly work to other work. As a matter of fact I have been doing that for some time now." TL, 7 April 1969.

17. "Pre-Party Papers, Draft V," 1, 2, 3, 13:21.

Enter the intellectuals, those who could help restore sight by bringing analysis to the people. Weinstein's group of intellectuals, intending to foster "a mass consciousness of alternatives," would do this through the formation of a new political party, but one that would not attempt to win electoral contests so much as seek to forge "an autonomous and comprehensive worldview" that would be "embodied in action," leading to the possibility of "a new culture." Catalyzing intellectual and political agitation under the aegis of a network of emergent socialist institutions, the movement would seek to influence politics and ideas in as many ways as possible. Lasch outlined key features of their strategy in a lead essay in the *New York Review* in July 1968 (and later published in *Agony of the American Left*), as Draft III was making the rounds. "What are needed," he wrote,

> are institutions that would parallel existing structures of government (city councils, for instance) and, without any recognized authority or immediate hope of implementing their decisions, undertake the social planning of which the existing institutions are incapable. In other words the Left has to begin to function not as a protest movement or a third party but as an alternative political system, drawing on the abilities of people who realize that their talents are often wasted in their present jobs. It has to generate analysis and plans for action in which people of varying commitments to radicalism can take part, while at the same time it must insist that the best hope of creating a decent society in the United States is to evolve a socialism appropriate to the American conditions.

Through this sort of politically indirect agitation they hoped to "create a broad consciousness of alternatives not embraced by the present system, to show both by teaching and by its own example that life under socialism would be preferable to life under corporate capitalism, and thus *in the long run* to fashion a new political majority." Earnest if not exactly hopeful, Lasch and (at least some of) the others envisioned this long road as the only one available at the present time — if even *it* was truly available. He ended his article on an ominous note: "The coming months hold both promise and the possibility of an almost unqualified disaster."[18]

18. "Pre-Party Papers, Draft V," 22, 32; CL, "The New Politics: 1968 and After," *New York Review of Books,* 11 July 1968, 4, 5, 4, 6.

He was right: Disaster befell both the larger radical movement and his group. Several major conflicts had threatened to destabilize the latter from the outset; by May 1969, one year after Lasch had joined it, the group had broken up over them. The week after Richard Nixon's victory in 1968, Weinstein raised one of the points of contention, informing Lasch that his broadsides against the new left in another *New York Review* article had disturbed some in the group. In a lead essay commenting on American political prospects in the aftermath of the 1968 Democratic convention in Chicago, Lasch had thrown aside all delicacy in pronouncing judgment on the student movement. "If SDS provides a foretaste of the future — a terrifying thought — we seem to be headed toward an implacable tyranny of inexperience and ignorance," he wrote, pronouncing with bitter pessimism that "Given the obscurantist anti-intellectualism that is increasingly prevalent among student radicals, there is no immediate hope of uniting the Left."[19]

Weinstein urged Lasch to soften his rhetoric — not necessarily because he disagreed with it, but for strategic purposes. His view was that "we should avoid all public criticism of the nihilists . . . particularly before we offer a set of alternatives, I think it is wrong to attack them in the liberal press." Lasch complied, pledging to "forthwith cease my attacks on SDS . . . unless provoked beyond endurance." He desisted from public attacks on the students, but tension on this front remained.[20]

Concerns and perspectives raised by feminists within the group emerged as a point of division — not surprisingly, at least in retrospect. How would the newly developing feminist perspectives on social justice and gender equality be integrated into the party's vision? In November Lasch sent back an addendum to the statement's section on women containing his perspective on "how the discussion of the 'woman question' can be connected to the discussion of socialism" (as he put it to Weinstein), and it underscored the extent to

19. James Weinstein to CL, 13 November 1968, TLS, 13:21; CL, "Where Do We Go from Here?" *New York Review of Books,* 10 October 1968, 5.

20. James Weinstein to CL, 13 November 1968, TLS, 13:21; CL to James Weinstein, TL, 21 November 1968, 2:13. Interestingly, the SDS group at Columbia asked Lasch this same month to come speak at a teach-in on the contributions of the American professorate to Cold War policy-making. See Michael Klare to CL, TLS, 5 November 1968, 2:13.

which his view of society and morality was diverging from the liberationist direction the left was taking. He criticized the "ideology of feminism" he saw gaining ground on the left, faulting it for producing in effect "a new class of alienated workers" by urging women to join men in the centers of corporate capitalism. To counter this, he urged the group to consider "how some of the family's former functions — the education of children, the cultivation of the inner life — might be partially restored to the family, as part of a general decentralization of the productive machinery."[21]

Here he was propounding a conviction that had surfaced briefly in earlier writings and that would become more central to his thought and politics in the 1970s. In a 1966 exchange in the *New York Review of Books* he had suggested that that "conflict between home and career" in the modern era had had untoward effects on not just women but on men as well. Five years later, in an essay also published in the *New York Review,* he touted Frankfurt School philosopher Max Horkheimer's description of "bourgeois domesticity" as "the last defense of a rich and autonomous inner life against the encroachments of mass society," even while it was also (quoting Horkheimer) "'adulterated with the dregs of all past cultures.'" While far from calling for separate spheres, Lasch certainly was convinced that the imperative of advancing the equality of men and women must also fortify "domestic life," which, he felt, if liberated from capitalist hegemony, "still has the capacity to nourish the best human qualities instead of some of the worse." These ideas, with their nineteenth-century tinge, did not sit well with some of the group, Lasch's qualifications notwithstanding. As he developed them more fully over the next decade, the distance between him and much of the left would expand.[22]

How to regard the university itself was another point of contention, perhaps the most serious source of division. SDS by 1968 tended to regard the university as hopelessly corrupt due both to its unholy union with government and business and its hierarchical and bureaucratic structure, and thus worthy only of abandonment. Lasch found

---

21. CL to James Weinstein, TL, 18 November 1968, 13:21; Lasch's addendum is in "Pre-Party Papers, Draft V," p. 21C.

22. CL, "Letters," *New York Review of Books,* 31 March 1966, 30; CL, "Can the Left Rise Again?" *New York Review of Books,* 21 October 1971, 48; "Pre-Party Papers, Draft V," 21C.

this view intolerable. While he certainly agreed that the university was compromised by these ties, he also believed it to be the richest reposi-tory of "humane values," "the most likely environment" from which a truly democratic socialism might emerge. Lasch and Genovese, con-vinced of the strategic necessity of making the university the primary seedbed of an emerging socialist movement — indeed, of the new cul-ture itself — began in 1969 to co-author a book, never completed, pro-posing a radical program centered on the fundamental importance of the university. "Either the university represents what is decent in America (along with much of what is lousy) and ought to be defended or it is thoroughly corrupt and ought to be by-passed," Lasch had in-sisted to Genovese in May 1968 as the Weinstein group was debating the matter. "How can the same movement embrace people who want to save what is worth saving and people who want to tear everything down?" Having just seen Tom Hayden on television "babbling about 'bringing down the university'" in the aftermath of the student revolt at Columbia University the previous day, he reacted strongly: "I can't see large numbers of intellectuals attaching themselves to a party which doesn't pretty clearly dissociate itself from the current SDS-PL leadership." This stance generated further tension. Those in the group closer to the students could not abide this sort of harshness, much less the more positive estimation of the university itself.[23]

The political ideal of the "pre-party" group was a radically decen-tralized socialism, the importance of which for Lasch was by now non-negotiable. "Centralized public ownership is surely no solution," Lasch wrote to Alperovitz in July of 1968, insisting that "an important part of the case for socialism" centered on "certain purely technologi-cal problems that present social and economic organizations seem unable to cope with, and which victimize *everybody* more or less indis-criminately, quite apart from class exploitation: population, pollu-tion, air traffic, the possibility that the very bases of natural life may be endangered by pollution of the atmosphere, etc." Returning to his own suburban Chicago high school to give a commencement address just a few days after the assassination of Robert Kennedy in June 1968, he traced the upsurge in violence at all levels of American life to "the destruction of tradition and continuity, the forcible destruction of

23. CL, "The New Politics: 1968 and After," 5; CL, "Where Do We Go from Here?" 5; CL to Eugene Genovese, TLS, 23 May 1968, 2:10.

people's lives." "The culture is violent," he charged, "because it is a culture in which machines take precedence over people" — machines that served the less-than-benign interests of a small and powerful minority. "Certain affluent white people derive tangible benefits from guns, bombs, napalm, cars, superhighways, bulldozers, and supersonic transports which impoverish the rest of the culture and make life in America for people who don't happen to be affluent and white, increasingly insupportable." Americans, in sum, were now living in a world in which "the bulldozer" had become "one of the prime instruments of official violence." In a letter the next winter to a former Iowa student he cogently stated his case for decentralism, a more locally oriented and governed way of life: "[A]ny vision of socialism which does not confront the need for a drastic scaling down of institutions, for the need to combine planning with as much regional and local control as possible, does not have much to offer Americans in the twentieth century and has little chance of attracting a following."[24]

On this conviction there was little dissent within the group. What divided them was strategy: how to confront the existing entrenched political and economic structure and thus effect real political change. Lasch and Genovese ended up arguing for what was, as Lasch put it, "in effect . . . a left social democratic position," in which an electoral component would be incorporated into the larger program of the party only after the party's identity was firmly and broadly established. Those within the group who were closer to the student movement saw this set of tactics as the pathway to compromise, a part of the disreputable legacy of the "old left," which had also sought revolutionary change from within the structure of liberal democracy. "I think this prospect terrifies many people in our organization, who fear that it would identify themselves with people like [Michael] Harrington and [Irving] Howe (and worse with the social-democratic defenders of imperialism) and would also cut us off from the students in the 'movement,'" Lasch told Alperovitz. The others insisted on joining the students, whose method of direct confrontation would more forcefully give the lie to the "political democracy" being practiced in the United States. To Lasch, this reliance on what Lynd, in an ex-

24. Draft of a letter, CL to Gar Alperovitz, TL, 24 July 1968, 2:9; CL, Commencement address given at Barrington High School, 9 June 1968, unpublished ms. in 12:23; CL to Martin Eisenberg, TL, 22 February 1969, 2:14.

change with Lasch in the *New York Review*'s letters section, called "direct action," was folly. Lynd's notion that "a minority of committed activists can make a revolution in an advanced country" was not just romantic — it was deadly to any radical hopes, Lasch wrote in reply. Rather than throwing their hopes behind "the movement kids" (as he put it in a letter to his parents), Lasch advocated an attempt to "cultivate a new constituency of disillusioned McCarthy followers, unattached intellectuals, and various others who are as dissatisfied with the 'movement' as they are with the 'establishment.'" Whereas "the radical student movement may well only be an ephemeral thing," he continued, socialism was only possible in the long *durée*. As he put it to another correspondent and sometime co-conspirator, his hope was for a "socialist civilization" — no mean project.[25]

In March 1969 Lasch described the group's status to the *Nation*'s editor Carey McWilliams as "at a stand-still" thanks to the deadly combination of fundamental disagreement and grandiose ambition. The group soon disbanded, and Genovese and Lasch decided to strike out on their own. "It seems to me an urgent necessity that the few of us who seem to be thinking along the same lines try as hard as we can to get ourselves together in one place," Lasch wrote to Alperovitz in April. "Gene and I have already decided that it is important to try to get positions at the same university, but I do not know whether this will be possible." Moving closer to Cambridge and Alperovitz's circle was one option; in the fall he considered an offer from the University of Massachusetts at Amherst. Somehow, despite the breakup of the Weinstein group, his hopes were not quite quashed. "While I am unsure of what action to take," he confided to Alperovitz, "I do find my isolation out here increasingly dispiriting, and apart from these personal considerations there is the larger consideration of whether we can work very effectively scattered around the country."[26]

In December 1969 he accepted an offer to join Genovese at the University of Rochester, where Genovese had been appointed department chair. "The next few years are going to be rough, but if we can

25. CL to Gar Alperovitz, TL, 15 February 1969, 2:14; quotations from Lynd and Lasch are in the Letters section of the *New York Review of Books,* 12 September 1968, 42, 43; CL to Zora and Robert Lasch, TL, 5 February 1969, 2:15; CL to Ann Lane, TL, 7 April 1969, 2:15.

26. CL to Carey McWilliams, TL, 6 March 1969, 2:16; CL to Gar Alperovitz, TL, 7 April 1969, 2:14.

survive them we'll have achieved something very valuable," he had written to Genovese in the fall of 1968. One year later their numbers were fewer, but their dream of spearheading a politically engaged contingent of leftist scholar-intellectuals was still alive. "I now realize that it is too early to attempt to organize" a socialist party, he wrote to the historian Martin Duberman shortly after their group disbanded in May 1969. "There is a great deal of work, both theoretical and practical, that must precede it," work that required "socialist intellectuals" to work *"collectively"* on analysis of "the character of neocapitalist society." And, he added, he was more and more convinced, unlike Duberman, that the students' countercultural ways were a step backward. "Hedonism, self-expression, doing your own thing, dancing in the streets, drugs, and sex are a formula for political impotence and a new despotism," he wrote, "in which a highly educated elite through its mastery of the technological secrets of a modern society rule over an indolent population which has traded self-government for self-expression." The "peasants" would be "happy and ignorant," while hopes for democratic renewal slipped further away. It was this prospect that, despite mounting disappointments, pushed him on.[27]

*   *   *

Those "next few years" ended up being far rougher than even Lasch was capable of imagining — beginning with a falling-out between him and Genovese almost immediately upon his arrival in Rochester in the fall of 1970.

Lasch's and Genovese's alliance had grown sturdy during the four years they had known one another prior to Lasch's move to Rochester, and it was perhaps their mutual dream of a radicalism that would forge "a new cultural synthesis, based on the rationalist tradition," as they put it in a co-authored *New York Review* essay in 1969, that provided their deepest point of unity. Interestingly, they announced in that essay that the "rationalist tradition" was "a tradition now almost

27. CL to Eugene Genovese, TL, 8 November 1968, 2:10; CL to Martin Duberman, TL, 20 May 1969, 2:14. Duberman had expressed his hope in the counterculture in his review of AAL in the *New York Times Book Review,* 23 March 1969, 34.

in ruins" — a perception that suggests a shared conserving instinct, one that made each wary of unnecessary cultural and social destruction of the sort they saw the new left championing. This conserving instinct, in service of their rationalist tradition and its home in the modern university, put them at odds with both the spirit and the shifting epistemology of the younger radicals. What Lasch, Genovese, and Weinstein referred to as "nihilism," many on the new left — like Lasch's new radicals of a few decades earlier — understood to be freedom itself.[28]

Martin Duberman in his review in the *New York Times Book Review* of *Agony of the American Left* had hammered Lasch on just this issue: he criticized Lasch's "unqualified faith in rationalism" while regarding the new left's "cultural revolution" as quite possibly the beginning of "a decisive break with our society's hitherto dominant values of rationalism, Puritanism, materialism, and individualism." But to Lasch and Genovese such a "revolution" was at best a diversion from serious business and at worst testament of a turning away from rationality and intellect, which alone afforded a foundation upon which the necessary cultural and social construction might take place. When Robin Brooks, a history professor at San Jose State College who was sympathetic to the new left, challenged Lasch on his sharp opposition to the student radicals, Lasch denounced their revolutionary schemes as mindless and undemocratic, and confessed his continued belief that "society is, at bottom, rational." "I hope," he wrote, "that assumption won't prove to have been a mistake." The modern university, launched on the basis of this rationalist foundationalism, needed to be more true to its founding principles — not reject them.[29]

Literary scholar Roger Lundin, in his discussion of the deadly intellectual battles within American universities in the 1960s, saw that "The paternalistic liberal humanism that had ruled American schools for decades proved unequal to the challenge mounted by the subversive power of genealogical critique." Lasch later described the mission that he and Genovese undertook as an "ad hoc defense of liberal

28. CL and Eugene Genovese, "The Education and University We Need Now," *New York Review of Books,* 9 October 1969, 27.

29. Duberman, review of AAL, 34; CL to Robin Brooks, TL, 12 October 1967, 2:6.

culture" that sought nonetheless to dethrone "liberalism as a political ideology." But all that was happening at the time, within the university and without, only darkened their prospect. This was yet one more battle they had no chance of winning.[30]

A commitment to rationalism was not enough to stave off Genovese's own destructive tendencies, which took a devastating toll on their friendship as well as their political hopes. Genovese had arrived at Rochester with the express purpose of building a nationally prominent department with a decidedly left-wing cast. He was in the fall of 1969 trying to attract, among others, the African American historian Harold Cruse, Civil War historian William Freehling, nineteenth-century historian Winthrop Jordan, and even the sociologist Philip Rieff. None of these ended up coming, which provoked Lasch's doubts about whether he should go through with his own move to Rochester. "In your eagerness to get me to Rochester, you've consistently oversold the place," he wrote in November 1969.[31]

A more disturbing omen had taken place at the December convention of the American Historical Association, where Genovese had stridently opposed the attempt of the organization's "left caucus" to force the eminent historian of the American South C. Vann Woodward from the presidency and install Staughton Lynd instead. Genovese's opposition to Lynd by now had a long history, and stemmed from his deep distaste for the student movement, and his deeper distaste for Lynd's romantic radicalism. Genovese also opposed any formal politicization of the AHA, convinced that such a turn would end up weakening the scholarship it was supposed to foster. Lasch had urged that Genovese desist from opposing Lynd publicly, confident that Lynd's bid would fail anyway, and not wanting Genovese to turn into, as he put it to his parents, "the darling of the right" for his opposition to Lynd. But instead, he wrote them afterward, "Gene took matters into his own hands and delivered a long harangue" against the left caucus, "urging the convention to 'put them down hard and put them down once and for all '" Not only did this incendiary showdown at the AHA upset Lasch (even as it made it into newspapers such as the *Washington Post*), it also seemed, by 1969, dis-

---

30. Roger Lundin, *The Culture of Interpretation: Christian Faith and the Postmodern World* (Grand Rapids: Eerdmans, 1993), 21; CL, WN, 334.

31. CL to Eugene Genovese, TL, 21 November 1969, 2:15.

turbingly familiar. He wrote to Genovese just after the convention that he was "puzzled and worried. . . . Your break with our friends in New York seems to me unnecessarily bitter and total." He confessed to being uncertain about how this would play out at Rochester. "Over the past two years, our political position has steadily deteriorated," he wrote. "In the foreseeable future we can afford to entertain none but the most modest expectations." There was no room to alienate the rest of the left on such matters. He had, consequently, "developed real reservations about coming."[32]

Despite his doubts (and the warnings of Ann Lane, a historian, member of the Weinstein group, and also, it turns out, Genovese's first wife, who feared that such close quarters with Genovese would diminish "the subtlety, the use of language and essentially the human concerns" she saw in Lasch's work), he decided to accept the offer, explaining to his parents that the decision "seemed in the end to boil down to a question of staying here or moving into an admittedly uncertain situation which nevertheless has the possibility of developing into something really exciting." Besides, Northwestern's history department was "not a department at all," he wrote. (He had once called Northwestern "the kiddie corner, where the department is largely controlled by the bag-lunch and basketball set — a more obnoxious collection of young fogeys would be hard to find.")[33]

Lasch arrived at Rochester in the fall of 1970 only to find that the senior Europeanists in the department were already siding against Genovese. By October Lasch and Genovese were at odds over the latter's desire for control of a journal of Marxist scholarship they were trying to launch. Genovese insisted that his wife, the historian Elizabeth Fox-Genovese, be made the managing editor, to which Lasch strongly objected. The situation deteriorated quickly. In January Lasch sided with a group of three Europeanists and the labor historian Herbert Gutman, another of Genovese's erstwhile allies, in asking him to resign on the grounds that his control of the department had become authoritarian, a "mixture of democratic forms and autocratic content." Genovese refused, and the administration, when the

32. CL to RL & ZL, TL, 2 January 1970, 2:21; CL to Eugene Genovese, TL, 3 January 1970, 0:38.

33. Ann Lane to CL, TLS, n.d., 2:21; CL to ZL & RL, TL, 10 February 1970, 0:38; CL to RL & ZL, TL, 2 January 1970, 0:38.

five opponents made their allegations known, backed Genovese. Some attempts at reforms were made, to no avail. To a friend at CUNY Lasch described Genovese's chairmanship as "an unmitigated disaster." His own wound was severe: "The bust-up of a close friendship causes both of us a great deal of daily pain. It is all a very sorry and sad business."[34]

In July 1971 the efforts to launch a journal "completely collapsed," Lasch wrote his parents. The most hopeful reasons for going to Rochester had now evaporated. He began to look into other opportunities, including an opening at Amherst. The young intellectual historian John Patrick Diggins asked him to consider an appointment as chair of the department at UC-Irvine, but Lasch felt no desire to move to California. His colleagues at Northwestern, hearing of his distress, offered his position back to him, but in the end he turned it down because he had "never been joyously happy" in that department, he told his parents, and, besides, he was hoping to land in New England. He never did. Ironically, after leaving two friction-free appointments at major universities, Lasch ended up staying at friction-filled Rochester for the duration of his career.[35]

In the midst of the destruction of his friendship with Genovese and the larger disappointments at Rochester, Lasch's mood became more subdued, and his writing more quiet. "Surveying the wreckage of the sixties," he wrote to his parents in the spring of 1970, "one is amazed at how little has been accomplished. Just in the last two years the outlook has changed completely." He recalled how in 1968

> Paris, Columbia, McCarthy's candidacy, Johnson's withdrawal, and the emergence of Kennedy: all seemed to give hope that the monolith was really beginning to break up, and that the intense political activity of the sixties, however chaotic and discordant, was going to produce important changes.

34. CL to George Frederickson, TL, 5 October 1970, 2:18; CL to Marvin Becker, TL, 23 January 1971, 3:2; CL to Warren Susman, TL, 26 October 1970; Marvin B. Becker, Herbert G. Gutman, Christopher Lasch, A. William Salomone, and Perez Zagorin, to the University of Rochester department of history, TL, 11 January 1971, 3:3; CL to John Cammett, TL, 12 January 1971, 3:2.

35. CL to RL & ZL, TLS, 2 July 1971, 0:39; CL to John Patrick Diggins, TL, 17 July 1972, 3:8; CL to RL & ZL, TLS, 17 April 1972, 0:39.

But nothing enduring had happened. He sensed that the seventies might be a time for more thinking and less agitating: "In my own case the occasion seems to call for an abandonment of political activities and occasional political writing and an effort to get down to fundamentals . . . undistracted by political alarums and excursions."[36]

In October 1970, shortly after moving to Rochester, he penned a reflective letter to Richard Hofstadter, with whom he had fallen out of touch as he had moved leftward following the publication of *The New Radicalism*. He expressed a sense of hope about the journal he and Genovese were trying to launch, which would stake out "a strong position not only against trivial and mindless empiricism but against the facile leftism so much in vogue among younger scholars and students — not only such absurdities as 'street history,' 'guerrilla history,' etc., but the whole notion of 'radical history' itself, of scholarship enlisted in the service of the revolution." He sensed, he admitted, the need to return to serious scholarship, to honor the claims he had for years been making about its importance. He mentioned "a number of other projects, all abortive," with which he had been involved, including "new political parties (which turned out to consist of about fifteen people, none of which could agree on anything), a proposed journal that would be purely political (and would immediately rally the whole country behind it), and others of a similarly fantastic nature."[37]

When the letter was mailed back to him he was stunned to learn that it had arrived at Hofstadter's address on the day of his death. Lasch described Hofstadter's passing to his parents as "extremely saddening," and remarked that he had been "somewhat sobered" by

36. CL to RL & ZL, TLS, 26 March 1970, 0:38. See also his opening statement in a *New York Review* essay in the fall of 1971: "An interminable war in Indochina; the revolutionary movement elsewhere in disarray; the American left fragmented and driven on the defensive; Nixon acting belatedly but with apparent success to disarm his opponents; public services in decline; the quality of public discussion lower than ever; demoralization and drift on every side — the political scene has seldom looked more dreary. Only three years ago the glacial rigidity of American politics appeared to be breaking up . . . Columbia, Paris, the dumping of Johnson seemed so many proofs that the diverse strands making up the new left had finally coalesced as a movement, a political force." But he continued, "Now it appears that the new left, even in the moment of its apparent triumphs, has already passed the peak of its influence. The Chicago convention was an end rather than a beginning." "Can the Left Rise Again?" 21 October 1971, 36.

37. CL to Richard Hofstadter, TLS, 22 October 1970, 2:20.

it. This subdued mood came through when, having been asked by Hofstadter's widow shortly after his death to write the introduction for the twenty-fifth-anniversary edition of *The American Political Tradition,* Lasch reflected on his own generation of historians, which had been so influenced by, yet so dismissive of, Hofstadter's writing. Admitting that Hofstadter's "undivided devotion to his craft" had once "puzzled" him, especially in the light of the political and even professional debates that would seem to have demanded his more devoted engagement, he acknowledged that for all its avowed activism and reforming spirit his generation had fallen sadly short. In tones of piercing lament he wrote, "For whatever reasons, we have written much less history than they did; nor can we console ourselves that at least we have reformed the university and the political system of which it is a part." His conclusion struck a sharp autobiographical note:

> Our generation has seen too many brave beginnings, too many claims that came to nothing, too many books unfinished and even unbegun, too many broken and truncated careers. As activists, we have achieved far less than we hoped; as scholars, our record is undistinguished on the whole. It is not too late to achieve something better, but it is no longer possible to be complacent about our accomplishments or the superiority of our own understanding of American society to that of the generation before us, whose finest historian was Richard Hofstadter.[38]

As the sixties began to dissipate, and his own place in the center of ideological debates diminished along with it, Lasch began a long season of searching reconsideration. "I can't remember more discouraging times," he wrote to one of his former students at Northwestern, Richard Klimmer, in spring of 1971. "A letter this morning from Robert Coles puts it well: 'I don't think it's only a matter of the economic recession; there seems to be something else receding, something spiritual and moral.'"[39]

Put one way, the collapse of what the historian Robert Crunden

---

38. CL to ZL & RL, TLS, 31 October 1970, 0:38; CL, "On Richard Hofstadter," *New York Review of Books,* 8 March 1973, 12, 13. This essay appeared as the introduction for the 1973 Knopf edition of *The American Political Tradition.*
39. CL to Richard Klimmer, TL, 8 March 1971, 3:4.

has called a "climate of creativity" had occurred, leaving those who had thrived in that other climate feeling exhausted, bewildered, and reflective. William Taylor, recently moved to the University of Chicago, remarked to Lasch that it was very much like the 1950s there, spurring Lasch to retort, *"Everything* looks like the fifties, except that unfortunately it is not quite the same this time around. The students are just as intent on their grades, but alas! They're a lot stupider, having been badly educated all along the line."[40]

These sorts of educational concerns were a part of a larger complex of issues that were beginning to drive his research and writing, as his faith in intellectuals diminished and his search for alternate sources of politically decisive, communally embodied hope took him in other directions. But before he started that quest, what would become a quite different but even more publicized campaign in the second half of the seventies, he continued to sort out the sixties. In 1973 he published a longer collection of essays as *The World of Nations: Reflections on American History, Politics, and Culture,* containing everything from his historical writings from the early sixties to his more political fare from the later part of the decade. He began and (finally) completed a novel during the summer of 1973, a parody of contemporary America written during the early days of the Watergate fiasco. His Knopf editor, though, discouraged him from trying to get it published. In his opinion, said Lasch to a friend, it was "'just a rehash of the history of the last thirty years,'" with "'mawkish'" humor and characters that were "'thinly disguised' caricatures of real people and hence aren't believable."[41]

But the novel was believable as a creation of Christopher Lasch, and it gave a satirical preview of what was to come. His narrator, "Harold Fox," styled himself "a skilled surgeon presiding at the birth of a new American culture, a culture more advanced, more mature, stronger and healthier than the old culture, which was stunted by puritanical repression and the harsh work of taming a virgin continent." Finally, though, in America's triumphant "post-puritan society" a "new race of men" was "finally beginning to emerge."[42]

40. Robert Morse Crunden, *Ministers of Reform: The Progressives' Achievement in American Civilization, 1889-1920* (New York: HarperCollins, 1982); CL to William R. Taylor, TL, 8 November 1972, 3:10.

41. CL to Gerald Graff, TL, 26 November 1973, 3:12.

42. CL, "The Life and Times of a Libertine," unpublished ms. in 65:5-8; quotes are from p. 2.

A new race and a new culture — but not the kind Lasch had been fighting for. This "new race" was an alien one to Lasch, and he felt the dissonance and distance acutely. His hopes for radical change of any sort had severely diminished, and his political excursions beyond academe by and large ended. "I really feel terribly disconnected at the moment from anything concerning radicalism," he wrote to a professor at the University of Virginia in 1973. "I haven't been 'keeping up.' I've spent most of the last year reading about courtly love, fabliaux, clandestine marriage and the suppression thereof . . . and to tell you the truth I feel remote not only from radicalism but from the modern world in general — the same way I always felt, only more so." Hopes for a new culture were giving way to visions of a culture of narcissism.[43]

---

43. CL to Dante Germino, TL, 9 June 1973, 3:12.

CHAPTER SEVEN

The Collapse of a Common Culture

I'm determined to try to provide my children with some inner resources against the contemporary madness, the youth culture, and the enormous temptations to total cynicism and despair.

Christopher Lasch to Zora and
Robert Lasch, 26 March 1970[1]

But the question for serious historians is not whether progress exacts a price but whether the history of modern society can be considered progress in the first place.

Christopher Lasch, "What the Doctor Ordered,"
New York Review of Books, 1975[2]

A s the 1960s began to cool, Christopher Lasch began to redirect his energies away from intensive engagement in politics and toward a more searching, satisfying understanding of the altered national circumstance. Once more the intersection of politics and scholarship was forcing him to re-examine his most basic assumptions about the country's past — and, inevitably, about life itself.

It was not a merely cerebral activity. While preparing to move to

---

1. CL to RL & ZL, TLS, 26 March 1970, 0:38.
2. Christopher Lasch, "What the Doctor Ordered," *New York Review of Books,* 11 December 1975, 53.

Rochester in the summer of 1970 he wrote to Gerald Graff of an "agonizing reappraisal" of his "own position on a number of issues," a period of "reevaluation" that was yielding "a clearer idea than I've had before of the kind of work I should be doing." His ironic "Yours for the counter-revolution" at the close of the letter hinted at the nature of his emerging stance.[3]

Lasch was, to be sure, experiencing little affinity with the intellectual peregrinations of the nascent "neo-conservatives," that group of erstwhile liberals and leftists that, having watched the collapse of the midcentury liberal consensus, was now making a new home on the right. Such prominent figures as Irving Kristol, the editor of the *Public Interest,* Norman Podhoretz, the editor of *Commentary,* and Gertrude Himmelfarb, the eminent British historian (and Kristol's wife), were veering rapidly away from the left, repelled by, as Patrick Allitt puts it, their "experience with student rebellion, urban riots, antiwar protest, and a general deterioration of civility." But Lasch showed little sympathy for their quest; in fact, he seldom passed up a chance to ridicule it. "Norman Podhoretz was in town yesterday, lecturing on Jewish writing and predicting a wave of anti-semitism and the balkanization of American culture," wrote Lasch in the fall of 1971 to his friend the leftist sociologist Norman Birnbaum, then residing in Italy. "At the same time he tells me that I ought to be more sanguine about the country: people do really like their jobs, walk with a bounce in their step (in contrast to decadent Europe). I would be grateful for your impressions of the degree of bounce in the gait of the Turinese; comparative statistics seem to be in order here." Writing later that fall as a referee for *American Quarterly,* he decried "the extreme intellectual poverty of right-wing thought," which "makes an analysis of it somewhat pointless, except as a case of social pathology." "Conservatism," in its contemporary ideological guise, continued to be a weak and unworthy foe, "resting," as he noted dismissively in a *New York Review* essay, "in religious assumptions that can be taken seriously only at risk of ridicule." As Lasch's sometime comrade David Kettler remembered, "We all had nothing but contempt for these writers, whose work and whose constituency appeared merely ideological in the worst sense."[4]

3. CL to Gerald Graff, TL, 11 July 1970, 2:19.
4. Patrick Allitt, *Catholic Intellectuals and Conservative Politics in America,*

Various luminaries on the left tried to recruit Lasch in their efforts to regroup in the early seventies. *Dissent* editor Irving Howe, professedly "distressed by the evident waste of energies, idealism, hope" he had witnessed in the rise and fall of the new left, wrote of trying to assemble a group of forty or so "serious intellectual people on the left (no party hacks, no ranters, no fixed-position takers)" for "an afternoon of quiet discussion." Lasch, apparently, did not respond. When Birnbaum urged Lasch to accept an invitation to participate in a conference sponsored by *Partisan Review,* a venerable New York literary and cultural journal of leftist sensibility, Lasch replied by mocking the pretensions of those in the journal's orbit. It would no doubt be simply a "P-R promotion," he wrote, "with all the 'well's,' 'er's,' and 'ahem's' preserved in the stenographic record." "This rage for symposia and conferences," he muttered, "for high-level intellectual chit-chat, where you get to see 'personalities' of the various participants, seems to be itself a symptom of serious cultural disorder." He did respond, minimally, when inveterate leftist organizer Michael Harrington in 1973 issued a call for a "new socialist organization" that would position itself on the "Democratic Left." In a personal letter to Lasch, Harrington acknowledged that Lasch would "probably consider our orientation toward the Democratic Party too conservative," but he stressed his conviction that "what is now crucial is to re-establish some kind of socialist *presence* in this country," which would demand "an ingathering of all the exiles in a loose, communicative, open-minded socialist organization of the Democratic Left." Lasch, joining Howe, Birnbaum, Lewis Coser, and other intellectuals of varying leftist stripes, agreed to be a "Signer of the Call" for the "founding convention" of the organization, slated to take place in October of 1973 in New York City.[5]

But Lasch himself embodied the post-sixties leftist disarray; he was in no condition to help man the ramparts of any new political movements. Disturbed and disoriented by the course of not just the student movement but also his own personal alliances, his season of re-thinking and self-examination had taken a dark, interior turn. "I

1950-1985 (Ithaca: Cornell University Press, 1993), 161; CL to Norman Birnbaum, TL, 27 October 1971, 3:2; CL to Murray G. Murphey, TL, 8 December 1971, 3:2; CL, "Inequality and Education," *New York Review of Books,* 17 May 1973, 19n.2; David Kettler to author, private email of 6 November 2006.

5. Irving Howe to CL, TLS, 20 January 1972, 3:8; CL to Norman Birnbaum, TL, 18 August 1972, 3:7; Michael Harrington to CL, TLS, 18 July 1973, 3:13.

don't know if I can get up the energy for any more calls or manifestoes," he had in 1970 written to Kettler, a political theorist who had just lost his position at Ohio State University. He noted, in addition to the failure of the James Weinstein party, "all the other prematurely organized socialist parties, the closing in of the whole political landscape over the past two years" and "the collapse of even the prospects for university reform." In a letter to Kettler two years later he voiced his keen sense of personal and political disappointment in a brief, quiet confession: "The collapse of the department here . . . the collapse of the left, have left me high and dry, in spirits far from sociable. Bourgeois domesticity (of which I am also trying to write the rise and fall) provides some solace." He noted that nineteenth-century British socialist William Morris had termed himself a "revolutionary culturalist" and wondered if this was the only remaining political option since, according to Morris, "the problem of culture was inseparable from the 'social question,' and . . . the meeting ground was the problem of work, the debasement of work under capitalism."[6]

Work at the University of Rochester continued to pose considerable problems of a debased sort for Lasch; he stayed away from that lamentable scene as much as possible. The Lasches had opted to buy a house well outside of Rochester in Avon, a small town which could very well have served as the inspiration for Frank Capra's Bedford Falls in *It's a Wonderful Life;* their house was on one of the main streets, lined with old trees and large, rambling wood-frame homes. From the outset it became a welcome retreat from the departmental chaos. In a letter to former Northwestern colleague Robert Wiebe written shortly after his arrival, Lasch confessed, "Twenty miles to the north lies the great metropolis, with its university teeming with intrigue, factions, conspiracies, and higher learning, but I only go in occasionally, so I only hear about those things."[7]

Indeed, in his first year the climate of the department had become so poisonous that Genovese had chosen to not recommend salary increases for Lasch and the four other vocal opponents of his chairmanship, and university officials, not keen on intradepartmental insubordination, had supported his decision. This ac-

6. CL to David Kettler, TL, 30 March 1970, 2:20; CL to David Kettler, 6 December 1972, 3:9.
7. CL to Robert Wiebe, TL, 26 October 1970, 3:1.

tion prompted Paul Forman, not one of the five dissidents, to write a letter to the entire history faculty protesting that Genovese had "humiliated and compromised the rest of us," since "any financial rewards that one accepts under such a regime must be at the cost of one's self-respect, for it is impossible to escape the suspicion that one is receiving either a bribe or a pay-off." Finally, after five semesters at Rochester, Lasch in January 1973 wrote to Genovese asking for a raise, his brief appeal freighted with the quiet sarcasm that intimacy alone, however strained, makes possible: "I know that you will not allow personal considerations to stand in the way of the advance of historical knowledge." Still Genovese did not yield, and in the inflationary summer of 1973 Lasch mentioned to *New York Review* editor Robert Silvers the "serious toll" that "the freeze Genovese has put on my salary" had begun to take. It is no wonder that he described himself to Birnbaum in the winter of 1973 as living in "an almost perfect vacuum."[8]

Within two years of Lasch's arrival four professors and several graduate students had left the department over the controversies surrounding the Genovese chairmanship, including Herbert Gutman, a leading labor historian and onetime Genovese ally. Remarkably, despite inquiries from various universities around the country, including Stanford and the University of Pittsburgh, Lasch stayed on. He was beginning to attract talented graduate students, including David F. Noble, Russell Jacoby, Leon Fink, Maurice Isserman, Thomas R. Cole, William Leach, and Casey Nelson Blake, all of whom would go on to prominence as scholars and intellectuals. Cole, a Yale philosophy undergraduate who began at Rochester in 1975, recalls that Lasch "seemed to revel in the sort of network of students and colleagues and families that would come and drink and make music and talk," so much so, in fact, that "the boundaries between his students and his family sometimes blurred." Cole, Leach, and Lasch "spent an awful lot of time playing arias and Gilbert and Sullivan," remembers Cole, with Cole and Lasch singing together while Lasch or Leach played piano. "We just spent hours and hours and hours making music, and it was very gratifying, and lots of fun."[9]

8. Paul Forman to University of Rochester History Department, TL, 3 March 1971, 3:3; CL to Eugene Genovese, TL, 4 January 1973, 3:12; CL to Robert Silvers, TL, 6 July 1973, 3:15; CL to Norman Birnbaum, TL, 5 February 1973, 3:11.
9. Interview with Thomas R. Cole, 3 August 2007.

Despite such welcome forms of extracurricular relief, Lasch's discontent with his vocational and political life was deep. The rapid decrease in faculty openings for historians in the early seventies only added to his funk, as he watched one student after another struggle to find work. "I curse the job market, academia, capitalism, and modern life generally," he wrote in 1971 to Richard Klimmer, one of his Northwestern Ph.D.s, "every time (which is often) that I consider that a person of your obvious and perfectly indisputable abilities can't find a job in this profession." In 1975 he described himself to Roger Nash, another Northwestern student who had just been released from a faculty position at Wayne State University due to financial cutbacks, as "increasingly bitter about the academic depression in general." The jobs that were available, he lamented, were tending to go to Ivy League candidates, who were "as dismal a bunch of dullards as we have every right to expect considering who's teaching them." He shuddered as he considered "the long-range effects of these practices on the intellectual well-being of the academy, somewhat attenuated already. . . ." [10]

In the aftermath of the 1960s Lasch did continue to address one core dimension of his earlier vision: education, especially higher education, his preoccupation with which became the bridge between his sixties activism and the more far-reaching cultural matters that in the seventies began to absorb him. Still certain, as the sixties dissipated, that the university, and education more generally, were foundational to any serious hope of cultural renewal, he narrowed his vision and directed his energies toward the only sphere he had a serious prospect of altering. The stance he came to, though, differed in dramatic ways from the emerging cultural consensus on the university. By the decade's end his feisty combination of cultural traditionalism and leftward political economy — what his future colleague Stewart Weaver would classify as "Tory Radical" — would be highly anomalous.[11]

Lasch's work as a college teacher gave him steady, direct exposure to the culture he was trying to understand, and over the years his parents proved to be sympathetic listeners to his sporadic observations and complaints. In one letter in 1973 he described even his better students as "semi-literate." "They write 'enormity' when they mean that

10. CL to Richard Klimmer, TL, 8 March 1971, 3:4; CL to Roger Nash, TL, 25 February 1975, 4:3.

11. Stewart Weaver, Introduction to CL, PS, 15.

something was enormous," and "they are permanently and incurably confused about the number of Latin nouns like 'criterion' and 'phenomenon.'" "Every discipline has 'parameters' and is informed by certain 'paradigms,'" he wrote, finishing with the sort of tirade brought on by stacks of student papers:

> This barbaric jargon is almost impenetrable, and it is difficult to correct it because the students don't know the grammar of their own language. . . . Never having heard of a participle or a gerund, they can form sentences only by accretion, by adding endlessly onto one fragile stem; the result is that although they can form only simple sentences, they produce sentences that are anything but simple — dense tangles of syntactical undergrowth, perfect in their opacity. . . . Assuming that the quality of writing is closely related to the quality of thought, and there is no reason to believe otherwise, I do not see a bright future for the life of the mind in America.[12]

In a 1973 *New York Review* piece on education Lasch took the opportunity to try out some of his developing ideas regarding the interplay between education and cultural decline and renewal, which had shifted considerably in the preceding years. "Many of us in the mid-sixties," he wrote to one correspondent in 1971, "were too ready to assume that changes in education would have repercussions throughout the rest of society. We were closer perhaps than we realized to the American tradition of overvaluing education, or, more precisely, attaching to it an inflated social significance." How to "break the school's monopoly on culture while restoring some richness ('culture') to the rest of life" was, he thought, the new challenge.[13]

Lasch took it up with a decidedly programmatic edge. The book under review in his 1973 essay was sociologist Christopher Jencks's much-discussed *Inequality: A Reassessment of the Effect of Family and Schooling in America.* By arguing that the decisive variable in educational success was not equality of opportunity but social class, Jencks had ignited a firestorm, and Lasch jumped to his defense. Jencks's study, he underscored, defied the progressive assumption that social equality could be achieved through the current structure of public ed-

---

12. CL to ZL & RL, TLS, 15 January 1973, 0:39.
13. CL to Jonathan Galassi, TL, 13 August 1971, 3:3.

ucation. "Even if it were possible to give everyone the same amount of schooling," Lasch emphasized, Jencks had shown that "this would have little effect on the distribution of income. A direct political attack on inequality therefore makes more sense than an attempt to equalize educational opportunities."[14]

But he then veered toward a deeper criticism of the "system of universal compulsory education" itself. Displacing the older more local systems in the nineteenth century (systems that "whatever their obvious shortcomings, had roots in the neighborhoods and reflected — although with many distortions — the interests of their constituents"), the modern system was operated by "new educational bureaucrats" who tended to see students — especially those from immigrant families — as "clients," "so much raw material to be processed as expeditiously as possible." Progressives, backed by the industrialists, had seized on the opportunity to use public schools to conform the nation to their own enlightened ideals and standards, and by the 1970s the deplorable effects were on full display. By wantonly dismantling local, familial educational networks, the industrial economy and public education had worked in tandem to create "a youth culture that is at least partially self-created and autonomous, a culture created on the streets but having a large, perhaps decisive influence on the schools." "The schools," he wrote, "are plagued by boredom, disruption, violence, drugs, and gang warfare," all indicative of "the crumbling of authority, and the replacement of authority with violence."[15]

He was working up to a counter-proposal — one that many readers found unpalatable, even offensive, but that was his attempt to etch a fuller vision of the decentralized socialism he was advocating. Nodding backward to early American educational debates, he affirmed Jefferson's cardinal assumption that all citizens need a basic education. But he followed Jefferson well beyond this point, and well beyond the now-hardened postwar consensus on the desirability of a college education for all. Jefferson, it turns out, had also been right in believing that higher education should be available only to those able to appreciate it. Here Lasch's judgment was startlingly unequivocal: "The dream of bringing culture to the masses by making higher edu-

14. CL, "Inequality and Education," 20.
15. CL, "Inequality and Education," 21, 22, 23, 24.

cation widely available has failed; mass higher education has only facilitated the spread of mass culture, impoverishing popular culture and higher culture alike." To those who viewed such opinions with egalitarian disdain, he threw out an extra jab: "Higher education is necessarily 'elitist' if it is to mean anything" and should be available only to those with a "pronounced taste for intellectual matters."[16]

This educational program fit within and expanded Lasch's larger defense of liberal culture and the socialist political economy he believed was necessary for its preservation. It was not for the faint of heart. Underlining both the socialist and the ascetic dimensions of his stance, he concluded that in an attempt to avoid the scandal of a careerist professorate, college faculty should not be paid well, should in fact "live on the edge of austerity" in order to safeguard the sanctity of the university ideal. And in a socialist economy, crucially, people could afford to skip college. "If incomes were roughly equalized, the demand for extended education would diminish drastically; the over-developed educational bureaucracy would wither at its source. Is it possible to imagine a fairer prospect?"[17]

Apparently so. Just a few weeks after the article appeared, Lasch wrote his parents that it had "provoked a predictable outcry among leftists because of its 'elitist' views." Indeed, one of his erstwhile allies, the historian Ann Lane, then teaching at John Jay College of Criminal Justice in New York City, wrote in scolding tones that he needed "the humility imposed by one year's contact with John Jay–type students . . . before you should allow yourself to repeat those pious phrases about the impossibility of 'bringing culture to the masses' and why higher education is only for people 'completely committed to it.'" Robert Lasch, however, saw hope for his son in the piece. "Having read your article in the New York Review I feel constrained to welcome you to the 18th century. I have always felt like an 18th century rationalist, and you are evidently beginning to feel the same."[18]

Indeed, there was a lot from an older world — the eighteenth century as well his parents' early-twentieth-century Midwestern world —

16. CL, "Inequality and Education," 24, 25.
17. CL, "Inequality and Education," 25.
18. CL to RL & ZL, TLS, 28 May 1973, 0:39; Ann Lane to CL, TLS, 10 May 1973, 3:14; RL to CL, TL, 2 June 1973, 3:14.

that was becoming more self-consciously integral to Lasch's social vision in the aftermath of the sixties, from an intensely local, familial vision of education to a hierarchical understanding of learning and knowledge itself. As America in the seventies became at once less traditionally religious and less "modern," Lasch was slowly forced to reckon with the growing sense of attachment he felt to these overlapping, contending cultural identities that had given that older American world its shape.

Canadians observers might have recognized Lasch's emerging stance as reflecting many of the impulses and assumptions held by those known in that country as "Red Tories," traditionalists who in the middle decades of the twentieth century embraced a socialist political economy while eschewing the liberationist individualism of the left. The foremost Red Tory intellectual, the philosopher George Parkin Grant, in 1961 claimed, for instance, that socialists "must be able to show that the social morality they propound comes to grips more cogently with our problems than does the present capitalist ethic," with its attendant liberationist effects — effects he believed most socialists foolishly welcomed.[19]

In a 1999 reflection James Neuchterlein, an American historian and then-editor of the neo-conservative magazine *First Things,* noted that Lasch was one of the few American critics who "wrote in a manner that brought Grant to mind," due to his joining of perspectives conventionally found on either the left or the right but not both. Recalling his days teaching at Canada's Queen's University in the 1960s, Neuchterlein noted that the Red Tories, like Lasch, fought with vigor to maintain traditional academic ideals and structures: "I found that most of my most regular allies on curricular issues were people who belonged to Canada's leftist New Democratic Party but who had not a taint of progressive sentiment when it came to educational standards." In 1955 Grant had already observed that in the name of democratic ideals — equality — students were attending the university only to end up as "servants of the expanding economy." He saw this as a paradox not easily addressed. "How does one reconcile one's deep loyalty to the tradition of democracy with the undoubted debasement of education that our democracy brings?" he asked, not rhetorically.

19. William Christian and Sheila Grant, eds., *The George Grant Reader* (Toronto: University of Toronto Press, 1998), 66.

David Kettler, who was teaching in Canada in these years, suggests that had Lasch "been working in Canada, just across Lake Erie . . . he might have found congenial companions among the 'Red Tories' active at the time — anti-American, humanistic, collectivist, stylish. American conservatism could offer no such home." Kettler's perception of Lasch rings true: "He was a very lonely man, I think."[20]

But it may have been the experience of parenting, not teaching, that was the most immediate occasion of Lasch's lonely reckoning with the cultural legacy of the West, forcing him to think in ways he previously had not about morality, culture, and society. In an autobiographical essay published in 1989 Lasch recalled that while the direction his research had taken him in the 1970s was certainly connected to his ongoing study of the family in America, it probably "grew more deeply out of my experience as a husband and father." When he and Nell married in the mid-fifties, they had, he recalled,

> wanted our children to grow up in a kind of extended family. . . . A house full of people, a crowded table, four-hand music at the piano, non-stop conversation and cooking, baseball games and swimming in the afternoon, long walks after dinner, a poker game or *Diplomacy* or charades in the evening, all these activities mixing children and adults — that was our idea of a well-ordered household and a well-ordered education.

Having "no great confidence in the schools," he wrote, "we knew that if our children were to acquire any of the things we set store by — joy in learning, eagerness for experience, the capacity for love and friendship — they would have to learn the better part of it at home." Of course they had not framed their hopes so self-consciously at the time, he noted — "but some such feelings helped shape the way we lived, along with much else that was not thought out but purely impulsive."[21]

Child-rearing, though, had turned out to be "unexpectedly rigorous." "[O]ur 'child-centered' society's icy indifference to everything

20. James Nuechterlein, "Confessions of a Contrarian," *First Things* 90 (Feburary 1999), 9; Christian and Grant, *George Grant Reader,* 176, 177; David Kettler to author, email, 6 November 2006. My thanks to Professor Kettler for turning me toward the Red Tories.

21. CL, "The Obsolescence of Left and Right," *New Oxford Review,* April 1989, 11.

that makes it possible for children to flourish and grow up to be responsible adults" had come as a particularly disturbing revelation, leading him to remark grimly that "to see the modern world from the point of view of a parent is to see it in the worst possible light." Being a parent had exposed for him, with stark clarity, the "unwholesomeness, not to put it more strongly, of our way of life"; indeed, he had come to see all too clearly "why the family issue had come to play such a large part in the politics of the 1970s and 1980s, and why so many Democrats had drifted away from their party." By the 1970s being "liberal" had come to mean "sexual freedom, women's rights, gay rights, denunciation of the family as the seat of all oppression, denunciation of 'patriarchy,' denunciation of 'working-class authoritarianism.'" But what to Lasch (and others who eventually were labeled "cultural conservatives") were disturbing signs of "moral collapse," liberals and leftists saw as at worst a mixed bag and at best heartening signs of progress. This outraged him. During the seventies, he recalled, he had reached the conclusion that "'Middle Americans' had good reason . . . to worry about the family and the future their children were going to inherit." To illumine and validate that judgment had become a critical element of his scholarly-political program.[22]

By 1975 the Lasch children ranged in age from seventeen (Robert) to ten (Christopher), with Elisabeth and Catherine in between. Having struggled for years at the intersection of career, politics, and family, Lasch in the 1970s began more fully to perceive just how the commercial milieu of American family life was militating against their efforts — a reality that had not escaped the watchful eye of his mother. Back in 1965 Zora, following a visit to Iowa City, had expressed concern to Kit and Nell about "Robbie's and Betsy's passion for buying things." But she did not fault Nell and Kit so much as the ever-expanding powers of the consumer culture, remarking with a grandmother's long view that now "parents have the whole economic and social system to fight." "I wonder," she asked Kit, "if you would have spent so many hours on building your little theaters and characters" if such items had then been so readily available to children. Now "kids get bored with them and don't know it. Like a drug addict they look to another toy to relieve the boredom. It is a sick, sick world we live in," she sighed. But she wanted Nell and Kit to know that she and Robert

22. CL, "The Obsolescence of Left and Right," 12, 13.

had "faith in your resolution and the children's intelligence to fight it through." "Don't be afraid of a little moralistic lecturing in a mild, affectionate manner," she added.[23]

Five years later Lasch found himself writing to his parents, with some desperation, about the academic struggles twelve-year-old Robby was having. He expressed hope that their move to Avon along with his own "partial retirement . . . from public distractions" would aid both Robby's performance as a student and his own performance as a dad. "I'm determined," he vowed, "to try to provide my children with some inner resources against the contemporary madness, the youth culture, and the enormous temptations to cynicism and despair." Robert responded by writing Kit a long, sympathetic letter. He recalled how he had read Homer to Kit at bedtime, and how Zora had conducted "adult conversations" with him "at a most tender age." He reminded him of how they had "rationed" the less challenging books for the "good books" until he had lost his desire for the "trashy" ones. "Of course we had two extreme rationalists in the house from the day you were born and it is not surprising that you were a rationalist too," he wrote. He gently chided Kit for neglecting his family responsibilities in the previous years, and followed up with words of counsel: "I do think the critical point is respect for the intellect, the mind, the rational process, learning for the joy of learning, and so on." He and Zora had shown Kit a better way, one that had sought to transcend the consumer culture that was gaining ground in the 1930s and 1940s, and now Kit needed to do the same.[24]

While admitting blame for the educational failures of his children, Lasch continued, more in the manner of his mother than his father, to point to the marring influence of deeper, malevolent historical forces and patterns on his children's world. Most of the current nostrums in public education, he remarked in reply to Robert's letter, were examples of "the same old progressive permissiveness." This was something his parents had long ago taught him to guard against — and their warnings had taken root. Indeed, in a book report he had written on Horace Greeley at age fourteen, Kit had opened with a remarkable page-and-a-half typed diatribe against "progressive educa-

23. ZL to CL and NL, TL, 2 December 1965, 1:18.
24. CL to RL & ZL, TLS, 26 March 1970, 0:38; RL to CL, TLS, 31 March 1970, 2:21.

tion" and its "project system," of which he considered the assignment in question to be a troubling manifestation. The youthful critic derided the "project system" as a "lowly device invented . . . for the purpose of 'encouraging the pupil to think for himself,'" which, boiled down to cold, hard facts, means to 'encourage the pupil not to think.'" The progressive educators, he warned, were trying to "pull all good students down to a certain grade and to elevate all bad ones. . . ." (One "Miss Strauss," with bemused patience, responded gently to her young charge, allowing that he was "an individual who likes to do things in his own way." Although she gave him an A+, she served him notice that she would not allow him "to become too satirical. I hope you retain always your own loveable traits.")[25]

This carefully ingrained distaste for "progressive education" was still detectable thirty years later, but it was now accompanied by a newer element, a settled, increasingly fierce affection for older, traditional ways and means that had once achieved "education" in a manner Lasch now thought of as both more effective and rich. The old culture, far from being as retrograde and unappealing as most now saw it, had been guided by a wisdom largely unknown to modern Americans. He had become "more and more convinced," he wrote his parents, "that the real trouble . . . is in the school's monopoly of education." Whereas once the schools had been centered on basic academic instruction, now they had become "an alternative to the family, to the job, and to all the other institutions that used to be intimately implicated, in one way or another, in education. The school," he scorned, "claims to be able to teach you how to live, how to cook, drive a car, get along with people, and all the other things that were formerly left, wisely, to agencies better equipped for this kind of training." Due to this inadequate way of preparing American children for adult life, the universities were turning out to be, "in effect, trade schools for overgrown adolescents," a college degree having become both a "prerequisite for admission to the working force" and a "universal right." He felt certain that "As long as education is compulsory, and particularly as long as it is not only compulsory but prolonged well into the twenties," Americans would continue to "suffer generation gaps, the alienation of youth, Vietnam or no Vietnam;

25. CL to ZL & RL, TLS, 30 April 1970, 0:38; CL, "Horace Greeley, Printer, Editor, Crusader," unpublished ms. dated 10 January 1947, 69:11.

and higher education will continue to be for the most part a meaningless ritual."[26]

Of course, the central "agency" in the older world he was lauding with more and more vigor had been the family, and throughout the sixties and early seventies Lasch had watched with growing discomfort as this institution, on rapidly shifting ground throughout the twentieth century, had begun at best to reconfigure and at worst to crumble, and along with it the ideal of lifelong monogamous marriage. When he had begun his career he had not felt so deeply concerned about these shifts, he recalled in a 1991 *New Oxford Review* symposium "On Transcending Ideological Conformity." His own "friends and contemporaries," he stressed, "did not grow up in the dark ages," but were "children of light, raised by good liberal parents on good liberal principles." Consequently, "The old sexual code, the mid-Victorian code as we thought of it, had no meaning for us. Premarital chastity, strict sexual monogamy, a rigorous division of sexual labor — we could no longer take these ideas seriously."[27]

But by the time he renewed his work on the family in the early seventies, he had, he wrote with marked understatement, "begun to have doubts about the desirability or even the feasibility of an open-ended experimental approach to sexuality, marriage, and childrearing." Inspired by the bravery Frankfurt School philosopher Max Horkheimer had displayed in renouncing his formerly negative opinion of the "authoritarian family," Lasch followed suit. Horkheimer's "willingness to modify his theoretical and ideological preconceptions in the light of empirical evidence," he recalled, "gave me a model of intellectual integrity and courage, at a time when such models were in short supply." In retrospect, Horkheimer's courage of conviction had helped Lasch to "brave the abuse that was in store for me, once my 'apostasy from the Left' became public knowledge."[28]

This political and philosophical reorientation toward what Lasch would in this 1991 symposium term "cultural conservatism" was, of course, slow, only surfacing in quiet and subtle ways. While auditing a

26. CL to ZL & RL, TLS, 30 April 1970, 0:38; CL to ZL & RL, TLS, 3 June 1969, 0:38.

27. CL, contribution to "Symposium on Transcending Ideological Conformity," *New Oxford Review,* October 1991, 20.

28. CL, "Symposium on Transcending Ideological Conformity," 21.

course on the family at Iowa in 1962, he had noted in a letter to William R. Taylor that most scholars of the family "are simply propagandists for a more permissive attitude toward sex," treating sexual freedom as "a kind of panacea"; this, he thought, amounted to "the accommodation of liberalism to points of view which tend to undermine it." By 1971, in a lengthy *New York Review of Books* essay titled "Can the Left Rise Again?" Lasch highlighted Horkheimer's contention that "bourgeois domesticity," in Lasch's words, was "the last defense of a rich and autonomous inner life against the encroachments of the mass society." "Today," he warned, "family life increasingly exists in a vacuum and has become vacuous." The next year, in a deceptively breezy letter to John Updike, he expressed with an anecdote his growing unease. "Because almost everyone I know has been divorced at least once, I have taken to calling mine, with an arrogance that as always provides rich satisfaction but does not amuse the other members of the family, 'the last marriage.'" He supposed that "Others who cling to this obviously archaic mode of reproduction doubtless experience similar feelings of historical obsolescence."[29]

Lasch was trying to keep his balance while making his way through newly difficult terrain on all fronts, professional, political, familial — even religious. Although he had assured Updike that 1970s college students were, contrary to the popular conception, not the exact counterparts of their own generation, since they did not seem to feel a "passionate desire to be saved," his own children had managed to come into contact with at least one popular expression of 1970s-style Christianity. Chris and Kate, he wrote his parents in 1974, were helping to stage a rendition of *Jesus Christ Superstar* at a local Episcopal church. Lasch had seen the film version of *Superstar* and declared it to be "utterly without musical, dramatic, or moral interest, to say nothing of redeeming social value." He suspected, though, that "perhaps it filled a need for religious instruction in our children's lives that I have been derelict in meeting." Call it the nagging doubt of a child of "extreme rationalists."[30]

29. CL to William R. Taylor, TL, 19 February 1962, 7d:7; CL, "Can the Left Rise Again?" *New York Review of Books,* 21 October 1971, 48; CL to John Updike, TL, 6 November 1972, 3:10.

30. CL to John Updike, TL, 6 November 1972, 3:10; CL to RL & ZL, TL, 13 February 1974, 3:18.

*   *   *

When Lasch wrote his never-delivered letter to Richard Hofstadter in the fall of 1970, he enclosed an essay he had recently published on the French sociologist Jacques Ellul, whose *The Technological Society* had won a broad readership in the United States after its publication in English in 1965. The essay on Ellul, he told Hofstadter, suggested "some of my growing misgivings about current leftism." It also provides an illuminating documentary starting point for a fuller understanding of Lasch's shift toward an outspoken cultural conservatism in the 1970s.[31]

His "growing misgivings" about the left, if the Ellul essay is any indication, centered on the relationship of moral character to political and cultural renewal. Discussing Ellul's book *The Political Illusion,* Lasch explained that for Ellul the "illusion" — so prevalent among leftists on both sides of the Atlantic — was that "a change in political structures, without an attendant spiritual or cultural transformation, will bring about a genuine democratic society." In exposing this fallacy in such convincing fashion Ellul, almost alone among "contemporary radicals," had decisively identified "the cultural dimensions of the twentieth century crisis," which, he thought more and more, centered on clashing understandings of freedom. Whereas it was the hope of those he called the "cultural radicals" to "seek salvation in drugs, sexual liberation, and communal arrangements," Ellul proffered a different vision of freedom, one that of necessity included such elements as "privacy, order, and continuity," the centrality of the family, and the "belief that institutionalized tension should be clearly present in human affairs." Ellul's understanding of liberty, sourced in what Lasch termed "Christian humanism," enabled him "to see the modern obsession with personal liberation as itself a symptom of pervasive spiritual disorder." It was the "*creation* of order," rather than mere "revolutionary violence," that radicals must pursue. No radical shift in political economy could ipso facto create the good society that revolutionaries had in mind; just social structures were impossible apart from properly ordered selves.[32]

31. CL to Richard Hofstadter, TLS, 22 October 1970, 2:20.
32. CL, "The Social Thought of Jacques Ellul," in WN, 274, 276, 292. In a 1974 letter he mentioned, cryptically, that he considered this one of his best essays. See CL to Linda Smithson, TL, 4 December 1974, 3:19.

Ellul was a lay Protestant theologian as well as a sociologist, and Lasch's essay appeared in *Katallagete,* a small journal of opinion edited by James Y. Holloway, a professor at tiny Berea College in Kentucky. It was published by the "Committee of Southern Churchmen," which had been called into existence in 1964 through the vision and leadership of Yale-trained Baptist minister Will Campbell, a former civil rights activist and director of religious life at the University of Mississippi. Populist in spirit, neo-orthodox in doctrine, and radical in vision, the committee sought, in its own words, to aid "those who must live in the new life emerging from the struggle between the revolutionists and the resistors." It was pursuing the "reconciliation" between the former enemies that must take place if the justice achieved through the civil rights movement was to fulfill its promise.

The English translation of the journal's awkward but fitting Greek name, "Be Reconciled," appeared on the masthead, along with the names of the members of its editorial board, among them Ellul, the Catholic novelist Walker Percy, and eventually Lasch himself. The journal's circulation was small, ranging between 3000 and 7000 in the 1960s and 1970s, but it attracted major writers, including Thomas Merton, Reinhold Niebuhr, and Robert Penn Warren. Significantly, the editorial team of Campbell and Holloway centered a good deal of their energies on an unsparing critique of liberalism, and particularly its willingness to believe that legislative reform would lead inexorably to uplifting cultural change. Six years after the publication of his Ellul essay, when Lasch wrote a fundraising letter for the magazine, he commended it as a publication that "speaks for Christian radicalism, forged in the class struggle," noting in particular its "impatience with slogans and abstractions" and its "respect for concrete experience." *Katallagete,* he wrote, was "something rare and precious."[33]

But if while seeking to define his reaction to the sixties Lasch

---

33. CL, fundraising letter, TL, 18 August 1976, in 4:7. This discussion of *Katallagete* is based on Jennifer Ford, "Will Campbell and Christ's Ambassadors," *Journal of Southern Religion* 3 (2000), http://jsr.fsu.edu/ford.htm, and Steven P. Miller, "From Politics to Reconciliation: *Katallagete,* Biblicism, and Southern Liberalism," *Journal of Southern Religion* 7 (2004), http://jsr.fsu.edu/volume7/Millerarticle.htm; the quotation from the Committee's statement is in Ford, "Will Campbell."

found himself in general agreement with these expressly religious thinkers on the need for order, continuity, and authority, he was working from an ontology different from theirs, and he continued to look to the towering rationalists of the modern era as guides for a naturalistically supported moral conservatism. Freud and the leftist social theorists who followed him became particularly indispensable to Lasch for his conception of order as he in the 1970s turned his attention toward marriage and the family in modern America. Freud, in fact, became a true intellectual beacon to him, one who, far from being a "'prisoner' of his age," as many critics by the 1970s were contending, had "struggled heroically to transcend it," according to Lasch. In the previous decade Freud had been a much smaller part of Lasch's thinking; now he became much more central. Eventually Lasch's understanding of Freud became so impressive that he would be asked to give the annual Freud Lectures at the University of London in 1981.[34]

As usual, most of Lasch's schooling in Freud came by his own solitary efforts, although he found helpful companions along the way. He was most appreciative of Russell Jacoby, whose dissertation (later published as *Social Amnesia: A Critique of Contemporary Psychology from Adler to Laing*) Lasch supervised when Jacoby's erstwhile mentor, Hayden White, departed Rochester. Their conversations began in 1971, and if anything it was Jacoby who ended up becoming a sort of mentor to Lasch, at least regarding things Freudian. "I've waited for a long time to read something on Laing and Cooper that made this kind of sense," he wrote excitedly to Jacoby in 1972, remarking on an introduction Jacoby had sent to him for a proposed anthology on twentieth-century neo-Freudian debate. Trying to help Jacoby land a teaching position in 1974, Lasch described him to Donald Meyer as "an absolutely brilliant student in modern European intellectual history" and gave him perhaps the highest praise he could offer at the time: "I don't know anyone who is better equipped to teach Marxisms, psychoanalysis, and European social theory in general." Jacoby would help Lasch sort out the Frankfurt School and its implications for his study of the family; he later told *New York Review* edi-

---

34. CL, "Freud and Women," *New York Review of Books,* 30 October 1974, 12. For an early use of Freud, in which he castigates the new radicals for their upbeat use of Freud, see CL, NR, 143-45.

tor Robert Silvers that he had "learned more from Jacoby than he has learned from me."[35]

Since his introduction into American intellectual life in the early twentieth century, Americans had embraced Freud in the way most people embrace that which is alien: by refashioning it in their own image. Softening Freud's jarring contentions about childhood sexuality and rejecting his somber, stoic outlook on human possibility (Freud had famously defined the aim of psychoanalysis as moving from "hysterical misery into normal unhappiness"), Americans made him over with astounding success, in what historian Richard Wolin dubs a "textbook Oedipal revolt." Some Americans resisted this makeover, of course, Jacoby among them. He joined other left intellectuals — most notably Herbert Marcuse in *Eros and Civilization: A Philosophical Inquiry into Freud* — who in the sixties and seventies were arguing that classical Freudian understandings of the human condition must be defended and embraced if a mature, radical theory of society was to take root in the United States.[36]

Lasch followed in their train. To misunderstand or reject Freud in such fundamental ways, he began insistently to argue, was to misunderstand the world itself, with deleterious political consequences. Jibing with Lasch's own stoical sensibilities, Freud (sounding at times like a secular Augustinian) helped to provide Lasch with a theory of human experience that buttressed both his solidifying moral conservatism and his ongoing attack against enlightened liberalism. Freud, he believed, gave him sturdy support in the war against, as he put it in a 1974 essay, "cultural relativism, historicism, [and] an empiricism hostile to theory in almost any form." Each of these vaunted aspects of mainstream intellectual life he saw not as signs of intellectual integrity or political generosity but rather as signs of disorder and evasions of moral and intellectual judgment. The biological, instinctual basis of culture, he insisted, made it not just possible but *necessary* to judge — rather than remain "neutral" about — the ways of a people. A people's conduct and character, to Freudians like Lasch, was the truest

35. CL to Russell Jacoby, TL, 1 June 1972, 3:9; CL to Donald Meyer, TL, 12 June 1974, 3:18; CL to Robert Silvers, TL, 11 November 1978, 5:1.

36. Richard Wolin, "Freudianism," in *A Companion to American Thought*, ed. Richard Wightman Fox and James Kloppenberg (Cambridge, Mass.: Basil Blackwell, 1998), 250. The quotation from Freud is also in this entry.

measure of their political structure and the only solid basis for real political hope. The quest for "tolerance" and "empirical evidence," on the other hand, was for him the fruit of the liberal inability to apprehend the human condition itself, a troubling refusal to render difficult judgment on that which must be understood. "A society that no longer is able to define the difference between right and wrong," he explained to a young historian in 1976, "is all too eager to accept the impartial, 'objective' evidence of the medical and 'social' sciences as a substitute source of such distinctions and to tolerate the abnormal as long as it acknowledges its need for treatment."[37]

"Morality," on this view, did not consist in a set of precepts but was, most basically, the organic yield of a proper symbiosis between social structures and the most elemental of human ties, kinship relations. If the structures of society — economic, governmental, educational — were properly framed and calibrated, families could develop in such a way that the elemental psychic tensions, conflicts, and deceptions that threaten all human beings would be confronted and corrected within the family, the sphere in which biology required this crucial process to take place. To evade family relations was to evade the possibility of selfhood itself, and to consign oneself to regressive, perhaps pathological, patterns of behavior. So that which was right — or "moral," to put it differently — was right because it produced men and women who were themselves able to become good fathers and mothers: those with the will and ability to nurture children to maturity and foster societies aligned, rather than opposed, to this task. If biology provided the ontic baseline of the political project while psychoanalysis made possible an epistemic roadmap for it, politics be-

---

37. CL, "Freud and Women," 17; CL to Richard Wightman Fox, TL, 7 June 1976, 4:6. He put the same view somewhat differently to another correspondent: "It is perfectly fitting that a harried humanism at the end of its tether, utterly unable to explain why anyone should be moral, should declare in desperation that people who keep asking why they should be moral are sick in the head." Here again, Lasch insisted that "we need to know more about the historical setting in which the authority of ethical philosophy has collapsed, and about the social and cultural reasons for this development." CL to Ched Noble, TL, 25 May 1977, 4:15. In *Haven in a Heartless World* he noted that "Cultural relativists are so strongly impressed by cultural differences that they overlook what human beings share simply by virtue of being human" — namely, this biological basis (201n.26).

came the necessary protector of the proper, fragile, symbiosis of family and society.

Clearly, Lasch was turning to Freud for an ontology, scientifically supported, that could both underpin and give shape to his somewhat inchoate but nonetheless strong beliefs about the relations between society, culture, power, family, masculinity, femininity, and sexuality. How did this worldview function in Lasch's criticism? His attack on the Austrian psychiatrist William Reich for his advocacy of "a new and supposedly less repressive sexual morality" as a means of political and social improvement serves as a good example. Warning that psychoanalysis had long established that the hopes proffered by Reich were illusory, he reminded readers that "the battle between nature and culture inheres in the very fact of culture and is irreconcilable." "The human mind," he wrote, was no isolated, self-existing, autonomous entity but rather "the product of an unrelenting struggle between instinct and culture." Accordingly, "the miseries of existence" were unavoidable, and those who rejected this insight were invariably left grasping for the sort of "sweeping spiritual consolations" that would only turn them into ever-weakening pawns for corporate and state manipulation. In response to the outrageous success in the 1970s of the bumptious purveyors of personal and social salvation through psychology, Lasch loudly championed Freud's "skepticism about spiritual transformation and about psychoanalysis as its agent."[38]

Marx, another towering rationalist, also continued to be very present in this emerging counter-vision, offering a materialist, naturalistic theory of history to complement Freud's vision of the human person. As late as 1978, in a letter to *New York Review* editor Robert Silvers protesting what Lasch perceived to be an editorial shift away from Marxist perspectives in the aftermath of the Vietnam War, he averred that Marxian "intellectual traditions" offered "the only hope of understanding the contemporary world." But Marx and Freud were uneasy co-inhabitants of his mind. With Marxist eschatology jostling and agitating against his Freudian gravity, some sense of hope remained intact, if not always persuasively. For all of his disdain of modern psychological enthusiasms, Lasch continued to believe that social transformation and improved human character might somehow dia-

38. CL, "Freud and Women," 15; CL, "Sacrificing Freud," *New York Times Magazine,* 22 February 1976, 71, 72.

lectically emerge. A genuine collective elevation of human experience, he insisted, required change in social structures, not mere psychological therapy; yet changed social structures alone, as he had insisted in his essay on Ellul, were themselves not wholly adequate to the task. He ended one 1974 review by on the one hand hailing "the renunciation of messianic political visions" on the left as necessary, while on the other hand rejecting a complete dismissal of the ideal of cultural renewal: "The revolutionary movement, whatever its idiocies and absurdities, at least kept alive the idea of spiritual rebirth. This idea must not be allowed to fade."[39]

Lasch was clearly no friend of easy polarities, whether intellectual or political. His vision of the human prospect possessed a certain Aristotelian quality, a fundamental intuition that tension of all kinds was to be aimed for, and was in fact the best hope of discovering the way to health. Most immediately, though, it was the assumptions and aspirations of the Frankfurt School that continued to guide in a general way his appropriation of Marx and Freud. Their dedicated probing of the dialectic between economic structures and human character was reflected in Lasch's contention that "Any lasting improvements in the human condition . . . would have to come not from psychotherapy but from social action." Their unstinting insistence on cultural and political possibility beyond the present — indeed, their relentless damning of those who accepted, in Horkheimer and Adorno's piquant phrase, "the eternity of the now" — helped keep Lasch hoping for what he had tellingly called "spiritual rebirth," which would manifest itself in the transformation of capitalism into a more humane, life-generating political economy, a structural change that would somehow be enfolded within a profoundly renewed and reformed vision of human possibility and character. He continued to hold — continued to hope — that capitalism had reached a state of "historic obsolescence," that the "objective conditions" for revolution were now in place. The moment only required an understanding of why the "subjective conditions" necessary for revolution had not yet obtained. This quest for insight into the barriers to spiritual renewal he took as his task, even as he warned against the progressive fantasies that so seduced Americans.

39. CL to Robert Silvers, TL, 4 November 1978, 5:1; CL, "Learning from the Thirties," *Working Papers* 1:4 (Winter 1974), 47.

It was a tough and tense line to walk, even for the intellectually elastic, politically driven Christopher Lasch.[40]

The more he sought this pathway to renewal, the more he perceived post-sixties American culture to be fracturing into jagged pieces. In a lengthy 1970 letter to a correspondent seeking his perspective on the state of the historical profession, Lasch poignantly spoke of "the collapse of a common culture," which he described as "disastrous," and he underscored especially its epistemic fallout. Historians, he wrote, had once believed in the "unity of knowledge" and "objective historical truth," but such assumptions were now in near complete disrepute. The humanities had "abandoned any pretense of addressing themselves to objective reality," leaving their practitioners "demoralized" and "deprived . . . of any absolute standards of truth by which to measure the importance and meaning of their work" — not just for scholarship, but for the common life itself.[41]

Lasch professed to be unsure if "there are any ways out of these difficulties." It all reflected, he wrote (citing Norman Birnbaum's recent book of the same name), "the crisis of industrial society," a crisis with "roots in social life." Given its origins, he suggested that "a general attack on prevailing forms of social organization" might result in some sort of restored cultural unity, along with the return, presumably, of confidence in "objective reality," assuming that the realization of humane social conditions would correct the failing epistemic vision. With such a broad philosophic and political restoration, specialists from the various disciplines might once more begin to "relate their work to the work of other specialists." But questions loomed: How decisively could anyone pronounce on "meaning" within the epistemological framework of "objectivity"? Could the pursuit of objectivity ever lead to an objective morality of the sort Lasch seemed to imagine? Could "reason," in short, hold the world together?[42]

As Lasch's sense of fragmentation and disintegration increased, he, in desperate fashion, found himself fighting to maintain his hope

---

40. CL, "Sacrificing Freud," 70; *Dialectic of Enlightenment: Philosophical Fragments,* ed. Gunzelin Schmid Noerr, trans. Edmund Jephcott, Cultural Memory in the Present series, ed. Mieke Bal, Hent de Vries (Stanford: Stanford University Press, 2002), 20; CL, "Freud and Women," 16.

41. CL to "Mr. Kellman," TL, 8 January 1970, 2:20.

42. CL to "Mr. Kellman," TL, 8 January 1970, 2:20.

in broad social and political reconstruction. Thomas Cole describes him as slowly "becoming disillusioned with traditional Marxist explanations," and "beset by a feeling of loss, a world that had gone, sources of inspiration that were gone" — always there was "this yearning in him and his work," Cole underscores. His 1960s dream of fulfilling his political ideals in expansive fashion was turning slowly into the more narrow hope of merely salvaging them, as American liberalism continued its morally and politically eviscerating course. It was a time for minimalist, not maximalist, aspiration. "The development of political freedom," he wrote to a correspondent in 1973, "went hand in hand with the growth of a system of private enterprise that ravaged the land, eradicated the past, destroyed older traditions of communal life, and accentuated class conflict." "Liberalism," to be sure, had led to the "growth of individual freedom in the 19th century," but such freedom had gained a footing "at the expense of public traditions of culture and of the public, common life in general." What was a nation without these? Certainly not one he could believe in. "The growth of liberalism gave rise to problems that could no longer be solved within the framework of liberalism." As an ideology it had proven incapable of spawning a culture that was as decent and just as it had once hoped it might become.[43]

Perhaps most alarming of all to Lasch was the fact that as he was coming to a deeper perception of the nation's jagged fracturing, he found himself surrounded by friends, colleagues, and citizens who seemed to be blind to the catastrophe. When he warned of increasing fragmenting and decay, more and more, it seemed, they heralded rising moral integrity and health. His sense of crisis was met by their air of celebration. This failure *to see* only confirmed his foreboding about the profoundly corrosive effects of the modern circumstance. Americans were losing the ability to preserve in the most basic of matters the hard-won skills of discernment and judgment.

Tellingly, he thought, academics and intellectuals, far from rising above the progressive delusions of the broader public, were simply dressing them up in a more sophisticated guise. Nowhere did he find this mimicry more evident than in the widespread acceptance of "modernization theory" among American scholars in the sixties and

43. Interview with Thomas R. Cole, 3 August 2007; CL to Jerry Walker, TL, 12 January 1973, 3:15.

seventies. Modernization theorists, he wrote in the *New York Review* in 1975, tended to think of liberal capitalist society as the end at which all nations and peoples were bound to arrive. By these lights, personal freedom, constitutional democracy, and scientific advance were triumphantly leading the world to economic equality and the cessation of conflict among all nations, classes, and races. While employing modernization theory to christen "Western 'postindustrial' society as the prototype of the future," they dismissed "the turmoil and pain of the present as a mere incident of 'transition.'" Lasch believed they could not be more wrong.[44]

Historians were particularly guilty of this wrongheaded thinking. Rather than examining the past with rigorous and imaginative inquiry that might illumine the troubled present, historians were habitually allowing faith in "modernization" to skew their vision. Confident that they were riding the crest of the world-historical progressive wave, they wrote histories that mainly served to sustain the broad, uncritical acceptance of current political and cultural conditions. For Lasch this civic and scholarly failure replicated the political failure of the optimistic, enlightened liberals he had scored fifteen years earlier in *American Liberals and the Russian Revolution* and the cold war intellectuals he had scorned throughout the sixties. Their mental habits and features gave them away as members of the same corrupted lineage, starry-eyed believers in America's progressive destiny who couldn't keep their eyes on the actual historical reality — to their own peril and everyone else's.

He held up Edward Shorter's *The Making of the Modern Family,* blurbed by the cutting-edge colonialist historian John Demos as "Truly a *tour de force* of scholarship, of organization and of writing," as a prime example. In attempting to explain the erosion of the premodern social forms that had given marriage and family their distinctive power and shape in the West, Shorter, Lasch argued, "confuses the disintegration of communal restraints with freedom and privacy, the collapse of parental control with the 'exploration of per-

44. CL, "The Family and History," *New York Review of Books,* 13 November 1975, 37. Lasch emphasized, quoting political scientist Samuel P. Huntington's classic 1965 definition, that these theorists saw modernization as a "'multifaceted process involving changes in all areas of human thought and activity' — a 'systemic' process that 'reappears,' moreover, 'in virtually all modernizing societies on all continents of the world, regardless of race, color, or creed,'" 36.

sonality.'" Shorter had failed to note that as the modernizing jugger-naut was paving the way for a brighter tomorrow, the working class, on Lasch's reading of the evidence, had "persistently sought to coun-ter the demoralizing effects of industrialism by reviving the very tradi-tions of communal action which, according to Shorter, it eagerly repu-diated in the interest of sexual freedom." In spinning his fairy tale of progressive triumph, Shorter had, in sum, merely projected the "en-lightened prejudices of our own time" — the "therapeutic conception of the world in its current form, the ideology of sexual liberation, per-sonal liberation, and psychic health" — back into the nineteenth cen-tury, while imagining those in the past as "having seldom attained our heights of feeling."[45]

All of this was conclusive evidence, Lasch contended, that mod-ernization theory was simply the latest expression of the myth of prog-ress, serving to obfuscate and abet the present state of cultural and so-cial disrepair rather than address it. Far from being a "tour de force," Shorter's study was itself testament of the poverty of intellectual life in the midst of a massive, truly world-historical wrong turn. In a slash-ing 1978 *New Republic* review of Lawrence Stone's book *The Family, Sex and Marriage in England, 1500-1800,* he extended this critique by countering Stone's "unilineal theory of history" with a "dialectical theory." Rather than a straight line of progress, modern history, he proposed, had paradoxically brought back the "return of the re-pressed, a new war of all against all." The emancipated individual, the glory of modernization theory, was in reality the victim of "new forms of slavery inherent in sexual liberation," since, without local commu-nities and kinship networks to superintend domestic life, children of the modern era "belong not to their parents but to the state," and thus have no possibility of confronting their libidinal instincts in a way that might lead to health rather than destruction. He attacked the lib-eral myth of individual emancipation, managing a nod to de Sade, Huxley, and Foucault at once: "sexual freedom under capitalism ends not in personal autonomy but in the universal obligation to enjoy and be enjoyed." Progress was the illusion; servitude — a deep, sinister, psychic servitude — was the reality.[46]

45. CL, "What the Doctor Ordered," 50, 53, 52, 53.
46. CL, review of *The Family, Sex and Marriage in England, 1500-1800* (New York: Harper and Row, 1978), in *New Republic,* July 8 & 15, 1978, 36, 37.

Lasch propounded another vision of freedom, a freedom rooted not in personal liberation but in the dignity of privacy, kinship ties, moral order, and civic duty. On this matter he was far closer to the Christian humanist vision of a Jacques Ellul than to the secular liberationist vision of a Herbert Marcuse. Seen from this vantage, sexual life, to be free, must be guided and protected by a community that understands the inalienable connections between sexual mores and the health of the community, especially its families. Absent such conditions in the modern world, sex had become just one more means for the control of the populace by powers ready to exploit it for their own ends. Favorably reviewing Foucault's *The History of Sexuality, Volume One: An Introduction* in *Psychology Today,* Lasch stressed that, per Foucault, "The superstate has not only survived the 'sexual revolution,' it has enlisted the sexual revolution in its own campaign, undertaken on the whole with the best intentions, to eradicate the last remnants of secrecy and private life." Lasch's sights were set on another way of conceiving human freedom, one that was more tribal, more centered on intergenerational continuity, coherence, and stability. These elements, rapidly receding in his own time, must be at the heart of any "new culture" worth working toward; it was only under these conditions that any sort of human flourishing could take place.[47]

Since the early 1960s Lasch had been looking toward the left for a movement that might embody these ideals. Gradually even this hope began to fade. In a 1973 symposium in *Commentary,* he remarked that the left seemed to have "nothing to offer except an extension of meaningless personal freedom Americans already enjoy," the mere "freedom to do your own thing." Two years later, after lecturing around the country, he wearily remarked to Gerald Graff that he had found "a widespread determination to believe that experimentation with alternative lifestyles, the woman's movement, etc., are going to make everything all right again." As his vision of fragmentation enlarged, his sense of alienation from the left, and from the professional classes as a whole, was mounting. And if he had misgivings about the left, it was responding in kind, as he would come to see all too clearly.[48]

---

47. CL, "Talking about Sex: The History of a Compulsion," *Psychology Today,* November 1978, 158.

48. CL, contribution to a symposium on "Nixon, the Great Society, and the

*　　*　　*

As the 1970s wore on Lasch's Marxist assumptions joined with his own Midwestern progressive heritage to predispose him to look toward the working classes — that part of the populace least implicated in the advance of the modern world — for at least a modicum of political hope, if not actual intellectual companionship. If in the mid-sixties Lasch viewed the student radicals as a possible portent of political transformation, by the mid-seventies he was turning a similarly critical-yet-hopeful eye toward what was being tagged "the new populism." In fact, in a retrospective essay published in 1981 he would credit the new left's "populist strategy" for its early success, and charge that its failure was rooted precisely in its turn away from this populist approach and toward a program more "revolutionary" and less oriented toward a "broad movement for social change." His sympathy for "the people" flowed as easily from his pen in the 1970s as it had from his father's thirty years before. "Having no control over his work, over governmental policy, over the press and television, or over the education of his children, the citizen feels himself manipulated to suit the interests of the rich and powerful," he wrote in 1972 in a review of *A Populist Manifesto: The Making of a New Majority* by Jack Newfield and Jeff Greenfield. On the broad spectrum of post-sixties politics he saw the "new populism" as "one of several candidates hoping to inherit what remains of the new left," and of those candidates it was clearly the one to which he was most attracted; as a "revolt against economic injustice" the new populism was for many a "more appropriate answer to the crisis in American society than the radicalism of the sixties." Although he faulted the new populism for, among other things, its inadequate understanding of the connections between class, society, and culture, he warned the left not to arrogantly dismiss it, as it had other such political movements. "Wisdom is not the monopoly of any political position," he reminded his readers; the left should take seriously the new populism "if only because it is closer to the country's mood than the new left ever was."[49]

Future of Social Policy," *Commentary,* May 1973, 45; CL to Gerald Graff, TL, 19 May 1975, 4:1.

49. CL, "The Conservative 'Backlash' and the Cultural Civil War," in *Neo-Conservatism: Social and Religious Phenomenon,* ed. Gregory Baum (New York: Seabury Press, 1981), 8; CL, "Populism, Socialism, and McGovernism," *New York Review of Books,* 20 July 1972, 15, 20.

The power structures of liberal capitalism had long prevented populism from having an adequate voice in the American party system, and in a 1973 essay on the Jeffersonian lineage — one of his few overtly historical pieces of the decade — Lasch described the new populism as a modern embodiment of that venerable but embattled tradition. Its nineteenth-century forebears had held a "radical democratic interpretation" of property rights, what Lasch dubbed "radical agrarianism" (indeed, he took care to point out that "the nineteenth century often used 'agrarianism' and 'socialism' as synonymous terms"). The People's Party of the 1890s, along with turn-of-the-century working-class radical organizations, had flickered on the American political scene as earlier embodiments of the Jeffersonian tradition, but these had died out when twentieth-century Democratic presidents chose to center their energies on building the welfare state rather than altering economic structures. Such liberals, Lasch charged, had repudiated Jefferson's "ideals of limited central power" and instead devoted themselves to building a "global empire."[50]

Things had not improved over the course of the century for Jefferson's progeny. As Lasch noted in the summer of 1972, Democratic party candidate George McGovern had chosen to center his presidential campaign on contentious and problematic policies like school busing and abortion, thus giving the lie to the populist overtures he had been making. McGovern, Lasch wrote as the election neared, was sure to alienate working-class voters over cultural issues rather than unify them around collective economic concerns. McGovern was, in the end, a "liberal" and not a populist, never having "been able to understand or identify himself imaginatively with the distress of the working class communities," especially their concern over the deterioration of both their livelihoods and their neighborhoods.[51]

Lasch's growing conviction of the significance of the new populism emerged again in a 1973 *Commentary* symposium, where he guardedly mapped out the American landscape in the martial terms that would come to dominate political commentary in the last quarter of the century. "The ethnic backlash against the blacks," he wrote, "is

---

50. CL, "The Jeffersonian Legacy," in *Thomas Jefferson: The Man, His World, His Influence,* ed. Lally Weymouth (New York: G.P. Putnam's Sons, 1973), 242, 243, 245.

51. CL, "The Election II," *New York Review of Books,* 2 November 1972, 6.

only one aspect of what has been called, perhaps too sweepingly, a cultural civil war." He perceived the "conservative" side of the divide, though, to be animated not simply by racist backlash, as liberals tended to tell themselves, but by a diffuse opposition to cultural radicalism, what he termed a "generalized, ill-defined revulsion against 'permissiveness.'" He sympathetically suggested that "a vague sense that things are out of joint, that values and standards are collapsing, that respect for authority has declined, troubles people at almost every social level." At this historic juncture especially, the sentiments of "the people" needed to be not dismissed but respected, and perhaps followed.[52]

At a conference co-sponsored by *Change* ("The Magazine of Higher Learning") and the Rockefeller Foundation in late 1974, Lasch delivered a paper that captured succinctly and determinedly his evolving response to fracturing post-sixties America. Along with Harvard physicist Gerald Holton and Amherst historian Leo Marx, he was to address "The Future of the Humanities"; afterward these three, along with twenty other academics and writers of various sorts, from Timothy Healy and John Knowles to Roger Rosenblatt and Doris Kearns, would join together for a follow-up symposium. In his paper Lasch etched out a complex and novel thesis on the connections between cultural fragmentation, education, and the current conflict between the professional and working classes. The picture of twentieth-century American history he presented would remain foundational for him for the rest of his life.

Lasch titled his address "The Democratization of Culture: A Reappraisal," and it certainly was all of that and more. Reiterating the argument regarding education he had made in his *New York Review* essay on Christopher Jencks's *Inequality* the previous year, he noted that since "universal education" had replaced traditional means of education it had required a "heavy emphasis on the nonacademic side of the curriculum," which had in turn led to the increasing domination of the state in everyday life. But now Lasch focused his argument not on the powers of the state but rather on those whom he believed the state was attempting to control. He described "the emergence of two 'cultures,'" one "based on technique, critical self-awareness, and the

---

52. CL, contribution to a symposium on "Nixon, the Great Society, and the Future of Social Policy," 45.

refinement of exact knowledge, the other based on stubborn popular resistance to the spread of modernity." It was, he contended, the historical unfolding of these dueling cultures that had incited the "cultural civil war raging around us," with "universal education" (which since the middle of the nineteenth century had served as an "initiation into modern culture") a burgeoning battlefront. The humanities he singled out in particular as guilty of thrusting the "cultural modernism" of the educated classes upon the masses, a worldview and way of life that had only quickened the dissolution of "provincial, familial, and ethnic loyalties." "The ideal product of such education," Lasch charged with palpable repugnance, was "a person with no roots, without prejudices," "tolerant," and "able to move about freely." These were no virtues, he made clear. In fact, he went so far as to conclude his address with the remarkable contention that the "plebeian revolt against modernity," with its suspicion of "personal liberation and technique," represented a way of life superior to what modern, professional classes were preferring. It was, in the end, with the least modern that any hope for the modern world resided.[53]

Norman Birnbaum, the moderator of the symposium that followed, admitted to being "genuinely bewildered" by Lasch's contention that "a large segment of American society is more reality-oriented than our culturally saturated elitists." Noting that Lasch had been "careful not to develop" this notion with particular political or social prescriptions, he now gave him the opportunity to do so. "I didn't come to any firm conclusions," replied Lasch evasively, "because I can't come to any firm conclusions, and I think I would rather distrust any that were stated at the present moment, which seems to me so confusing and puzzling." There were "so few historical precedents," he remarked, leaving him "pretty baffled about the direction that we are going in."[54]

Despite his coy responses Lasch struck a chord with Charles Muscatine, who admitted that he had found Lasch's paper "terrifying," exposing for him a "new type of obscurantism, based precisely on the formalization, analysis, articulation, and all the other things

53. CL, "The Democratization of Culture: A Reappraisal," *Change* 7:6 (Summer 1975), 15, 19, 20, 15, 20, 22.
54. CL, et. al., "A Symposium: The State of the Humanities," *Change* 7:6 (Summer 1975), 42, 43.

we thought were necessary to rational life." Lasch's perspective also resonated with Kearns, who agreed that "liberal education" was "creating a populace hungry for information as opposed to truth," "mere consumers of culture" who were "mobile and rootless." Given the extent of these developments, she wondered how it could be changed. Lasch, less evasively this time, agreed that the possibilities for change indeed seemed "limited," but he proposed that at least teachers could cease preoccupying themselves with trying to "deparochialize people" in response to what he deemed a "nonexistent problem." The restless, self-aggrandizing "modernist sensibility," so characteristic of their students, needed to be seen as the enemy, not the ideal.[55]

To the extent that the ideal he was erecting had ever been realized in the West, it had occurred in a more deeply rooted, local way of life, one that invariably had been bound up in and constituted by religious structures, beliefs, and practice. But Lasch grounded his early advocacy of what in the 1980s he would call the populist tradition not in a religious framework but rather in the functionalist, secular language of his own class — the side of the "culture war" he was, of course, attacking. Concepts like "rootlessness" and "permissiveness," not to say "morality" and "religion," provided him only vague behavioral direction and little moral specificity, certainly not enough to launch a vision of a fully developed alternative to the cultural modernism against which he was inveighing. Lasch was facing the ironic predicament of trying to criticize the world the professional classes had made from within its own linguistic constraints — with the language that had made that world possible, that had effectively distanced it from earlier, religion-centered cultures. As the decade moved along it became increasingly evident that his own critique of the culture of modern America existed in uneasy tension with the "tradition of critical rationalism" he had long touted, and that had given him the functionalist, social-scientific vocabulary that was making it difficult for him to articulate his concern for "morality" in convincing ways. His enlarging perspective on modern history, in sum, seemed to be rooted in ideals and perceptions that predated the rationalist tradition that was his more immediate inheritance. Trying to sort through and take the measure of his own assumptions, inclinations, and attitudes proved difficult and painful — but the arduous nature of his efforts yielded a brilliant, poignant record of in-

55. CL, et. al., "A Symposium: The State of the Humanities," 59, 60.

ward wrestling and critical encounter. And that effort, in the end, would lead him to a measure of fame, even celebrity.

When in his pivotal 1976 *New York Review* essay "The Narcissist Society" Lasch cited what he perceived to be key aspects of the current mood of "desperation," he wrote in a pained manner, as one watching the disintegration of his very way of life. What most disturbed him was the fact that the left seemed not to care about this destruction, much less have anything to offer in the midst of the crisis. Having habitually evaded "the terrors of the inner life," the left, he thought, now faced a daunting struggle for its own credibility and viability. The way he framed the cultural crisis in this essay pointed up with particular clarity his own deepest cultural affinities:

> The problem for the Left — the problem for everyone — is to understand why personal growth and development have become so hard to accomplish; why the fear of growing up and aging — of "becoming a man" — haunts our society; why personal relations have become so brittle and precarious; and why the "inner life" no longer offers any refuge from the dangers around us.

This was a pathos thinly veiled by his social-scientific vocabulary. From the preoccupation with "personal growth" and "the inner life" to the gendered reference to maturity, Lasch revealed himself to be bound up in an acute and bitter reaction against the ongoing, inexorable drift of Western civilization away from its older moorings, to which he was more attached than he perhaps understood. "Now the dissolution of a unitary system of common belief, accompanied, as it must be, by a certain disorganization of personality, may have run its course": this was the way the sociologist Philip Rieff had described this civilizational moment ten years earlier, and Lasch was registering and responding to it in a manner acutely personal and highly analytical at once. But his intellectual commitments left him in the unenviable position of trying to explain and defend this attachment by using the tool chest of what in many respects had long lived as the declared enemy of the (old) West: his own tradition of critical rationalism, which by now was forcing scare quotes around words — "freedom," "morality," and dozens more — that reflected his truest concerns.[56]

56. CL, "The Narcissist Society," *New York Review of Books,* 30 September

He tried in the "Narcissist Society" essay to root "the devastation of personal life" in structural conditions, underscoring the "social origins of the suffering that is painfully but falsely experienced as purely personal and private." Yet he seemed to struggle satisfactorily to understand the "emptiness and isolation" of his own experience in purely Marxian and Freudian terms. Indeed, he was perhaps already sensing that Marx, Freud, and friends were themselves implicated in this general malaise, as he himself had suggested in his *Change* symposium address, when he had drawn a line from the modernist thinkers to the rootlessness of contemporary culture.[57]

Good politics demanded a certain kind of person: this he knew. He also knew that what was happening around him was destroying that kind of person. As he put it in a 1975 exchange with Norman Birnbaum published in *Partisan Review,* he was convinced that the "personality" that had been developed in the context of Western history, for all of its "pathological side effects," was "irreplaceable." Birnbaum pointed out that this contention put Lasch "clearly in the camp of the cultural traditionalists." Lasch did not dissent. As he examined what was to him a devastated landscape in the mid-seventies, he found himself siding with "the people," disdaining the modernizing elites, and abhorring the direction American society as a whole was taking. But he had little idea what could be done about it in any concrete manner. Where did one go for the "spiritual transformation" of which Ellul spoke? And how could such deeply entrenched social structures be changed without it?[58]

1976, 8; Philip Rieff, *The Triumph of the Therapeutic: Uses of Faith after Freud* (New York: Harper & Row, 1966; reprint edition, Wilmington, Del.: ISI Books, 2006), 2.

57. CL, "The Narcissist Society," 10, 13.

58. CL and Norman Birnbaum, "America Today: An Exchange," *Partisan Review* 42:3 (1975), 365; CL, WN, 274.

CHAPTER EIGHT

Different Roads

I'm now satisfied . . . that I've written something that is guaranteed to bore and possibly offend almost every class of reader. The initial response to fragments that I've shown to various readers is highly encouraging. I've been told that reading too much sociology has corrupted my style . . . that my own opinions about sex are "Victorian," and that in any case my approach is too "monographic" to be of any interest.

Christopher Lasch to Gerald Graff, 7 August 1975[1]

As Lasch was beginning (yet another) attack on the history of the family in 1975, competing for his attention was the grisly spectacle of Watergate. That spring he exclaimed to his parents with a certain glee, "I can't get over the appropriateness of it all, how absolutely characteristic from start to finish." It was a perfect ending: Richard Nixon had long been the eminently laughable symbol of the Republican party in the Lasch family, and if the Watergate fiasco caught the Lasches off guard, it certainly did not surprise them. Back in 1968, as the presidential election was approaching, Zora was chagrined to note that the Soviets, having just put down a revolution in Czechoslovakia, were "doing silly things," which she feared would only increase public sentiment for Nixon. "And I doubt not that Ike will contribute his bit by dying at an appropriate moment with blessings on his boy Dick," she drily remarked. Lasch carried the family

---

1. CL to Gerald Graff, TLS, 7 August 1975, 4:1.

scorn with him as he participated in conferences on Watergate in New York and California.[2]

Lasch's distaste did not end with Nixon and Watergate, though. The scandal, he thought, revealed far-reaching dysfunctions not only in Nixon's psyche and party but in American society itself. Reviewing J. Anthony Lukas's *Nightmare: The Underside of the Nixon Years* in 1975, Lasch seemed most dismayed that, in just a matter of months, the notion that Watergate "constituted no more than a regrettable interlude in American politics — a minor spasm from which the body politic has fully recovered" had already become an "article of national faith." The old, reliable progressive self-image had recovered all too quickly. True, Nixon and his deputies had managed a singularly appalling "juxtaposition of old-style graft and corruption with the techniques of a sophisticated police state." But to exaggerate the uniqueness of "the bizarre combination of crimes, peccadilloes, usurpations, felonies, abuses of power, crackpot capers and violations of constitutional law" that Watergate featured was to risk missing something of far greater consequence, a major development in American political history: "the emergence of the Presidency as a fourth branch of Government, wielding vast powers, conducting much of its business in secret, justifying illegal actions in the name of 'national security' and accountable, in its own eyes, to no one but itself." The White House's handling of the situation was powerful testament to the fact that in American public life the "very distinction between truth and falsehood has receded into obscurity," undermining the very possibility of active, meaningful citizenship.[3]

The Watergate crisis and all that it meant only intensified Lasch's mounting sense of unease and disillusionment as the sixties receded. Having been awarded both the Ford and Guggenheim Foundation Fellowships for the 1974-75 academic year, he began in the fall of 1974 to work in earnest on the project that had been focused at varying times since the early 1960s on women, marriage, and the family. By 1974 he had finally settled on the family as his subject, and in Octo-

2. CL to ZL & RL, TLS, 28 May 1973, 0:39; ZL to CL and NL, TL, 21 August 1968, 2:11; CL to ZL & RL, TLS, 3 November 1973, 0:39.

3. CL, "Nightmare," *New York Times Book Review*, 25 January 1976, 23, 24. For a more full statement of his thinking about the presidency in the aftermath of Watergate, see his "Paranoid Presidency," *Center Magazine* (March/April 1974), 23-32.

ber he reported to his parents that he had "a much clearer idea of where I'm going and what remains to be done." By early November he told them he had written fifty-six pages — "which isn't much for fourteen years work but is a lot more than I had a few weeks ago." He later remembered it as the "most difficult of all the books that I ever wrote." He had gone "through draft after draft," with much uncertainty along the way. But by the end of 1974 he in a letter to a friend would sketch the argument that would drive the book: the modern family, he was arguing, "far from being isolated," is "well integrated into the surrounding structures; or better, it is invaded by them."[4]

By May 1975 Lasch had finished the first draft of the manuscript that would be published in the fall of 1977 as *Haven in a Heartless World: The Family Besieged.* The book had long been under contract with Knopf, but they were anticipating something along the lines of the contracted title, "American Womanhood." Explaining this shift, Lasch told his editor Ashbel Green that "the burning question of women and women's liberation" was best explored "in connection with the family"; he had decided, accordingly, to launch his history of the family with (what he would later term) a "theoretical introduction" to the topic. The book had taken the form of a "critique of sociology," he wrote to Green, because he was convinced that "progress in historical understanding of marriage and the family could take place only if historians clarified their underlying theoretical assumptions," which were usually grounded, whether knowingly or not, in sociology. His book was not "a contribution to intellectual history" but rather "a contribution to social theory in its own right: one that criticizes other theories in order to develop its own." All of this represented Lasch's most strenuous attempt yet to achieve that which since the 1960s he had been insisting was imperative: the doing of history from within the most sophisticated and rigorous theoretical framework possible — the only way by which "the facts" of the past had a chance of speaking with force to the contemporary situation.[5]

4. CL to RL & ZL, TL, 8 October 1974, 3:18; CL to RL & ZL, TL, 4 November 1974, 3:18; Richard Wightman Fox, "An Interview with Christopher Lasch," *Intellectual History Newsletter* 16 (1994), 11; CL to Erik Wensberg, TLS, 26 December 1974, 3:19.

5. CL to Ashbel Green, TL, 19 March 1975, 4:1; Fox, "Interview," 11. Lasch confessed the heterodoxy of this approach as he was writing in the fall of 1974: "This procedure is backward, of course; I should pretend to ground my observa-

Green was not exactly taken. Lasch's 1973 collection of essays *The World of Nations* had not done well for Knopf — they were by 1975 reducing their warehouse stock — and Green was hesitant to back this next project. Lasch had admitted to Green that he feared he had "another non-seller" in the works; to Graff he was more frank: "I'm now satisfied," he wrote in August of 1975, "that I've written something that is guaranteed to bore and possibly offend almost every class of reader." He had shown parts of it to various people, and the results were "highly encouraging. I've been told that reading too much sociology has corrupted my style . . . that my own opinions about sex are 'Victorian,' and that in any case my approach is too 'monographic' to be of any interest."[6]

These in fact became the arguments Knopf marshaled against the *Haven* manuscript when they rejected it. Lasch's hopes plummeted; he later told Graff that he had begun to accept the probability that the book would prove unattractive to trade houses, leaving him at the mercy of the university presses and their cohort of academic reviewers — "practically," he thought, "a guarantee of non-publication;" especially since some of the reviewers would likely be sociologists with reservations about a historian barreling onto their turf. But in October 1976 he received word that Basic Books had accepted the manuscript, news he greeted with "great relief." Soon after he told Graff he was "thankful to be rid of the family for a while," and that he had already "started a little book tentatively titled *Life without a Future: Cultural and Personal Life in an Age of Diminishing Expectations.*"[7]

Haven in a Heartless World, released in late 1977, turned Lasch's life into a swirl of publicity and argument that would not begin to slow for three years, after which his place in American intellectual life would be fundamentally altered. By 1980, rather than standing

tions about the contemporary family in a profound study of the past, instead of admitting that the study of the past reflects one's assumptions about the present. This secret has been out for a while now, however, and should no longer shock anyone." CL to Erik Wensberg, TLS, 26 December 1974, 3:19.

6. CL to Ashbel Green, TL, 18 October 1975, 4:1; CL to Gerald Graff, TL, 7 August 1975, 4:1. At the end of 1973, its year of publication, Knopf editor Harold Strauss reported to Lasch that as of December 1 they had sold 2050 copies of *World of Nations;* a paperback was due out in March of 1974. Harold Strauss to CL, TLS, 7 December 1973, 3:15.

7. CL to Gerald Graff, TL, 14 October 1976, 4:6.

stridently in the vanguard of left intellectuals, he would be standing virtually alone — a radical looking in bewilderment for his erstwhile friends on the left and shunning many on the right who were beginning to warm up to him. "It was only when I saw how [*Haven*] was received by the Left that I realized how far we had traveled down different roads," he later recalled. He was becoming, somewhat unwittingly, a central, singular figure in the emergence of what came to be known in the last quarter of the century as "cultural conservatism." More widely known than ever, he would also become more lonely than ever.[8]

In retrospect, the left's hostile reception of Lasch's book should not have been surprising, especially since Lasch's 1975 three-part *New York Review* series on the family ended up being incorporated in varying forms into the book, along with material from several previously published essays. Lasch himself was aware that a chasm had widened between him and at least one large segment of the left, those he dubbed "cultural radicals." But the extent of the divide only seemed to register when in a careful but slashing style he laid out his views in a book densely scholarly and deeply political at once. No amount of Freud and Marx, however nuanced, could cover the fact that he was now defending a way of life that American radicals since the age of his own "New Radicals" had in the main been militating against. What did one really make of the sixties? Reading *Haven* was a good way to find out.[9]

The questions that drove his argument had personal dimensions obvious and deep, and he did not hesitate to assume that scholarship should be used to address them. The fact that most contemporary scholarship on the family explained "everything except the things we most want to know" was precisely what drove his own inquiry. His tone throughout was sermonic and argumentative, his language public and objective, his words sharp and slicing. "Why has family life be-

8. Casey Blake and Christopher Phelps, "History as Social Criticism: Conversations with Christopher Lasch," *Journal of American History* 80:4 (March 1994), 1328.

9. The three-part series included "The Family and History," *New York Review of Books,* 13 November 1975, 32-38; "The Emotions of Family Life," *New York Review of Books,* 27 November 1975, 37-42; and "What the Doctor Ordered," *New York Review of Books,* 11 December 1975, 50-54. See also "Freud and Women," *New York Review of Books,* 3 October 1974, 12-17.

come so painful, marriage so fragile, relations between parents and children so full of hostility and recrimination?" he asked at the outset. His answer came in the form of a thesis as simple as its implications were alarming: democratic society depends on tightly knit families that consist of a husband, wife, children, and a larger kinship network. Under the aegis of corporate capitalism this basic structuring of family life, essential for democratic civilization, has collapsed. It was no wonder that by the seventies Americans were experiencing a general sense of confusion, not to say trauma, in both their personal and political lives. What else could such severe familial disintegration be expected to yield?[10]

Lasch was clearly among those feeling this trauma. His own pain was palpable on nearly every page of the book, sometimes as outrage, often as bitterness, but always as an enveloping sensitivity to a threatened domestic ideal. He described a "savage and warlike society," filled with "storms" that "threaten." "The sense of man's isolation and loneliness" he himself sensed acutely, and at one level he traced it back to "the collapse of public order and the loss of religion." But these forms of demise he saw as themselves the result of "the waning of parental authority and guidance," which had left the country with no place to go but down.[11]

He turned to Freud to construct his argument on the necessity of the traditional makeup of the family and continued to echo voices in the Frankfurt School (with significant quarrelling) on his thinking about the historical effects of capitalism on personality, family, and culture in the West. But if the underpinnings of his argument in this book (as in all of his books) were self-consciously dependent on the ideas of big thinkers, his argument itself was sourced in a distinctive vision, a vision that had been steadfast now for many years. Indeed, it was the shape and articulation of this fundamental vision that lay at the heart of Lasch's originality, which emerged as he placed his intensely critical, often revisionist appropriation of others' ideas in service to his own expressly moral and political intent. What Raymond Williams said of D. H. Lawrence in *Culture and Society* can also be said of Lasch: "Lawrence's position, in the question of social values, is an amalgam of original and derived ideas. Yet, because of the intensity

10. CL, HHW, xvi.
11. CL, HHW, xiii, 178.

with which he took up and worked over what he had learned from others, this is, in practice, very difficult to sort out." Lasch's work could not be read as "objective" scholarship, however scholarly his framework. "My subject is the intersection of theory, ideology, and social practice," he wrote in *Haven*'s introduction. But he wrote as an intellectual, with the soul of a citizen, the mind of a scholar, and the eyes of a judge, aiming for the kind of discriminating, learned observation that might offer a way beyond the present. If one of the most startling elements of *Haven* was the remarkably intricate, even tedious level of scholarly disputation in which Lasch engaged, it was a reflection of the high stakes he saw in the ongoing battle to define the true condition of contemporary America.[12]

For Lasch, such an understanding had to begin with the home. Why? "Without struggling with the ambivalent emotions aroused by the union of love and discipline in his parents, the child never masters his inner rage or his fear of authority," he declared, making the child likely to develop "personality traits more compatible with totalitarian regimes than with democracy." The family, for Lasch, provided what no surrogate could: the natal, biological locus of the "divided self," which irrationally "insists on its own wholeness" and so inclines humans toward forms of destruction both passive and active, with inescapable political effects. But the family also provided the best means of taming these impulses and turning them toward the public good. "The union of love and discipline in the same persons, mother and father, creates a highly charged environment in which the child learns lessons he will never get over — not necessarily the explicit lessons his parents wish him to master," Lasch explained. The politically

12. Raymond Williams, *Culture and Society, 1780-1950* (Garden City, N.Y.: Anchor Books, 1960, originally published in England, 1958), 213; CL, HHW, xiv. It was the creative, tense dynamic between Lasch's influences and his own political and cultural vision that his Harvard mentor Donald Meyer noted when several years after Lasch's death he described Lasch's use of Freud as "always opportunistic" (see Donald B. Meyer, "Spinning Wheels," *Intellectual History Newsletter* 21 [1999], 79). Regarding the Frankfurt School, Lasch covertly acknowledged his debt even as he criticized *The Authoritarian Personality,* for instance, for failing to establish its premise: that "authoritarian personalities are rooted in authoritarian family structures." Lasch's conclusion, following what Frankfurt School philosopher Max Horkheimer had written elsewhere, was that "'authoritarian types suffer less from a strong family than from a lack of family,'" 92. For his most extended discussion of the Frankfurt School, see 85-96.

imperative "reproduction of culture" requires a home, not a school; it was here that, with manifest pain and struggle, parents could form citizens capable of self-government and mutual endeavor. Mere "formal instruction and discipline," the liberals' enduring hope, were not enough to form the kind of human being democracy required.[13]

With the emergence of the modern, capital-created world had come the gradual but fundamental disruption of the old world of familial authority. If in the face of a rapidly industrializing nation Americans had in the nineteenth century retreated to the home in refuge from the morally vacuous, ever-enlarging market, by the twentieth century the market had so penetrated the home that it had become little more than a source of shelter and vestigial emotional warmth — a refuge no more. "The development of capitalism and the rise of the state," Lasch intoned, "reverberate in the individual's inner being," wreaking "spiritual damage." By removing work from the home — first the father's work, then the work of the mother and children in maintaining the home — the primal experience of family had been eroded, yielding woeful results in all aspects of American life, now given over almost completely to "the machinery of organized domination." Parents were no longer parenting; children, in turn, were being manipulated by institutions and influences they had neither the strength nor the acuity to resist. Far from guiding them through childhood into adulthood, these surrogates were presiding over mass psychological regression and cultural destruction, with overweening dominance emerging more powerfully than ever as the engine of historical change. The state was now manipulating malleable, fear-driven individuals who had never attained the psychic maturity to overcome their self-destructiveness and take part in the building of a good society.[14]

The basic contours of this argument about the family and modern society Lasch had been formulating — absent the dense Freudian thicket — for many years. As far back as 1961, just out of Columbia, he had mused to William R. Taylor that "the progressivism movement

13. CL, HHW, 123, 66, 3, 4. The comment on "totalitarian regimes" is in Lasch's "Preface to the Paperback Edition," published by Basic Books in 1979; see p. xiv.

14. CL, HHW, 4, 168. Lasch summarized his point of view: "Instead of liberating the individual from external coercion, the decay of family life subjects him to new forms of domination, while at the same time weakening his ability to resist them," HHW, 91.

can be explained as a stage in the taking over by the state of functions previously exercised by the family; which would explain why the progressives' favorite metaphor for society was precisely the family itself." He now presented his case in carefully honed neo-Marxist form: the professional classes, under the aegis of the corporate state, had entered the home with all of the authority of the modern world itself, armed with glistening new ideas and roseate visions for the home and other spheres that had formerly been guided by the "ignorant" and "repressed."[15]

Nothing was more striking in Lasch's argument than the scorn with which he treated the members of the "helping professions," the university-trained professionals who for him amounted to practitioners of a new enlightened form of priestcraft:

> With the rise of the "helping professions" in the first three decades of the twentieth century, society in the guise of a "nurturing mother" invaded the family . . . and took over many of its functions. The diffusion of the new ideology had the effect of a self-fulfilling prophecy. By persuading the housewife, and finally even her husband as well, to rely on outside technology and the advice of outside experts, the apparatus of mass tuition — the successor to the church in a secularized society — undermined the family's capacity to provide for itself, and thereby justified the continuing expansion of health, education, and welfare services.

Expounding the new pieties — "the new gospel of relativism, tolerance, personal growth, and psychic maturity," all rooted, ironically, in "the unmediated authority of the fact" — these professionals only ended up serving the ends of the dominant political-economic powers, who themselves had a huge stake in the "liberation" of the family. The bourgeois family, centered on communal authority, fidelity, and thrift, actually turned out in Lasch's argument to be "the last stronghold of precapitalist modes of thought and feeling," the great, unsurpassable seedbed of political transformation. While to be sure the bourgeois family had invariably "passed along the dominant values" of a given society, it had also "unavoidably provided the child with a glimpse of a world that transcended them, crystallized in the

15. CL to William R. Taylor, TL, 26 December 1961, 7d:7.

rich imagery of maternal love." Its demise would lead inevitably to "the decline of transcendent ideals," and a resultant inability to perceive a reality beyond the capitalist, consumerist present. Put simply, at its healthiest the traditional western family had made possible that realm of experience which most clearly showed liberal capitalism to be, both in its practices and in the culture it spawned, the enemy of the good.[16]

"Liberationist ideologies . . . often support pseudo-liberations," Lasch noted bitingly, and Americans as he presented them certainly were not free. Slowly ceasing to know themselves as citizens, they had become instead "full-fledged consumers, perpetually restless and dissatisfied," plagued by the psychological and political disorders such a way of life helped to advance. With the demise of the family, the great conserver of "separatist religious traditions, alien languages and dialects, local lore, and other traditions that retarded the growth of the political community and the nation state," moderns had become flimsy and weightless, impotent before the immanent powers that now controlled all, and lost in a world in which "society" — the necessary friend of freedom — was now regarded as "something alien, impersonal, remote, and abstract — a world from which pity and tenderness had fled in horror."[17]

Lasch did not hesitate to lay out the worldview underlying this unrelentingly negative argument in precisely the terms Americans, including psychoanalysts, had mainly rejected — reflecting, perhaps, his perennial refusal to, as one of his editors later put it, "seduce" the reader. "The repression of sexuality, in one form or another, remains the very condition of culture," he contended. Indeed, "the most important insight" of psychoanalysis was its premising of an "an irreconcilable antagonism between culture and instinct," an antagonism that showed progressive, utopian hopes to be a form of infantile delusion, rooted in the most fundamental forms of denial and evasion. If a true culture is to be formed, he averred, the deeply sexual "forbidden

16. CL, HHW, 18, 98, 23, 36, xvii, 92. Here he was echoing Theodor Adorno, who maintained that "The end of the family paralyses the forces of opposition. The rising collectivist order is a mockery of a classless one: together with the bourgeois it liquidates the Utopia that once drew sustenance from motherly love." *Minima Moralia: Reflections from Damaged Life* (Frankfurt: Surhkamp Verlag, 1951; Englsh edition trans. E. F. N. Jephcott, London: NLB, 1974), 23.

17. CL, HHW, 50, 20, 13, 8.

impulses" that beset every child must be confronted within the bounds of thick, daily parent-children relationships; this was the only way a child could ever "internalize authority" and act responsibly in the world. Absent this painful process, children, unable to turn their aggressions outward, end up retreating from strong emotions of any kind and acquiescing in chaotic personal and political propensities. "New ideas of sexual liberation — the celebration of oral sex, masturbation, and homosexuality — spring from the prevailing fear of heterosexual passion," Lasch contended, which weak and fearful moderns were unable to achieve in its most satisfying and necessary forms. "The repudiation of monogamy expresses an accurate understanding of possessive individualism extended to the emotional realm," he offered, the social foundations of intimacy having eroded. "Yet it also expresses a rejection of intimacy and a search for sex without emotion." Paradoxically, "the contemporary cult of sensuality implies a repudiation of sensuality in all but its most primitive forms."[18]

Such arguments help to explain why Lasch did not greet women's liberation, feminism, and "cultural radicalism" in general as friends either of the family or democracy. These enthusiasms he dismissed as "the new psychiatric morality," with its exaltation of "healthy, well-adjusted, cooperative, achievement-oriented, and upwardly mobile" individuals on the pathway to "liberation." He certainly did not elevate the Victorian family as the perfected ideal — that era's "domestication of woman" had "simultaneously degraded and exalted" her. Yet Lasch found little comfort in the fact that more and more women were by the 1970s finding employment in, of all places, corporate America, and were thus active contributors to the vast economic and ecological wasting, even as in their absence from home they diminished the possibility of rich, countercultural domestic experience of family life.[19]

If anything, Lasch's criticism of fathers, rooted in his understanding of oedipal dynamics, was harsher than his criticism of mothers. "The father's withdrawal into the world of work has not only deprived his sons of a 'role model,'" he argued; it has "transformed the contents of the superego so that archaic, instinctual, death-seeking ele-

18. Interview with Edwin Barber, July 6, 2007; CL, HHW, 201, n. 26; 77; 177, 178, 183.

19. CL, HHW, 104, 108-9, 6.

ments increasingly predominate," leaving the son "a slave to pre-Oedipal impulses and external stimuli, with which he is bombarded by a culture devoted to consumption and immediate gratification." Violence, or repression of anger and violence in the form of prolonged immaturity, were the invariable results in boys reared in this disintegrating familial environment. Fathers needed to raise sons; instead, they had abandoned their sons to surrogates who ensured that they would remain in a perennial state of boyhood or worse, fodder for consumer culture and useless in society.[20]

For Lasch, in sum, the older political economy in which the family had been the "center of production" was superior because it enabled children and parents to work together and so mature together. Rejecting this arrangement and moving instead toward the industrialization not just of the economy but of education as well, the "progressive," liberal twentieth century had witnessed by the 1960s "the emergence of a youth culture that condemned American society in the most sweeping terms, repudiated the desirability of growing up in the usual way, and sometimes appeared to repudiate the desirability of growing up at all." And most sinister and telling was the fact that American elites, far from condemning this development, had actually hailed it:

> That the new youth culture represents more than adolescent rebellion is suggested by the way its attack on the family reverberates, appealing to a great variety of other groups — feminists, advocates of the rights of homosexuals, cultural and political reformers of all kinds. Hostility to the family has survived the demise of the political radicalism of the sixties and flourishes amid the conservatism of the seventies. Even the pillars of society show no great inclination to defend the family, historically regarded as the basis of their whole way of life.[21]

But was there no one, in the end, who had been capable of sounding an alarm, of halting this disaster? Lasch's answer was a familiar one. Consonant with his 1960s work, Lasch placed a large share of the blame for this massive political failure on his own kind: intellectuals

20. CL, HHW, 123, 124.
21. CL, HHW, 6, 129, 130.

and other professional observers of society, those whose paychecks were justified by the charting, monitoring, and reporting of such matters. Twentieth-century American social scientists, and the many who followed them, he contended, had as good liberals given themselves over to "seeing society as an evolving body of ideas and attitudes, an essentially harmonious equilibrium," and so had failed to grasp that "beneath the appearance of contractual freedom, individual autonomy, and the rule of reason, domination still continued as the motor of history, class rule as the basis of wealth and economic power, and force as the basis of justice." For this more accurate if less pleasing understanding they substituted holistic abstractions and fuzzy obfuscations, misconstruing the nature and direction of capitalist society, and of human existence itself. Continuing his assault on modernization theory and the structural-functionalist school in particular, Lasch dissected thinker after thinker, in discipline after discipline, for what he had come to see as fundamental, consequential errors of perception. Society did not simply cohere as a matter of course, as the structural-functionalist school preached in its jargon-laden sermons. Rather, fundamental forces rooted in capitalist domination created the appearance of a naturally unified, fluid society with only occasional, anomalous difficulties. Humans were not, in the end, essentially unified, harmonized beings who could expect as a matter of course unified, harmonious relations with one another, as the neo-Freudians proclaimed; rather, humans were essentially and painfully divided and could only mature by learning to embrace that divided condition in the context of long-term family relations. Liberal truisms like "community," so enthusiastically advocated by contemporary intellectuals, were far from adequate to enable this critical process.[22]

What became evident with the publication of *Haven* was that by the mid-1970s Lasch had erected a theoretically dense, historically informed framework that strengthened the case he had been mounting for years against a dominant tendency among Americans: the instinct to assume a basic, elemental wholeness, even goodness, at the heart of their national life and indeed their national history. Misled by yet another generation of elites purveying "enlightened opinion" and boasting the same liberal confidence that had led the nation into the Vietnam catastrophe, the cold war, and before that World War I,

22. CL, HHW, 69, 24.

Americans in the 1970s desperately needed leaders who could broadcast an accurate understanding of their truest condition. Instead, the elites, caught up in their "crusading zeal to harmonize the world," were only abetting its deterioration at all levels.[23]

Lasch, writing during the cold war and in the not-so-distant aftermath of World War II, believed that "personal and political freedom" were at stake, that "Today the state controls not merely the individual's body but as much of his spirit as it can preempt," as he put it in the book's conclusion. As it turned out, *Haven's* perspective and thrust made the possibility of any change look miniscule, if not impossible — even the left, his own greatest hope, was overrun by "pseudoradicals who confuse the individual's emancipation from the family with social and cultural progress." Still, despite his utterly bleak analysis, Lasch continued to insist that there was a solution, and it was, of course, *truly* radical change. "Americans can preserve what is valuable in their culture only by changing the conditions of public life itself," he wrote. Fundamentally altered social structures were the family's — and democracy's — only hope.[24]

Despite its theoretical density and despairing message, it was from beginning to end a heady argument, testament, among other things, to the remarkable quality of mind Lasch by the mid-seventies had attained. While writing in 1977 what would become *The Culture of Narcissism* he told his parents (one suspects only half-jokingly) that he had come to love "the exhilaration and dangerous excitement of playing the social scientists on their home field, not to mention the excitement of winning hands down." Now in his mid-forties, Lasch was achieving in key respects his peak intellectual performances, or at least his most dazzling ones. His tone by then had become more quietly authoritative without losing its aggressive edge. His continual stream of commentary carried a deeper sense of confidence, due in part to his continual, perceptive reading, along with his developing ability to defer to his argument, allowing it, rather than his voice, to carry a passage along. Intellectually he was more convinced than he ever had been (or ever would be) of the integrity of his worldview, a conviction built upon the mastery he had attained of the canon of twentieth-century leftist social thought. The upshot was a brilliant

23. CL, HHW, 100, 111.
24. CL, HHW, 189, 115, xviii.

clarity of vision: confident that he was truly *seeing,* he tossed off critical judgment after critical judgment. Increasing numbers of readers, and students, came to bathe in the light — or to at least check it out.[25]

What Lasch by this time was exhibiting, though, was not simply a critical vision sourced in a powerful intellect and a particular political vantage. His unusual ability to see, and so to make judgments, was also bound up in a distinctive kind of hope — an existential dimension not easily described or classified. In the history of modern politics much of what has made the left the left has been its fierce protecting and cultivating of this experience of hope: the unyielding, corporate conviction that there *must* be a better way for humans to live together, that a world profoundly better than the present is possible. If Christian theology has long regarded despair as a thoroughly corrupting sin, turning humanity toward self-absorption and often destruction, the genius of the political left has come from its longstanding battle against despair, its uncompromising guarding of a vivid sense of both the partialness of our present experience and of the fullness that must yet come. Lasch's most powerful, compelling criticism would not have been possible apart from his embrace of this tension between the ideal and the present — apart from the tendency to see the ideal, in fact, *as* the real. If some manifestations of the left in the nineteenth and twentieth centuries tragically sought to force such transcending upon a recalcitrant world, leftist political traditions also conserved the possibility of an embodied hope, keeping alive in Lasch and others the prospect of vital human flourishing — without which hope dies.

It was, finally, this left-inspired moral stance that gave *Haven* both its archly critical angle and its sharp, radical thrust. For some its brilliance afforded spectacular views. Lasch was both bemused and chagrined to discover that conservatives were offering some of the loudest applause for the book. "I wonder, with some misgivings," he wrote to Graff, "what you would make of the rave review of *Haven* that has just appeared in the *National Review,* which praises it as a 'marvelously reactionary' book." (He was sure to emphasize that it was Genovese who had called his attention to the review; he certainly did not read that magazine.) Indeed, the *National Review*'s George Gilder called *Haven* "shrewd and brilliant," except for the "complex and un-

25. CL to RL & ZL, TL, 11 October 1977, 4:14.

intelligent" arguments about the crisis being rooted in capitalism. "Even if there are warps of caricature in his depiction of the experts," wrote Gilder, "Lasch is essentially right about the inner logic and observable effect of their ascendancy." Historian Robert Crunden, writing in the conservative *Modern Age,* agreed: "The enemy throughout is liberal manipulation," and Lasch had "clearly, even savagely argued" his case. Crunden, curiously, failed even to mention the central role capitalism played in Lasch's argument.[26]

Most reviewers did take note of the overweening role of capitalism in it, though, and faulted Lasch for it. In the *Harvard Educational Review* Bella Rosenberger ridiculed the reductive quality of the argument in a pithy summary: "Social scientists . . . were the strategists, professionals merely the soldiers, government and public institutions the fortresses, and social policies the martial laws of the great occupation force of capitalism." Rosenberger was herself engaging in caricature, but most reviewers echoed her criticism. The political theorist Marshall Berman offered the lowest blow of all in a lengthy piece in the *New York Times Book Review,* calling Lasch's understanding of domination "perhaps the most conventional form of pseudo-Marxism, a conspiracy-theory." Whereas Marx believed, Berman contended, that "every emerging form of socialization is ambiguous, not only oppressive but liberating," he saw Lasch affirming "no contradiction or complexity; socialization is nothing but an unmitigated evil." Far from a Marxist analysis, *Haven* was merely Lasch's expression of "a generalized hatred for modern life."[27]

Many of Lasch's interpretive assumptions were indeed troubling, and none more than his perspective on the people whose story he was purporting to tell, both the malign professionals and the victimized masses. In the case of the former he left no room for ambiguity about mission, motive, or performance: the professional classes marched in lockstep to the beat of the capitalist drummers, destroying everything that crossed their path. In the case of the latter, Lasch either tended to portray them as passive and innocent or as passive and contemptu-

26. CL to Gerald Graff, TLS, 28 February 1978, 4:19; George Gilder, "The Therapeutic State," *National Review,* 17 February 1978, 220, 222; Robert Crunden, "Enemies of Civilized Life," *Modern Age* 22:3 (Summer 1978), 330.

27. Bella H. Rosenberg, "Private Lives, Public Lies," *Harvard Educational Review* 49:2 (1979), 235; Marshall Berman, "Family Affairs," *New York Times Book Review,* 15 January 1978, 20.

ous. Strangely, he allowed neither for significant skepticism (much less resistance) on their part, nor for any sort of complicity in embracing and helping to forge capitalism's destructive world. His own fundamentally sentimental stance toward "the people," ironically, only reinforced his depiction of the overweening intellectual conceit of the professionals.

The whole book, in fact, was a telling example of how Lasch's generalizing, abstracting vision, for as much as it made possible his remarkable interpretive reach, tended at the same time to undercut his analysis and diminish his ability to win converts. His failure to complement his powerful perception of historical movement and cultural form with a careful, sympathetic examination of life on the ground made it too easy for critics to dismiss him as a cranky, if brilliant, ideologue. In an era of fragmenting political traditions, Lasch's singularity of stance, conveyed through his tough, sweeping style, made him of interest to many but finally less compelling than he might have been with a more cautious, conciliatory approach.

But in view of this writer-reader dynamic, Berman's review is worth returning to. If Lasch's overstated analysis and biting style incited dismissal, it also loosened writers like Berman into less guarded expressions of their own points of view — precisely the kind of exposure Lasch wrote to force. Berman tipped his hand when he suggested that Lasch was not "fully in touch" with his "deepest and most hidden feelings about himself and his life"; a book whose "movement" was "jagged, clotted, gnarled" surely was the fruit of such denial, he thought. The therapeutic drift of Berman's politics was of course precisely what so troubled Lasch about America's plunging twentieth-century course. And the ad hominem form of his criticism could quickly be turned back on the author — one man's gnarled narrative is another's complex portrait. The fact that Berman regarded *Haven* as "one of the strangest and most disturbing books to have appeared in years" said more about him and about the moment than it did about Lasch. That, at least, is what Lasch hoped discerning readers would see.[28]

Perhaps most telling about the book's reception was the way in which reviewers used *Haven* to grapple not just with Lasch's recent turn, when, as Christopher Shannon puts it, "the moral concerns that

28. Berman, "Family Affairs," 20, 7.

had driven Lasch's political critique began to take center stage," but also his distinctive and peculiar movement in the context of the strange post-sixties aftermath that was the 1970s. Yale historian David Brion Davis lauded Lasch's lengthening track record of "provocative independence" and "disturbing honesty of mind," but freely speculated that Lasch had "clearly been shaken, to the point of shrill overreaction, by the recent divorce rate, the trend of avoiding or postponing marriage, and the more bizarre attacks on the family and celebrations of experimental styles of life." Berman too began his review with a long section lauding Lasch as "a trenchant critic and an independent spirit," with a mind that "fuses political sense with psychological sensibility," and one who possessed a "brave readiness to take big risks." But Berman found himself lamenting the disappearance of a Lasch he thought more complex and fair-minded — the author of *The New Radicalism*. "Those who remember his brilliant, critical appreciation of Jane Addams a decade ago cannot help but mourn," he sighed. Lasch now seemed "seized by just the sort of nihilistic fury that marked the New Left at its worst. He seems to have become one of the people he warned us against."[29]

But however angry Lasch was — and he clearly had no interest in hiding it — he certainly was not "nihilistic." Far from darkly delighting in his own self-absorbed world of hopeless rage, Lasch was trying to preserve himself and others from such a world, the world both he and Berman inhabited, but that Berman and others seemed not to sense — *would* not sense. In fact, it was precisely this refusal that sparked Lasch's anger, his fierce intent to unmask. True, as Berman noted, a crucial human element had dropped out of his writing in the decade since *The New Radicalism*. But Lasch had at the same time added what that book lacked: a prescriptive framework, the normative nature of which was aimed directly at the foundations of progressive, liberal culture. This attack, and the vision beneath it, may have been what drove critics like Berman to their own kind of fury. Any normative critique of the evolving mainstream liberal culture — and es-

29. Christopher Shannon, *Conspicuous Criticism: Tradition, the Individual, and Culture in American Social Thought, from Veblen to Mills*, New Studies in American Intellectual and Cultural History Series, ed. Dorothy Ross and Kenneth Cmiel (Baltimore: Johns Hopkins University Press, 1996), 181; David Brion Davis, "The Invasion of the Family," *New York Review of Books*, 23 February 1978, 37, 38; Berman, "Family Affairs, 6, 20.

pecially one made forcefully in its own language of rational objectivity — was bound to incite and offend.

This incendiary atmosphere that swirled around *Haven,* and Lasch himself, is what Lillian B. Rubin was observing when in a 1979 review she wrote that *Haven* had become "a verbal Rorschach test," uncovering "a special place where rage and fear hide." Certainly among the most raging and fearful were Lasch's erstwhile friends, the radicals, who by the late seventies had developed a maturing network of intellectual societies and publications while, paradoxically, becoming virtually absent from the broader political sphere: what John Patrick Diggins has described as "the Academic Left." "*Haven* continues to receive bad reviews from almost everyone on the left," he wrote his parents in September 1978. "Criticism from knee-jerk socialists doesn't bother me; but it is a bit disconcerting to find that there don't seem to be many socialists who don't fit this description."[30]

That same month *Theory and Society* published an example of such left-wing infighting and incivility. Written by psychologist Adrienne Harris and historian Edward Shorter, the article-length review of *Haven* was contemptuous and sarcastic. "Most people who have ever had anything to do with either 'revolution' or psychotherapy" were bound to find Lasch's "carelessly researched and defiantly wrongheaded" book "infuriating." Especially incensed by Lasch's charge that working mothers were implicated in the ruin of modern society, they accused him of turning a blind eye to the bourgeois family's shadowy history of domestic violence. The book, to them, was merely "a crusty example of male backlash, or conservative backlash" from one who, remarkably, had once been one of the leading "prophets of the New Left."[31]

Winifred Breines, a young feminist sociologist at Boston College and an acquaintance of Lasch's, engaged in a lengthy and animated correspondence with him in the spring of 1978. Both her reactions to the book and Lasch's defense of it graphically underscore the divisions that were emerging on the left, not just at the level of politics but

30. Lillian B. Rubin, review of HHW, in *Society* (March/April 1979), 98; Diggins, *The Rise and Fall of the American Left,* ch. 7, "The Academic Left," 279-306; CL to RL & ZL, TL, 2 September 1978, 4:20.

31. Adrienne Harris and Edward Shorter, "Besieging Lasch," *Theory and Society* 6:2 (September 1978), 279, 291-92.

at the level of worldview. Like Harris and Shorter, Breines found odious Lasch's accusing "recent movements, particularly the women's movement, of making things worse," but she was especially troubled by the insubstantial, faceless quality of his rendering of the world. "There is some way in which real people in their everyday lives drop out of your analysis (very male, by the way)." She prodded him: "Do you know people who have narcissistic personalities? Really, are there people you relate to who you would describe that way?" She, accordingly, could not accept Lasch's contention that in the recent past prospects for radicals had actually dimmed, that the gains of radicals in the sixties were largely chimerical.[32]

Lasch wrote a four-page letter in response. "Can anyone deny that prospects for socialism were much brighter a hundred years ago than they are today," he asked. "Then, the memory of communal traditions antedating capitalism kept alive the vision of a post-capitalist society," but the movements that had sprung from these traditions had "died, or were hounded out of existence, without leaving a legacy of socialist politics." Twentieth-century radicalisms, he claimed, "pale in comparison to that of earlier periods," all suffering the same dim fate in the teeth of the capitalist state. "And surely," he wrote, "the women's movement is eminently susceptible to the same kind of co-optation, eminently assimilable to the 'rampant present-minded individualism' you criticize." The contemporary "women's movement" consisted of much that merely reflected "the dominant culture of acquisitive individualism" rather than "a real alternative to modern capitalism," he thought. He even admitted, strikingly, that he too had begun with a bias against the family in its traditional structure, but his analysis of "historical experience" had caused him to change his mind. At the letter's end he apologized for its "too harsh" tone. "I've been absorbing a lot of punishment from feminists lately and find it increasingly difficult to keep a civil tongue."[33]

Breines wrote back several months later, at the end of 1978 and in the aftermath of the mass suicide by the members of Jim Jones's "People's Temple." That ghastly event had shaken her, forcing her to wonder about the real, current possibilities for "resistance to capitalism." She found herself identifying, she admitted, with the longings

32. Winifred Breines to CL, TLS, 10 April 1978, 4:17.
33. CL to Winifred Breines, TL, 21 September 1978, 4:17.

of the followers of Jones to "be part of a group, a community, of building something better than they had." People did look for means of "resistance," she insisted, even if such resistance did not turn out to be "a political force for socialism." She saw "minimal networks, arrangements, cooperation, activities" that helped "sustain people, prevent them from being completely overwhelmed, connect with one another in ways impossible to maintain in other institutions of society"; these "residential patterns" were especially significant for women, she argued.

She also pressed Lasch on his failure to acknowledge that there was "systematic inequality" between men and women in both the traditional and contemporary American family. In response to his contention that mothers and fathers needed to be far more present in the caretaking of their children, she charged him with unfairly placing the burden of care upon the mother, and again contested his notion that feminists had played a serious role in "breaking up the family." By the letter's end she found herself reacting against his overall outlook: "Your vision seems to me one in which the individual puts up with an enormous amount of suffering, masochism, punishment if *he* (or she) is to become an individual." Why was this dreary outlook worth holding on to, much less engaging in political battle over? "Heterosexual monogamy, dutiful love, hierarchy, suffering, grim fucking come to mind; are they values and experiences we want to preserve? And again, why attack those who try to find a way out?"[34]

In response, Lasch persisted in his contention that "deterioration of care for the young" was "one of the central facts of contemporary society," and it was due to *this* brute fact that feminists needed to acknowledge the decline of the family — "not," he wrote, "because they are primarily responsible for it," a contention he insisted he was not making. He did not believe, he repeated, that women should be forced to stay at home, and again averred that "a reorganization of work" needed to occur that would allow for men to be involved in childrearing and "women to have useful and interesting careers without sacrificing the prospects for a satisfying family life." It was thus the contemporary structure of work that posed "the central problem" that feminists should be confronting, rather than the "currently fashionable outcry against the repressive nuclear family." And to her

34. Winifred Breines to CL, TLS, 12 December 1978, 5:3.

rejection of his stoical conception of life, he rejoined that he was "not convinced of the dispensability of hardship and suffering." In the end, he wearily wrote, he was simply trying to speak in behalf of a "decent society," one that "would make concern for the future its central preoccupation, merge work and nurture, and do everything possible to assure that new generations will inherit a more hospitable environment." He signed off with his ironic "Yours in the counter-revolution."[35]

Fortunately for Lasch's own sense of equilibrium, it was not just the right that welcomed the culturally conservative direction he had taken; other friends, scholars, and activists praised the book and drew attention to his voice in the increasingly chaotic cultural battlefield. In the *Chronicle of Higher Education,* to take one example, Richard Wightman Fox, a Stanford Ph.D. who had considered attending Rochester to study with Lasch and who was becoming one of his most discerning and sympathetic readers, called the book "fascinating, alarming, profound." Lauding it as "a major advance in historically and theoretically informed social criticism," Fox sought to forestall easy dismissal of it by underscoring Lasch's rhetorically self-conscious use of incendiary overstatement in the prosecution of his argument — an old, time-honored approach, one that in the minds of writers like Lasch and his early guide, Richard Hofstadter, was made necessary by the entrenched intellectual and political formations of the day. Less publicly, Lasch found himself encouraged by personal notes and letters, some of which gave him a sense of how the book was actually being put to use. At SUNY-Cortland, a group of professors assigned the book in an interdisciplinary course titled "Advanced Industrial Society." In a letter to a friend, Lasch noted that he had received a few letters from people "who confront the disintegration of family life in their daily experience and who are no longer beguiled by pseudo-radical slogans about the politics of the family and the urgent need to smash monogamy." Such letters had given him some hope that "the book may have done some good in places that really matter; and this knowledge makes it easier for me to put up with the enlightened nonsense of academic reviewers."[36]

35. CL to Winifred Breines, TL, 16 January 1979, 5:3.
36. Richard W. Fox, "A Relentless Critique of the Standard View of the Fam-

For some the book resonated in intensely personal ways, and became a source of moral illumination. David F. Noble, a Rochester Ph.D. teaching at M.I.T., wrote that he and his wife had been "deeply troubled" by the book, which "put into words some of the more disturbing aspects of what it means to belong to the 'modern generations.'" Historian William Appleman Williams wrote with particularly keen autobiographical force, disclosing how the book had aided him and his children as they had sought to understand and move beyond the painful complexities of a family life disrupted tragically by divorce. Williams' confessional spirit and open appreciation moved Lasch to reply with equal warmth. "Your letter is worth more to me than the opinion of those who have reviewed the book," he wrote.[37]

Before confronting what he would later characterize as the "hostile reception" to the book, Lasch received one early review that must have given him a lasting sense of gratification. He had dedicated the book to his daughter Elisabeth, then in her first year at the University of Virginia, and had sent her a copy before it was released. "To Betsy," he inscribed on the dedication page, followed by a line from George Meredith's 1885 novel, *Diana of the Crossways:* "A witty woman is a treasure; a witty beauty is a power." Upon receiving the book Betsy wrote to her father:

> How wonderful to get your book! Isn't it beautiful? Right now it lies there on the table before me . . . Even with the slight frown, your picture almost brought me to tears; it looks just like *you.* . . .
>
> The dedication, though, did fill my eyes. In fact, every time I think of those words, those words of Meredith's given to me through you, they hit me harder. I went outside in the cool brisk air and danced around and around and ran and raced and sang until my throat hurt from drawing in cold breaths.
>
> Father, I am deeply touched.[38]

---

ily," *Chronicle of Higher Education,* 6 February 1978, 15, 16; Frank Burdick to CL, TLS, 18 September 1978, 4:17; CL to Robert Neuman, TL, 30 May 1978, 4:21.

37. David F. and Ched Noble to CL, TLS, 17 January 1978, 4:21; William Appleman Williams to CL, TLS, 18 February 1978, 5:1; CL to William Appleman Williams, TL, 28 February 1978, 5:1.

38. Blake and Phelps, "History as Social Criticism," 1328; Elisabeth Lasch to CL, ALS, 14 November 1977, 4:13.

By the late seventies, Christopher Lasch and Gerald Graff were each plagued by a growing confusion. "The problem of strange bedfellows," wrote Lasch to Graff at the end of 1977, just after the release of *Haven,* is "growing more insistent as the lines of political and cultural debate progressively grow more fuzzy. You never know who your friends are going to be from one minute to the next, and one hardly knows how to conduct himself." His own solution was to "adopt a surly demeanor toward one and all in the hope of offending *everybody.*" Graff wrote Lasch that he had recently found himself in the ironic position of being applauded by the neoconservative he had just attacked, the influential *New York Times* art critic Hilton Kramer. Lasch recounted his own tale of unnerving neoconservative encounter. He had spoken on a panel with Midge Decter, a writer and the wife of *Commentary* editor Norman Podhoretz, and he found himself

> agreeing with many of the things she was saying about the family, even though I suspected that what she was saying about the importance of kids having parents instead of professional day-care sitters was part of a larger argument about a conspiracy of communists, homosexuals, and appeasers to subvert our liberties. And sure enough, there appeared a piece by Norman Podhoretz in Harper's about the communist-homosexual conspiracy to subvert our liberties and how the "culture of appeasement" was playing into their hands. Yet, even here, I blush to say it, I found much to agree with.[39]

This was bewilderment. What such shifts in the moral bearing of American society meant, and where the trajectory was leading, were the questions occupying popular and elite conversation, and few raised them as fiercely or intelligently as did Lasch. But he found himself in the uneasy position of more loudly than ever being proclaimed a seer and prophet at just the moment he was most ideologically alone. Not surprisingly, he felt misunderstood by all sides. In late 1977, in a letter to friends living in France, he spilled out his sense of the moment. "At a time when social and political criticism not only has to challenge the status quo but to call into question many sentimental egalitarian pieties that have become absorbed into the official ideology," he wrote, "it's becoming more and more difficult to talk about

39. CL to Gerald Graff, TL, 15 December 1977, 4:12.

what's wrong with modern society without encountering accusations of 'elitism' and 'nostalgia.'" The rapid hardening of ideological lines, he thought, was shutting down genuine, necessary argument about any number of matters that he believed required sustained, intelligent, free debate:

> If you talk about the erosion of academic standards which threaten to produce a state of universal stupefaction, it's assumed that you're against women and blacks and want them to be excluded from higher education. If you talk about the growing tensions that so often seem to characterize relations between men and women, it's assumed that you want women to return to the kitchen. If you defend the importance of intellectual clarity, you're an elitist. If you take the position that children should be raised by their parents instead of by professional experts, you're participating in a "sentimental" cult of the home.

He concluded: "In a society where everything from the price of oil to the quality of workmanship to traffic to telephone service to reading skills seems to be visibly and demonstrably getting worse, to talk of things getting worse has become the cardinal heresy."[40]

America in denial was of course Lasch's perennial story, and perhaps at no point in his lifetime was this story more difficult to deny than in the 1970s. If Vietnam and Watergate had forever altered the way Americans perceived their political structures and culture, the economic crises of the era, including the rise of the Middle East as geopolitical power, were forcing an abrupt encounter with the provisioning structures that industrial capitalism required and the broader way of life that they proffered. At another level, the complicated process of assessing and judging the ongoing liberationist detonation of pre-1968 America — a land where *The Andy Griffith Show* had ruled the Nielsen roost — was slowly dividing Americans along culturally "conservative" and "liberal" lines in a way that earlier political divisions did not necessarily reflect.[41]

40. CL to Ed and Sheryl Gould, TL, 19 December 1977, 4:12.

41. For a survey of the cultural and political debates of the decade, see Peter N. Carroll, *It Seemed Like Nothing Happened: America in the 1970s* (New Brunswick, N.J.: Rutgers University Press, 1990, reprint). Among the most widely

If the rise of Jimmy Carter was on one level an expression of the old state of sentimental denial (Carter as virtuous outsider — a farmer, even — sent to Washington to restore national standards and morale), it was also an indication of a general willingness to examine the national circumstance in a more honest, less-politicized way. Carter's ability to have "an unpleasant talk" with Americans, as he put it three months into his presidency in an address on the energy crisis, was, in the end, made politically possible by the questioning, confused populace then searching for direction and leadership. In a short time, and in an exceedingly odd turn, it would be Carter's willingness to approach the presidency in this pastoral way that would bring Lasch and him together; Carter would end up as the one American president linked to Lasch's name in historical memory. But perhaps their meeting was not so odd. After all, Carter had farmed and governed in Georgia, a vital hub of the populist movement just a few generations back.[42]

But at this moment, in the midst of the exhilarating, exasperating reception of *Haven*, Lasch was also managing to put the finishing touches on his next book. If it was *The New Radicalism* that made Christopher Lasch an intellectual, *The Culture of Narcissism: American Life in an Age of Diminishing Expectations* turned him into a celebrity. It would also, on the heels of *Haven*, confirm once and for all his status as a pariah — a well-known pariah, to be sure, but nonetheless an outsider to any of the dominant political camps.

Prior to its publication Lasch had some sense that *Narcissism*, like *Haven*, would excite serious attention. In a February 1977 letter to Robert Silvers he noted that his September 1976 "The Narcissist Society" piece for the *New York Review* had provoked the strongest reader response he had yet received (in fact, in November 1977 he would attend a conference at the University of Michigan on narcissism that was in part inspired by that essay). His book on narcissism was, he

---

regarded of the sociological interpretations of changes in American life during the 1970s are Daniel Yankelovich, *New Rules: Searching for Self-Fulfillment in a World Turned Upside Down* (New York: Random House, 1981); Robert Bellah et al., *Habits of the Heart: Individualism and Commitment in American Life* (Berkeley: University of California Press, 1985).

42. Jimmy Carter, speech given to the nation on April 18, 1977. In *Jimmy Carter and the Energy Crisis of the 1970s: The "Crisis of Confidence" Speech of July 15, 1979*, ed. Daniel Horowitz (Boston: Bedford/St. Martin's, 2005), 36.

told Silvers, centered on "issues that seem to be on a lot of people's minds at the moment," so "it seems important to me to get it out as soon as possible." (He was also rushing it out because, as he had admitted to Genovese in the fall of 1976, he hoped that it would "sell well," Tom Wolfe's celebrated essay on "The Me Decade" having just been published in book form.) He had fallen into "a good writing rhythm," and by February 1977 had finished five of seven projected chapters, all of which were comprised at least in part of various pieces that had been previously published. Supposing that his "reputation" was "probably going to have to rest on these two books more than any others," he had been attempting to "avoid other writing commitments," he told Silvers. By September, just before the release of *Haven,* he had finished a draft of the manuscript — "the second of two books," he wrote his parents, "on which I've been working simultaneously for exactly a year."[43]

Knopf looked but was not compelled by it. Lasch remembered their reaction years later with some pique: "When people at Knopf said 'All this is just one more book of essays,' they were out of their minds. I could see that much." He had, in fact, gone "to much more trouble to try to produce an integrated book," and had "satisfied myself that it wasn't just a collection of occasional pieces but that it added up to one coherent argument," unlike his earlier Knopf books *The Agony of the American Left* and *The World of Nations.* He ended up signing with Norton, a decision they certainly never regretted. Published a year after *Haven* in January of 1979, *Narcissism* within weeks made *Time* and *Newsweek,* which devoted articles to it; *Time* featured a picture of a grim Lasch leaning against a fence outside of their newly purchased house in Pittsford, New York, just south of Rochester. The picture matched the tone of the article. "Like a biblical prophet, Christopher Lasch appears at the gates of our culture with dire pronouncements," the article began. In two months the book sold 26,000 copies, and paperback rights were almost immediately auctioned off to Warner Publications for advanced royalties of $140,000, of which 60 percent went

43. CL to Robert Silvers, TL, 5 February 1977, 4:16; CL to Eugene Genovese, TL, 28 September 1976, 4:6; CL to RL & ZL, TL, 8 September 1977, 4:14. On the Michigan conference: Lasch attended it, and afterward wrote to his parents that "I must bear some of the blame for this event, since I am told that it was my article on narcissism a year ago in the *New York Review* that prompted much of this speculation." CL to RL & ZL, TL, 20 November 1977, 4:14.

to Lasch. By April 22 the book had sold 45,000 copies; in November Lasch could complain to his parents that in one advertisement for the book it was touted as belonging "in the company of such classics as Alvin Toffler's *Future Shock* and Charles Reich's *Greening of America.*" As he later put it, "If I'd known in advance [that it would be so widely read] I would have written it somewhat differently."[44]

Haven had led to an enormous number of requests for interviews, lectures, and speeches. (In early May of 1978 Lasch, on the run, had written to his parents, "In a couple of hours I'm off to Atlanta, then to Evanston for a total of five talks in four days. This is the last trip of the season.") But this was mere spring training for what *Narcissism* would bring. "I've been hounded all month by people wanting interviews," he wrote to his parents at the end of January, "one of which turned out disastrously, and I've decided not to give any more." Not in the habit of satisfying the public relations requirements the media demanded of literary commodities, he quickly tired of trying to spell out the book's main thrust. "Having taken the trouble to lay out an argument in print," he wrote his parents, "it seems pointless to go on explaining over and over again." This frustration did not stop him from hitting the lecture circuit hard, however. He detailed a particularly grueling itinerary for his parents: he was on his way to Columbia University, then to Ohio Wesleyan, Northern Illinois University, Wisconsin-Milwaukee, Wisconsin-Kenosha, SUNY-Cortland, Colby, Berea, Columbia again, and then to a conference of social workers in Amsterdam.[45]

Even *People* magazine got into the act. Olivia Newton-John was not exactly the first person one would expect to find sharing a billing with Christopher Lasch, yet in July 1979 *People* featured both of them in a single issue. (Lasch was interviewed, but Newton-John, with a white cowboy hat, hot pants, and roller skates, trumped him on the cover.) Having been coaxed, against his better judgment, into the *People* interview for commercial reasons, he was surprised and chagrined to learn that a family photograph was part of the deal. Clustered together in the backyard, the Lasches looked every bit the anti–Brady

44. Fox, "Interview," 11; Valerie Lloyd, "Me, Me, Me," *Newsweek,* 22 January 1979, 75; R. Z. Sheppard, "The Pursuit of Happiness," *Time,* 8 January 1979, 76; CL to RL & ZL, TL, 6 March 1979, 5:8; CL to RL & ZL, TL, 22 April 1979, 5:8; CL to ZL & RL, TL, 17 November 1979, 5:8.

45. CL to RL & ZL, TL, 9 May 1978, 4:20; CL to RL & ZL, TL, 30 January 1979, 5:8.

Bunch, with Lasch sternly glancing down at a book, Nell lying on the ground and gazing up into the sky, and the children, ranging in age from fourteen to twenty-one, striking various hip poses. The *People* interviewer asked whether "the ferment of the '60s" offered "an antidote" to narcissism. "On the contrary," corrected Lasch, "it seems clear that the counterculture celebrated many of the values of narcissism." The next question was just as informed as the previous: "Might things take a turn for the better?" Lasch gave his now standard reply: "I have no easy solutions." But he did underscore in particularly concise fashion the direction to which he looked for whatever hope he felt: "The will to build a better society . . . survives, along with the traditions of localism, self-help and community action. These traditions only need the vision of a new and decent society to give them vigor." How was he "coping"? the interviewer asked. "I guess I agree with Freud," he replied. "The only things worth living for are love and work. I have a family I like to live with and work I enjoy. Every day I make compromises, but I don't know how else to live. Maybe I have a stable life and family because we live here in the provinces. Or maybe I just got lucky."[46]

Winifred Breines may not have thought of Lasch's success as "lucky," but she certainly had an understandable reaction to the *Narcissism* craze, jotted on a postcard in August of 1979: "Saw you in *People* magazine — Jesus, what a phenomenon, you on narcissism in *People* magazine!!"[47]

* * *

Lasch quickly tired of pronouncements that his latest book was dark, somber, sobering. To a childhood friend he wrote that "It appears to some readers as a 'pessimistic' book only in the current climate of escapism, and also perhaps because it doesn't propose 'alternatives,' 'solutions,' etc." His reaction to such criticisms contained more than a hint of evasion: "I don't see much point in discussing solutions until people have a better idea of how deep the problems go."[48]

46. CL to Robert Silvers, TL, 21 May 1979, 5:11; CL, "Gratification Now Is the Slogan of the '70s, Laments a Historian," *People,* 9 July 1979, 36.

47. Winifred Breines to CL, ALS, 16 August 1979, 5:3.

48. CL to Paula Cronin, TL, 19 June 1979, 5:3.

He was seeking to provide them with that sense of depth, if not actual solutions. If in *Haven* he focused on explaining the sociological process by which family experience — and democracy itself — had been corrupted in America, in *Narcissism* he zeroed in on the psychological effects of this process on the individual. Following in the traces of such critics as David Riesman and Theodor Adorno, Lasch was probing the connections between particular social structures and the shaping of personality, seeking to detail the human toll of what he termed "the wreckage of capitalism."[49]

Again, he spoke in a voice that was scholarly, normative, and anguished at once. Like Riesman in *The Lonely Crowd,* he based his study on the premise that "Every society reproduces its culture — its norms, its underlying assumptions, its modes of organizing experience — in the individual, in the form of personality." America's "current malaise," in this light, was etched in the dominant personality type of the day: the narcissist. Not simply a pleasure-seeking hedonist or a selfish egoist, the narcissist's condition was far more grave. Capitalism's triumph, he contended, had by the 1970s weakened dramatically the ability of Americans to act as individuals; lacking the "inner resources" that could be nurtured only in the family, the typical American hungrily turned to persons and institutions beyond the family to prop up his or her own neglected and underdeveloped self. The result was a person whose "apparent freedom from family ties and institutional constraints" merely "contributes to his insecurity, which he can overcome only by seeing his 'grandiose self' reflected in the attentions of others, or by attaching himself to those who radiate celebrity, power, and charisma." It was at root a self-flattering form of romantic identity, "a wish," he wrote, "to be vastly admired, not for one's accomplishments but simply for oneself, uncritically and without reservation." In actuality, this means to a mature identity only weakened the person and impaired a more searching and fruitful understanding of "the human condition." Riesman's "other-directed" twentieth-century person — which he had depicted hopefully, as regaining a more healthy form of both social connectedness and autonomy — was being directed, along with the vast lonely crowd, right into an abyss.[50]

49. CL, CON, xv.
50. CL, CON, 34, xiii, 210, 10, 232, 231. On Riesman's essentially liberal hopes

Such, at least, was his argument in brief, clearly an extension of his theoretical work in *Haven*. But the book itself was no neat and dry exposition. Lasch was writing with less caution and more fire than in *Haven*. Rather than surveying abstruse scholarly literature, he was slicing his way through American culture with a razor edge, using for evidence the assorted artifacts and exhibits from contemporary American life he had collected over the years. In this vein he resembled Adorno far more than Riesman. Adorno — fierce, brooding, and alienated — reacted to the culture of industrial capitalism with biting repugnance, deeming it, in the most bitter of tones, a vast moral failure. "Every visit to the cinema leaves me, against all my vigilance, stupider and worse," he confessed in his remarkable 1951 collection of brief meditations and essays, *Minima Moralia: Reflections from Damaged Life.* "Sociability itself connives at injustice by pretending that in this chill world we can still talk to each other." Adorno's honesty, acuity, and pessimism bore striking resemblances to Lasch; indeed, one of Lasch's closest students notes that Adorno in the 1970s was "probably the most important philosophical influence on him." It was with a critical passion and literary verve similar to Adorno's that Lasch crafted this sophisticated jeremiad, masterfully displaying once more his Marxian-Freudian framework. Novels, films, current events, magazine articles, politicians' follies: all became fodder for his roving eye able to find just the right place within his larger explanatory framework for everything, it seemed. He was, he claimed, describing "a way of life that is dying," and he coolly but angrily pronounced its last rites.[51]

What, precisely, was this expiring way of life? He described it as "the culture of competitive individualism, which in its decadence had carried the logic of individualism to the extreme of a war of all against all." The old Protestant American quest for "salvation," which had once fostered a decidedly public, communal politics of moral im-

---

for modern Americans, see for example chapter fifteen, "The Problem of Competence," where he applauds the "choices in styles of life and leisure available to millions" through "Hollywood movies." David Riesman, with Nathan Glazer and Reuel Denney, *The Lonely Crowd: A Study of the Changing American Character,* abridged and revised edition, with a foreword by Todd Gitlin (New Haven: Yale University Press, 2000), 291.

51. Adorno, *Minima Moralia,* 25, 26; interview with Casey Nelson Blake, 18 June 2007; CL, CON, xv.

provement, had devolved into the pursuit of "mental health," which in reality meant "the overthrow of inhibitions and the immediate gratification of every impulse." What was spawned as a result was not a new culture so much as an anti-culture. This was an argument indebted to University of Pennsylvania sociologist Philip Rieff, whose 1966 book *The Triumph of the Therapeutic: Uses of Faith after Freud,* recalls Thomas Cole, possessed "the aura of a sacred text" while he was a student at Rochester in the 1970s. Whereas for Rieff "faith" had in earlier times been the "compulsive dynamic of culture, channeling obedience to, trust in, and dependence upon authority," modernity and its "analytic attitude" had brought "the creation of a knowing rather than a believing person, able to enjoy life without erecting high symbolic hedges around it." But this process of "deconversion" carried a huge cost: the willful destruction of that which had historically unified humans in those "communal purposes in which alone the self can be realized and satisfied." "The new anti-culture," Rieff warned, "aims merely at an eternal interim ethic of release from the inherited controls."[52]

The engines of corporate capitalism had, of course, pushed hard in this all-consuming, anti-cultural direction. Advertising provided particularly powerful tutelage for the barren post-Protestant soul. Lasch dissected its spirit and purpose:

> Advertising serves not so much to advertise products as to promote consumption as a way of life. It "educates" the masses into an unappeasable appetite not only for goods but for new experiences and personal fulfillment. It upholds consumption as the answer to the age-old discontents of loneliness, sickness, weariness, lack of sexual satisfaction; at the same time it creates new forms of discontent peculiar to the modern age. It plays seductively on the malaise of industrial civilization. Is your job boring and meaningless? Does it leave you with feelings of futility and fatigue? Is your life empty?

52. CL, CON, xv, 13; Thomas R. Cole, "The Uses of Faith after Rieff: A Personal Response to *The Triumph of the Therapeutic,*" in *Figures in the Carpet: Finding the Human Person in the American Past,* ed. Wilfred M. McClay (Grand Rapids: Eerdmans, 2007), 273; Philip Rieff, *Triumph of the Therapeutic: Uses of Faith after Freud,* with an Introduction by Elisabeth Lasch-Quinn (New York: Harper & Row, 1966; reprint edition, Wilmington, Del.: ISI Books, 2006), 9, 23, 17, 16, 3, 17 (page numbers are to reprint edition).

Consumption promises to fill the aching void; hence the attempt to surround commodities with an aura of romance; with allusions to exotic places and vivid experiences; and with images of female breasts from which all blessings flow.

Lasch was here demystifying what had been coyly obfuscated by those who saw their fellows not as neighbors or citizens but as simply one more variety of "natural resource" useful for their exploitative ends. A deep and abiding anger drove his argument, the anger of one who himself felt violated by such wanton disregard for the foundational ideals of decency and mutual respect upon which a democracy might be built.[53]

A more personal dimension pervaded this book. If in *Narcissism* Lasch did not render actual historical figures, his focus on personality rather than social structures did give him opportunity to display his capacity for sensitive interpretation of human behavior. Humans, to him, were "creature[s] of instinct, whose partially repressed or sublimated drives always threaten to break out in all their original ferocity." Fragile, delicate, and weaker than they believed themselves to be, humans needed just the right conditions in order to thrive, conditions that capitalism certainly could not produce, as evidenced by the mass emergence of the narcissist, with his repressed rage against authority and inability to touch and shape the real world. Locked within herself, the narcissist, whatever her own self-perception, was unable to break loose from her solitary cell. "All of us, actors and spectators alike, live surrounded by mirrors," sensed Lasch. "In them, we seek reassurance of our capacity to captivate and impress others, anxiously searching out blemishes that might detract from the appearance we intend to project." This was the antithesis of Lasch's ideal for the human person, of course; this was, in fact, precisely the kind of person who, tragically, had nothing to offer to the building of "the decent society." And it was, alas, the only kind of person capitalism, with its "anti-culture," could form.[54]

Once more, Lasch's Freudian eyes took the reader into a tight, at times suffocating interiority, as he depicted what he called "the spiritual desolation of modern life." Abandoned by those whose pain

---

53. CL, CON, 72-73.
54. CL, CON, 64, 92.

might impart strength and make love possible — parents — contemporary Americans fought hopelessly against, or gave way to, the self-destruction their elemental impulses wrought. As the destruction proceeded, perception only diminished, leaving the narcissist on a steep, precarious ledge, unaware of his need of rescue, of a guide. A world of safe solidity awaited, but for the narcissist it was far, far away.[55]

In *Narcissism* Lasch took care, subject by subject, to develop a historical narrative that explained the emergence of this new cultural condition. Whether discussing sports, aging, or politics, he insisted that the story of America was centered not on grand, heroic movement from authoritarian control to freedom, as most Americans supposed, but rather on the shift from one form of overweening social control to another. "Most of the evils in this book originate in a new kind of paternalism," he wrote. "Capitalism has severed the ties of personal dependence only to revive dependence under cover of bureaucratic rationality." To be sure, there had existed a counter-surge throughout American history, a collective push-back against the dialectical re-emergence of authoritarian rule. Jeffersonian republicanism, manifesting itself in "populism, localism, and residual resistance to centralized progress," had, since colonial times, been the last, best hope for true freedom, the native alternative to mass domination.[56]

But it, alas, was forced to battle, both without and within, what Lasch described as a powerful "new ruling class," which had "elaborated new patterns of dependence." Itself profoundly dependent economically, intellectually, and psychologically on the world that liberal capitalism had made, the "managerial and professional elite," often with the best intentions, had propounded an ethos, outlook, and set of institutional dependencies that undermined with increasing force more promising ways of conceiving of politics, community, and the human person itself. It was this subtle and kindly form of control that had, over the course of decades, led to "dependence as a way of life," and so the emergence of narcissism, which in this new climate was not denounced as a pathology but, strangely, heralded as an ideal, an attainment, the state of being that ensured success and approval in the new paternalist order. Thus, Lasch concluded, it is only through

55. CL, CON, 73.
56. CL, CON, 218, 227.

an understanding of the history of this professional and managerial class that we can see "how our current difficulties arose."[57]

Was there a way back, or forward? Lasch claimed to see signs of promise. He pointed to "earlier traditions of local action, the revival of which holds out the only hope that a decent society will emerge from the wreckage of capitalism." Vaguely he reported that "In small towns and crowded urban neighborhoods, even in suburbs, men and women have initiated modest experiments in cooperation, designed to defend their rights against the corporation and the state" — even the so-called "retreat from politics" may actually be "the beginnings of a general political revolt." But resistance was not his subject in this book. "Much could be written about the signs of new life in the United States," he claimed, but until the malignant effects of capitalism were exposed and understood, such activism was unlikely to develop the critical power and political anger capable of overthrowing the behemoth. A renewed examination of America's condition would, he hoped, lead to a quest to truly understand the nation's past, a collective inquiry he believed to be essential for any future cultural transformation. The past, he wrote, is a "political and psychological treasury from which we draw the reserves . . . that we need to cope with the future." But the past was precisely what the American narcissist was increasingly unable to apprehend.[58]

The postal response Lasch received to the book is better described as a flood. *"What should bother everyone,"* exclaimed one enthusiastic reader, a retired elementary school teacher, "is that by the late 60s new teachers were entering the classroom unable to read, write, or spell the most common words." "I have just finished trying to read your book," wrote another, more agitated reader. "I started every chapter but finished none. My problem was mid-chapter gagging. . . . It makes that stuff written by the John Birchers in the early 1960s look positively thoughtful." A clinical psychologist in New York City wrote that the book "came into our lives at an opportune time . . . Personally and professionally our lives are rewarding, yet there is a recurrent feeling of living on a hard won little island of sanity in a sea of insanity." A correspondent with *Veja,* a weekly Brazilian news magazine, wrote to ask for an interview, sure that "your approach and ideas can have a

---

57. CL, CON, 222, 221, 230, 222.
58. CL, CON, xv, xviii.

tremendous repercussion at this time in Brasil." A Rochester minister invited Lasch to address an ecumenical group meeting regularly during Lent. When in June Lasch mentioned to his editor, Jeannette Hopkins, the overabundance of mail he had been receiving, she remarked that this was "not a usual response even for best-selling books." "Perhaps you'll be glad to hear that sales are slowing down, to about 5-600 a week," she wrote.[59]

It took the published reviews a very long time to slow down. Close to 100 periodicals chose to review *Narcissism* in the two years following its publication. And despite the acutely varying reactions to it, at some crucial points the reviewers spoke in a common voice.

"The quintessential doomsday book," Paul Zweig called it in *Harper's*. Lasch was "Biblical and relentless, a Jeremiah without the horizon line of God and hope"; like similar recent literature, the book "speaks the language of science while reciting the perennial narrative of the Apocalypse." Frank Kermode, in a page one review in the *New York Times Book Review*, called it "a civilized hellfire sermon, with little promise of salvation." Kenneth Lynn in *Commentary* dubbed Lasch "our apocalyptic author." Daphne Merkin in the *New Leader*, while acknowledging that "it would be sheer foolishness to deny that much of Lasch's case rings true," suggested that Lasch "denounces with an almost unseemly vigor, relishing his doomsday role a bit too much." Allen Lacy in the *Chronicle of Higher Education* put it succinctly: Lasch is "very long on acid distaste for our time, and very short on transforming visions."[60]

In sum, amidst the by now familiar and often accurate charges — that Lasch exaggerated the power of capitalism, that he neglected the study of ideas, that he buttressed his claims with little concrete evidence, that he tended to caricature his subjects rather than render them sympathetically and with particularity — hung this one, cumula-

---

59. Raymond Belanger to CL, ALS, 13 March 1979, 5:2; Phillip J. Trainor to CL, TLS, 16 March 1979, 5:12; Judith March Goldrich to CL, ALS, 17 March 1979, 5:5; Judith Patarra to CL, ALS, 29 May 1979, 5:10; Converse P. Hunter to CL, TLS, 8 October 1979, 5:6; Jeannette Hopkins to CL, TLS, 8 June 1979, 5:6.

60. Paul Zweig, "Collective Dread," *Harper's Magazine,* July 1979, 75; Frank Kermode, "The Way We Live Now," *New York Times Book Review,* 14 January 1979, 1; Kenneth S. Lynn, "Self and Society, " *Commentary,* April 1979, 84; Daphne Merkin, "Paradise Lost and Defended," *New Leader,* 26 February 1979, 13; Allen Lacy, "Visions of Narcissus in a Decadent World," *Chronicle of Higher Education,* 22 January 1979, R-12.

tive, larger charge: Lasch had little to point toward, and what he did offer seemed to most of his critics to be a step backwards toward a benighted past. By underscoring (and denouncing) what amounted to Lasch's affinity for central elements of Western, Christian civilization — including the moral priority of the traditional family and a dismissal of post-sixties liberation — his reviewers were forcing Lasch to become more concrete and historically particular about his own moral proclivities. While those on the left such as Kermode or Winifred Breines were unable to muster any sort of affection for the "bourgeois" American past, and dragged out the usual catalogue of crimes to denounce it, Lasch found himself just as unable to dismiss it.

As he was pressed on the matter of "religion" following *Narcissism's* publication, Lasch more and more began to defend it, something he had not done in any extensive way in the book. Invited to participate with the British author Henry Farlie in a "National Town Meeting" on "The Me Decade: Narcissism in America" in 1979 at the John F. Kennedy Performing Arts Center in Washington, Lasch took questions from the audience on his book. Those who had read it were no doubt stunned to find that the "apocalyptic author" standing before them seemed quiet, earnest, gentle, and sympathetic. When a member of the audience asked Farlie, who had just published *The Seven Deadly Sins Today,* whether the "elimination of a supreme being" had helped to foster the current narcissism, Farlie's response was that "Western civilization without its god is a very anchorless, drifting thing." Lasch, surprisingly, nodded that he "agreed" with this perspective on the relationship between religion's decline and the rise of narcissism in the West, and added that, for all of the wisdom that the great nineteenth-century thinkers like Freud and Marx brought to bear on the condition of the world, they possessed what he referred to as a "blind spot" in disregarding religion. Their failure to see religion as a positive and necessary element "begins to look very old-fashioned," remarked Lasch, and "exposes the limits" of their thought. Lasch noted that he was not propagating a return to the Christian church so much as what he called a "new worldview" that could critically embrace the insights of Christianity. But religion, he insisted, was indispensable: "Religion is the substitute for religion," he averred; to be rid of it was both impossible and undesirable.[61]

61. CL, CON, 96; audio tape, "The Me Decade," in the Library of Congress, in

When had this conviction gained this sort of ground? Thomas Cole, who was at the time slowly wending his way toward a re-embrace of his own Jewish heritage, says that he and Lasch "didn't really talk about religion *at all* in those days" — except in one indirect but very personal way: through the process of Cole's work on his dissertation, a cultural history of aging in America (which was later nominated for a Pulitzer Prize). Cole recounts that he himself had had "a kind of conversion experience" as he was writing it, coming to believe that it is impossible to "make sense existentially of the experience of growing old and dying if you don't have access to some transcendent framework of meaning." He and Lasch had together read Puritan theologian Jonathan Edwards on "the idea of true virtue as absolute love of God and benevolence toward being in general," and Cole sensed that this "resonated . . . with [Lasch] at the time." They had "lots of exchanges and conversations about these issues, mediated through the work — through my writing and through the research. But of course these were deeply personal and spiritual things that were happening to us . . . in ways that were half-acknowledged, but not quite." Lasch was, Cole reflects, "in the middle of a transition, too — or at the beginning of a transition, I think."[62]

There was, simply put, too much in the older Western world — including its way of understanding the world — that Lasch wished to see preserved for him to pitch it all onto the bonfire of cultural radicalism. In an exchange with sociologist David Riesman following the book's publication, he referred with appreciation to "the great bourgeois liberal culture of which the culture of narcissism is a feeble echo." His long-present conserving instinct had developed by the end of the 1970s into a readiness to support and sustain an embattled moral tradition, transmitted in part through his native twentieth-century Midwestern progressivism, that he was becoming convinced was necessary for human flourishing — even as many American intellectuals, now beginning to fancy themselves "postmoderns," were drawing the opposite conclusion.[63]

He endeavored to sustain these convictions through the means

---

the Recorded Sound Reference Center of the Madison L.O.C. Building, Washington, D.C.

62. Interview with Thomas R. Cole, 3 August 2007.

63. CL to David Riesman, TL, 27 September 1979, 5:10.

available to him from within his own tradition of critical rationalism. Bella Rosenberg had noted the awkwardness of this effort in her review of *Haven,* when she pointed out that Lasch's understanding of family and its relation to society relied not on the reality of cultural transmission so much as on his Freudian positing of "psychic mechanisms" that govern life. In fact, she argued, Freud's anthropology and Marx's philosophy of history provided for Lasch a scientific, rational "natural" sphere that would structure human endeavor; for Lasch, "the laws of orthodox Freudian psychology . . . are as iron-clad as the earlier principles of nature." And she was, of course, right: for Lasch their natural quality was indeed their attraction, though this version of "nature" was grounded in power and instinct rather than the older understanding of nature as the sphere of law and love.[64]

But was Lasch's religiously sensitive variant of Freudian Marxism enough, philosophically, politically, or personally? If *Haven* and *Narcissism* added up to a scorching damnation of the liberal world in all possible ways, had his own vigorous and intelligent alternative to it actually furnished him with a worldview sufficiently capacious and rich to satisfy his own personal and political longings, not to mention sustain his cultural critique? Jean Bethke Elshtain, a political theorist who in later years would become one of Lasch's closest friends and allies, thought not. In her review of *Haven,* published in 1979 in *Commonweal,* she noted that "Culprits and malefactors abound" in the book, among them "bourgeois domination and its antithesis, feminism," "schools and social welfare agencies," and "all self-righteous and priggish forces of organized virtue" (she went on to list Lasch's villains for an entire column). Her quarrel, though, was not just with Lasch's book but, more seriously, with his worldview: In compiling his "roll call of horrors Lasch could not go on to proffer any hope that private virtue might flourish despite all and the beleaguered family might survive." Reading the book left one with the sense that "Lasch has not so much frightened us as put us on guard that we are reading some things that are true but are by no means either the whole truth or the simple truth." The strange irony was that those who were "credulous" enough to accept Lasch's depiction of the family and of the world itself would likely go on to abet a "further erosion of the family's normative significance coupled with the extension, paradoxically, of

64. Rosenberg, "Private Lives, Public Lies," 235, 236.

precisely that brutalization of social life Lasch himself indicts as characteristic of our age."[65]

Elshtain made it clear, without actually saying so, that Lasch was writing satire: Exit from the muddle was as a matter of course impossible — not a particularly desirable endpoint for a writer with the variety of political longings that were fueling Lasch. What he most fundamentally needed, Elshtain and others seemed to suggest, was an answer to the philosophic problem of *goodness,* a problem in many respects as old and perplexing as the more immediate and disturbing problem of evil. Lasch could not abide what he termed the "hedonism" of the "cultural radicals"; goodness, whatever it was, certainly did not flow from unrestrained submission to base impulses. He supported this assumption by recourse to Freud, and took up the satirist's pen in an effort to capture the devastating absurdity of the liberationist turn progressive culture had taken. But satire's social usefulness ends if it fails to be enfolded within and corrected by a stronger and truer accounting of reality, one that, among other things, brings human beings more fully into focus. Satirists who would be reformers eventually must depart from satire and account for the presence, amidst the abounding folly, of goodness and hope.

Lasch was certainly not prepared to be done with hope, and his search for a surer source for it opened him up to a reconsideration of religion and its place in human efforts to live the sort of life he believed to be necessary and possible. For all of his immersion in Freud, Marx, and their kin, he could see that in leaving out religion they had excluded something substantial, even necessary. They could not satisfactorily explain, let alone sustain, this realm of experience that to him now seemed increasingly important, and that seemed connected to this question of goodness. Might "religious" insight help provide a basis for his assumptions about what human existence was, and what, finally, was good? He began to hedge in this direction.

In her review of *Haven* Elshtain commended to Lasch the writings of the prolific Harvard psychologist Robert Coles, whose "thirst for moral uplift," she remarked, "is as pronounced as Lasch's impulse to quash each and every hint of solace in sight." Coles, like Lasch, had

---

65. Jean Bethke Elshtain, "Under the Lasch," *Commonweal,* 16 March 1979, 155, 156.

achieved a platform with his social activism in the sixties — in the Catholic Workers Movement and the civil rights movement — and had also been a contributor to *Katallagete*. He and Lasch had been occasional correspondents since the mid-sixties, when they had met through Lasch's friend William R. Taylor. Coles later remembered his earliest impressions of Lasch, as they had with Taylor discussed the state of the family in America. "For a few memorable moments," he wrote, "I was privy to a prescient mind at work." Lasch had spoken "earnestly, passionately, and with evident alarm about what, even then, he saw happening: a decline in the persuasiveness of various religious and cultural norms, with serious consequences for the family life of our nation."[66]

The topic had shifted only slightly over the years, but this time Elshtain was trying to get Lasch to tune more closely into Coles, who possessed the virtue of "treating us to complex, thickly textured portraits of real human beings," she wrote, "men, women, and children in real social locations, living in and through genuine political and moral crisis." It was perceptive counsel, but also a bit late; Lasch, it turns out, had already been reading Coles. One year before Elshtain's *Haven* review appeared, Lasch's review of Coles's *Privileged Ones: The Well-Off and the Rich in America* had been published in *Psychology Today*. He had been especially pleased to discover in Coles's research evidence for his own understanding of human maturity as fundamentally a struggle. "I can think of no other book that demonstrates so vividly why growing up, under any circumstances, has to be regarded as above all a process of accommodation, compromise, and renunciation," Lasch wrote.[67]

Lasch's writing had struck a chord with Coles as well. Coles was one of the reviewers who found much to heed in *Narcissism,* and he published a long, meditative review of it in the *New Yorker*. Unlike many critics, he found Lasch's argument for pervasive narcissism to be ably rooted in "a growing psychoanalytic literature," and commended Lasch as "one who has looked back hard and looked around keenly," his overstated analysis notwithstanding. "We possess no

---

66. Elshtain, "Under the Lasch," 156; Robert Coles, "Remembering Christopher Lasch," *New Oxford Review* (September 1994), 16.

67. Elshtain, "Under the Lasch," 156; CL, "To Be Young, Rich, and Entitled," *Psychology Today,* March 1978, 124.

larger, compelling vision that is worth any commitment of energy and time," Coles agreed. "We shun the elderly, reminders of our own mortality. We worship super-athletes, promoted by endless and sometimes corrupt schemes. We cultivate postures — ironic cynicism, skeptical distance — meant to keep us from the inevitable difficulties of human involvement." In short, wrote Coles, "We play it cool, play it fast, and, in the clutch, place our faith in lotions and powders and soaps and dyes and surgical procedures so that we can stay — we hope, we pray — in the game as long as possible."[68]

The one cultural and moral corrective Coles was advocating in the face of Lasch's America was religion. Religion, he wrote, far from being "a joke," or "inconsequential," or just "a mere ritual," provided a means to combat the narcissism. Lasch was, of course, coming to the same conclusion. In the spring of 1979 a correspondent asserted that religion was to blame for the widespread emergence of narcissism. Lasch's response? "Religion is better understood as a powerful *antidote* to narcissism." Coles's and Lasch's sense of being kindred spirits deepened in the coming years. In fact, Coles, after Lasch's death, mentioned that he, Lasch, and Elshtain had become something of a threesome, embarking together on a search for "a spiritual home in a contemporary world full of all too unequivocal political and cultural categories."[69]

The question of which particular religion or religions might be the antidote to narcissism was not particularly absorbing to Lasch at the time. Religion was a category to be incorporated into the modern, rational frame, not the other way around. In so supposing he was in the company of many social critics and theorists with similar concerns and orientations. Jackson Lears, in a perceptive review of *Narcissism* published in the *Nation,* suggested that Lasch had with this book truly emerged as a "cultural conservative" in the company of "other powerful critics of capitalism" who "looked backward rather than forward. From William Morris to Lewis Mumford," Lears wrote, "they have arraigned capitalist 'progress' for promoting untrammeled individualism and eroding loyalties to family, craft, commu-

---

68. Robert Coles, "Unreflecting Egoism," *New Yorker,* 27 August 1979, 98, 104.
69. Coles, "Unreflecting Egoism," 103; CL to Jiro Nakasato, TL, 21 May 1979, 5:9. For Coles' account of their friendship, see his "Remembering Christopher Lasch"; the quotation is on p. 18.

nity or faith." These critics believed that "any serious critique of capitalism requires a stable set of alternative values," and Lasch had become "one of the most vigorous critics working within this tradition." But where, even within the bounds of "religion," Lasch was going to go to find epistemic support for that "stable set of alternative values" was a lingering question.[70]

Lasch began to cross paths with religious people more often in the 1970s. In 1979 he exclaimed to his former student William Leach that "For the first time, I've begun to get students in my courses who see life from a religious perspective. Another alarming sign of the times, probably. Unnerving, too. I'm not used to dealing with the argument that the trouble with the left is that it is godless." That winter he received a letter from an evangelical Protestant who had heard him lecture in Appleton, Wisconsin. "Are you happy," he asked Lasch, and proceeded to inform him that "a true believer in Christ knows an inner peace which the shallow secular man doesn't." Lasch was astonished at this claim — or at least nettled — and wrote back with some theological disputation:

> Happy? I thought Christ came to bring not peace but a sword. I don't remember his saying anything about happiness. One hardly needs religion for that. If it's happiness you're looking for, try rolfing [*sic*]. Religion is a real drag. So says Kierkegaard — not to mention Erasmus, who says it is also folly.

As his father once noted, Lasch did not suffer fools gladly — nor foolish religionists. He criticized Philip Rieff's "resort to religious categories" in a 1979 talk on Freud at Columbia University that he had attended. Rieff's use of religion, he wrote to Robert Boyers, the editor of *Salmagundi,* was "not backed up by any sensitivity to the sociology and psychology of religion. In stating these objections, I suppose I am merely falling into the critical style that Rieff deplores, not without reason." But he was at a loss to discern where else one could go other than to the tradition of critical rationalism to understand religion: "I don't see any alternative short of a full-scale restoration of Christian theology that is intellectually untenable."[71]

---

70. Jackson Lears, "Therapy's Triumph," *Nation,* 27 January 1979, 91.
71. CL to William Leach, TL, 16 October 1979, 5:8; David Becker to CL, ALS, 1

In the aftermath of *Haven* and *Narcissism,* Lasch began, as he later put it, "to rethink issues that I thought I had more or less resolved to my satisfaction. Now I no longer felt comfortable with the traditions I'd inherited." The question remaining was where, and how far, would he go?[72]

February 1980, 5:13; CL to David Becker, TL, 14 February 1980, 5:13; CL to Robert Boyers, TL, 27 February 1979, 5:3.

72. Blake and Phelps, "History as Social Criticism," 1328.

CHAPTER NINE

The Need for Roots

A radical movement capable of offering a democratic alternative to corporate capitalism will have to draw on traditions that
have been dismissed or despised by twentieth-century progressives and only recently resurrected both by scholars and by en-
vironmentalists, community organizers, and other activists. It
will have to stand for the nurture of the soil against the exploitation of natural resources, the family against the factory, the
romantic vision of the individual against the technological vision, localism over democratic centralism. Such a radicalism
would deserve the allegiance of all true democrats.

Christopher Lasch, "Democracy and
the 'Crisis of Confidence,'" 1981[1]

President Jimmy Carter, whose easy Southern Baptist piety had
helped propel him into the White House, became the cynosure of
the 1970s revival of "born-again" Christianity. In fact, *Time* declared
the year of his election, 1976, "The Year of the Evangelical." Lasch had
esteemed Carter highly in 1976. For one thing, his political ascension
had kept another Kennedy from the White House — "a man whose
rise has already buried not only Wallace but the Kennedys can't be all
bad," he quipped to his parents. Predictably, Robert Lasch was turned
off by that which helped make Carter attractive to Kit: his religious

1. CL, "Democracy and the 'Crisis of Confidence,'" *democracy* 1:1 (January
1981), 40.

and moral earnestness. "I distrust a man who claims to have a hot line to God," he grumbled. Kit was not so disturbed. In a letter to Eugene Genovese (with whom he was in the midst of, as he put it to his parents, a "mild reconciliation"), he opined that even though Carter had been "nervous, edgy, and evasive" in the first presidential debate against the Republican Gerald Ford, he was still "the most intelligent politician to have risen to national prominence in a long time." Lasch thought it would be "a great pity if, thanks to his own mistakes, he doesn't get elected."[2]

Carter was elected, of course, and Lasch's tagging of the 1970s as "an age of diminishing expectations" resonated with Carter's perception of the nation's condition. More surprisingly, it led him to seek out Lasch for counsel. Lasch was stunned in May 1979 to receive an invitation to a private dinner at the White House, where he joined, among others, Harvard sociologist Daniel Bell, civil rights leader Jesse Jackson, and journalists Haynes Johnson and Bill Moyers for a discussion of what Lasch in *Narcissism* had termed the nation's "current malaise." The dinner was at least mildly ironic for Lasch, who had launched his career by denouncing intellectuals who spurn critical detachment for direct political influence. But Lasch gingerly, and not without considerable reservations, took a step in that direction.[3]

Carter adviser Jody Powell had been vague in his invitation, Lasch remembered, not even indicating if Lasch would meet with the president alone or come as part of a group. He simply informed Lasch that Carter had been reading *The Culture of Narcissism* and was interested in discussing its "political implications," as Lasch recounted a few days after the event in a lengthy letter to his parents. At the dinner ("a frugal meal consisting of crabmeat-oyster salad, lamb chops, asparagus, and ice cream") he was seated next to the president's wife, Rosalynn Carter, who, Lasch told his parents, "spoke with feeling of the

2. CL to ZL & RL, TL, 24 July 1976, 4:8; RL to CL, TL, 30 July 1976, 4:8; CL to ZL & RL, TL, 13 February 1974, 3:18; CL to Eugene Genovese, TL, 28 September 1976, 4:6.

3. CL, CON, xiii; CL to ZL & RL, TL, 11 June 1979, 5:8. The other members of the dinner party were Pat Caddell and Jody Powell, both on Carter's staff; John W. Gardner, founder of a citizen's lobbying group called Common Cause; and Charles Peter, the editor of *Wasington Monthly*. See *Jimmy Carter and the Energy Crisis of the 1970s: The "Crisis of Confidence" Speech of July 15, 1979: A Brief History with Documents,* ed. Daniel Horowitz (Boston: Bedford/St. Martin's, 2005), 65-66.

difficulties of getting anything through the federal bureaucracy." He later remembered their dinner conversation as "heavy going"; he was uncertain "she had any clearer idea than I did about the purpose of the meeting."[4]

According to Lasch, during the formal discussion that followed the dinner Carter's pollster, Patrick Caddell, documented "a sharp rise, since 1977, of pessimism about the country's future and about the personal prospects for individuals; of cynicism about politics and politicians; and of lack of interest in public issues." But "the real issue" that was driving everything, according to the White House, was "a profound moral crisis, and also a crisis of confidence in the system as a whole." "Perhaps this is where my book is thought to come in," Lasch speculated. Carter had told him over drinks that thanks to having "mastered the art of speed reading" he had read *Narcissism,* along with the recent books by the other authors present. But throughout the night Lasch did not "talk much," he recalled in a 1993 interview, "being overawed by this distinguished company, and feeling a little uncomfortable too because of having written so much about the perils of intellectuals as advisers to people in power. I wasn't sure whether I should even be there in the first place."[5]

Daniel Bell took particular note of Lasch's silence. In September he circulated to those invited to the meeting a fifty-eight page document filled with wandering observations and speculations about the evening. In it he stated that Lasch had seemed "puzzled by the role that he was being asked to play." Lasch, he noted, "certainly has thought of himself as a critic of American society and probably a severe critic of Mr. Carter." Yet "here he was being called upon to give Mr. Carter advice as to how to deal with the society." Bell thought it "likely that he felt perplexed as to what he could or should say."[6]

He was right. While Carter seemed to think that the cynical, pessimistic mood of Americans called for a chastising lecture, Lasch's sense, as he explained to his parents, was that Americans actually had "a fairly realistic awareness of the economic prospects facing the

---

4. CL to ZL & RL, TL, 11 June 1979, 5:8; Richard Wightman Fox, "An Interview with Christopher Lasch," *Intellectual History Newsletter* 16 (1994), 12.

5. CL to ZL & RL, TL, 11 June 1979, 5:8; Fox, "Interview," 12.

6. Bell's "personal memoir" is included in the Lasch Papers with a cover letter from Bell dated 1 September 1979, in 20:6.

country, of the failure of public policy to come to grips with the situation, of the absence of real political choices, and of the powerlessness of the ordinary citizen." Carter's political struggles, in short, were to be expected: "I think any president would find it difficult to govern the country, at least within the framework of existing assumptions, programs, and policies." By the time the evening ended he could see that "the gloom and pessimism registered in the polls was confirmed by the discussion that took place in the President's living room." He doubted that "there has ever been a time, except perhaps for the eve of the Civil War, when those charged with governing have been less able to govern."[7]

Unlike Carter, Lasch understood this dire condition to be sourced in a political system that lay in a shambles, the historical effects of a corrupting economic framework. Sensing that Carter had not grasped the radical nature of his analysis, Lasch within two weeks of the meeting had typed a thirteen-page letter to Jody Powell (who had elicited continued discussion), emphasizing that the president's reformist, moralistic politics were inadequate to halt the rapid cultural erosion. He urged the president to consider another vantage, one more historically informed. The triumph of industrial capitalism had been possible, he explained, due to a "historic compromise in which people accepted a lower standard of work in exchange for a higher standard of consumption — too often confused with a higher standard of 'living.'" This unparalleled level of consumption was "now threatened by interlocking economic crises that have called into question the underlying assumption of unlimited growth." It was this historical development, surfacing in dramatic fashion in the seventies, that accounted for "the pessimism registered in the polls."[8]

He tried in the letter to convince Carter's inner circle that, given the inevitable shortages of supplies industrial economies require, "the future will call for discipline and sacrifice" in some form, whether through the voluntary action of the citizenry or the coercive power of an authoritarian regime. Thus the moment demanded "bold executive leadership" that would almost certainly be "divisive rather than unifying in its initial impact," but which might in the end lead to "a new consensus . . . after a period of upheaval and conflict." "A thor-

7. CL to ZL & RL, TL, 11 June 1979, 5:8.
8. CL to Jody Powell, TL, 10 June 1979, 20:6.

ough democratization of politics" was needed, and the president's challenge was to work toward fostering "a society composed of citizens, rather than clients and consumers," a people who would "insist that the distribution of scarce resources, the distribution of sacrifices, and the nature of the discipline imposed by economic adversity are all collective decisions that should be made not by elites but by the people as a whole, who have to bear their costs."[9] This was Lasch at his apocalyptic-socialist best, distilling the critique that had won him acclaim.

Alas, he received no reply from Carter or the White House. But in Carter's famed July 15 "malaise" speech he did appropriate some of the more negative rhetorical flourishes of *Narcissism,* a pirating which did not fail to capture Lasch's attention and arouse his ire. In a letter to a friend a few weeks after the speech, Lasch complained that although he had "recognized certain phrases of mine in Carter's famous speech," the "ideas were torn out of context and came across as moral denunciation of selfishness, selfish interest groups, and a plea for personal sacrifices without any assurance that the sacrifices sure to be imposed on us by our economic troubles would be fairly distributed." Alarmed by this very public misreading of his stance, Lasch on July 18 mailed a seven-page protest to Caddell and warned him that following the speech he had been besieged by interview requests from all sorts of places, including CBS News. Having at the president's request pledged secrecy regarding their discussion at the May meeting he was withholding public comment, he told Caddell, even though he knew the media "might for their own reasons welcome criticism of the President, or anything that could be construed as criticism, from a left-wing author claiming that his ideas had been misused, bowdlerized, or put to purposes he had not intended and could not now countenance." Vexed by his forced silence, he lamented that he was not in a position to "forestall charges from the Left that I've been seduced and co-opted by too close proximity to power."[10]

9. CL to Jody Powell, TL, 10 June 1979, 20:6. Lasch sent a copy of this letter to his parents, along with his own account of the evening.

10. CL to Doug Lowell, TL, 29 August 1979, 5:8; CL to Patrick Caddell, TL, 18 July 1979, 20:6. Carter biographer Leo Ribuffo notes that Carter did read the first letter and underline a few phrases from it. Remarkably, as Ribuffo points out, the word "malaise" never actually appeared in the text of Carter's speech. See Ribuffo's discussion of Carter's summer of 1979, "'Malaise' Revisited: Jimmy

He wanted the president and his brain trust to understand, he instructed Caddell, that although he had found the speech "courageous, powerful, and often moving" (though he later confessed to Bell that he had "overpraised the speech" in this letter), he was disturbed by the way Carter had misconstrued and distorted his perspective. While Carter had berated the country at large for its selfish, inward turn, in describing a "culture of narcissism" Lasch had sought to expose "above all the culture of . . . the managerial and professional elite that gets most of the social and economic advantages from the existing distribution of power." The blame needed to be more justly assigned. "These people have sold the rest of us on their way of life, but it is their way of life, first and foremost, and it reflects their values, their rootless existence, their craving for novelty and contempt for the past, their confusion of reality with electronically mediated images of reality." Future homilies and policies should be directed at the professional classes, not ordinary Americans. And if the lot of these ordinary Americans was to improve, more radical economic and political policy must be enacted. The "choice," he wrote, is "between centralization and concentration of power on the one hand and localism and 'participatory democracy' on the other" — which, he added, "remains a good idea no matter how outrageously the new left may have perverted it."[11]

The Carter-Lasch episode illustrates dramatically the reasons behind the constructive turn that Lasch's thinking in the early eighties began to take. The critical attention he had won, from the White House on down, was forcing him both to refine his analysis and to think more architectonically. His stress on the genesis of America's narcissism in the professional classes in his letter to Carter was a crucial rhetorical shift — not just for the president's sake, but also for the integrity of his own political vision. Had this more careful, more pointed perspective achieved a more central place in *Narcissism,* fewer copies might have been sold — decrying the state of the "managerial and professional elite" is much less riveting than pronouncing

---

Carter and the Crisis of Confidence," in *The Liberal Persuasion: Arthur Schlesinger, Jr., and the Challenge of the American Past,* ed. John Patrick Diggins (Princeton: Princeton University Press, 1997), 164-84.

11. CL to Patrick Caddell, TL, 18 July 1979, 20:6; CL to Daniel Bell, TL, 8 November 1979, 5:2.

upon the condition of "America" — but it also might have afforded Lasch greater respect from those readers who had chafed at the one-dimensional nature of his analysis.

Most of his readers, it is worth pointing out, were not "the people" but the "professional-managerial elite." Lasch was not seeking to rally them; he was chiding them. Above all, he wanted these highly educated, culturally refined readers to confront the brute historical fact that they, America's ruling class, were superintending a period not of prosperity and liberality but of poverty and domination.

It was a difficult case to make. If the entire decade of the 1970s, and particularly the Carter presidency, had left most Americans feeling beleaguered and confused, it did not seem to be the case that they felt "dominated." Nor did it seem that those in the upper-middle class perceived themselves to be doing the dominating. How to break through the illusions of freedom and progress to actually *move* people? This kind of penetration required prophecy, and as Lasch continued his outpouring in the aftermath of *Narcissism* he did not soften his rhetoric. Could college-educated professionals be made to see that their abandoning of crucial public standards — their redefining, for example, of "sin" as "a kind of sickness, curable by psychiatric intervention" — was helping to perpetuate a soul-killing, democracy-denying historical turn? Much of the avowed liberation in the great modern march had been, Lasch hoped they would grasp, *welcomed* by those who ran America, since the increasingly unfettered citizenry would have no choice but to fall back on the corporate state for sustenance, and so forfeit the possibility of true, meaningful self-government. But did "the professional-managerial elite" notice? Did they have eyes to see the "sentimental lie" that was their supposed "democratic" way of life?[12]

---

12. CL, "The Cultural Civil War and the Crisis of Faith," *Katallagete* 8:1 (Summer 1982), 15, 16. See also his comments in a 1980 symposium on "History in America" published in *Salmagundi,* where in response to a paper by John Lukacs he noted that "The new elite governs not so much by attempting to elicit or impose a consensus about values as by defining normal behavior increasingly by arriving at a statistical definition of normal behavior." This elite, he wrote, has "little use for humanistic learning . . . It asks only that the solutions to these problems which it has uncovered, the management of these crises be turned over to the appropriate experts for further study." "Response: History in America," *Salmagundi* 50-51 (Fall 1980–Winter 1981), 188.

The evidence seemed to say, in no uncertain terms, No. "Democracy survives as an ancestral memory even as it disappears from political practice," he wrote in 1981. "Our government has ceased to be in any important sense a government of, by, and for the people. At its best, it functions merely as a government for the people, a benevolent paternalism. At its worst, it represents a warfare state, with the potential of developing into a thoroughgoing form of totalitarianism."[13]

This brand of forecasting and analysis was too often abstract and angry, bombast that was doing little to augment Lasch's argument or stature. But whatever its deficiencies, it was certainly not mere rhetoric; Lasch was neither faking nor dissembling. His urgency was genuine. He agreed with a correspondent who in 1980 noted similarities between his outlook and that of Huxley and Orwell, and confessed,

> Lately I have had a discouraging thought: we have lost the collective capacity, the traditions of moral discrimination and consecutive thinking (not to mention such discarded concepts as the dignity and moral accountability of the individual), which alone would enable us to recognize the world of 1984 even if we were living in it.

He paused, and added: "This thought is followed by one more discouraging still: we *are* living in it." Accordingly, he felt continued indignation toward those who, calling themselves "radicals," had fallen for the "sentimental lie" of the professional-managerial elite, proving themselves unwilling to apprehend the nature of their circumstance and thus take the political action the moment demanded. To Princeton political philosopher Sheldon Wolin in 1979 he wrote deploringly of the lack of "urgency even in the most 'radical' analyses of the crisis in contemporary society. Often the writer betrays a comfortable sense that it will go on indefinitely so that he can go on analyzing indefinitely." And this endless analysis was itself far from adequate. "I've felt for some time that we're rapidly losing the ability to recognize the 'future' when it arrives — as in most areas of life it already has."[14]

"The future" had already arrived for the family. Families were at the heart of the narrative of devastation Lasch had been telling since

---

13. CL, "Democracy and the 'Crisis of Confidence,'" 26, 27.

14. CL to Naomi Lizard, TL, 14 February 1980, 5:18; CL to Sheldon Wolin, TL, 13 November 1979, 5:12.

the mid-seventies, and nothing in the early eighties caused them to be displaced from that position. He welcomed the recently translated volumes by the French poststructuralist Michel Foucault and his student Jacques Donzelot, for their work only reinforced his contention that the nineteenth-century elites who advocated enlightened family practices were actually agents of elite, capitalist domination. When the *New York Times Book Review* asked him in 1980 to join various other luminaries in recommending books for "summer reading," Lasch archly urged readers to take Donzelot to the beach — he could help them "explore the ways in which they have been reduced, even in family life, to consumers of expert services." In a more lengthy discussion of Donzelot's *The Policing of Families* and Foucault's *The History of Sexuality, Volume One* in the *New York Review of Books,* Lasch used their studies to rip holes in the more progressive analysis of Carl N. Degler in his recent book *At Odds: Women and the Family in America from the Revolution to the Present.* Foucault and Donzelot had a "better understanding of these issues," wrote Lasch, and he went on to integrate their understanding of political domination into his own narrative of the Progressive era. The French poststructuralists, he wrote, reinforced Charles Beard's contention that American progressivism was a "'counter-revolution,'" a "highly successful attempt to deflect Populism, labor radicalism, and other potentially revolutionary movements by reforming society from the top down." Contra Degler, Lasch saw American feminists as implicated in this coercing, power-seeking juggernaut, expressing as they did "a boundless faith in disinterested scientific expertise" while disdaining the worldview and politics of the Populists. Ironically, women had availed themselves of the nascent culture of professionalism to "improve their position in the family only to fall into a new kind of dependence," in which they would rely on experts not just for "the satisfaction of needs but for the very definition" of them.[15]

15. CL, contribution to "Guide for the Perplexed," *New York Times Book Review,* 8 June 1980, 40-41; CL, "Life in the Therapeutic State," *New York Review of Books,* 12 June 1980, 27, 26, 27. The other books that Lasch recommended for summer reading were Harry Braverman's *Labor and Monopoly Capital* (New York: Monthly Review Press, 1974), which was "the best analysis of the division of labor between the design and execution of industrial production, which underlies all our social arrangements," and Lawrence Goodwyn's *Democratic Promise* (New York: Oxford University Press, 1976), which "explores one of the last genuinely

The vehement attacks from feminists Lasch had incited in the seventies were not exactly leading him to back down, although the wounds he suffered still seeped. In the summer of 1979 he had remarked to friends in France that the "hysterical reaction" of feminists to his recent work was "compounded no doubt by the rising popular backlash against feminism," and in the process of attacking him they had demonstrated a "seemingly endless capacity for misrepresentation, slander, vilification, and character assassination." His bitterness was palpable. To fellow historian and longtime friend Carol Gruber he in October 1980 listed the mounting misunderstandings of his position:

> When I point out that in endlessly attacking the nuclear family the Left is beating a dead horse, this is mistaken as a defense of the "patriarchal" family. When I point out that relations between men and women have deteriorated (drawing on the writings of feminists to make this point and to illustrate it and support it), this is mistaken as a statement that feminism *caused* the deterioration. When I say that men and women should learn to live with their differences, this is mistaken for a defense of the sexual status quo.

He could not help but conclude that they had not simply "misread" him but rather had "willfully and maliciously distorted" his thinking. The fact that many of his critics tended "to resort to personal vituperation instead of argument" only confirmed his suspicion. His own stance on the matter of feminism and the family remained steady: "the dominant feminist tradition in the West instead of criticizing the division of labor has tried to extend it even to childrearing and housekeeping," and this was destructive of the family and, consequently, of democratic civilization. While feminism had indeed brought "indisputable gains" for women, the gains were "largely confined to women in the professional and managerial class — not because working-class people are hopelessly benighted and 'authoritarian' in their sexual attitudes but because the feminist program has always had so little to offer them."[16]

---

democratic movements in American politics, Populism, and clarifies the far-reaching consequences of its defeat," 40.

16. CL to Ed and Cheryl Gould, TL, 3 August 1979, 5:5; CL to Carol Gruber, TL,

If such arguments left Lasch encountering a less-than-enthusiastic embrace from feminists and other former friends on the left, one circle that welcomed him and whose embrace he returned was centered around *Salmagundi,* a "quarterly of the humanities and social sciences" published by Skidmore College and edited by Robert Boyers. Boyers had in 1975 asked Lasch to write an introductory essay for the journal's tenth-anniversary issue, noting that there was "no one else I'd rather think of reading the magazine and considering its 'position' in the context of the cultural moment." According to Gerald Graff, a longtime editorial board member and frequent contributor, *Salmagundi,* in maintaining sympathy with radical ideals yet criticizing many of the "aberrations" of the "counterculture," was then trying to achieve "in a sort of different way the synthesis of politics and art that had been represented by *Partisan Review,*" which was then "becoming very neo-conservative." Lasch, as the most eminent representative in the mid-seventies of this enigmatic stance, was an attractive figure for *Salmagundi;* for his part, Lasch gave the journal a glowing tribute. In the anniversary issue Lasch nodded affirmingly at the magazine's refusal to celebrate "cultural radicalism" as "cultural renewal" — rather, *Salmagundi* had at times dared even to decry cultural radicalism as "decay." Most important of all for Lasch, the editors had grasped that the "'cultural history' of cultural collapse had become the most pressing intellectual task of the twentieth century," and their eagerness to engage both Marxists such as Peter Sedgwick and more conservative critics like Philip Rieff (with his "sweeping bleakness," as Lasch put it) had demonstrated both the seriousness of their intentions and their unwillingness to involve themselves in self-protective partisan politics or evasive pursuits of scholarly "objectivity." Thus *Salmagundi* had managed to assume an "indispensable position . . . in our intellectual life."[17]

Boyers was pleased, to say the least, with this assessment. In the ideological controversies that would buffet him throughout the rest

---

3 October 1980, 5:16. In response Gruber wrote, sympathetically, that it was "regrettable, to say the least, that people seem to forget that you were way ahead of the crowd in asking serious theoretical questions about the relations between men and women." TLS, 9 October 1980, 5:16.

17. Robert Boyers to CL, ALS, 14 April 1975, 3:20; Robert Boyers to CL, TLS, 3 May 1975; interview with Gerald Graff, 2 August 2001; CL, "Introduction: Ten Years of *Salmagundi,*" *Salmagundi* 31-32 (Fall 1975–Winter 1976), 7, 9.

of his career, *Salmagundi* became one place Lasch would go, whether as a participant in their periodic conferences or as a writer, and experience a sense of belonging. For the quietly communal Kit Lasch this was no small thing; it became, in fact, a sort of lifeline. Perhaps most importantly, the journal brought together leading figures to address divisive issues, including intellectuals with varying perspectives on feminism. In the *Salmagundi* orbit Lasch found the freedom to express his heterodox views, and even discovered the occasional ally, one of which was Jean Bethke Elshtain, whom he had first met at a *Salmagundi* conference in 1980. Elshtain, "in the position," as she later put it, "of the young scholar who sees before her a vast array of famous people" (including, she writes, Susan Sontag, Dwight Macdonald, and George Steiner), had at a reception introduced herself to Lasch. Finding him "droll and rather diffident," she was won over by his mix of a "deadpan sense of humor" and his "moral seriousness." As their friendship grew and their political affinity became more apparent, she became for him over the next few years a trusted critic and confidant. Like Lasch, Elshtain was herself receiving harsh criticism from many feminists for her defense of "parental authority," and within just a few months of their meeting some leftists began to denounce her and Lasch as leading representatives of what political scientist Paul Breines dubbed the "'new authoritarianism.'" The controversy enlivened the friendship. Lasch began sending her copies of his various manuscripts for her comment, which shocked Elshtain; she was "flabbergasted that he had that much confidence in my judgment." But confidence he had. In support of her application for a Guggenheim fellowship to work on a project titled "A Theory of Children and Politics," Lasch summarized the value he saw in her work: she was "forcing us to consider this whole range of issues — women, the family, authority, child-rearing — in new ways, and to reject the received wisdom of feminism and anti-feminism alike."[18]

18. Robert Boyers to CL, TLS, 15 September 1975, 3:20; Jean Bethke Elshtain, letter to author, 15 February 2001; Jean Bethke Elshtain to CL, TLS, 31 October 1980, 5:14; CL, letter of recommendation for Elshtain, 1 January 1981, 5:14. Breines's comments on the "new authoritarianism" came in the context of *Telos* magazine's symposium on *Narcissism;* he grouped Lasch and Elshtain with the journal's editor, Paul Piccone. See *Telos* 44 (Summer 1980). For a good example of Lasch and Elshtain joining to hammer out a common "feminist" position, one which Lasch claimed would not be recognized by most as "feminist," see the pub-

If *Salmagundi* provided a forum for broadening discussion and debate, another magazine appealed more directly to the persisting longing Lasch felt for participation in an actual movement. With the backing of philanthropist Max Palevsky, whose Common Good Foundation had backed McGovern's candidacy in 1972, the first issue of the quarterly *democracy* appeared in January 1981. Sheldon Wolin, its editor, had contacted Lasch in November 1979 about plans to launch the effort and invited Lasch to play a central role in it. Wolin's political stance, what Stephen Holmes has recently tagged "left-wing antimodernism," bore notable similarities to Lasch's. In the *New York Review* in 1975, for instance, Wolin had, in the aftermath of Vietnam, called for a "politics of reversal" — not the return to a "pastoral society" but rather an "undoing of our own necessities and seeking the intensive fulfillments that can only be found in smaller scales where we cannot evade the consequences of our own actions." Stylistically more didactic than prophetic, Wolin nonetheless shared with Lasch a common concern to map out a radicalism that would move beyond the cultural politics that dominated what was left of the left at the end of the seventies.[19]

Lasch was elated with Wolin's invitation. "This is the most encouraging news I've heard in a long time," he wrote in reply. He had "pretty much reached the end of what it seems possible to do in political and intellectual isolation," and looked forward to seeing what might happen with a journal that encouraged an "undogmatic and unsectarian analysis of the contemporary crisis." Lasch assumed a position on the editorial board that included the historians Joyce Appleby, Lawrence Goodwyn, and his own former student David F.

---

lished transcript of a 1985 panel discussion, which followed a paper by Elshtain on "the new feminist intellectual": "The New Feminist Intellectual: A Discussion," *Salmagundi* 70-71 (Summer 1986), 32-43.

19. CL to ZL & RL, TL, 19 December 1979, 5:8; Stephen Holmes, "Both Sides Now," *New Republic,* March 4 & 11, 2002, 34; Sheldon Wolin, contribution to the symposium "The Meaning of Vietnam," *New York Review of Books,* 12 June 1975, 23. See also his essay on "The New Conservatives," *New York Review of Books,* 5 February 1976, 6-11. In it he sounds a very Laschian note in remarking that "Our best hope, paradoxically, is in the pessimism of the present, in our disillusionment. It may signify that as a nation we are finally ready to abandon childish fantasies of collective omnipotence and overflowing abundance, that we are repelled at having made legitimate the corpulent powers that now govern us and at having accepted gratefully their tawdry benefits" (10).

Noble. He began to recruit authors, describing the venture to one potential contributor as "devoted to a radical but non-Marxist politics, if that isn't a contradiction in terms"; the magazine, he emphasized, had a "stated determination not to be content with received political answers." To Winifred Breines he pitched it as a means for "people on the left today to try to reassess the sixties and come to terms with the political experience of that period," a task that was "obviously imperative." He told his parents that "it remains to be seen just what radicalism is when its no longer Marxist, but the effort to explore the issue might just inspire a higher level of commentary than is anywhere to be found currently." As these remarks indicate, Lasch was by this time ready and even eager to search for sources of illumination beyond Marx. If he was not abandoning the Marxist tradition, he was certainly judging it inadequate.[20]

Why? The question bedevils. Lasch at no time made a direct and thoroughgoing critique of Marx, much less issued a full repudiation of Marxian thought. And it had only been one year since he had earnestly described Marxism's indispensability to *New York Review of Books* editor Robert Silvers. So why the sudden crisis of confidence?[21]

One of Lasch's companions through the 1980s, Casey Nelson Blake, witnessed this shift firsthand. Arriving as a graduate student at Rochester in 1979, he quickly joined his own political pilgrimage to Lasch's, having been, as he puts it, "marinated in Marxism" himself and "already aware of the limits of certain aspects of that tradition." Much to his own benefit he found that Lasch too was "undergoing his own process of de-marxification." It is Blake's sense that Lasch's rapid shift away from Marx around 1980 was triggered in part by the tumult he was experiencing in the wake of *Haven* and *Narcissism*. Marx, it turns out, was providing little defense against those who charged Lasch's regard for past social structures and practices as "nostalgic." "I think he came to see such accusations," says Blake, "as rooted in a progressivist ideology that underwrote both Marxism and modern liberalism alike." Whereas Lasch had abandoned by *Narcissism* his earlier, neo-Marxist hope that industrial capitalism was pre-

20. CL to Sheldon Wolin, TL, 13 November 1979, 5:12; CL to Henry Davis, ALS, 17 August 1980, 5:14 (this letter apparently was never sent); CL to Winifred Breines, TL, 13 October 1980, 5:14; CL to ZL & RL, TL, 19 December 1979, 5:8.
21. CL to Robert Silvers, TL, 4 November 1978, 5:1.

paring the way for socialist democracy, the left's continuing recourse to Marxian theory and eschatology gradually revealed for him its inadequacies. "The rise of fascism and Stalinism furnished premonitory signs of a reversal in the direction of history," Lasch in 1981 suggested. "What if industrial civilization should prove to have been itself an aberration in the course of history, not its climax? Future developments may show that industrialism was a step fundamentally in the wrong direction, the mounting costs of which mankind can no longer afford. Is it still too soon to consider how some of our mistakes might be undone?" If Marx had been blind to such monumental mistakes, certainly more scrutiny and searching were required. "Neither liberalism nor Marxism provides an adequate explanation of the destructiveness that has erupted in the twentieth century," he concluded a couple of years later in *The Minimal Self: Psychic Survival in Troubled Times.* He, as he put it in *democracy,* was in search of a way of seeing that "cut sharply across the grain of progressive, Marxist, enlightened modern thought," which were all captive to "the same myth of historical progress."[22]

The ways in which Lasch's politics and ideas were changing were subtle but of a piece with larger shifts taking place in American intellectual life in the 1980s, as postmodern assumptions and sensibilities began to alter whole academic disciplines and rearrange political alliances. Having been a defender and exponent of the "rationalist tradition" throughout the sixties and seventies (even as he himself was heavily engaged in an early species of deconstructive, genealogical criticism), Lasch in the eighties began — along with virtually the entire American professorate — to rethink the basic epistemic assump-

22. Interview with Casey Nelson Blake, 18 June 2007; CL, "Democracy and the 'Crisis of Confidence,'" 26, 39; CL, MS, 240; CL, "Democracy and the 'Crisis of Confidence,'" 39; CL, "Mass Culture Reconsidered," *democracy* 1:4 (October 1981), 17. In a 1980 letter that may never have been sent, he wrote that "There are many aspects of contemporary society — and I would include here the whole problem of 'information' — which Marxism alone, no matter how Gramsci-ized and updated, is simply not able to analyze." CL to Hilary Davis, ALS, 17 August 1980, 5:14. The heterodox left-wing sociologist Paul Piccone noted that *Narcissism* "remains couched in the traditional Marxist framework of inevitably intensifying economic crises," even though the "socialist pot of gold at the end of the rapidly disappearing capitalist rainbow" was now gone. Paul Piccone, "Narcissism after the Fall: What's on the Bottom of the Pool?" *Telos* 44 (Summer 1980), 116.

tions that lay beneath his worldview. He was especially affected by his reading of two looming figures of the decade, philosophers Richard Rorty and Alasdair MacIntyre. Both argued persuasively that the Enlightenment's foundationalist project was dead, which helped Lasch understand his own waning confidence in figures such as Freud and Marx. Rorty spoke for a secular pragmatism, while MacIntyre wrote as an ex-Marxist turned Thomist. Lasch listened intently to both. What he seemed mainly to take away from them and others was an increasing desire to listen to past human perceptions of the world, rather than to turn so confidently to analysis of it, as had been his usual method. "Now that modern history is itself beginning to recede into the past," he noted in 1981 with a sense of awakened apprehension, "we can see that modernism in the arts depended much more heavily on tradition than pioneers of modernism believed; and the same point extends to modern culture as a whole." His writing began to focus not so much on the conditions that might lead to cultural and personal transformation as on the actual people to whose political and moral traditions he found himself attracted. In effect, this led to his moving in the direction Elshtain had in her review of *Haven* urged him to take, one that probed with more nuance and respect the historical particularities of human experience, focusing less on reifications like "society" and more on the lives of those who comprised societies.[23]

This postmodern moment, gaining strength in the eighties, brought with it a "neo-traditionalism," in Wilfred M. McClay's term, that filtered through American society and culture in these years. A genuine (if mild) longing among Americans to restore their rapidly eroding connections to their past once more surfaced, as seen in instances as varied as the nostalgia-soaked rhetoric of Ronald Reagan, the self-consciously traditional jazz of Wynton Marsalis, the popularity of Ken Burns's documentary series on the Civil War, and books like E. D. Hirsch's *Cultural Literacy,* Robert Bellah's *Habits of the Heart,* and Allan Bloom's *The Closing of the American Mind.* Following in

23. CL, "Mass Culture Reconsidered," 21. For Lasch's mid-1980s perspective on MacIntyre and "communitarianism," see CL, "The Communitarian Critique of Liberalism," *Soundings* 69:1-2 (Spring/Summer 1986), 60-76. Lasch noted both Rorty and MacIntyre in a letter to SUNY-Plattsburgh Vice President for Academic Affairs: "The most interesting books I've read recently are by two philosophers, *After Virtue* by Alasdair MacIntyre, and *Philosophy in the Mirror of Nature,* by Richard Rorty." CL to Jerome H. Supple, TLS, 20 November 1984, 7:12.

train, American academics, in the process of abandoning universal categories of human experience for the particularities of place and time, began embracing with a certain ardor the analytic category of "tradition." As scholars shifted toward seeing in the past not fodder for analysis but a body of experience to absorb, language became the object of more intense scrutiny, forceful debate, and political hope. Decades of scientific rationality had suddenly left American academics wondering how humans construct "meaning" after all. After a long season of neglect, what people *said* became central, once more, to understanding what they *did*.[24]

Was this postmodern moment in some respects a massive turning away from "rationality" itself and toward the very "religion of experience" Lasch's new radicals had pioneered decades before — an inevitable macro-swing away from the modern, scientistic cast of mind and toward blind sensate experience of the kind Lasch had in *The New Radicalism* deplored?

Lasch did not think so. After all, the earlier generation of wayward intellectuals had professed, even in the midst of their quest for "experience," ultimate belief in a universalizing scientific rationality. And it was this belief that had eroded, replaced by an intensive search not for a "religion of experience" so much as, more basically, a framework for it: a stabilizing, provisionally and pragmatically coherent structure with which to meet the world (since, as John Milbank puts it, "the necessity of an ultimate organizing logic cannot be wished away"). It is in this context that the revived notion of tradition began to seem so necessary and appealing, providing as it did a structure and telos that was not universal but historically embedded — contingent, proximate, and, indeed, dependent on "experience." Late-twentieth-century scholars, increasingly aware of what under the aegis of science their society's rejection of the past had cost, began in some fashion to seek it anew, through the pathway of "tradition." Crucially, though, they usually did so in the classic modern mode, defined in McClay's telling by the "liberation from the guide-

24. Wilfred M. McClay, *The Masterless: Self and Society in Modern America* (Chapel Hill: University of North Carolina Press, 1994), 282. For an essay that illumines how this general postmodern critique affected the practice of intellectual history, see John E. Toews, "Intellectual History after the Linguistic Turn: The Autonomy and the Irreducibility of Experience," *American Historical Review* 92 (October 1987), 879-907.

posts of traditional or authoritative institutions." If they sought connections to the past, they did not cede authority to it. They were still very much on their own.[25]

Lasch had denounced the antinomian "cultural radicalism" latent in this great modern quest for knowledge and freedom at each of its earlier stages. But he had done so, it must be noted, with the authority and language of science, using it to make a case for a more sober moral conservatism. With that authority diminishing (at least for such uses as Lasch had made of it), would he find a comparable source of authority, one persuasive enough to sustain his critical stance? Or would it be his critical stance, finally, that would have to go? These were the underlying questions he was confronting as he began wandering into the postmodern thicket, searching for a way to move beyond *Narcissism,* or perhaps to fulfill its promise.

It was in this moment of transition that *democracy* — with the tagline "a journal of political renewal and radical change" — was launched. It was a timely, earnest, even desperate attempt to articulate a post-sixties vision for the American left, as well as the reflection of a more instinctual effort to begin collectively to consider what post-national (yet also proto-national) cultural construction and recovery might require in the radically globalizing present. If the culture of liberal capitalism was a sham, no match for the weight of history, fundamental dependencies of all kinds had to be re-examined. Americans needed more sustainable forms of connecting.

"Why democracy?" Wolin asked in the opening editorial of the first issue. His answer to that question reflected the sense of cultural and political malaise that had been so palpable throughout the electoral season that was just then concluding with Reagan's triumphant ascension. "Every one of the country's primary institutions," Wolin wrote — "the business corporation, the government bureaucracy, the trade union, the research and education industries, the mass propaganda and entertainment media, and the health and welfare system" — had devolved into forms that were "antidemocratic in spirit, design, and operation." Americans had been "hypnotized so long by the ideology of economic and technological progress that we have scarcely noticed that, politically, we have become a retrogressive soci-

25. John Milbank, *Theology and Social Theory: Beyond Secular Reason* (Cambridge, Mass.: Blackwell, 1990), 1; McClay, *The Masterless,* 275.

ety, evolving from a more to a less democratic polity and from a less to a more authoritarian society." In the face of this progressive mythos, *democracy* was aiming to "help repair the democratic fabric where it has been rent and to invent and encourage new arrangements that will point the way toward a better society." This would involve both conservation and innovation, Wolin stressed; "the crucial challenge to radical democracy is to be as zealous in preventing things of great value to democracy from passing into oblivion as in bringing into the world new political forms of action, participation, and being together in this world. Radicals," he urged, in a note that surely resonated with Lasch, "need to cultivate a remembrance of things past for in the capitalist civilization . . . memory is a subversive weapon."[26]

Lasch struck a similar note in his inaugural article, "Democracy and the 'Crisis of Confidence.'" He pointed directly to the place he thought the left needed to look for guidance and hope. Noting the manifest failure of "the new machinery of social discipline" to achieve stability, the United States found itself in "a state of permanent crisis," led there by those who tried to present themselves as democracy's truest purveyors. "Liberalism," Lasch explained, "never developed an adequate idea of the common good in the first place" and so historically had been susceptible to the misdirecting influence of elites whose ends reflected little interest in or understanding of democracy. But the democratic vision had persisted, Lasch wrote, manifested especially in the Populists of the late nineteenth century, who had preserved "preindustrial traditions of work and preindustrial definitions of the political community." Their heirs still haunted the nation; theirs was the legacy radicals must recover and reclaim. Following Harry Braverman in *Labor and Monopoly Capital* — a book Blake describes as "crucial" to Lasch at this moment — he placed more emphasis than he ever had on the degradation of work that had occurred with the advent of industrial civilization. Invoking the nineteenth-century British socialist William Morris, Lasch argued that "the goal of social reconstruction" must be to make it possible for work to be "artistic and varied." "The development of a democratic left in the 1980s," he added, "depends first of all on the recognition that when the worker forgot how to build his own home, and his wife forgot how to cook, they lost control over much else besides." In the place of liberalism and its industrial

26. Sheldon Wolin, "Why democracy?" *democracy* 1:1 (January 1981), 3, 4.

detritus Lasch was calling for a decentralized world where craftsmanship would be not only practiced but honored, and where family life would be strengthened in and by the world of work.[27]

Wolin and Lasch, this first issue made clear, intended *democracy* to do battle for the soul of the American left, believing, as Lasch declared, that the future of democracy itself "depends on the revival and transformation of the Left." Markedly absent from this editorial and general political vision was the cultural agenda of the post-sixties left, which had come to center on issues surrounding sexuality, gender, and race. Instead, Lasch, Wolin, and company were attempting to shift the ideological focus of the left back to matters of class, power, technology, and labor: in sum, to the political ideals and objectives — indeed, to the political culture itself — of the Populists. The articles *democracy*'s editors solicited early on left no doubt about this aim. Lawrence Goodwyn, author of the groundbreaking 1976 study of populism, *America's Promise,* wrote on "Organizing Democracy: The Limits of Theory and Practice." Staughton Lynd, now out of academia and working as a labor lawyer for a union in Youngstown, Ohio, assessed "Reindustrialization" in two different industrial sites. Jean-Christophe Agnew, a Yale historian, discussed and critiqued the history of the idea of the "new class," while William Appleman Williams wrote on "Radicals and Regionalism." The magazine was seeking to counter John Patrick Diggins's "Academic Left" — "academic insurgents" who, as Lasch put it in the fourth issue of the first number, were foolishly "celebrating the demise of bourgeois culture and the rise of a liberated, revolutionary sensibility that promises to deliver mankind from its age-old submission to drudgery and duty." This journal aimed instead to develop "a coherent strategy of political and economic change, designed to reverse the long-term drift toward financial consolidation and centralized decision making." It sought to revive the memory and push for the development of an older, alternative political economy, where "artisanal activity and craftsmanship," along with "informal agencies of cultural transmission like the kinship group, the neighborhood, and the voluntary association" were at the center.[28]

27. CL, "Democracy and the 'Crisis of Confidence,'" 34, 35, 36, 37, 38; Blake interview, 17 June 2007.

28. CL, "Democracy and the 'Crisis of Confidence,'" 35; Goodwyn, "Orga-

In groping toward a more architectonic vision in the early eighties, Lasch was continuing his long trek toward finding a home within a tradition — or, perhaps better, inclination — that had barely survived the first half of the twentieth century and that possessed no singular, recognizable title. "Populist," "agrarian," "decentralist," "localist," "distributist," "Jeffersonian," "revolutionary conservative": all had been used by various movements within the broad tradition, but none of the titles seemed adequately to capture it in its latter-day form. After years of grappling, Lasch would, with elaborate if not fully satisfactory justification (even to himself), end up embracing the term "populist" as the most useful title. But the difficulty in naming the tradition only signaled the degree to which what it stood for had been devastated — a devastation that lent credence to Lasch's insistent rendering of the American twentieth century as a site of far-reaching invasion and domination.[29]

Lasch was not without personal ties to late nineteenth-century Populism; his maternal grandfather had been a Democratic politician and manager of a grain elevator in turn-of-the-century Nebraska, a stronghold of Populists just a few years prior. Although Lasch had little direct contact with his mother's side of the family during his childhood, their political sensibilities certainly molded his own family's political ideals, managing to survive in some form within the cosmopolitan world of major metropolitan newspapers, universities, and political organizations. As Lasch in the 1970s had grown disaffected with leftist politics and mainstream American culture in general, his admiration and affection had deepened for that sector of America that had mounted a fierce, credible, collective revolt against the in-

---

nizing Democracy: The Limits of Theory and Practice," *democracy* 1:1 (January 1981), 41-60; Staughton Lynd, "Reindustrialization: Brownfield or Greenfield," *democracy* 1:3 (July 1981), 22-36; Jean-Christophe Agnew, "A Touch of Class," *democracy* 3:2 (Spring 1983), 59-72; William Appleman Williams, "Radicals and Regionalism," *democracy* 1:4 (October 1981), 07-98, CL, "Theme Note," *democracy* 1:4 (October 1981), 5, 6.

29. For general coverage of this political tradition in the twentieth century, see Allan Carlson, *The New Agrarian Mind: The Movement toward Decentralist Thought in Twentieth-Century America* (New Brunswick, N.J.: Transaction Publishers, 2000), and Paul V. Murphy, *The Rebuke of History: The Southern Agrarians and American Conservative Thought* (Chapel Hill: University of North Carolina Press, 2001).

roads of the "progressive" culture he was devoting his career to de-constructing. As the promise of the left dimmed in his thinking, he began to move more aggressively toward a stance and a tradition he increasingly saw as distinct from it.[30]

Among contemporary writers with populist leanings, Wendell Berry, who after a decade of writing and teaching literature had de-cided in the mid-sixties to return home to his native Kentucky to farm, teach, and write, became an important influence on Lasch in these years. Blake remembers Lasch being not only "very drawn to Berry's perspective" but "intellectually close" to it. Berry's 1977 manifesto *The Unsettling of America: Culture and Agriculture* had in particular captured Lasch's attention in a sustained and sustaining way. Lasch, asking historian Steven Hahn to review the book for *democracy*'s first issue, mentioned that Berry had "taught me a lot and helped me to re-formulate some of my own thoughts." He believed the book "deserves to be better known, and the issues it raises need to become the focus of sustained debate."[31]

It is not difficult to see why. In *The Unsettling of America* Berry de-picted a nation that historically had been peopled by two general types: those committed to nurturing the land and those dedicated to exploiting it. This was a division he saw extending back to the earliest days of European life on the continent. Throughout the nineteenth century those dedicated to "unsettling" America had become cultur-ally ascendant, but not without a steep price, as traditional communi-ties and the earth itself were laid waste. For Berry, healthy human cul-tures could only emerge as people responsibly cultivated the earth. Accordingly, the emergence of industrial capitalism, with its wanton

30. See Zora Schaupp Lasch, "The Life and Times of Zora Schaupp Lasch," n.d., unpublished manuscript in the possession of the author. Upon the publi-cation of Kit's defense of populism, *The True and Only Heaven: Progress and Its Critics,* Robert wrote Kit a letter of skeptical protest against his ideological turn: "Zora's father ran a cooperative elevator in rural Nebraska about the turn of the century, he told me why it failed. The farmer members, he said, insisted on tak-ing their grain to the commercial elevator if it offered a few cents more a bushel. If they had waited till the end of the year their dividends would have given them a bigger total return, but they wouldn't wait." RL to CL, TL, 21 August 1991, 7b:12.

31. Interview with Casey Nelson Blake, 18 June 2007; CL to Steven Hahn, TL, 13 October 1980, 5:16.

destruction of rural traditions and the earth, had left in its wake a moral and political crisis that now pervaded all aspects of contemporary life. On this view, the effect of the industrial revolution on human existence itself was corrosive — a perspective quite distant from the Marxist mainstream. Berry's memorable depiction of the state of the soul under industrial capitalism underscores the degree to which he and Lasch were in the 1970s thinking within a common moral and political tradition. Describing the late-twentieth-century American, Berry wryly wrote:

> The fact is . . . that this is probably the most unhappy average citizen in the history of the world. He has not the power to provide himself with anything but money, and his money is inflating like a balloon and drifting away, subject to historical circumstances and the power of other people. From morning to night he does not touch anything that he has produced himself, in which he can take pride. For all his leisure and recreation, he feels bad, he looks bad, he is overweight, his health is poor. His air, water, and food are all known to contain poisons. There is a fair chance that he will die of suffocation. He suspects that his love life is not as fulfilling as other people's. He wishes that he had been born sooner, or later. He does not know why his children are the way they are. He does not understand what they say. He does not care much and does not know why he does not care. He does not know what his wife wants or what he wants. Certain advertisements and pictures in magazines make him suspect that he is basically unattractive. He feels that all his possessions are under threat of pillage. He does not know what he would do if he lost his job, if the economy failed, if the utility companies failed, if the police went on strike, if the truckers went on strike, if his wife left him, if his children went away, if he should be found to be incurably ill. And for these anxieties, of course, he consults certified experts, who in turn consult certified experts about *their* anxieties.

"It is rarely considered," Berry concluded, "that this average citizen is anxious because he *ought* to be — because he still has some gumption that he has not yet given up in deference to the experts. He ought to be anxious, because he is helpless." For Berry, if there was any political and cultural antidote to this crisis of culture, it lay in a return to the

basic Jeffersonian vision of personal independence through the cultivating of the land in the company of other citizens.[32]

It would be difficult to come up with a portrait more reflective of
Lasch's "culture of narcissism." Lasch echoed Berry and others in this
decentralist vein in his initial *democracy* essay, declaring that "A radical movement capable of offering a democratic alternative to corporate capitalism" would have to "stand for the nurture of the soil
against the exploitation of natural resources, the family against the
factory, the romantic vision of the individual against the technological vision, localism over democratic capitalism." In a later issue he decried the fact that most theories of democratic "cultural revolution"
had featured programs that removed people from "familiar contexts,"
fracturing "kinship ties, local and regional traditions, and attach-
ments to the soil." These "allegedly outmoded forms of particular-
ism" had, contrary to most modern democratic theory, actually furnished "people with psychological and spiritual resources essential
for democratic citizenship and for a truly cosmopolitan outlook, as
opposed to the deracinated, disoriented outlook that is so often confused, nowadays, with intellectual liberation." Those interested in democracy needed to understand that "Uprootedness uproots everything except the need for roots."[33]

In departing from *Narcissism*'s Marxian-Freudian framework and

---

32. Wendell Berry, *The Unsettling of America: Culture and Agriculture* (San
Francisco: Sierra Club Books, 1977), 20-21. Blake interview, 18 June 2007. For
Berry's place in what Allan Carlson calls the "New Agrarian project," see his *The
New Agrarian Mind,* chapter eight, "The Agrarian Elegy of Wendell Berry," 177-201.
In *The Rebuke of History,* Murphy, in a book that began as a dissertation under
Blake, makes a brief but persuasive attempt to locate Lasch within the same broad
political tradition as Berry. Tracing the history of the Southern Agrarians and their
heirs, he notes that "In certain, limited ways, *I'll Take My Stand* resonates most
clearly with contemporary communitarians or with the late Christopher Lasch, an
idiosyncratic critic of progress." The agrarians, Murphy writes, in this volume
were issuing a "call to resist progress, to remember the superiority of inherited
ways of life and to prevent their destruction." He deemed Wendell Berry "The contemporary critic who best embodies this central aim," despite his self-conscious
distance from current "neo-Agrarian political thinkers" (274).

33. CL, "Democracy and the 'Crisis of Confidence,'" 40; CL, "Mass Culture
Reconsidered," 9, 22. In this last sentence Lasch was nodding toward Simone
Weil, whose book *The Need for Roots* (New York: Putnam, 1952) he had just quoted
from.

heading instead in this populist, decentralist direction, Lasch was also beginning to shed aspects of the "uprooted" analytical framework that had in the previous two decades marred his own critical vision. His very understanding of "theory," in fact, began to shift, away from (in Philip Rieff's formulation) seeing theory as "the creator of power" and toward the perception of theory as a "way of understanding the ideal," the conforming to which became the hope for a society's health. The social-scientific language in which Lasch had so hopefully immersed himself in the sixties and seventies had done much to forge the abstracted, hollow vision of history featured in *Haven* and *Narcissism,* which critics like Elshtain and Winifred Breines read as vacuous, misleading, and harmful. To look at the world and see simply a "society," they knew, was to miss that world, or at least that which was central to it. The discourse that so privileged the notion of "society" and other similarly reified concepts tended to confuse its own abstract rendering of the world with reality itself, and in so doing fostered a way of seeing that lacked a deeply human dimension — a dimension critical, presumably, for any vital political vision. It was precisely this dimension that Lasch's social criticism, for all its power, had been missing. In seeking to measure the "society" he had lost sight of the country.[34]

By turning toward populism, in short, and to the moral and religious traditions in which it was rooted, Lasch gradually gained confidence in another way of seeing, and his identity as a Marxist began to diminish as he started to explore this other, older moral and political tradition.

But did this turn have significant effects on — or reflect changes in — his own inner life, his own manner of perceiving others and himself? Some who knew Lasch well describe something like a personal transformation in these years. Lasch, Thomas Cole notes, was never a confessional person, even among close friends, and though at one level he was "very warm and open" he was also "very shy." One's "feelings," Cole recounts, were not a topic of fluid and frequent conversation — in the 1970s Lasch seemed more or less to think "it was intel-

---

34. Philip Rieff, *Triumph of the Therapeutic: Uses of Faith after Freud,* with an introduction by Elisabeth Lasch-Quinn (New York: Harper & Row, 1966; reprint edition, Wilmington, Del.: ISI Books, 2006), 73 (page numbers are to reprint edition).

lectually vapid that you would actually describe feelings" apart from "theoretically controlled or precise analysis of the feelings themselves"; for Lasch, ideas were sometimes "a defense against experience," Cole sensed, as well as a means to illumine it.[35]

Cole had learned much from this orientation, and came to prize it — particularly the refusal to elevate "experience" at the expense of a hard-headed, sober attempt to understand it. But in turning toward Judaism and working as a medical humanist at the University of Texas following his years at Rochester, Cole started in a different direction. In a fascinating autobiographical essay on his own encounter with Rieff, Lasch, psychoanalysis, and religion, Cole concludes that "The antidote to personal and cultural loss lies not in restoring absent authority" — what he interpreted Lasch's earlier hope to be — "but in pursuing identity, meaning, and connection." And it was this search for connection, this embracing of "sources of rootedness and meaning," that Cole began to detect both in Lasch's work and personal life in the 1980s.[36]

This sense of finding himself on a new path pervaded one of Lasch's *Salmagundi* essays in a particularly keen way, and though it was framed very much as a non-confessional, historical piece of writing, its confessional undertones were difficult to miss. The 1980 essay probed the social thought of the American cultural critic Lewis Mumford, who had been writing for most of the twentieth century. An arch critic of industrial capitalism and an advocate of decentralized regionalism, Mumford had devoted a good portion of his career to advocating the need for regaining control over the technological albatross he believed to be misshaping modern life. Lasch was quite obviously taken (while at the same time bemused — he wrote Graff that Mumford has "a fatal weakness for, as you'd put it, Humane Values, Creative Interpretation, and Meaningful Change"). He found especially insightful Mumford's "critique of the 'metropolitan mind' with its educated contempt for roots." Mumford, Lasch noted, could see that the "progressive tradition" had undertaken a "misguided at-

35. Interview with Thomas R. Cole, 3 August 2007.
36. Thomas R. Cole, "The Uses of Faith after Rieff: A Personal Response to the Triumph of the Therapeutic," in *Figures in the Carpet: Finding the Human Person in the American Past,* ed. Wilfred M. McClay (Grand Rapids: Eerdmans, 2007), 283; interview with Thomas R. Cole, 3 August 2007.

tempt to emancipate the individual from his past, from family ties, from the sense of place, and from nature itself." After beginning his career in his early twenties as a smart but innocent radical of Greenwich Village vintage, Mumford, Lasch pointed out, had become a critic of the left, arguing for instance that "the modern socialist utopias . . . live off the 'unearned increment of religion,'" and disdaining the fact that "Progressivism scorns the discipline gained through manual labor, the endurance of discomfort, the nurture of the young."[37]

As Lasch made these observations it became obvious that in tracing Mumford's progression he was not only showing the redemptive path one erstwhile "new radical" had discovered; he was also self-consciously writing his own autobiography, a brief, indirect *apologia pro vita sua:*

> If the political implications of Mumford's work can be characterized neither as conservative nor "progressive," this is not because he pretended to stand above politics or, as superficial readers might be inclined to say, because he combined a conservative critique of modern culture with a progressive political program. Mumford's work defies political categorization because the conventional terms of political debate have lost their meaning. Work that transcends conventional categories, like Mumford's, will naturally be seen as a form of "cultural conservatism" by those who cling to the certainties of an outmoded progressive mystique. It is the champions of leftist orthodoxy, however, the "avant-garde minds cast in this old-fashioned 'progressive' mold," as Mumford once called them, who are now living in the past.

The deft strokes with which Lasch interpreted Mumford recalled his earlier biographical prowess in *The New Radicalism,* except that now he was not debunking but discovering. Lasch had found a new lineage; the work of genealogy lay ahead.[38]

Had *democracy* survived he surely would have done some of that genealogy in its pages. Alas, it went the way of most little magazines,

---

37. CL to Gerald Graff, TL, 12 January 1979, 5:5; CL, "Lewis Mumford and the Myth of the Machine," *Salmagundi* 49 (Summer 1980), 12, 13, 16.

38. CL, "Lewis Mumford," 28.

and with it went perhaps the most impressive attempt since the 1960s to shift the program of the American left away from cultural radicalism. From the outset Lasch and Wolin, despite having attracted many established and reputable writers and scholars, had been disappointed with the quality of its writing and commentary. As the journal was about to begin its second year, Wolin, in a letter to its editorial board, described its shortcomings as "the result of a failure to attract contributors of a caliber that we want." Ten months later, after peaking at 10,000 subscribers, it had plateaued at 8000, Lasch told his father. "There seems to be a general feeling that the magazine is a bit dull," he wrote, "but no one seems to have any good ideas about livening it up." He had complained to Norman Birnbaum in July 1981 that they were "forced to rely mostly on academic contributors, which means of course that we're dealing most of the time with functional illiterates. Furthermore," he added, "they can't meet deadlines."[39]

After three years Palevsky made what Lasch described to Agnew as an "abrupt and unexpected decision to pull out." Lasch was disappointed and frustrated. (Almost a decade later he turned down an invitation from Genovese to help launch yet another journal of opinion because "When *democracy* collapsed, I swore I'd never have anything more to do with journals.") In September 1983, just after Palevsky had made his decision, Lasch wrote Wolin of an essay he hoped to write that would ask "whether it's really very useful any longer to think of the political spectrum in the old way," in part because "The idea of a 'left'" failed to "commit people, in itself, to any deep feeling for democracy." But with *democracy*'s demise, sadly, he could not "think of any place else it might be published without appearing to be part of a growing conservatism." The magazine had become, he wrote Agnew the next month, "just about the only journal on the left that showed much interest in the small-is-beautiful tradition on the left (if it is even correct to identify it as a left-wing tradition)." It was also the only journal interested "in trying to persuade the left to scrap its tired old dogma of progress," and was on its way to making "a far more rigorous case for localism and 'soft' technology" than its rivals, in part by its effort to "pare away the metaphysical mumbo-jumbo and mysticism and 'personalism,' . . . that so often seems to go along with this

39. Sheldon Wolin to the editorial board, TLS, 13 January 1981, 6:10; CL to RL, TLS, 6 November 1982, 6:16; CL to Norman Birnbaum, TL, 21 July 1981, 5:21.

kind of politics." After correspondence and conversation with many of the contributors he had come to see, he wrote Wolin, "how much we have all come to depend on *democracy.*"[40]

Despite its short-lived career, though, the journal had helped give shape to Lasch's post-seventies political direction and set him on a course from which he would not depart. His thought had taken a more deeply ecological turn, one less attuned to the enlightened confidence in human powers and prospects and more to the necessity of achieving a modest point of health for human persons, communities, and the earth. A vision of cosmic yet earthy participation in the world and its past had captured him, giving him a way to transcend the destructive fallout of the modern, spectatorial way of seeing and living. Lasch's "populism" was here to stay, and with it his participation in a late attempt to resurrect an older way of conceiving and constructing the world, one centered on the guarding of place and adherence to — and delight in — the human scale. At the very center of this vision stood the conviction that human life has its best chance of flourishing when it embraces the reality of limits — the very limits his own self-consciously progressive civilization was determined to conquer.

40. CL to Jean-Christophe Agnew, TLS, 16 October 1983, 6:20; CL to Eugene Genovese, TLS, 16 September 1992, 7c:17; CL to Sheldon Wolin, TLS, 30 September 1983, 7:6.

CHAPTER TEN

Our Fallen State

I'm less inclined than ever to stress the social production of narcissism; the social factor now seems to me to lie in the erosion of certain cultural defenses against it . . . If the "structural contradictions" of narcissism remain "unsystematized" in my work, that's because I see it not chiefly as a sociological issue but as an existential, moral, and religious issue.

Christopher Lasch to Jeff Livesay, 5 August 1988[1]

Lasch had agreed to give the Freud Lectures at the University of London in the winter of 1981 — as ideal a time as any for him to leave the country, given the imminent ascendance of Ronald Reagan. By the primary season of 1980 Lasch had lost any inclination to vote for Carter. Lasch's last letter to the White House was sparked by Carter's decision to reinstate registration for the draft; indeed, so deep had his disregard for Carter become that he joined his father in backing Ted Kennedy's attempt to wrest the Democratic nomination away from him. (Robert told Kit in March of 1980 that while he had "reservations" about Kennedy, if he had the chance to choose between "a man with a real liberal record and one with Carter's record the choice is not difficult for me. With all his flaws of character, if any, this Kennedy has been a better senator than Jack and a more reliable liberal than Bobby.") After Kennedy's bid failed, Lasch threw himself behind fringe candidate Barry Commoner, a cell biologist and pio-

---

1. CL to Jeff Livesay, TLS, 5 August 1988, 7b:2.

neer of the modern environmental movement, whose Citizen's Party was calling for a socialist response to the ecological devastation of capitalism. "I am still persuaded," Kit wrote to Robert and Zora, "that a third party is just about the only hope of bringing about any real change." On election day he admitted to his parents that he had been "lured into voting for Carter at the last minute by projections indicating an extremely close election" — he "couldn't live with the thought of helping to elect Reagan." But Reagan had won without him — "a repudiation of liberalism," Kit speculated. What he did not know was whether it was a "temporary fit of madness, like 1946, of which voters will soon repent" or "a real turning point, like 1930, signaling perhaps decades of conservative government. What a prospect!"[2]

In the face of a barren political landscape England once more loomed as an attractive getaway. Just as Reagan was assuming power and the fifty-two Americans who had been held hostage for more than a year in Iran were being released, he traveled in January with his daughter Kate, then seventeen, to London. He had been given an office in the psychology department of the university, where he found himself able to work in peace. In the evenings he and Kate took to exploring London — going to the zoo, the theater, or just "walking in Regents Park" and "admiring John Nash's terraces." Shortly after his return he remarked to Carol Gruber that "for the first time in my life, almost, I worked in an office instead of at home, left my work there at 4:30, and didn't give it another thought until morning. I've discovered that there is a lot to be said for the '9 to 5 routine' — especially if you spend your evening going to plays and concerts."[3]

This casual side of his London stay turned out to be by far the most enjoyable aspect of this particular England experience for

2. CL to Patrick Caddell, TL, 9 February 1980, 20:6; CL to RL and ZL, TL, 27 March 1980, 5:18; RL to CL and NL, TL, 31 March 1980, 5:18; CL to ZL & RL, TL, 30 October 1980, 5:18; CL to ZL & RL, TL, 6 November 1980, 5:18.

3. CL to ZL & RL, TL, 16 February 1981, 6:6, CL to Carol Gruber, TL, 5 April 1981, 6:3. For a sense of the sort of academic conversation he was having in England (and perhaps why he was so easily able to leave his work at the office), see CL, "Family and Authority," in Barry Richards, ed., *Capitalism and Infancy* (Atlantic Highlands, N.J.: Humanities Press, 1984): 22-37, which reprints part of a lecture Lasch gave and transcribes a discussion on it among several scholars in England. A longer version of the same lecture was published as "The Freudian Left and the Cultural Revolution," *New Left Review* 129 (September-October 1981), 23-34.

Lasch. Whatever pleasure he experienced in England had little to do with the Freud Lectures. In fact, shortly after he had begun to prepare them in the fall of 1980 he informed his parents, with unveiled disgust, that he "should never have agreed to give these lectures in the first place. It turns out that I have little left to say in the Freudian vein." Returning to Rochester in April 1981, he told his father-in-law that he had intended to give twelve lectures, but had ended up cutting that number in half: "After the inaugural lecture, the audience dwindled to thirty-five or forty regulars, and I had the feeling that the six I did give taxed their patience to the limit." His self-deprecating quip provided cover for his increasing dissatisfaction with the psychoanalytic tradition. He put it much more strongly in an interview twelve years later: "After *The Culture of Narcissism* I was sick of psychoanalysis and I didn't want to hear any more about it," but due to having committed to give the Freud Lectures "was forced much against my will to immerse myself all over again in this stuff."[4]

The book that eventually emerged from Lasch's last tango with Freud, his 1984 volume *The Minimal Self: Psychic Survival in Troubled Times,* ended up marking a decisive moment in his journey from his 1970s Marxian-Freudian politics to the self-conscious populism that took root in the last decade of his life. After *The Minimal Self* Lasch would almost completely cease speaking in a psychoanalytic tongue, but the concerns and convictions that marked the book would guide his work for the next decade. More distant from the crises of the 1960s, the chaotic aftermath of which had so sparked and stamped both *Haven* and *Narcissism, The Minimal Self* was less apocalyptic in tone and not as tightly governed by the airtight neo-Marxist eschatology that had helped give these earlier books their clipped, dramatic pace. This book, in fact, he called an essay. Yet he also addressed his readers in a more self-consciously scholarly way than he had in *Narcissism;* indeed, the book seemed primarily an effort to engage the scholarly critics of *Narcissism* rather than to extend his readership. Still, it was not merely an academic book. He moved easily throughout from disputation to exhortation, attempting to point the way toward a more adequate conceptual basis for understanding politics and hu-

4. CL to ZL & RL, TL, 30 October 1980, 5:18; CL to Henry Steele Commager, TL, 28 April 1981, 6:2; Richard Wightman Fox, "Interview with Christopher Lasch," *Intellectual History Newsletter* 16 (1994), 13.

man experience itself. If his style was less dazzling, his assessment was more useful. By the time the reviews began to appear in the fall of 1984 Lasch-watchers recognized that a significant shift was taking place in his thinking. And once more the varied critical reception provided an index for the diverging ideological viewpoints dotting the political spectrum.

Confronting the critics of *The Culture of Narcissism* at the outset, he acknowledged that in retrospect the concept of narcissism was "a difficult idea that looks easy — a good recipe for confusion." He stated once and for all that in describing a "culture of narcissism" he was not writing against "contemporary 'hedonism,'" as he was broadly understood to have done. He tried to convey this by reframing the historical backdrop of his basic thesis. The previous two decades, he suggested, had been a time of sustained "emotional retreat from the long-term commitments that presuppose a stable, secure, orderly world," one consequence of a destructive historical shift that had left Americans with little choice but to withdraw in the face of "personal disintegration." The self that survived this epochal collapse, he proposed, was neither "imperial" in the classic nineteenth-century sense nor "narcissistic" in the sense in which this term was popularly understood, but "simply beleaguered." In a *U.S. News & World Report* interview he put his new formulation succinctly: in a time in which people were "dominated by total systems of power absolutely unamenable to any kind of control or understanding," Americans were now "desperately trying to just survive the general wreckage." It was this distress, he sensed, that was responsible for creating "the peculiar concern with the self that seems so characteristic of our time" — along with, strangely enough, the increasing fixation on "community." "Now that the public or common world has receded into the shadows," he wrote in the book's opening passage, "we can see more clearly than before the extent of our need for it." Such regnant obsessions were a sign not of presence but of absence.[5]

At this point Lasch settled into an intricate and roving discussion of what he called "the survival mentality," speaking quietly, not despairing so much as properly desperate. The twentieth century was far from the fundamentally sound, basically innocuous habitat for hu-

5. CL, MS, 25, 15, 16; CL, "Why 'the Survival Mentality' Is Rife in America," *U.S. News & World Report,* 17 May 1982, 59; CL, MS, 32.

manity Americans tended to believe it to be. This troubling misconception, he argued, was in fact a self-protecting response to the vast crisis of the age, the understandable reaction of a people that had been savaged by history. The Holocaust, the knowledge of which westerners had now lived with for forty years, was just one of several macro-events and overarching developments that had sent them into dark retreat and despair — albeit often in the misleading guise of the "detached, bemused, ironic observer," itself a "mode of moral armament."[6]

In probing the cultural and psychological effects of the Holocaust — indeed, in invoking the Holocaust at all — Lasch was seeking among other things to open up a more fruitful way of construing the reality and nature of evil in history, the public discussion of which had after the 1960s narrowed to a confining and comfortable focus on "oppression." The vantage Lasch was trying to introduce went back two decades more, to the post–World War II, post-Holocaust moment — the time of his own youth — when academics, writers, and intellectuals, convinced anew of the reality of human corruption, had forcefully spoken about human evil to a civilization in crisis. Attempting to expose progressive sentimentality about the nature of history and revive a discarded understanding of it, Lasch insisted that this world of catastrophe and carnage, and more importantly, its ethos, were far from past, though Americans of the educated classes in particular seemed unwilling to grasp its still forceful, bitter presence. The late twentieth century's "heightened interest in the 'Holocaust,'" he wrote, "coincides with a diminished capacity to imagine a moral order transcending it, which alone can give meaning to the terrible suffering this image is intended to commemorate." Having absorbed the pummeling barrage of the twentieth century, westerners, shocked by their own "unsuspected or forgotten depths of destructiveness," were left morally bereft, unable or unwilling to perceive their circumstance and condition, much less make an appropriate response to it. For many modern survivors, Lasch sensed, there was by now "no reality . . . beneath or beyond what meets the eye, no heaven or hell, no inner depths and no transcendent heights, no utopia in the future, nothing except this moment."[7]

6. CL, MS, 96.
7. CL, MS, 129, 224, 153.

As he made such claims a certain familiarity with his audience gave the book a conversational quality, at least in places. (He went so far as to use the first person pronoun "me" in his preface — "Do not mistake me . . ." he began one sentence — something that had rarely if at all been present in his earlier writing; in his earlier writings he had nearly always maintained what Gerald Graff described as a strong "public-private split.") But this more familiar authorial voice tended, tellingly, to sound defensive. Clearly he felt as "beleaguered" as anyone he was purporting to describe, for the same reasons and more. But if he was defensive, he was, to his credit, engaging his critics in honest debate, presenting himself not as a shrewd analyst making an invincible case so much as a fellow sufferer and a co-combatant, calling for "a collaborative assault on the difficulties that threaten to overwhelm us," and for "political opposition to these evils" — trying to shake his readers free of the prevailing "refusal of moral and emotional commitments."[8]

To those feminists who had countered *Narcissism* with the argument that, far from being pathology, the phenomenon of narcissism was actually a salutary female corrective Lasch offered sympathetic but sharp debate. For these critics, promethean males had created a world devoid of the processes of nurture and mutuality; what critics like Lasch termed narcissism, they argued, was in reality a recovery of these deeply human, feminine qualities. Lasch did not dismiss this perspective but rather sought to absorb it into his. While he was still convinced that "the effort to uphold narcissism as a theoretical alternative to possessive individualism rests on shaky ground," as he had put in an article published in 1983, he conceded that at least since the eighteenth century women had preserved the values of "mutuality and union" more successfully than had men. Indeed, in a letter to Harry Boyte written in February of 1984, Lasch suggested that "some of the wider implications of feminism" could help to buttress what he termed an "environmental or ecological perspective," one that might forcefully call into "question many of the values commonly associated with masculinity and with masculine models of personal liberation" that, he was now seeing, were at the root of many of the disorders of the age, and of history itself.[9]

8. CL, MS, 17, 18, 75; Graff, interview, 2 August 2001.
9. CL, "A Society without Fathers: Cooperative Commonwealth or Harmoni-

While this feminist line of argument had opened another vista on the origins and nature of the cultural domination he had long had in his sights, in *Minimal Self* he still held to his contention that to view narcissism as an ideal was to indulge a ruinous form of denial: "the illusion of absolute unity with nature." This, he thought, was a sure route to a passive, permissive form of "self-annihilation," a psychological acquiescence that would only lead to the refusal to take the decisive steps that could lead toward wholeness, both personally and socially. But the opposite response to that of the defenders of narcissism — the complete *dismissal* of this longing for primal union — he regarded as equally dangerous. This he called the "illusion of self-sufficiency," the promethean impulse, the triumph of which had led to the atomized, sterile, destructive modern world. While suggesting that in the history of the West women had tended toward the former while men had tended toward the latter, Lasch insisted that the pathway to health depended not on the triumph of one over the other but rather upon the collective ability to hold the two tendencies in tension while rejecting the regressive elements in each. The way out of the beleaguered state, he urged, was to live in fruitful (and necessarily painful) tension between the impulses toward narcissistic one-

---

ous Ant-Heap," in *Face to Face: Fathers, Mothers, Masters, Monsters — Essays for a Nonsexist Future,* ed. Meg McGavarn Murray (Westport, Conn.: Greenwood Press, 1983), 4; CL to Harry Boyte, TLS, 21 February 1984, 7a:8. In a bibliographic note in *The World of Nations* Lasch gave one statement of his longstanding complaint about current academic criticism, and afforded a glimpse at the dialectical quality of his own thinking: "As so often in the past, a new wave of historical revisionism, instead of absorbing and transcending the work of its immediate predecessors, threatens merely to reverse its political direction, substituting new heroes . . . but leaving the underlying issues where they were before, or in some cases at a more primitive level of awareness," 325.

Against those who blanketed all of Western history as a long epoch of destructive male domination, Lasch in 1983 presented the unlikely counter-case of the Puritan male. Far from rejecting the "feminine" qualities of mutuality and unity, as the current caricature of Puritan "patriarchy" told it, seventeenth-century Puritan men had actually embodied these qualities far more fully than did most contemporary American men, Lasch argued. Puritan men and women "rightly saw the acknowledgment of dependence and inferiority as a precondition of spiritual growth. Their imagery of rebirth, moreover, stressed its difficulties, obstacles, and pain." Lasch believed the "complexity of premodern psychological perceptions" needed to be more carefully understood. See CL, "A Society without Fathers," 7.

ness and promethean domination — a "creative tension between separation and union" — aiming for an ethic that would foster a measure of union with one's fellows and one's world, however short that union might fall of utopian longings.[10]

If in *Minimal Self* Lasch understood contemporary westerners to be suffering in profound ways, his writing in this book suggested that his own asceticism and "critical detachment" were giving way to a more empathic perception of their condition. Westerners, he believed, needed above all a more complex and true notion of selfhood — a renewed vision of human existence itself — and his attempt to offer one moved his book beyond the realm of social criticism and into the province of wisdom literature. Christopher Lasch the analyst was now presenting himself as a teacher, and as he elaborated on the nature and difficulties of selfhood his tone and language became genuinely, if generically, religious. "The painful awareness of the tension between our unlimited aspirations and our limited understanding, between our original intimations of immortality and our fallen state, between oneness and separation" was at the heart of the human condition, and must be the starting point for the pathway toward maturity. "The achievement of selfhood," he wrote, requires the "acknowledgment of our separation from the original source of life, combined with a continuing struggle to recapture a sense of primal union by means of activity that gives us a provisional understanding and mastery of the world without denying our limitations and dependency." A culture and politics could be judged sound inasmuch as each aided this process. Critically, religion's great historic achievement was the direction it had provided humans in their quest to "restore the original sense of union," leading them into a way of life that did not evade but rather acknowledged "the fact of alienation." Religion and art, in fact, had this in common; each was the fruit of a "hard-won restoration of the sense of wholeness, one that simultaneously reminds us of the sense of division and loss." Given the condition of the west, the "need for a renewal of religious faith" was pressing.[11]

10. CL, MS, 20, 177.

11. CL, MS, 20, 164, 247, 112. For his later reflections on these themes, and on the general themes addressed in his work in the psychoanalytic tradition, see his 1990 interview "The Crime of Quality Time," *New Perspectives Quarterly* 7:1 (Winter 1990), 45-49.

In a fascinating retrospective essay on *The Culture of Narcissism,* published in 1990, Lasch recounted the journey he had made between that book and *The Minimal Self,* and it sheds light on the evolving interplay between religion and psychoanalysis in his thinking. In *Narcissism,* he wrote, he had preoccupied himself with the psychoanalytic discussion of "secondary narcissism," which he described (quoting the psychoanalyst Thomas Freeman) as resulting from the self's attempt both to "'annul the pain of disappointed love'" and protect itself from the abiding anger that came from disappointment. In the early eighties, though, he had begun "to see that the concept of narcissism had much broader implications than I had suspected," that "it also described enduring features of the human condition." Accordingly, his starting point in *Minimal Self* shifted from secondary to primary narcissism, which he described as the "infantile illusion of omnipotence that precedes understanding of the crucial distinction between the self and its surroundings" — the distinction the acknowledgment of which makes constructive, purposive action possible. Following the writings of Melanie Klein and Janine Chasseguet-Smirgel, he now posited a more general and universal tendency toward narcissism, which any true culture develops distinctive ways to combat. And it was, crucially, this battle that twentieth-century Americans had given up. He credited this portentous shift to "Three lines of social and cultural development": "the emergence of the egalitarian family, socalled; the child's increasing exposure to other socializing agencies besides the family; and the general effect of modern mass culture in breaking down distinctions between illusions and reality."[12]

Lasch, in sum, was not rejecting the theoretical underpinnings and overarching argument of *Narcissism* and *Haven* so much as refining them, unfolding a more persuasive set of assumptions on the nature and interrelations of personhood, culture, and politics. The overwhelming power of social structures in his earlier analysis began to diminish as he made room for elementally destructive tendencies within all humans that tended to work against the realization of the much longed-for "decent society." But at the same time he was affirming a kind of inviolability of the human person that his earlier work had lacked — a "core of selfhood not subject to environmental determina-

---

12. CL, "The Culture of Narcissism Revisited," reprinted in CON, 1991 Norton paperback edition, 240; MS, 185.

tion, even under extreme conditions," as he put it. This was, he explained, "an older conception of personality, rooted in Judeo-Christian traditions." As a result of these new discoveries and affirmations, Lasch's sense of both the beautiful and the tragic took on new depth, and his rendering of human history became more convincing.[13]

With this shift in worldview came a deeper perception of the political spectrum, rooted in the inescapable connections between economics, ideas, ideology, and selfhood, the volatility and intricacy of which the modern world had immeasurably intensified. In chapter six, "The Politics of the Psyche," Lasch presented what he termed an "ideal typology," a Freudian construct that helped explain "the growing importance of cultural issues" in contemporary politics. Those who tended in contemporary political debate to be tagged "conservative" were, he suggested, reflecting one particular reaction to the larger "crisis of the superego"; they sought a "restoration of the social superego and of strong parental authority as the best hope of social stability and cultural renewal." The other side, which represented what Lasch termed "the essence of the liberal, humanist tradition," tended to advocate further freedom for the ego, the "rational faculty," an ever-expanding release from the old "forbidding structure of moral prohibitions and commandments." People of this latter inclination harbored immense "respect for human intelligence and the capacity for moral self-regulation"; not surprisingly, many "democratic socialists and even . . . many revolutionary socialists" worked from these assumptions.[14]

As his schema suggests, Lasch found both options wanting. The superego, he wrote, was never a "reliable agency of social discipline," noting that "Its relentless condemnation of the ego breeds a spirit of sullen resentment and insubordination," which usually meant rule by "intimidation and threats of retaliation." With this in mind, in his bibliographical essay at the end of the book he found wanting not only Rieff's *Triumph of the Therapeutic* but also his own *Culture of Narcissism,* which, he now judged, was "not sufficiently critical of superego controls." With a sense of affinity he contrasted this so-called conservatism to "a truly conservative position on culture," one that "attempts to hold society together by means of moral and religious

13. CL, MS, 59.
14. CL, MS, 197, 198, 199.

277

instruction, collective rituals, and a deeply implanted though not un-critical respect for tradition." He took care to note that when one who occupies this position "speaks of discipline, it refers to an inner moral and spiritual discipline more than to chains, bars, and the electric chair." A "cultural conservatism" of this type, he stressed, "is compatible with political liberalism, even with democratic social-ism" — a perspective that once more recalled the Frankfurt School, and in particular Max Horkheimer's comment, in his 1968 preface to *Critical Theory,* that "a true conservatism which takes man's spiritual heritage seriously is more closely related to the revolutionary mental-ity, which does not simply reject that heritage but absorbs it into a new synthesis."[15]

The party of the ego, on the other hand, in its self-flattering quest for independence, had rationalized every conceivable aspect of life, giving the modern world an oppressively dehumanizing technologi-cal cast and structure. This was, among other things, politically de-structive. "What if," asked Lasch, "the drive to make ourselves entirely independent of nature, which never succeeds in reaching its goal, originates in the unconscious attempt to restore the illusion of infan-tile omnipotence?" Both "conservative" and "liberal" parties, in sum, had manifested profound deficiencies, and Americans were being forced to swallow the bitter fruit of each. Each side tended toward its own form of regression, and neither was capable of leading the nation to a morally and ecologically sustainable way of life.[16]

The moment called for a third way, and Lasch in fact saw one aris-ing, almost spontaneously and unself-consciously, in the last half of the century. Oddly enough, it was not his usual third way, the one he was elsewhere touting: populism. In fact, *The Minimal Self* did little (on the surface, at least) to advance his advocacy of populism. This was a telling indication of the limits of his psychoanalytic typology, which schematized history to the point of obscuring it behind the the-oretical assessment of its actual development; to probe historical populism within the framework of *The Minimal Self*'s argument would likely have required him to skewer either his framework or the popu-

15. CL, MS, 203, 287, 201, 202. Max Horkheimer, *Critical Theory: Selected Es-says* (New York: Seabury Press, 1972; reprint edition, New York: Continuum, 1982), ix.
16. CL, MS, 222.

lists. But perhaps his neglect of populism also denoted his own persisting attachment to the discourse and culture of the decidedly nonpopulist educated classes. His smart, heated arguments with them in Freudian language were not the screed of an outsider but rather a sign of his ongoing membership.

Remarkably enough, *The Minimal Self*'s third way was the "party of Narcissus," and his pronounced, even shocking sympathy to it revealed his own searching reevaluation of not just "the culture of narcissism" but also the new left and the counterculture, the party of Narcissus's chief twentieth-century embodiments. For all its untoward tendencies, the party of Narcissus, he now argued, was at its best trying to find its way toward the ideal of union that was so dangerous and yet so psychologically and politically necessary. If liberalism had cohered in subservience to the ego and conservatism to the superego — and together they had driven the "modern," "free," "democratic" world into such overwhelming brutality and carnage — the party of Narcissus had by midcentury slowly arisen out of modernity's ruins as a chastened revolt against both ways of imagining freedom. Following Chasseguet-Smirgel and Dorothy Dinnerstein in particular, Lasch saw this desperate, instinctual political impulse as at its best a courageous attempt to affirm the reality of what those in the Freudian tradition termed the "ego ideal": that dimension of the mind that "holds up admired, idealized images of parents and other authorities as a model to which the ego should aspire." This construct, much debated and discussed in current post-Freudian psychoanalytic theory, he deemed "indispensable," a means of breaking free from the deadening grip of the flattened "realisms" of both left and right and into a way of life more consonant with the deepest human hopes. The ego ideal, he wrote, "helps to remind us that man belongs to the natural world but has the capacity to transcend it." Those who kept it in view would find ways to devote themselves to practices that realized it, however partially. "Critical self-reflection," "adherence to the most demanding standards of conduct," "loving explorations of the world through art," "playful scientific curiosity," and "moral heroism": all of these were the yield of a proper, healthy devotion to the ego ideal. If the party of Narcissus, in short, was prone to fantasies of perfect union, this was in key respects a sign of health, evidence that it maintained and guarded a vision for a more fully human life, something the other parties had almost totally lost sight of. He approvingly quoted Samuel Novey: "'One dies for one's ego ideal rather than let it die.'"[17]

The party of Narcissus, insistently probing the political implications of these ideals, had over the course of the previous half-century raised "disturbing questions" about the nature of rationality, technology, and morality — indeed, about the whole drift of modernity. This had first sparked Lasch's admiration in the 1960s, and it was doing so now again in the eighties. It had manifested itself initially in the new left and in the counterculture, and in the seventies and eighties had given birth to political movements in varying stages of development, including feminism, environmentalism, and the peace movement. Amidst the unparalleled devastation of the twentieth century, in short, a "cultural politics" had emerged, seeking to "renew the capacity for devotion on the modest scale of personal friendship and family life" while at the same time guarding a profound skepticism of the ability of massive modern social structures to foster it. Its animating ideals — from "faith in small groups" to the "repudiation of power and 'power trips'" — all extended from its defining premise, which Lasch, quoting from the 1970 manifesto of the San Francisco Redstockings, identified as "our politics begin with our feelings."[18]

This line of thinking amounted to a formidable critique of the modern world and the politics that had made it, he held, and in making this contention Lasch was expressing not only sympathy but the hope of alliance, trying to make clear that however "conservative" his politics may have appeared to become, he was not in the process of defaulting to one of the two established ideological orientations. "I believe in the goals of these movements" he insisted, "and join in their demand for realignment of political forces, an abandonment of the old political ideologies, and a reorientation of values." Like them he was convinced — as he had been since the late sixties — that "a

17. CL, MS, 178, 179, 180. Lasch would later equate "ego ideal" with the "faculty of conscience," which rests, he said, "in the capacity for forgiveness, remorse, and gratitude." See CL, "The Crime of Quality Time," *New Perspectives Quarterly* 7:1 (Winter 1990), 47. While in MS he did not put it this explicitly, he did stress that in his view conscience was not "adherence to a received body of law" but rather "an awareness of the dialectical relationships between freedom and the capacity for destruction." It "originates not so much in the 'fear of God,'" he wrote, "as in the urge to make amends" (258-59).

18. CL, MS, 223, 225, 227, 226.

'cultural revolution' is an essential precondition of political change, though not a substitute for it."[19]

This warm and unexpected reappraisal of the new left and its progeny, more reflective of his 1965 than his 1975 stance, could not have developed apart from the personally harrowing course he had taken in the 1970s, as he with such intensity had sought to reckon with the events and shifts of the previous decade and still salvage his own guiding ideals. It was as good an example as any of, as Gar Alperovitz puts it, Lasch's driving "sense that *you had to follow the trail*," that history demanded nothing less than an all-out quest for understanding, even if it resulted in costly backtracking, or the loss of allies along the way. "When I think about Lasch," Alperovitz says, "I think of him really trying to understand what the hell's going on, not taking anything at the surface level" but "doggedly trying to grasp what was happening — not fearlessly, but relentlessly, in a kind of painful way." In *The Minimal Self* Lasch was attempting to turn the pain he had absorbed from the left in the previous decade into a stance open and sturdy enough for politically constructive engagement with people on the left.[20]

As he was laying out this argument and appeal, though, he surely knew (as he had also known in the sixties) that the odds for such engagement were long, for as much as he lauded its impulses and ideals, he saw the persisting deficits of the "party of Narcissus" — its "anti-intellectualism," its "taste for destruction" — as deadly. His final estimation of this leftist current, and his relationship to it, for all the years that had passed, continued to bear the same striking marks that it had in the sixties: while he genuinely admired and affirmed its political ideals and longings, he was in the end unable to accept its fundamental assumptions about human nature and the human prospect. Still he sought alliance, as he had in the sixties, and sought it through the medium of argument. A "new politics of conservation," he insisted in the book's final section, must "rest on a solid philosophical foundation." He briefly suggested three arenas of inquiry that might lead to this end: "purposefulness," "nature," and "selfhood."[21]

19. CL, MS, 253.
20. Interview with Gar Alperovitz, 18 December 2006.
21. CL, MS 227, 253.

Rather than rejecting the "purposefulness" of life in favor of play (as people in this party from the yippies to Norman O. Brown had urged), Lasch, following Alasdair MacIntyre, urged the party of Narcissus to consider the Aristotelian conception of "practical reason," which held play and purpose together. On this view purposeful virtue was the yield of playful "practices" (from oratory to athletics) that promoted "the development of character" and the "moral perfection of life." This was Lasch's attempt to address in some foundational way the moral libertinism he had long disdained on the left. Regarding nature, Lasch agreed that there must be "respect" for it, yet also insisted that such respect must not devolve into "mystical adoration"; he held instead that the "subject-object distinction" must be maintained, which alone would lead to "purposive intelligence" and adequate self-understanding.[22]

This led to his third corrective, which was in many respects not only the lynchpin of the book but the foundation of his entire worldview. "Selfhood" — the true end for which he was aiming — was possible only through embracing "the inescapable awareness of man's contradictory place in the natural order of things" — the existential tension the party of Narcissus insistently but wrong-headedly hoped to dissolve. "The distinguishing characteristic of selfhood," he underlined, is "the critical awareness of man's divided nature," which "expresses itself in the form of a guilty conscience, the painful awareness of the gulf between human aspirations and limitations" — the fundamental, unchangeable reality that the mind, "divided against itself," was not and would never be "whole and happy." However necessary it was to guard the utopian impulse, to *insist* on utopia, paradoxically, was to lose the self. This bedrock belief he would not waver from (nor venture far beyond), though it was in fact a stark departure from the core anthropological and political assumptions held by many in the party of Narcissus. This did not, needless to say, augur well for his efforts to align himself with them or even be heard by them. Still, it was the counsel he believed they needed. Projecting toward the possible yet still living in the immeasurably fallen present was the necessary path. The tension between the possible and the present must be maintained, not collapsed. Humans must decisively press toward the ideal, even make themselves accountable to it, while at the same time

22. CL, MS, 253, 254, 253, 257.

resisting the regressive impulses that would lead to the violence of domination or the narcissism of acquiescence.[23]

The reality of the divided self — what William James in *The Varieties of Religious Experience* had famously described as the belief that "man's interior is a battle-ground for what he feels to be two deadly hostile selves, one actual, the other ideal" — was, of course, a conviction Lasch had long held, though less self-consciously and theoretically at first. In this book, the historical sources he cited for it were unlikely to endear him to his targeted audience. (He several years later would judge that "The New Left's defensive disengagement from the cultural traditions of the West doomed it to futility.") He had begun the book by pointing back toward "an older conception of personality, rooted in Judaeo-Christian traditions"; closing it, he urged his readers toward "what remains valuable in the Western, Judaeo-Christian tradition of individualism" for recovery from the twentieth-century crisis: "the definition of selfhood as tension, division, and conflict." Reinhold Niebuhr's "suggestion that psychoanalysis recaptures some of the deepest insights of the Judaeo-Christian tradition rests on a very solid intuition," he proposed. It began with the bracing supposition of the reality of "our fallen state," yes, but it also spoke to and even cultivated "our surprising capacity for gratitude, remorse, and forgiveness, by means of which we now and then transcend it." With these cryptic, enigmatic words he ended the book.[24]

And then he awaited the response. His most prized and targeted audience continued to be the left intelligentsia, and it reacted with both appreciation and critique. It is fair to say that it did not welcome him back as a returning hero. Alan Wolfe (announcing "a certain liking for Christopher Lasch") in the *Progressive* reduced the book to "a long footnote" to *Narcissism*. If the many "faults" of the earlier book had been "annoying," in this one they had become "exasperating." He found "no overall theme to unite the book" and thought Lasch's response to his critics "self-righteous, obfuscatory, and boring." He ended his review, though, by lauding Lasch for trying to steer a third

23. CL, MS, 257, 258, 176.
24. William James, *The Varieties of Religious Experience,* The Works of William James, ed. Frederick Burkhardt (Cambridge: Harvard University Press, 1985), 143; CL, "The Degradation of Work, Yesterday and Today," *New Oxford Review,* October 1990, 18; CL, MS, 59, 258, 301, 259.

way "between an emphasis on state planning and the unrestrained anarchy of the market." Much more taken was Thomas DePietro, writing in the *Nation,* who declared that Lasch's "prescription" for a reconstructed radicalism held out "the best prospects for genuine democratic renewal." Lasch's cautious, analytic, and politically modest vision was what the left needed, both in sensibility and program: "His tactical realism, in its very simplicity, defies progressive faith. His sober glance backward through history challenges radical nostalgia for a recently departed past." DePietro's response was not atypical. In general, Lasch's more guarded, qualified, and conversational approach led to a more sympathetic if muted reception, not only on the left but on all sides; within the first two years of its publication it was reviewed in over forty publications — still a remarkable showing, but a little less than half the number of publications that had reviewed *Narcissism.*[25]

While the book drew the usual reactions to Lasch's social criticism (the neoconservative psychiatrist-turned-pundit Charles Krauthammer, writing in the *New Republic,* began his review with the quip, "Rarely has a small book made such wearying reading"), it was the shift in Lasch's philosophic assumptions about the self and the world that struck certain readers with force. Richard Wightman Fox, whose biography of Reinhold Niebuhr Lasch would review a short time later, applauded Lasch for moving in *The Minimal Self* "beyond the historically rooted social and psychological analysis that marked all his previous work" to a reflection on "the ultimate meaning of human existence." Writing in the liberal Catholic journal of opinion *Commonweal,* Fox perceived that Lasch, always something of a "moralist," had "now embraced that role with a forthright discussion of the spiritual dimension of human life. He preaches no return to religion as such" — not entirely true — "but he does insist that progressive politics must root itself in a 'Judeo-Christian' view of human selfhood," having melded Freud and Niebuhr into a "cogent appeal for a resurgent liberalism built on a firm sense of human limits." In quietly exultant tones, Fox noted that Lasch had "decisively broken with the determinist tenor of

25. Alan Wolfe, "Rebuttal," *Progressive* 49:4 (April 1985), 43; Thomas DePietro, "Under Fire," *Nation,* 2 February 1985, 120. See also Robert Ehrlich's guardedly approving review in *Telos* 62 (winter 1984-1985), 223-30; Kent M. Brudney, "Christopher Lasch and the Withering of the American Adam," *Political Theory* 15:1 (February 1987), 127-37.

much of *Haven* and *Culture*," and he urged the left to heed Lasch's call to seize what was valuable in its Jewish and Christian heritage.[26]

Another Catholic magazine of a more conservative stripe noted this shift with even more enthusiasm. "We may have here the opportunity for a bit of bridge-building," wrote John J. Thompson in the *New Oxford Review*. "Christopher Lasch is not a Christian," but "a careful reading of *The Minimal Self* shows that Lasch admires much of the Judeo-Christian tradition" and believes "its loss of vigor . . . accounts for the malaise that grips so many Americans." "At the risk of offending Lasch," wrote Thompson, "one might suggest that he is something of a fellow traveler with Christianity."[27]

*　　*　　*

Bridge-building indeed. Within a month of publishing that review, the *New Oxford Review*'s editor, the former socialist and Catholic convert Dale Vree, had contacted Lasch about writing a piece on how "it might be possible to transcend the apparent chasm between agnostic democratic socialists and religious conservatives." Lasch replied that this problem "or more generally of breaking out of existing ideological categories has been much on my mind." Already a reader of Vree's magazine, he found himself, he professed, in "agreement with most of what appears in *New Oxford Review*." He agreed to submit an essay, and by October 1986 he had accepted an invitation to become a contributing editor to the magazine just as his first piece for it was being published.[28]

Lasch's willingness to contend as a leftist intellectual for the importance of "religion" in a largely secular intellectual culture was by now unusual, to say the least. He was coming to see in new ways that the realms of inquiry that most consistently compelled him — selfhood and politics — met forcefully within the sphere of religion, and he seemed to be pushed along by the possibility that a deeper probing

26. Charles Krauthammer, "Little-Big Book," *New Republic*, 10 December 1984, 90; Richard Wightman Fox, "Limits and the Solid Self," *Commonweal*, 8 February 1985, 86, 87, 88.

27. John J. Thompson, "Christopher Lasch: A Fellow Traveler with Christianity," *New Oxford Review*, January-February 1986, 23, 22.

28. Dale Vree to CL, TLS, 27 January 1986, 57:9; CL to Dale Vree, 4 March 1986, TLS, 57:9; Dale Vree to CL, TLS, 21 October 1986, 57:9.

of it might move him beyond a few well-fortified intellectual and political obstacles. "Whatever ails us doesn't have any quick secular fix,"
he remarked in a paper delivered at the "Future of the Self" conference at Louisiana State University in March of 1987. The most serious
questions Americans were facing had to do with whether there was
any way to retain "the capacity for moral judgment, self-sacrifice" and
"responsibility for one's actions" *without* holding to "religious perspectives." Would we truly be better off, he asked, thinking of "the
soul as a vestigial organ we can do without"?[29]

If by the time he went to work on *The Minimal Self* Lasch had
grown weary of soul-less psychoanalysis, his movement away from it
coincided with that of many other American intellectuals, as psychoanalysis, and the Freudian tradition in particular, began to fall from
favor. But Freud's demise came not at the hand of a single robust chal-
lenger; rather, he fell to a swarm of theories, hopes, and preferences
eager to plunder but able to do little to build upon existing conceptions of the self. Freud, it was becoming apparent, was located at the
end of a long tradition rather than poised at the beginning of a new
one. He was one of the most remarkable figures in the grand, relentless modern effort to map through secular means the inner reality of
the earthly world Christian civilization had imagined, but he came
along just as this civilization — including its conception of the self —
was disappearing. As Raymond Martin and John Barresi put it, "In
seeing humans as subjects who need to recover the repressed truth
about themselves — the secret of their sexuality — Freud dressed this
self in secular clothing." Freud's supposed "scientific" approach to
the self was actually a variant of an older, pre-modern way of imagining human existence, and by the late twentieth century the larger civilization that had brought that vision to life was in a heightened state
of dissolution, the evasively referred to period of "postmodernity."[30]

The collapse of the Freudian tradition was just one facet of the
erosion of a broader civic language that had been formative in American political culture, one that even in its scientistic phase had kept

29. CL, "Beyond Left and Right: Notes on the Cultural Civil War," a lecture delivered at Louisiana State University in March 1987; quotations are from the video-
tape of the performance, found in box 69.

30. Raymond Martin and John Barresi, *The Rise and Fall of Soul and Self: An Intellectual History of Personal Identity* (New York: Columbia University Press, 2006),
260.

alive a continuing public discussion of the proper and healthy ends of human being and endeavor. Its loss was consequently the loss of a common moral vision transcending the language of liberation. The deconstructive project that was both cause and symptom of this erosion was already leading some into the desert of "posthumanism," the utter dissolution of any abiding notion of a coherent self, a thorough hollowing-out of older notions of the human "person," which was now devolving primarily into a legal term. It was the dark portent of this shift that Lasch was reacting against in moving toward a more religiously grounded conception of the self. The earlier dismissal of older religious and philosophic traditions by leading modernist thinkers was bound to incite renewed interest in them among later intellectuals, and as the broader conception of the self upon which Freud had himself been dependent deteriorated, Lasch became one of those drawn to reopen the inquiry.

But inasmuch as American democracy had been built upon the language and authority of science (itself, as scholars such as George M. Marsden and Patrick Deneen have argued, framed and authorized by the broader religious context), it was not clear how successfully late-twentieth-century proponents of "religion" — including, now, Lasch — could leverage newly discovered religious insight into effective calls for moral and political transformation. Here, as Christopher Shannon argues, Lasch and like-minded intellectuals were up against the limits of what Shannon dubs the tradition of "conspicuous criticism," or what Alvin Gouldner terms "the culture of critical discourse," which by the last third of the twentieth century had almost fully supplanted in American public life older moral and philosophic traditions with diverging conceptions of authority. What meaning and authority could religious language have (however tied analytically to a particular "tradition") in a nation that had become so irreducibly defined by scientific authority, individual autonomy, and personal choice? Roger Lundin, in his recent study of what he calls "the American search for cultural authority," sums up this trajectory as the yield of the grand effort to "further a Protestant cultural agenda after the eclipse of Protestant belief," a project bound to lead to the centripetal dispersal of authority, to a world in which humans, whatever they are, can only wander alone, subject to none — and yet also, strangely, to all.[31]

31. Christopher Shannon, *Conspicuous Criticism: Tradition, the Individual,*

It was precisely this boundless fate that Lasch resisted, and this is why Shannon, who as an undergraduate had studied at Rochester with Lasch, describes him as the one who "more than any other intellectual since the 1950s carried on the struggle with modernity" as it took form in the ever-debating, never-arriving tradition of conspicuous criticism. As *The Minimal Self* displayed, Lasch had begun to turn to "religion" as a means of drawing Americans back to firmer moral and political ground. But could "religion" (as conceived in this way and introduced as such into this world) do what Lasch hoped it might? Could "religion," understood mainly as a resource for better living — or, what Lundin, in his discussion of Emerson, terms "a philosophy of insight rather than tradition" — take Lasch and his country to the end he for so long and so persistently had been pressing toward? The odds were long.[32]

Lasch may well have sensed that this thoroughly modern conception of religion did not have the weight to achieve the desired effects. And it is possible that Lasch, recognizing this, was gradually moving toward a full-orbed conception and experience of tradition in the older sense, rather than promoting the practice of *bricolage*, the collecting of "insights" from varying sources, including the religious, while essentially preserving the autonomy of the self. Although he usually appealed simply to "religion" rather than to any theologically particular tradition, he did display a marked affinity for the Calvinist tradition; Dale Vree would write after his death that Lasch had once admitted to him that "Calvinism was his theological inspiration"

---

and Culture in American Social Thought, from Veblen to Mills, New Studies in American Intellectual and Cultural History Series, ed. Dorothy Ross and Kenneth Cmiel (Baltimore: Johns Hopkins University Press, 1996); Alvin W. Gouldner, *The Future of Intellectuals and the Rise of the New Class* (New York: Seabury Press, 1979), 1; Roger Lundin, *From Nature to Experience: The American Search for Cultural Authority,* American Intellectual Culture series, ed. Jean Bethke Elshtain, Red V. McAllister, and Wilfred M. McClay (Lanham, Md.: Rowman & Littlefield, 2005), 7. George M. Marsden's *The Soul of the American University: From Protestant Establishment to Established Nonbelief* (New York: Oxford University Press, 1994) offers a compelling argument on the religious authority of science in the construction of American democracy. In *Democratic Faith* (Princeton: Princeton University Press, 2005), Patrick Deneen powerfully renders the relationship between religion and the development of American democracy.

32. Shannon, *Conspicuous Criticism,* 181; Lundin, *From Nature to Experience,* 53.

while also assuring Vree that "he was not a Calvinist." In a wry confession to the leftist social critic Barbara Ehrenreich, Lasch traced his attraction to the theological universe of the sixteenth-century Reformation back to his Harvard days. "Calvinism (via Perry Miller) was my downfall," he wrote. "Or was it Luther's commentary on Paul's epistle to the Romans, taught to me by Sidney Ahlstrom? Some ancestral throwback to some distant German past? Or just orneriness and perversity? I kept it under wraps for years," he joked, "but it was bound to come out in the end."[33]

Indeed, it did begin to come out, but usually in a generic and at times functionalist way. He had come gradually to understand and affirm Norman O. Brown's statement, he later recounted, that "Psychoanalysis restates certain ancient religious insights in new form." He had concluded, finally, that if psychoanalysis was "approached as a science or would-be science" or "as a source of a certain kind of literary criticism" there was "nothing there," but if on the other hand it was "assimilated to a very old tradition of moral discourse . . . its real meaning begins to emerge." If in the 1980s Lasch still held, as Dennis Wrong in the *New York Times Book Review* had declared in his review of *The Minimal Self*, that "the only full-fledged theory of human nature is Freud's," he was by then calling for a significantly less dogmatic account of it, frequently entwining religious and psychoanalytic language. In his retrospective on *Narcissism*, published in 1990, he discussed the phenomenon of psychological regression first "in psychological terms" and then "in religious terms," merging the two vocabularies into a common framework. Both helped him to develop what he called a "moral realism," one that "makes it possible for human beings to come to terms with existential constraints on their power and freedom." He was not willing to hedge much farther than this on the matter of religious commitment.[34]

All of this ontological revising and re-visioning in turn required a rethinking of politics and society — and, in particular, what each person could and should be held accountable for. "I'm less inclined than

33. Dale Vree, "Christopher Lasch: A Memoir," *New Oxford Review,* April 1994, 5; CL to Barbara Ehrenreich, TLS, n.d; 7b:9. The letter was written sometime after Ehrenreich's *Fear of Falling* was published in 1989.

34. Fox, "Interview," 13; Dennis Wrong, "The Case against Modernity," *New York Times Book Review,* 28 October 1984, 7; CL, *"Narcissism* Revisited," 244, 249.

ever," he wrote in August 1988 to Jeff Livesay, a sociologist at Colorado College, "to stress the social production of narcissism; the social factor now seems to me to lie in the erosion of certain cultural defenses against it." Narcissism, in short, was not primarily a "sociological" issue but rather "an existential, moral, and religious issue." He contended, in fact, that the "cultural defenses" against narcissism that were still available to Americans by the 1980s were those the cultural left had for decades been assaulting: he wrote in 1984 that in order to foster "a new culture based on conservation and stewardship" Americans may well need to "recognize that our own Western traditions . . . provide the necessary basis for such a culture." He then suggested that "Christianity itself . . . may provide a better basis for an 'ecological conscience' than the mélange of exotic Eastern imports usually recommended."[35]

These sorts of statements show that Lasch had at least in part arrived at his views on religion in an intuitive and pragmatic fashion. He seemed little interested in metaphysical speculation or doctrinal debate, but he was eager to probe Christianity's broad ontological framework and its general moral teachings. In his first *New Oxford Review* essay, to take one example, a 1986 piece on "The Infantile Illusion of Omnipotence and the Modern Ideology of Science," he seized upon the ancient Christian condemnation of Gnosticism, which had denied the inherent goodness of the material world, and compared this ancient framework to the habits of mind of twentieth-century "educated" elites. "The modern scientific project is not to reduce man to a machine but to elevate him — through his control of machines — to godlike status." Like Gnosticism, modern science believed "salvation" to come through "knowledge (as opposed to contrition)." And of course the purveyors of said knowledge became, on this view, the agents of salvation.[36]

In this essay, it is worth noting, Lasch referred to "the natural order of things," a rejection of the *au courant* notion of the world as socially constructed through and through. "Alienation is the normal condition of human existence," he wrote in a 1991 *New Oxford Review*

35. CL to Jeff Livesay, TLS, 5 August 1988, 7b:2; CL to Harry Boyte, TLS, 21 February 1984, 7a:8.
36. CL, "The Infantile Illusion of Omnipotence and the Modern Ideology of Science," *New Oxford Review,* October 1986, 18.

essay, "The Soul of Man under Secularism." "Rebellion against God is the natural reaction to the discovery that the world was not made for our personal convenience. . . . it is the comfortable belief that the purposes of the Almighty coincide with our purely human purposes that religious faith requires us to renounce." Were such statements metaphysical affirmations? Or was Lasch merely glossing the ideas of others, using religious language in a loose and symbolic way but still speaking well within the frame of "critical discourse"? It is difficult to say.[37]

In correspondence during the summer of 1990 with the self-consciously Calvinist and feminist psychologist Mary Stewart Van Leeuwen, whose book *Gender and Grace* he had just read, Lasch noted that despite commenting at length in his letter on her book he had neglected to say "anything about the theological side of your argument . . . because I'm not competent to do so." He did tell her, though, that he found her "interpretation of the fall" (and its particular effects on men and women as distinct sexes) "altogether persuasive." "Indeed," he wrote, "I like your theology best of all — not least because it rules out the hope of an easy or utopian solution of these difficulties." Clearly his theological exploration was serious, and where he was willing to go in public argument may not have fully reflected the inner workings of his evolving worldview or religious encounter. Jean Bethke Elshtain refers to Lasch's tendency to "compartmentalize" his conversations according to the beliefs and sensibilities of the particular conversation partner; she herself recalls "a number of conversations about religion," in which they discussed central doctrinal elements of Christianity, as well as Elshtain's own Christian affirmation.[38]

In an illuminating 1987 review essay of a book Lasch described as "a hand-me-down specimen of one of the ideologies of the day" — namely, the belief that scientific psychology should replace religion — he pointed to William James's notion of the "twice-born" for a counterpoint. But it was Lasch's description of the "twice-born" that was most arresting, tinged, it seemed, with his own longing, and per-

37. CL, "The Infantile Illusion of Omnipotence," 18; CL, "The Soul of Man under Secularism," *New Oxford Review*, July-August 1991, 18.
38. CL to Mary Stewart Van Leeuwen, TLS, 2 July 1990, 41:6. Interview with Jean Bethke Elshtain, 23 August 2007; Jean Bethke Elshtain to author, TLS, 15 February 2001, copy in possession of author.

haps even his own experience (though probably not in any strictly confessional sense), in the years since the release of *Narcissism*. The "twice-born," he wrote, "have such a powerful awareness of . . . wrongs and misfortunes that they are driven to distraction and despair before experiencing an unexpected, unsought, and overwhelming sense of the beauty and fitness of a world that nevertheless includes evil." If something like this had not been his experience, much of his writings from the mid-1980s until his death nonetheless held up this experience as an end to which humans, and human cultures, should make their way. His concluding statement in *The Minimal Self,* in which he evoked and underscored "our surprising capacity for gratitude, remorse, and forgiveness," revealed poignantly his continuing hope for what he had long since called spiritual renewal. He seemed to be struggling to find a way out of what Lundin calls "the school of suspicion," where he had long been a resident scholar — a place, in Lundin's words, where "there are no ideals grounded in a transcendent reality but only a spate of initially inarticulate urges, or preferences, that govern from the shadows the drama that unfolds in the light of common experience."[39]

Questions of his personal quest or his experience aside, one message Lasch was willing to take public beginning in the mid-eighties centered on the need to acknowledge the reality of "limits," as he simply put it, and he now turned to religious and ecological thinking as he made this case. Contrary to our common assumptions, humans were bound by discernible, immovable limits at all levels, he averred. "It is a lie, this gabble of having it all," he wrote in an editorial in the *New York Times* at the end of 1989, "a bigger lie by far than anything we used to make up about George Washington." Both for their own psychic health and for the survival of the earth, humans needed to circumscribe and discipline their restless desire for cheap, yet terribly costly, gratification. "Neither the Right nor the Left addresses the overriding question of our time, the question of limits," he wrote in an opinion piece in the *Daily Telegraph* of London in December of 1986; he urged readers to consider the possibility that "the problems confronting us are cultural and spiritual rather than political. To take the position that sufficiency for all, not superabundance, is the goal

---

39. CL, "Review Article — Scientists of the Mind," *Educational Theory* 37:2 (Spring 1987), 205, 204; CL, MS, 259; Roger Lundin, *From Nature to Experience,* 19.

we ought to aim at is to propose a fundamental revision of our ideas about the good life." He suggested that westerners call up an "important piece of oral wisdom inherited from our unenlightened, pre-emancipated past," the conviction that "happiness comes only to those who have renounced the search for it, having learned, in other words, that human happiness is not the grand design behind the natural order of things." "We need," he wrote, "to impose limits not only on economic growth and technological development but on human pretension and pride." A "politics of limits" would require "the abandonment of the whole ideology of progress and the recovery and restatement of old religious insights, ones that stress the finitude of human powers and intelligence."[40]

This task of vital restatement was now driving his writing. His philosophic and ideological sojourn had once more led him to a seemingly satisfactory resting place. Now, as the long-developing "cultural civil war" was facing a fierce turn, the matter of allies and audience posed his biggest challenges.

40. CL, "The I's Have It for Another Decade," *New York Times,* 27 December 1989, A23; CL, "The Politics of Limits," *Daily Telegraph,* 16 December 1986, 16.

CHAPTER ELEVEN

The Real Promise of American Life

I can't imagine a less attractive prospect than a society made up of intellectuals.

Christopher Lasch, in *democracy*, 1982[1]

The term you're looking for is "populist."

Christopher Lasch to Michael Lerner, 25 July 1987[2]

B y the middle of the 1980s Lasch was as politically free as he had ever been, much to his despair, as the left became increasingly theoretical and Ronald Reagan took center stage.

The sunshine of Reagan's "morning in America" wasn't reaching the decidedly chilly Russell Jacoby, who in the decade since the publication of *Social Amnesia* had become a free-floating intellectual and a nearly unemployable academic, trying with wit and punch to provoke a broadening readership to leftwing response. He warned in a widely read book published in 1987 that Americans were witnessing "The Last Intellectuals" — the book's title. His subtitle, "American Culture in the Age of Academe," underlined his contention that a major source of the recent loss of politically decisive argument was the feudal, walled-in university itself: that alleged source of light, the place to

1. CL, "Popular Culture and the Illusion of Choice," *democracy* 2:2 (April 1982), 88.
2. CL to Michael Lerner, TLS, 25 July 1987, 7a:18.

which radicals had run to hide, their academic pyrotechnics doing little to expose, much less halt, the spreading darkness. In contemporary America, Jacoby lamented, it was nearly impossible for intellectuals to make a living outside of academe and out on the street. Both the street and the academy were worse for it.[3]

In a juxtaposition that reveals much about the 1980s culture-wars landscape, Allan Bloom's *The Closing of the American Mind,* a rarified polemic on the long-term drift of American history published just a few months before Jacoby's book, pointed accusingly to the university as well, but from an archly conservative position. It became one of the decade's surprising bestsellers, occasioning innumerable reviews, essays, columns, symposia, and very long strings of imprecations from liberal academics. Bloom, a University of Chicago professor who was a disciple of the German émigré political philosopher Leo Strauss and a representative of the lingering influence of Robert Maynard Hutchins at Chicago, charged that (as his subtitle had it) "higher education has failed democracy and impoverished the souls of today's students." Bloom's argument wasn't primarily sociological but philosophical, and was centered on his perception of the moral relativism he saw guiding education — and all of America — toward a deepening darkness. "There is now an entirely new language of good and evil," he wrote, "originating in an attempt to get 'beyond good and evil' and preventing us from talking with any conviction about good and evil anymore. Even those who deplore our current moral condition do so in the very language that exemplifies that condition," leading to "radical subjectivity." Far from heralding Reagan's dawn, Bloom too was cursing the night.[4]

Predictably, Lasch was drawn to both books — which only underscored his heterodoxy in the pitched ideological battles of the decade, in which the very possibility of one nation under anything transcending the self seemed to be rapidly eroding, as cultural critic Andrew Delbanco suggests in his book *The Real American Dream.* Lasch would feature both Jacoby's and Bloom's books in the annotated bibliography of his posthumously published *The Revolt of the Elites and the Be-*

3. Russell Jacoby, *The Last Intellectuals: American Culture in the Age of Academe* (New York: Basic Books, 1987).

4. Allan Bloom, *The Closing of the American Mind* (New York: Simon & Schuster, 1987), 141-42.

trayal of Democracy, insisting that "the book liberals love to hate," Bloom's *Closing,* "deserves closer attention than it has received from the academic left." He echoed Bloom in his chapter on "academic pseudoradicalism," noting that "many young people . . . cannot seem to grasp the idea that 'values' imply some principle of moral obligation," and indicted the university as indeed complicit in the broader state of decline, which was unraveling in all directions, right down to the composition of sentences. "I'm more than usually distressed by the collapse of our language," Lasch wrote his father in the winter of 1983. In fact, so dismayed was he that he had taken it upon himself to purchase for his graduate students copies of the classic handbook *The Elements of Style,* by William Strunk Jr. and E. B. White, and then quiz them on it. "It isn't just that they can't write — they can't read either," he complained. "Such experiences leave me with the feeling that there isn't even any point in trying to talk about our educational system. It's a total and unmitigated shambles."[5]

Yet this had the effect not of narrowing and intensifying his focus to the sphere of educational reform ("My tolerance for discussions of educational reform is much lower than yours has turned out to be," he noted in 1987 to his erstwhile colleague Gerald Graff) but rather of keeping him fiercely present in the larger debates of this conflicted decade, the peak of the late-twentieth-century culture wars moment.[6]

To be sure, Lasch's teaching became if anything more effective in these years. But it was precisely his ability to bridge the churning, changing world around the academy to the classroom that gave his teaching its distinct edge. The case of Dominic Aquila, whose atypical academic background was something of a norm among Lasch graduate students, is worth noting in this regard. An administrator and musician at the Rochester Philharmonic Orchestra, with a B.A. from Julliard and M.B.A. from New York University, Aquila was an unlikely candidate to abruptly shift directions and become a historian. But after hearing Lasch discuss the state of the arts on a panel at Rochester's Eastman School of Music in 1983, Aquila was so taken by Lasch's analysis and style that after a follow-up conversation with Lasch he decided

5. Andrew Delbanco, *The Real American Dream: A Meditation on Hope* (Cambridge: Harvard University Press, 1999), chapter three, "Self," 81-118; CL, RE, 253, 248, 180; CL to RL, TL, 15 February 1983, 7:4.

6. CL to Gerald Graff, TLS, 6 October 1987, 7a:17.

to pursue a graduate degree under Lasch's direction. "I mean, I had no *intention* of studying history," Aquila recounts. "I really wanted to know *him*. . . . I read everything that he wrote right away," and ended up feeling "an affinity of mind" that, as their friendship developed, led Aquila in very different directions. "Lasch intervened twice in my life," Aquila says, "in a way that steered my career, and even my own sense of vocation and religious sensibilities." It was Lasch's ability to "do history as an intellectual" that Aquila found so "refreshing." He sums up his experience with Lasch: "I mean, he *energized* me."[7]

Rochelle Gurstein, a Lasch student who once thought she might become a documentary filmmaker, changed her life's course after working with Lasch. On the verge of completing her Ph.D., she wrote to Lasch to express her "profound gratitude." "Coming to Rochester," she reflected, "has saved me from the despairing life of the consuming aesthete" — a self-conscious reference, she later remembered, to a cultural type Alasdair MacIntyre had described in *After Virtue,* which she had read with Lasch. Students came to Rochester, she noted, to become not historians but "intellectuals," and in studying with Lasch they found themselves forced into a confrontation between themselves and the world. He did not teach a discipline; he taught a way of seeing, one that in the morally and politically confused post-1960s world decisively affected dozens of students.[8]

Much of what Lasch saw in that world came through his experience in the classroom, and this had a profound impact on his writing. The dynamic also worked the other way, of course — a fruitful dialectic. "I believe that young people in our society are living in a state of almost unbearable, though mostly inarticulate agony," he wrote in a 1989 op-ed piece for the *New York Times,* sounding every bit the fifty-something professor who had spent thirty-some years listening to students discuss texts and ideas. "They experience the world only as a source of pleasure and pain. The culture at their disposal provides so little help in ordering the world that experience comes to them in the form merely of direct stimulation or deprivation, without

7. Interview with Dominic Aquila, 5 January 2007. Lasch published a version of the address Aquila heard as "The Degradation of Work and the Apotheosis of Art," *Harper's,* February 1984, 40-45.

8. Rochelle Gurstein to CL, ALS, n.d. [c. summer 1985], 7:14; interview with Rochelle Gurstein, 20 July 2007.

much symbolic mediation." Here he was trying to achieve in the broader political realm what he also aimed for in the classroom: a vivid depiction of the real state of affairs in which all were enmeshed. "There is only one cure for the malady that afflicts our culture," he told the *Times* readers, "and that is to speak the truth about it. Once we can bring ourselves to do that, it will be time to worry about 'constructive solutions,' 'practical proposals' and 'social alternatives' for our young."[9]

His heterodoxy in a polarized time notwithstanding, finding writing outlets was not a problem; he was by this time an inveterate social critic of the type called on by major publications for the occasional striking column. If he had fallen out of favor by then with the *New York Review of Books,* he was still being solicited by *Harper's* for regular pieces, where some of his best writing in these years would appear. But this was not what Lasch was after, the pleasure of knowing he had become so much parlor furniture. He craved not fame but that for which he had always longed: participation in a vital political movement, one that might speak sharply and persuasively to the nation. More than ever, though, he was having difficulty finding one, or even the remnant of one. In the culture wars of the 1980s, he was a soldier in search of an army.[10]

In this atmosphere of entrenched conflict, the moment when America's "uneasy pluralism," in sociologist James Davison Hunter's term, erupted from new depths, Lasch eyed the dominant ideological stances cagily, as his warm greeting of both Jacoby and Bloom suggests. Liberals continued to be his primary focal point and foil. "If there is a unifying theme in my work," he in 1984 wrote to a graduate student at Ohio University who was writing a paper on him, "it is an attempt to understand the political and cultural heritage of liberalism, the political culture in which I myself was raised, but the failures of which become clearer and clearer with the passage of time" — although every electoral season Lasch's early political formation surfaced in ways that seemed to belie the passage of time. "Did you see the great presidential debate?" he asked Gerald Graff that October. "I

---

9. CL, "The I's Have It for Another Decade," *New York Times,* 27 December 1989, A23.

10. On Lasch's difficulties with the *New York Review,* see CL to Milton Cantor, TL, 1 July 1985, 7:13.

thought Reagan was surprisingly inept and befuddled and Mondale surprisingly forceful. I relished his turning Reagan's 'there you go again' so neatly back on him." This instinctual cheering for the very Democrat he would in any public forum denounce revealed an inclination of soul argument could not dislodge.[11]

But this primal attachment continued also to go a long way toward accounting for the persistence of his war against it, the occasional high points of a Mondale candidacy notwithstanding. In his review of *Minimal Self,* Richard Fox had understood Lasch to be calling for a "resurgent liberalism" — a choice of terms Lasch almost certainly found unfortunate. His public invective in the mid-eighties against liberalism — which he certainly hoped was not resurgent — was as harsh as ever; he rarely gave either the political tradition or movement any sort of blessing. In fact, he tended to see the culture wars as a fate liberals had brought upon themselves. In 1983 he published one of his most damning essays against liberalism in a volume dedicated to "Rethinking Liberalism." The "liberal order should have collapsed a long time ago," he charged. Fronted by intellectuals who despite their showy pedigrees had proven unable to develop a "theory of the good society," liberalism had devolved into "a politics of the mass media," with no particularly solid and rooted constituency outside of the rootless professional class. The "liberal condescension toward the values of 'middle America'" was only continuing to increase, leading Democratic presidential candidates to defeat after humiliating defeat. Many Democrats had sided with the Republicans in the early eighties because of the failure of liberal elites to give them "some acknowledgement of the legitimacy of their commitment to marriage, their patriotism, their religion, and their belief that the differences between men and women cannot be reduced to cultural 'conditioning' and economic oppression"; their electoral revenge against the left was the price new class Democrats had to pay. Lasch believed that the "ascendancy of the new class rests not on its secure command of an intellectual and political tradition, but on its imagined superiority to the average unenlightened American bigot."[12]

11. James Davison Hunter, *Culture Wars: The Struggle to Define America* (New York: Basic Books, 1991), 39; CL to Beverly G. Childers, TL, 10 January 1984, 7:8; CL to Gerald Graff, TL, 8 October 1984, 7:9.

12. Richard Wightman Fox, "Limits and the Solid Self," *Commonweal,* 8 Feb-

As pundits and scholars began increasingly to use the culture wars framework to explain the turn American politics had taken since the sixties, Lasch, whose use of this phrase went back to the early seventies, also found it apt. But unlike most commentators, he remained convinced that the deepest divisions reflected not simply clashes of abstract "values" or "ideas" but rather "the cultural dimension of class conflict." James Davison Hunter, in his widely read 1991 book *Culture Wars: The Struggle to Define America,* argued that the political clashes were the "result of differing worldviews" — our "most fundamental and cherished assumptions about how to order our lives." Lasch did not deny this more ideational level of conflict, but as a historian (and ex-Marxist) he thought its emergence only made sense in the broader context of the nation's political and economic history. The clashes, he maintained, were fundamentally rooted in the "economic disparities that have characterized American society for a long time and are bound to widen as our economic resources shrink." As the secularizing new class had triumphed, it had pushed to the economic and political margins those who were now fighting to regain some of that lost influence and control.[13]

The twentieth anniversary of John F. Kennedy's assassination gave him a timely opportunity not only to cast some long-harbored doubt on the Warren Commission but also to show how the "official interpretation" of Kennedy's death figured as a key moment in this triumphal liberal ascendance, which assured that culture wars would eventually ensue. The "Kennedy cult," Lasch contended in a *Harper's* essay, had been "promoted by those who had lost faith in the real promise of American life: the hope that a self-governing republic can serve as a source of moral and political inspiration to the rest of the world, not as the center of a new world empire." Kennedy, with his courtly style, magnificently symbolized the latter, not the former, and Lasch reminded his cosmopolitan readership that "The identification of political leadership with the rule of the 'best and brightest,' the celebration of an 'advancing cosmopolitan sentiment' over local-

ruary 1985, 87; CL, "Liberalism in Retreat," in *Liberalism Reconsidered,* ed. Douglas Maclean and Claudia Mills (Lanham, Md.: Rowman & Allanheld, 1983), 105, 112, 113, 115.

13. CL, "The Cultural Civil War and the Crisis of Faith," *Katallagete* 8:1 (Summer 1982), 15; Hunter, *Culture Wars,* 42.

ism, as Hofstadter put it, and a celebration of 'heroic leadership' have no place in the classical theory of democracy." The "imperial style of leadership" was in fact a violation of democratic ideals and practice. The creation of an American Camelot poignantly registered the distaste the new American nobility felt for those whom they imagined to be living beneath them.[14]

Here the youthful anti-liberalism of *The New Radicalism in America* vintage met Lasch's seasoned post-socialist vantage in a potent encounter. Back in 1965, Lasch had noted that the liberal intellectuals who had surrounded Kennedy and were then fashioning the Camelot myth were doing so in utterly self-flattering ways. "But looking at the Kennedy administration from a distance," Lasch wrote, "one could not avoid the suspicion that what liberals called his style consisted largely of a Harvard education, a certain amount of conscientious concert-going, and a feeling, never very precise, that the arts ought somehow to be officially encouraged." In that book Lasch had denounced this foppery as the betrayal of "intellect" while pointing toward a more bracing and serious conception of the intellectual life and politics. Twenty years later the hope he was holding had changed — "I can't imagine a less attractive prospect than a society made up of intellectuals," he declared in 1982 — but betrayal was still his preoccupation and charge. What he was seeing in the eighties was not simply the new class betrayal of "intellect" but rather its betrayal of the democratic ideals the mere existence of "ordinary people" required. It was this haughty, vulgar dismissal that now sparked his disdain.[15]

Lasch's turn away from the left in these years had everything to do with this same brand of conceit, which he believed so plagued liberals; if anything, his twenty years of active membership on the left had made its political arrogance even more outrageous to him, given its ostensibly higher and purer commitment to democracy. In fact, he began to doubt not just the viability of a left but its very usefulness as an ideological category. Writing to Winifred Breines in the summer of 1983 after reading her recent book on the new left, he speculated that the new left might not have been the start of something new at all, but rather the "end of an older tradition." In a letter written a few weeks later to Casey Nelson Blake, he tossed out the possibility that "the left

14. CL, "The Life of Kennedy's Death," *Harper's*, October 1983, 33, 40.
15. CL, NR, 311; CL, "Popular Culture and the Illusion of Choice," 88.

is simply finished as a serious intellectual force, and that the very concept of the left now has to be discarded." Still pondering the matter the next year, he suggested to Harry Boyte, an activist and advocate for a new populism, that "the idea of a left" was "part of a legacy, including other outmoded ideas like progress and cosmopolitanism and enlightenment, that no longer serves any useful purpose." Perhaps it was in the end "the product of a definite historical epoch — the epoch of industrialization and revolution — now drawing to a close."[16]

He was not sure what he was seeing. But he was convinced that enlightened, progressive new class mores and premises now guided the left, preventing it from listening to the experience and testimony of its potential constituency. Nowhere did Lasch more cogently express his quarrel with the left than in a 1983 letter to Victor Navasky, a *Nation* editor who was soliciting an essay from Lasch for a book with the working title "The Radicals and the Liberals: A Study in Contrasting Styles, Tactics, Strategies and Goals on the Left." Reading Navasky's proposal provoked in Lasch a moment of lightning-strike clarity:

> The left believes in progress, technology, education, enlightenment. It believes that people ought to be uprooted from tradition and liberated from provincial superstitions and constraints. It believes in cosmopolitanism and critical thought. It believes in socialism — revolutionary or social democratic. . . . It believes in science and scientific method [*sic*] and the scientific spirit. The reason the left is no longer a very useful category is that the best people on the left have been questioning every one of these dogmas and finding, furthermore, that there really isn't much room on the left for the kind of questioning that is really serious. The left hasn't come to terms with the critique of bureaucracy, centralization, technology, science, progress, modernity, feminism, androgyny. It hasn't even listened, since it already knows that criticism of these idols is reactionary. To label a position reactionary naturally settles the issue.

In other words, he saw failure of intellect, yes, but also a failure of heart — a very troubling combination for Lasch.[17]

16. CL to Winifred Breines, TLS, 21 July 1983, 6:21; CL to Casey Nelson Blake, TLS, 26 August 1983, 6:21; CL to Harry Boyte, TLS, 21 February 1984, 7a:8.

17. Victor Navasky to CL, TLS, 8 August 1983, 7a:5; CL to Victor Navasky, TLS, 11 September 1983, 7a:5.

Tellingly, Lasch in this letter and elsewhere framed his quarrel with the left as a failure on its part to follow what amounted to common sense, or an inability to faithfully uphold its own historic values, all the while underplaying the extent to which unfolding perspectival differences — including, for instance, underlying philosophic assumptions on matters related to personhood — were driving him and the left in diverging directions. This shying away from the probing of philosophic first principles was in part a habit of mind rooted in the social-scientific tradition he had so thoroughly imbibed. By depicting the "cultural civil war" as grounded substantially in class division, for instance, he tended to minimize the core presuppositions of many on both the cultural right and left and, accordingly, overestimated the extent to which political unity might yet be achieved, serious disagreement of an axiomatic nature notwithstanding.

But his motivation to approach issues and concerns in this less philosophically probing way stemmed also from his abiding desire for Americans to simply live together peaceably, as citizens who despite their deepest differences and dividing creeds could practice what he was in the mid-eighties calling "a politics of fraternity." At a conference on "guaranteeing the good life," sponsored by Richard John Neuhaus and his Center on Religion and Society, Lasch argued that philosophic differences notwithstanding, a shared past and language was "all the agreement that's needed." He believed the crucial political and moral issues raised by technology and ecology to be sufficient for true democratic renewal, providing there existed a genuine, broad desire for earnest civic engagement. His perspective met serious criticism. Sidney Callahan replied that even in a democracy "family resemblance" and "core cognitive overlap" were necessary to "make the project go."[18]

But Lasch would not agree, showing, in Aquila's words, little "patience" with the philosophic inquiry and debate such a view implied. "I always thought the basis of his morality . . . was just the populist movement in America," Aquila says. This is certainly what Lasch

18. Lasch and Callahan are quoted in a chapter called "The Story of an Encounter" that narrated the discussion that followed presentation of papers. Richard John Neuhaus, ed., *Guaranteeing the Good Life: Medicine and the Return of Eugenics* (Grand Rapids: Eerdmans, 1990), 142. The phrase "politics of fraternity" is in CL, "Politics and Morality: The Deadlock of Left and Right," p. 67 of the same volume.

stressed in July of 1987 to Michael Lerner, editor of the journal of opinion *Tikkun*. One of the strengths of populism, he wrote, was its insistence that despite considerable, indisputable differences, "all of us nevertheless have a past in common" as well as a country, and this shared legacy afforded sufficient common ground for a renewal of civic unity. An indisputably noble hope, it nonetheless led Lasch to evade the reality of the profound philosophic differences at the heart of the culture wars, hoping all the while that common political cause might overcome the obstacles.[19]

To be sure, Lasch was far from positing the possibility of an idyllic, organic harmony as the proper and possible end of democracy; indeed, he came to regard this yearning as the central flaw of the "communitarian" movement of the eighties. But he did believe in the possibility of a deepening, maturing sense of common, constructive civic purpose that could emerge through democratic practice at local levels, directing people to center their lives on caring for their kin, their neighbors, and the earth.

In a different sense, Lasch's unease with debate over philosophic first principles and their connection to politics may have been, ironically, convincing testimony of one of his own fundamental philosophic convictions: the moral necessity above all of "democracy." Perhaps democracy was, in some way, his own first principle, or at least the communal expression of a first principle. Democracy seemed, at times, to be the end that he placed alongside the ends of other Americans active in the culture wars of the eighties and nineties, such as the protection of life in the womb or the enlarging of personal rights and civil liberties. Professing no submission to the teachings of any particular moral tradition or church, he lacked the epistemic certitude, the ethical particularity, and the communal center that other moral conservatives in public debates possessed, and that gave them guidance. Democratic polity, rather than traditional religious forms of community, had always embodied Lasch's political and spiritual hope. This is, of course, partly why the "collapse" of American culture unsettled him so thoroughly.

19. Interview with Dominic Aquila, 5 January 2007; CL to Michael Lerner, TL, 25 July 1987, 7a:18. Wrote Lasch: "Without minimizing the conflicts that divide American society, [populism] takes the position that all of us nevertheless have a past in common and that the only way to restore the moral dimension of politics and to avoid moral relativism . . . is to appeal to this common, contested past."

Although he was unable to establish a home in any one political movement or religion, the moral judgments he made as a public intellectual amidst the culture wars possessed a predictably Christian quality. In a 1990 *Harper's* forum Lasch made the memorable suggestion, during a discussion of how the Bill of Rights might be rewritten to suit contemporary America, that a new "Article I" should read that "Fathers have the responsibility to marry the mothers of their children" — here he was interrupted by Benjamin Barber's spontaneous "That's outrageous!" — and "to contribute a fair share to their children's support unless the mothers *release* them from these obligations." His Article II was even more startling: "Marriage should be undertaken only by those who view it as a lifelong commitment and are prepared to accept the consequences, foreseeable and unforeseeable, of such a commitment. No state shall pass laws authorizing divorce for any but the weightiest reasons. In the case of couples with children under the age of twenty-one, divorce is hereby forbidden." Convinced simply, as he put it, that "divorce is bad for kids" ("There's no question about that," he said, alluding to recent studies), he believed that America's deepest ideals required it to not merely liberate the individual but also to provide the best possible life for the individual; for him, this meant doing all that was possible to ensure a family life for all. Decency, in the end, required a thoroughgoing attempt to provide as rich and just a life as possible for those within one's midst.[20]

When it came to abortion, the decade's central, symbolic issue, Lasch was somewhat more equivocal. Not surprisingly, he understood the political controversy to be mainly rooted in the class divisions at the heart of the culture wars. It was no accident, he argued, that the loudest proponents of abortion rights were upper-middle class professionals ensconced in "lifestyles" of permissiveness and hitherto unimaginable personal liberties. For him, the willingness to destroy a human fetus for the sake of maintaining this variety of freedom bespoke a sinister commitment to the libertarian ethos that governed the professional classes. He cited the sociologist Kristin Luker's recent book *Abortion and the Politics of Motherhood* to argue that opposition to abortion began "not in abstract speculation about the rights of the unborn but in opposing views of life and more specifically opposing views of the future," views he rooted in social class —

20. "Who Owes What to Whom: A Forum," *Harper's*, February 1991, 48, 49.

despite the fact that Luker herself noted that of those she surveyed, sixty percent of those on the pro-choice side had no religious affiliation, while eighty percent of those who declared themselves pro-life were Roman Catholic. Given these findings, was Lasch's emphasis on class so illuminating? Did not other structures of perception deserve more attention?[21]

Here Lasch's inability to grant the possibility of an anti-abortion stance rooted in both philosophic conviction (what he dismissed as "abstract speculation") and a more general outlook on life might simply have been a reflection of his own epistemic uneasiness. He certainly opposed the practice of abortion — he did not waver on this. But how did he ground his views or make judgments about the legal dimensions of the debate? In a 1982 letter to his father, who found pro-life arguments unpersuasive and the religious right repugnant, Lasch mentioned that there were "purely secular arguments against abortion," and that although he was "uncomfortable with some of them, I'm equally uncomfortable with the pro-abortion argument and with the whole idea of morality as a series of strictly private choices. There must be something wrong with our politics and with our morality too when a woman's right to an abortion can become a litmus test of political rectitude." In the end, abortion was for him, as he put it in a 1990 interview, "more a lightning rod for other conflicts than an issue central to the family." In a letter to a Rochester colleague who was attempting to initiate a protest against the United Way for dropping support of Planned Parenthood in 1991, Lasch expressed his own ambivalence, as well as the sense of complexity and confusion with which he regarded the issue and the debate. Aware that "restrictions on abortion fall disproportionately on poor women," he nonetheless remained "convinced that abortion isn't the answer to the problems poor women face" — he certainly did not believe that laws should be passed that "make it easier for men to escape parental responsibilities." Still, he recognized the extent to which a host of encircling, conflicting social issues surrounded the question of abortion, and this explained why he didn't "favor a legislative ban on abortion." "But," he added, "neither do I think abortion should be encouraged."[22]

21. CL, "Conservatism against Itself," *First Things* 2 (April 1990), 17.
22. CL to ZL & RL, TLS, 1 August 1982, 6:16; CL, "The Crime of Quality Time,"

Despite the convictions he shared with conservatives on issues related to the family and human personhood in these years, Lasch still did not regard conservatives as allies in the trenches. If some part of Lasch's soul was still liberal in a natal sense, he had come to political maturity through the left, and it continued to pull at him like a first love. Upon hearing in 1990 that Midge Decter had in *Commentary* called him an advocate of sexual promiscuity, he told a correspondent "It's kind of nice to be attacked from the right for a change. It's the attacks from the left that still bother me." Tellingly, though, Lasch's disgust with contemporary conservatism seemed to stem from something more along the lines of a character judgment, and perhaps a political prejudice, than propositional disagreement: American conservatives were simply not honest enough to deserve the respect they were so convinced was their due. Back in 1966, while assessing for Yale University Press a proposed book on the history of divorce, he had wondered whether those "who spoke for moral values in the moral sphere, also defended them in the economic sphere, or whether they spoke for laissez-faire and economic individualism, in the manner of modern 'conservatives.'" This kind of inconsistency was at least one of the elements that had long kept Lasch at a marked distance from any alliances with self-proclaimed conservatives.[23]

But in the mid-eighties he began, finally, to look toward them for possible alliance in his neo-populist campaign. "Aren't we going to need a lot of support from people who call themselves conservatives (but who might be persuaded to see that their 'conservatism' doesn't stand a chance under advanced capitalism)?" he in 1989 asked Paul Piccone, editor of the radical journal *Telos* and one whom Lasch did consider an ally. Lasch thought conservatives needed to be hit hard with their own inconsistencies, their inability to understand, as he put it to Piccone, "the social developments that threaten them." He took up his pen in a nearly solitary effort to make his case against them in order to perhaps win them over, while continuing also his efforts to

---

New Perspectives Quarterly 7:1 (Winter 1990), 48; CL to Paula R. Backsheider, TLS, 11 December 1991, 7c:17. In a response to Kit's letter, Robert wrote: "Please don't think I'm strongly in favor of abortion. I am only in favor of women and their mates making their own decisions." RL to CL, TL, 7 August 1982, 6:16.

23. CL to Paul Gottfried, TLS, 22 March 1990, 7b:5; CL to Jane Olson, TL, 29 September 1966, 2:5.

win a portion of the left to his point of view — a somewhat desperate and certainly lonely attempt to dispel his ideological homelessness.[24]

He made strong, cutting cases to both sides, trying to goad them toward fundamental re-positioning. In 1986 he published an article titled "What's Wrong with the Right" in the premier issue of *Tikkun,* whose editor, Michael Lerner, was a Jewish rabbi and a former new left leader at Berkeley who had gone on to earn Ph.D.s in philosophy and psychology. It was Lerner's community-oriented activism that had led him to launch this new endeavor, which he hoped would open space among left-liberals for a more religiously infused politics. Lerner had fingered Lasch as a potentially important contributor and, for his part, Lasch hoped *Tikkun* might become a place where those on the left could make common cause with moral conservatives who might be led to a more consistent political economy. Arguing that by boosting capitalism conservatives were actually perpetuating "one of the central tenets of liberalism, the limitlessness of economic growth," Lasch in the magazine's first issue pointedly asked, "What is traditional about the rejection of tradition, continuity, and rootedness?" — all the easy, eminently desirable prey of corporate capitalism. The very fact that contemporary conservatism (or "false" conservatism, as he called it) "merely clothes an older liberal tradition in conservative rhetoric" was testament that "the old labels can have no meaning anymore." Over against either the left or right species of liberal individualism, Lasch proposed a civic ideal rooted in long-term membership in particular communities rather than a world of "individual rights, contractual relations, and the primacy of justice." "People still cherish the stability of long-term marital and intergenerational commitments," he concluded, but "find little support for them in a capitalist economy or in the prevailing ideology of individual rights."[25]

Lasch's language in this essay was heavily indebted to what had become known as "communitarian" political theory, a development that had emerged in the 1980s mainly as a critique of the regnant liberal tradition and especially of its dominant political philosopher, John Rawls. It especially provided a discursive wedge for Lasch's efforts to address those — including many in Lerner's orbit — who fancied themselves

24. CL to Paul Piccone, TLS, 28 August 1989, 7b:3.
25. CL, "What's Wrong with the Right," *Tikkun* 1:1 (1986), 27, 29; CL, "Why the Left Has No Future," *Tikkun* 1:2 (1986), 96, 94, 95.

"left-liberals." As Lasch in an appreciative 1986 *Soundings* essay put it, theorists like Michael Sandel, Alasdair MacIntyre, Jeffrey Stout, and Michael Walzer shared a disavowal of "the kind of liberalism that seeks to 'empower' exploited groups by conquering the state and by extending its powers on their behalf." Yet they did not advocate leaving the state-free populace "at the mercy of the corporations" either. Instead, they propounded a "general strategy of devolution or decentralization, designed to end the dominance of large organizations and to remodel our institutions on a human scale." With care Lasch emphasized communitarianism's governing motive: "It attacks bureaucracy and large-scale organization . . . not in the name of individual freedom or the free market but in the name of continuity and tradition." In a sense, Lasch had been long awaiting a school of this sort to emerge, and his excitement at its arrival revealed, among other things, the extent to which his political hopes continued to depend on theoretical developments and possibilities percolating within the university.[26]

In the aftermath of *The Culture of Narcissism* Lasch had been particularly taken by MacIntyre, who had famously moved from Marxism to Thomism by the time of the 1981 publication of *After Virtue,* an interpretation of the modern self that both echoed and deepened Lasch's (and others') depiction of the enlarging cultural narcissism. On MacIntyre's view moderns, having gradually abandoned the long-dominant Aristotelian tradition of virtue ethics, had devolved into emotivists, assuming as a matter of course that "all moral judgments are *nothing but* expressions of preference, expressions of attitude or feeling, insofar as they are moral or evaluative in character." "We live in a specifically emotivist culture," contended MacIntyre, one that locates moral order not in a benevolent, overarching *telos* but solely within the individual self.[27]

For MacIntyre, accordingly, the twentieth century was choked with chaos, with fractures and fragments of an older order strewn about the wilderness of the western world. "Each moral agent now spoke unconstrained by the externalities of divine law, natural teleology, or hierarchical authority; but why should anyone else now listen

---

26. CL, "The Communitarian Critique of Liberalism," *Soundings* 69:1-2 (Spring/Summer 1986), 62.

27. Alasdair MacIntyre, *After Virtue: A Study in Moral Theory,* 2nd ed. (South Bend: University of Notre Dame Press, 1983), 12, 22.

to him," he asked. Also, like Lasch, he made it clear that he was not yet another ex-lefty who had made a home on the right: capitalism, for him, was profoundly implicated in this destructive historical turn. The ecclesially rooted political tradition for which and within which he was arguing, he emphasized, "is at variance with central features of the modern economic order and more especially its individualism, its acquisitiveness and its elevation of the values of the market to a central social place." Those Reaganites reading him in the eighties could find only selective solace in his critique of the secular order. MacIntyre's treatise sharply exposed the great contemporary crisis of the liberal tradition. Liberals (including both the left-wing and right-wing varieties) had allowed their defining achievement — their grand vision of a world saturated in a plurality of goods — to lead them to their own demise: they had gradually lost the ability to define and order the very goods they were so intent on celebrating.[28]

Mailed an advance copy of the book, Lasch had read it in the summer of 1981 and written enthusiastically of it to Sheldon Wolin while the two were still trying to get *democracy* off the ground. "Although I can't claim fully to have assimilated the argument, it's clearly an important book we should pay attention to. It's a critique of liberal individualism. . . . I find it extremely suggestive on a whole range of issues, and I wish I could think of someone who could review it for us." Calling it a "masterpiece" in his *Soundings* essay, Lasch made assimilating the book into his thinking a priority. He participated in a faculty book discussion on it at Rochester, and brought MacIntyre to campus to give a lecture in the spring of 1983.[29]

The way communitarians such as MacIntyre understood the individual (MacIntyre tagged the individual that "newly invented social institution") became a central point of their allure for Lasch, one that helped him improve upon his Marxian-Freudian conception of the self by providing a more richly historical framework and an improved understanding of the formation of human beings in relation to com-

28. MacIntyre, *After Virtue,* 68, 254.
29. CL to Sheldon Wolin, TL, 10 August 1981, 6:10; CL, "The Communitarian Critique of Liberalism," 60; CL to Alasdair MacIntyre, TLS, 2 December 1982, 6:17. In this letter Lasch suggested that MacIntyre might address "the danger that your 'brilliant attack on the modern age risks assimilation,' as Benjamin Barber puts it, 'to points of view' — surely not his — 'that are conservative or even reactionary.' (Increasingly this seems to be the case with any analysis worth listening to.)"

munities. "The dispute between communitarians and liberals," Lasch noted in *Soundings,* "hinges on opposing conceptions of the self. Where liberals conceive of the self as essentially unencumbered and free to choose among a wide range of alternatives, communitarians insist that the self is situated in and constituted by tradition, membership in a historically rooted community." Although Lasch would later distance himself from many of the dominant tendencies of what became the communitarian movement, he remained indebted to it for his understanding of the self and tradition. Not only did this notion of the self give him a more full understanding of the "culture of narcissism," it also redirected and reinvigorated his long-standing search for an actual historical embodiment of political hope: by conceiving of and depicting populism as a full-orbed "tradition" as defined in this communitarian discourse, he had found a way to significantly advance his own ideological ends.[30]

But did communitarianism, for all the theoretical strides it made against an atomizing individualism, have the social wherewithal to actually affect politics and culture on a national — or even local — scale? Did its sophisticated critique provide an adequate intellectual basis for the embodied communities it championed, for the "traditions" it contended were so necessary for human flourishing? Or was communitarianism rather simply one more rear-guard "critical analysis" that marked too late the passage of something that was once taken for granted — one more example of the modern knack for sophisticated analysis of an existing frame without knowing how to (re)construct the required foundation?

Eugene Genovese affirmed something like the latter in a 1995 interview, less than a year after Lasch's death and a year before his own re-entry into the Roman Catholic Church of his childhood, an appreciative but unsparing judgment of what was by then more than an intellectual trend:

Certainly one criticism of the communitarian intellectuals is that while they keep talking about community, you have the sense that

30. MacIntyre, *After Virtue,* 228; CL, "The Communitarian Critique of Liberalism," 62. For Lasch's critique of communitarianism, see "Communitarianism or Populism? The Ethic of Compassion and the Ethic of Respect," chapter five of RE, 92-114.

there's no community out there that they can abide — that they are trying to construct ideal communities, and communities, I'm afraid, are things that grow up historically and in time and place. The notion that you can create community from the top, ideologically, is, I believe, a will-of-the-wisp, and bound to fail. I do appreciate what these chaps are trying to do and the kinds of moral questions they are raising. But whether in the end what they're proposing has anything to do with the creation, or re-creation, of real community life is another matter, and I'm quite doubtful about it.

At this point in the interview something triggered another association, one more personal. Signs of an old intimacy and old tensions came through strongly. Obviously still nettled at some level, he remarked that

> My old friend Christopher Lasch, whose premature death was an enormous loss to all of us, has written wonderfully on these questions, but you know I used to kid him and say, "Kit, your critique of the breakdown of communities is wonderful, and much of what you say about what should go into the making of communities is wonderful, but show me a community you've ever been willing to identify with." And he certainly had no sympathy for the southern conservative tradition or for southern communities as they really lived. That was a great problem for him. In a sense, it's a great problem for all of us.

Given that Lasch had moved his family to Rochester in order to try to forge an intellectual community with others, this is, to say the least, an unseemly judgment. But it did underscore the challenge Lasch faced, both personally and politically, in moving beyond his own new class roots — his own de facto tradition. Lasch's long and arduous intellectual efforts, Genovese's comments help make clear, were in fact not directed at transcending his own new class tradition so much as reforming it from within. For his part, Genovese, with his Sicilian, New York City roots, had never been so thoroughly ensconced within the new class. In 1986 he had moved with his wife, the historian Elizabeth Fox-Genovese, to Atlanta, where she began to teach at Emory University, and by the nineties he himself had become something of a defender of southern agrarian conservatism, publishing his 1993 Massey Lectures at Harvard as *The Southern Tradition: The Achievement and Limitations of an American Conservatism.* Elizabeth converted to Catholicism in 1995, and he re-entered the church the next year — all indications of political and religious impulses still uncannily similar to Lasch's yet at the same time distinct, and different in arc. If they weren't quite on the same path at this point, it seemed they still had, remarkably enough, the same destination in view. Occasionally they would come close enough to wave at each other, as their occasional correspondence showed.[31]

But all of Lasch's unusual political associations and heterodox views did not add up to an adequate communal basis for an alternate politics — this was the heart of Genovese's critique — despite his careful and persistent dedication to achieving such a basis in his personal life. Casey Blake's vivid recollections of the Lasch household underscore the extent to which Kit and Nell sought another way. "At any given day there would be faculty and grad students" in the home, he recalls, but also "quite a mix of people with different backgrounds," including their children and their friends, the teachers of the children, and neighbors. "And while some food might suddenly appear," Blake notes wryly, "the expectation was that you would pitch in and help, and just in some ways take care of yourself but also join in whatever was going on collectively." Lasch's piano-playing and general love of music often shaped the moment; Blake recalls "the revelation of his musicianship." "Thank you Kit for gathering so many different people around the piano in song," Dominic Aquila wrote in one note following a dinner party at the Lasches.[32]

Lasch also practiced carpentry. "He had bookcases all over his house," Aquila remembers. "It seemed like every inch — spaces over doorways — had books in them. He did them all, and they were very well done." He built an extension on the house and a reflecting pool

31. Eugene Genovese interview on *Mars Hill Tapes,* volume 11 (March April 1995); Eugene D. Genovese, *The Southern Tradition: The Achievement and Limitations of an American Conservatism* (Cambridge: Harvard University Press, 1994). Fox-Genovese recounts her passage into the church in "A Conversion Story," *First Things* 102 (April 2000), 39-43. Genovese qualified his comments on Lasch in an interview with the author, 25 June 2008.

32. Interview with Casey Nelson Blake, 18 June 2007; Dominic Aquila to CL and NL, ALS, n.d., 7:17.

for the yard. He was a committed gardener as well. "That kind of craftsmanship was very much an extension of the way he lived," Aquila says. His daughter Elisabeth, trying to etch this impulse and ethic in the meeting held in tribute of her father at the 1994 meeting of the American Historical Association, suggested that "Perhaps the most constant thread joining all of his endeavors — his piano playing, his writing, his fatherhood, his many home improvements, his fine cooking, and of the other activities he somehow squeezed into a day — was his natural tendency to make things grow."[33]

The whole point of political traditions, Lasch believed, was to make such growth possible. Politics existed to foster freedom, true freedom, and freedom, life. But where was this vision of life, which he had with such difficulty sought, in the dominant political traditions, much less in the parties that claimed to represent them? Their general insensibility to such vision and hope was, there could be no doubt, the sign of a great malignancy. What could possibly disrupt a disease of such awful strength? Could a reform movement within liberal intellectual culture such as "communitarianism" have the desired effect? Might a powerful journalistic presence help? Well aimed and crafted books? Educational renewal? Would it take catastrophe, in the end, to open once more the way to life?

Lasch's most practical public response to this quandary was to continue to press as forcefully as possible for America's populist tradition, which for him was at least a politically alive, deeply American alternative to liberalism. He tried to persuade *Tikkun* editor Michael Lerner to more definitively embrace populism and make the magazine a beachhead for it. "Populism," he wrote in a lengthy letter in 1987, due to its "respect for the power of the past . . . is the only tradition on the left that can challenge conservatism on its own grounds." It had "always put more emphasis on restoration and renewal, on the fulfillment of old promises, old covenants, than on 'making it new.' It doesn't endorse the illusion that the past doesn't count, that individuals or societies can start all over again whenever they feel like it." For its part, *Tikkun,* Lasch charged, needed to forsake its attempt at " 're-structuring the liberal agenda,' " as Lerner had put it in his opening

33. Interview with Dominic Aquila, 5 January 2007; transcript of "A Tribute to Christopher Lasch," held at the American Historical Association's annual meeting, January 8, 1994, San Francisco, California. Copy in possession of the author.

editorial. "The thing is to repudiate 'progressivism,'" for progressivism, Lasch believed, had

> come to be associated with uncritical support of the present moment, with the march of progress, with the proposition that the direction of historical change is somehow foreordained and that we have no choice except to "adjust" and "come to terms with it" . . . and finally with the curious notion that history is moving in a democratic direction. It isn't — which is why it is a fatal mistake to confuse "democracy" and "progress." How they ever came to be equated in the first place would be an interesting story to tell.[34]

Lerner did not convert, and the next summer Lasch complained to Lerner of the "depressingly left-wing flavor" of the magazine. "I don't think you understand the depth of my disagreement with the left or the seriousness of my commitment to a politics beyond left and right," he wrote. Reading a *Tikkun* essay that for moral authority appealed to the views of "most progressives" had set Lasch off — "if you only knew how much I hate that smug term!" he exclaimed to Lerner. He believed the central concerns facing the nation had to do with the relationship between "free-market economics" and issues such as eugenics — "That's where the debate, the real debate, *begins*," he wrote. "If you want to remain on the fringes of that debate, that is, of course, your decision. But don't expect me to stay there with you."[35]

Lasch and Jean Bethke Elshtain hoped, in the late eighties, to bring the questionable relationship between capitalism and conservatism before the right in a way that had not been achieved in the history of the modern conservative movement. They began plans for a conference, one in which various writers and activists who "think capitalism and cultural conservatism (for want of a better word) are incompatible" would gather to debate, discuss, and issue a compelling collective statement. Although Lasch admitted to Elshtain that his was a "very short list," it included such figures as Lawrence Goodwyn, Dale Vree, Michael Sandel, Michael Lerner, Wilson Carey McWilliams, and Julius Lester. In the end they could not pull it off, but later Neuhaus staged a

34. CL to Michael Lerner, TLS, 25 July 1987, 7a:18.
35. CL to Michael Lerner, TL, 29 June 1988, 7b:2.

conference thematically similar to the one they had had in mind. At it Lasch gave a paper, which Neuhaus later published in an early issue of his new venture *First Things* (something of a right-wing version of *Tikkun* — an attempt to create a more distinctly religious space within the solidifying neoconservative consensus). Lasch's essay captured many of his long-standing arguments; he entitled it "Conservatism against Itself."[36]

But the conference disappointed Lasch, and he sounded off about it in a letter to Vree at the end of December 1989. The occasion, he wrote,

> was designed to see if certain kinds of radicals and certain kinds of conservatives had anything to talk about. It turned out that we didn't. Neo-conservatives of this stamp are a lot more interested in capitalism than cultural conservatism. The latter interests them only insofar as hedonism and moral disorder are thought to under-mine productivity. The more thoughtful of these people, like Peter Berger, aren't cultural conservatives at all. They're liberals — in their values as in their economics. Berger defined cultural conser-vatism as the defense of privacy, the quintessential liberal good. *Privacy?!* The right to privacy is precisely the basis of *Roe* v *Wade,* which these people condemn.

To make matters worse, Neuhaus did not invite any of the people whom Lasch had encouraged him to invite. It was "Neocons all the way."[37]

He also mentioned to Vree his recent correspondence "with a dif-ferent breed of conservative," which he dubbed "the Rockford crowd." Self-termed "paleoconservatives" gathered around the Rockford Institute (in Rockford, Illinois) and its organ *Chronicles,* they stood self-consciously in the line of the Southern Agrarians, but with a less critical view of capitalism and a more definite commit-ment to Catholicism and Christian civilization, or what they unapolo-getically defended as "Christendom." Attracted to Lasch's moral con-servatism and cultural critique, they nonetheless felt little affinity to

36. CL to Jean Bethke Elshtain, TLS, 19 August 1988, 7c:15; CL, "Conserva-tism against Itself."

37. CL to Dale Vree, TL, 2 December 1989, 7b:3.

his reading of the effect of capitalism on American life. Lasch described them to Vree as "died-in-the-wool Burnhamites who think that everything that's wrong with this country can be attributed to the managerial revolution. Capitalism doesn't exist in America, they say. Not a very helpful assumption from which to begin, it seems to me." Indeed, in a fall of 1989 exchange with one Rockfordite, the social critic and historian Paul Gottfried, Lasch insisted that the "managerial revolution" alone could not satisfactorily explain how American culture had come to be "dominated by consumerist imperatives." "After a decade of Reaganism, everything is worse than before," he contended, "and everything is worse not because the managers have inflicted their utopian designs on the rest of us but because old-fashioned capitalist acquisitiveness seems to have made such an unexpected comeback and won such a happy new lease on life." After several years of serious argument with conservatives in the mid-to-late eighties, Lasch remained convinced of his "capitalism against conservatism" thesis, even as the right rejected him almost as thoroughly as the left.[38]

Dale Vree's *New Oxford Review* turned out to be about the only journal of opinion, along with *Salmagundi,* that greeted Lasch with anything resembling embrace as the culture wars wore on in the late eighties. But two journals did not a movement make. In the *New Oxford Review*'s 1987 "Symposium on Humane Socialism and Traditional Conservatism" Lasch wrote:

> If socialism means the common ownership of land, a labor-intensive economy, the restoration of craftsmanship, the conservation of scarce resources, and a more modest standard of living, the alliance of cultural conservatism and socialism ought to be irresistible. But socialism means none of those things today — which is probably why it elicits so little enthusiasm. Who needs socialism when we can enjoy most of its blessings under a more enlightened form of capitalism?

38. CL to Dale Vree, TL, 2 December 1989, 7b:3; CL to Paul Gottfried, TLS, 17 October 1989, 7a:21. On the "Rockford crowd," see Paul V. Murphy, *The Rebuke of History: The Southern Agrarians and American Conservative Thought* (Chapel Hill: University of North Carolina Press, 2001).

"Conservatives face a doubly daunting task," he continued. They needed to "take cultural conservatism back from the capitalists and socialism from the socialists. Not work for the faint-hearted!"[39] Of all people, he would know.

39. CL, contribution to "Symposium on Humane Socialism and Traditional Conservatism," *New Oxford Review,* October 1987, 26.

CHAPTER TWELVE

Hope against Hope

If progressive ideologies have dwindled down to a wistful hope
against hope that things will somehow work out for the best, we
need to recover a more vigorous form of hope.

Christopher Lasch, *The True and Only Heaven*, 1991[1]

J ust days after the democratic reformer Boris Yeltsin took the helm
of the Russian Republic in May 1990, Lasch addressed a group gathered in Washington, D.C., to pay tribute to the recently deceased American historian William Appleman Williams. An influential scholar of
foreign policy and a leading left-wing critic of cold war America, Williams' scholarship and politics had from the beginning of his career
inspired Lasch. The occasion, Lasch told the audience, presented an
opportunity to honor Williams by following "his example of looking
facts in the face without the distortion imposed by wishful thinking."[2]

The facts Lasch wished to scrutinize had precisely to do with the
stunning collapse of the USSR and the responses — political, ideological, historical — that were emerging in its aftermath. The left, Lasch
noted, had already taken to using the end of the cold war as a "loyalty
test": any who thought the West "won" failed it. For Lasch, this was
just the latest piece of evidence that the left was "impervious, as
usual, to the sobering influence of events." If the trajectory of reforms

---

1. CL, TOH, 529-30.
2. CL, in "Excerpts from a Conference to Honor William Appleman Williams," *Radical History Review* 50 (Spring 1991), 65.

and concessions initiated under the leadership of Mikhail Gorbachev, the final Soviet leader, didn't "add up to a victory for the West," he maintained, "the term surely has no meaning."[3]

Gar Alperovitz, whose Institute for Policy Studies had convened the conference, remembers that Lasch was "quite nervous" about the task he had taken upon himself that day — "that was the interesting thing," Alperovitz says. "It was my sense of him as a person that he really was willing to take stands that he knew were difficult — and it was difficult for *him*." The stand Lasch was taking here (and elsewhere: he would make this same argument in a *New York Times* op-ed as well as in a *Commentary* symposium) was difficult not simply because of what he had to say to the left, but because of what he felt compelled to say to *all* sides. He captured it in a two-sentence summary sure to pique everyone: Even if the West, as he maintained, did win the cold war, the United States "can hardly be said to have shared in the fruits of that victory. It would be closer to the truth to say that the Soviet Union and the U.S. have destroyed each other as major powers, just as many critics of the cold war predicted."[4]

He concisely reviewed the nation's descent in the previous half-century. The cold war had helped advance the consolidation of business, government, and education, escalating to high levels the degree of centralization in American society. In aiming for all-out military supremacy over the Soviets, educators had from the lowest levels to the highest skewed schooling toward science at the expense of a more civic, philosophic orientation; the "shallow concept of democracy" the cold war had led American leaders to cultivate had narrowed the nation's focus to "the equitable distribution of comforts rather than the character-forming effects of civic participation." And the Vietnam War, in all of its dimensions, had been "a national disaster from which the United States has never really recovered." Lasch's conclusion was familiar, but timed perfectly for maximum provocation: "By any standard, the United States is a society in decline."[5]

It was fitting that the collapse of the Soviet Union should provide

3. CL, "Excerpts from a Conference to Honor William Appleman Williams," 65.

4. Interview with Gar Alperovitz, 18 December 2006; CL, "The Costs of Our Cold War Victory," *New York Times,* July 13 1990, A27.

5. CL, contribution to "The American 80's: Disaster or Triumph" symposium, *Commentary* 90:3 (September 1990), 23; CL, "Excerpts from a Conference," 67, 69.

the historical setting for what would be the last full, and certainly the most important, book of Lasch's life. He had, in the midst of the cold war, launched his career with a reassessment of first-wave American responses to the Russian revolution; he would end it with a probing, hortatory call to a more perceptive way of apprehending and responding to the post-USSR, post–cold war, still crisis-laden world.

The True and Only Heaven: Progress and Its Critics was released in January 1991. Lasch had written it while on leave at Stanford University's Center for Advanced Study in the Behavioral Sciences during the 1988-89 academic year, and at 520 pages of text (with an additional 36-page fine-print bibliographic essay) the book, besides being a remarkable account of Lasch's intellectual and ideological travels in the seven years since *The Minimal Self,* was a testament of a lifetime of learning. In it he ranged from authors with whom he had engaged in the sixties, like Marcuse, Mannheim, and Riesman, to more recent inspirations like Alasdair MacIntyre and Hannah Arendt, to earlier writers he had rediscovered as he was writing the book, like Thomas Carlyle and Jonathan Edwards. Lasch wrote with a literary richness and intellectual virtuosity that was hard not to relish, politics aside. It bore all the marks of high and distinguished achievement.

In his tribute to Williams, Lasch, suggesting the possibility of socialism's permanent demise, had remarked all too knowingly that "An ideal without any concrete historical embodiment is unlikely to remain very compelling." *True and Only Heaven* was above all the culminating achievement of his 1980s effort to leave Americans with a starker sense of the meaning and the promise of the populist tradition that was indeed still in their midst — his most sustained effort, as Horkheimer and Adorno had once put it, to "rescue the past as something living, instead of using it as the material of progress." To those who for years had dismissed him as an embittered critic with nothing constructive to offer, it was his long-awaited book-length response. To any seeking illumination and direction in this confusing historical moment, it was in no uncertain terms a call to action, rooted in a deep understanding of a long and consequential story that was still playing out. What *was* the story of America? What was the America that might have been, and that still might be? These were the questions he forced the reader, page by page, to ponder.[6]

6. Max Horkheimer and Theodor W. Adorno, *Dialectic of Enlightenment: Philo-*

As numerous reviewers would note, the book's sprawling, dense quality defied easy understanding and evaluation. Lasch had no interest in making a sleek and quick argument in the *Culture of Narcissism* vein. This book's slow, meandering style invited a different kind of response, one more meditative. It recalled scholarship and writing from an earlier time, before market imperatives had turned books into trim little sports cars, quick but able to carry less and less. The reader of *True and Only Heaven* found herself on foot, sojourning through thickets and up slopes, progressing gradually toward a new vantage point on progress, and on America itself.

Right down to his selection of a title, Lasch was seeking to evoke this self-consciously outmoded pace, mood, and setting. He had taken the phrase "the true and only heaven" from a Nathaniel Hawthorne short story called "The Celestial Railroad," a witty and slicing update of *The Pilgrim's Progress,* the Puritan writer John Bunyan's seventeenth-century classic that, besides sending fiction writing in new directions, had reflected and restructured the minds of Protestants in the 150 years prior to the publication of Hawthorne's story. Bunyan's heavenward pilgrim had had no choice but to journey through arduous trials and unexpected difficulties on his way to the celestial city. Such was the way of the world for Bunyan's readers, but it was the way of salvation as well. Salvation, the authentic realization of their humanity, came only through the narrow way.

What so troubled Hawthorne by the nineteenth century was his sense that Americans, in the throes of an emergent modern civilization, were jettisoning the time-honored understanding of life-through-pilgrimage and exchanging it for the ill-begotten hope of life-as-ease, a treacherous drift accelerated by the explosive arrival of hitherto unimagined conveniences and pleasures. Hawthorne looked out and saw a nation of pilgrims making their way toward the celestial city not on foot, with weighty bundles strapped to their backs, but by train, merry and relieved, through sites that had once upon a time forced pilgrims to fight for their lives.

The lengthy passage Lasch selected from Hawthorne's story to begin *The True and Only Heaven* highlighted recent developments in the

---

sophical Fragments, ed. Gunzelin Schmid Noerr, trans. Edmund Jephcott, Cultural Memory in the Present series, ed. Mieke Bal, Hent de Vries (Stanford: Stanford University Press, 2002), 25; Lasch, "Excerpts," 66.

modern city of Vanity Fair. What had once been a seedy, unrepentant metropolis given over to sin had, it turned out, undergone revival — or, better, reform. "The Christian reader," Hawthorne's narrator informs, "will be surprised to hear that almost every street has its church, and that the reverend clergy are nowhere held in higher respect than at Vanity Fair." True, their names were a bit odd — "Rev. Mr. Shallow-deep" and "the Rev. Mr. This-to-day," to name two. But the residents didn't seem to notice. In fact, many passengers, upon discovering the new Vanity Fair, decided to stay — "such are the charms of the place that people often affirm it to be the true and only heaven."[7]

Lasch's turn toward Hawthorne and Bunyan at the book's start created an allusive layering Lasch used to great effect throughout. Through this old, familiar story Lasch, with the usual mixture of subtlety and direct assault, was preparing readers for the crucial points of the case he would lay before them: that they were fools to believe democracy — the "decent society" — would be easy; that people they knew well had beguiled them into this foolish assumption; that the pathway toward their true end could be found in their past; and that the nature of their circumstance required that they now assume the posture and perspective of the pilgrim — one committed to traveling a dangerous course toward a necessary end.

For at precisely this moment of seeming geopolitical triumph, Lasch warned, all Americans were facing "mounting difficulties that threaten to overwhelm us" — a grand (though certainly not unprecedented) historical irony. The tendency and certain temptation of the moment was to simply defer to the present leadership of the country. But this was a huge mistake, for all, whether right or left, were currently committed to the same destructive course. "The right proposes, in effect, to maintain our riotous standard of living, as it has been maintained in the past, at the expense of the rest of the world," and the liberals were following right along. Could the cost possibly be worth it? Would it even be payable? Lasch thought not. Gathering the nation around the aim of maintaining the current way of life, he prophesied, "will widen the gap between rich and poor nations, generate more and more violent movements of insurrection and terror-

7. Nathaniel Hawthorne, "The Celestial Railroad," in *Hawthorne: Tales and Sketches* (New York: Library of America, 1996), 817, 818.

ism against the West, and bring about a deterioration of the world's political climate as threatening as the deterioration of its physical climate."[8]

That the "characteristic mood of the times" was "a baffled sense of drift" was, in short, damning evidence of great, possibly cataclysmic political and ideological failure. "The premise underlying this investigation," Lasch stated, is that "the old political ideologies have exhausted their capacity either to explain events or to inspire men and women to constructive action." This judgment was exactly what both sides either evaded or denied. "Neither wants to admit that our society has taken a wrong turn, lost its way, and needs to recover a sense of purpose and direction." At their most gloomy, leaders of both the left and the right tended to greet the future with a nervous smile and clammy handshake, looking for better times just around the corner. Their progressive faith in a kind of economic and environmental exceptionalism left them only vaguely aware of the avalanche whose violent rush had already begun to pour down on the citizens below.[9]

Trying to penetrate this mystified cast of mind had long been Lasch's mission, and he now moved away from the kind of analytic framework that characterized his earlier work and toward a more historical, narrative-driven approach laced with moral meditation, hoping, as he always hoped, to call into question "the old terms of the debate." The book's eleven chapters fell nicely into two parts. After beginning the book's first half with an opening analysis on the current moment, he waded into a long and winding story about how the nation had arrived there, including a pair of illuminating chapters on the moral and intellectual effects of this "progressive" trajectory and the flawed attempts of elite observers to understand and take proper account of its course. He concluded the first half of the book with his rendering of the road not taken: the way of the populists, whose history he reconstructed from the early modern period to the defeat of the People's Party at the turn of the twentieth century. In the book's last five chapters he went on to trace to the end of the twentieth century the playing out of this progressivism-versus-populism story, with those who had welcomed and hastened the advance of progress meet-

8. CL, TOH, 39, 23.
9. CL, TOH, 22, 21, 23.

ing unusual and unexpected forms of response from those who were troubled by it.[10]

It was a brilliant, dense, and truly original reading of the American story, developed in intricate conversation with recent work in American and European history as well as a wide range of other humanistic and social scientific scholarship. In conversation years later, American sociologist Robert N. Bellah called it an "extraordinary" book, Lasch's "masterpiece." From start to finish Lasch depicted those of progressive orientation and those of populist inclination in a strange and gripping struggle, the former to lead the nation on a march toward the realization of the bright but elusive "vision of men and women released from outward constraints," the latter to maintain a way of life structured by an ancient "sense of limits." Both sides (though they weren't really "sides" or political parties so much as competing cultural impulses with varying and diverging forms of incarnation) had achieved significant levels of power and authority as the nation had developed. The power of the progressives extended from the authority of modern science and enlightenment thought more generally, which had yielded extraordinary levels of political, intellectual, and economic might. The populists, for their part, possessed a distinct kind of political and cultural power, rooted in notions of authority connected to old creeds and ideals and the communal practices to which they were attached. But the history of combat between these orientations — mainly indirect and subterranean — over the shape and identity of the nation had not yielded what either had in mind. The progressives had yet to achieve their own steady state of painless, liberated living, and the populists had failed to reverse the moral, political, and spiritual deterioration they decried, let alone contain or reverse the structural encroachments of the modern order. As by the last third of the century the clash devolved into "culture wars," Americans of all kinds were witnessing "the erosion," Lasch believed, of their "psychological, cultural, and spiritual foundations from within." The long battle had led not to triumph but to defeat — at least if gauged by the state of the nation.[11]

10. CL, TOH, 23.
11. Interview with Robert N. Bellah, 16 June 2008; CL, TOH, 76, 17, 24. The book's table of contents did not break it down in this manner — a costly editorial lapse, given the difficulty reviewers had tracing Lasch's argument.

This basic story of two grand, dueling parties was itself a very old story, of course. While Lasch's influences ranged from Arthur Schlesinger Jr.'s late progressive classic *The Age of Jackson* to Alasdair MacIntyre's *After Virtue,* he mentioned another inspiration in an interview with Casey Blake two years after the book's publication: Richard Hofstadter. "In many ways he was and remained the dominant figure on my intellectual horizon," Lasch remarked to Blake, and not just, Lasch was quick to note, for the "charming presentation of his ideas." In books like *The Age of Reform* and *Anti-Intellectualism in American Life* it was Hofstadter who had reinterpreted the history of modern America as a contest (and not much of one, by Hofstadter's lights) between the unthinking, outmoded, village-loving, old-stock Americans and the cerebral, analytical, tolerant, city-dwelling pluralists, those with whom the future of the country — and democracy itself — rested. "I've come to see Hofstadter as a latter-day version of H. L. Mencken, endlessly belaboring the 'booboisie,'" Lasch remarked to Blake. In *The True and Only Heaven* he set out not only to defend "ordinary Americans" (his term) but to challenge the entire overarching set of assumptions about the generally salubrious trajectory of modernity that Hofstadter's work so winsomely reflected. "When a historian's work retains such enormous influence," Lasch suggested to Blake, "you begin to suspect — as in the case of Frederick Jackson Turner — that it has some kind of mythic resonance. It's not just that Hofstadter was a wonderful craftsman and writer . . . but that he summed up a way of looking at history that was already familiar" — too familiar, in Lasch's view. Following Hofstadter in seeing modernity as leading to decisive confrontation between the new liberals and the old traditionalists, he both complicated Hofstadter's way of framing this story and fundamentally attacked it.[12]

Lasch's most brilliant work came in the book's first half, as he, through a series of vignettes, moved in and out of the deeper layers of the progressive and populist stories. Throughout the book his keenness of perception and breadth of learning surpassed what he had displayed in his previous work, giving the sympathetic reader at least the sense of getting not just truth but *the* truth about the fundamental

12. Casey Blake and Christopher Phelps, "History as Social Criticism: Conversations with Christopher Lasch," *Journal of American History* 80:4 (March 1994), 1317.

movement of American history. Those (including his father) who had lamented Lasch's turn in the seventies away from history writing and toward social-scientific analysis had reason to claim that social criticism's gain was history's loss.

In rejecting and attempting to reverse the guiding narrative of enlarging progressive achievement, Lasch sought to displace the political identities of some figures and movements by changing the criteria for what makes one "liberal" or "conservative." More consequentially, he moved the populist tradition (and the related decentralist and agrarian traditions) from the margins back into the heart of the American story, where historians such as Charles Beard and John Hicks, prior to the postwar period, had understood it to be. At the same time, and despite his "populist versus progressive" framework, he did not locate this duel within a Manichean universe, one in which light casts out darkness, and enlightenment and freedom contend valiantly against superstition and oppression, as such narratives are usually framed. Rather, he placed this story, and history itself, within a more Aristotelian and generally Greek universe, one in which there weren't two sides battling against each other so much as two poles positioned opposite one another, with human beings being drawn forcefully toward one pole or the other. Lasch's champions were certainly the people between the poles, but they weren't mere "centrists," taking instruction now from one side, now from the other, stationing themselves in the middle as wise and level-headed compromisers — the usual place of enlightenment in liberal narratives. Instead, in this universe of spiritual and moral contestation, Lasch depicted the space between the poles as a moral force-field, in the center of which lay the possibility of freedom, which human communities could only realize by collectively denying the malign, life-thwarting impulses represented by either pole and aim for the point of tension between them. This was a variation of the tripartite framework he had developed in *Minimal Self,* but for this formulation he turned to a very different language, which took him to very different places. His three ideological positions were now not a reflection of their orientations toward the psyche but rather toward being itself.

It was at the very center of the book that he unfolded this historical-ontological vision: the spiritual affirmation that made a just and decent polity possible. "'No Answer but an Echo': The World without Wonder," at seventy pages, with five chapters to one side and five to the other, was the bridge between the pre-twentieth century world of the book's first half and Lasch's own time and place, the twentieth century. Crucially, this bridge had an essentially spiritual quality, and it reflected Lasch's own slowly forged answer to the problem of goodness and the search for spiritual vitality, which had for so long left him restless. And his final resolution of these questions in *True and Only Heaven* ended up addressing in definitive fashion the matter of his own deepest political identity. Whatever anyone else might think, he was, he could now explain more satisfactorily, not a conservative, and not a liberal, but a radical.

This radicalism was rooted in the fundamental conviction that goodness inheres, not in a program, or in human willing, but in reality itself at its most basic level. Advancing gingerly into what he termed "the higher register of moral and ontological speculation," he had become convinced that the proper and necessary basis for sound thinking about politics, culture, and human health was the affirmation of the primary "goodness of life," or, as he also simply put it, "the goodness of things." In terms of metaphysics or ontology, he himself would not advance beyond this; rather, he chose to invite voice after voice into his argument who did speak with philosophic and theological particularity, thinkers ranging from Jonathan Edwards to Orestes Brownson to Ralph Waldo Emerson to William James to Reinhold Niebuhr. And as he introduced their voices in his story, he glossed them in a way that made it difficult — by intention, one suspects — to know precisely where their voices ended and his began.

The effect was choral, with Lasch as conductor. "Man has no claim to God's favor, and gratitude has to be conceived, accordingly, not as an appropriate acknowledgment of the answer to our prayers, so to speak, but as the acknowledgment of God's sovereign but life-giving power to order things as he pleased": this was Lasch on Edwards. But how much of it was Lasch? His later applause for Emerson's rejection of the Puritans' "anthropomorphic conception of God," along with his own supposition that a God of "pure being" was more conceptually coherent than the older view of a personal God, give a good indication of both his deepest beliefs and his rhetorical method. He had come to a convinced sense of the fundamental goodness of being, and seemed to hint at times at a belief in a God whose participatory activity preserves and directs this world. To those who too affirmed this general conception, whatever their accretions, he would listen keenly. But it was this primary ontic goodness, however untraceable in origin or end, that became the launching point for his moral reasoning.[13]

The dogmatic particulars, of course, were themselves of paramount importance for many of the thinkers he gathered, but this did not much preoccupy him. This was the "impatience" with metaphysics Dominic Aquila notes; Aquila's perception that Lasch seemed intuitively to operate as something of a phenomenologist seems especially apt here. It had never been the structures of reality that had absorbed Lasch, but rather the human response within them. And by the late 1980s he had come to believe that a particular kind of sustained, habitual human response to the ultimate structure of reality was of final and decisive importance for the fate of human beings and their communities. Given the ultimate reality of goodness, he now contended — and this was the heart of this chapter that lay at the heart of his book — that affirmation of or resistance to that reality were the final determinants of whether human action, whether personal or collective, moved toward virtue or toward evil, toward, in another of his formulations, hope or desiccation.[14]

In describing the political necessity of virtue and hope, Lasch himself, somewhat surprisingly, stepped forward to sing. Virtue was hope incarnate, and it consisted of far more than duty to others, he avowed. For the voices he was most intently listening to, and to which he emphatically joined his own, virtue was the visible expression of a spiritual state: the condition of the soul that was the manifestation of life itself, the fruit of a person's willingness, despite all manner of objections and obstacles, to affirm the goodness of reality. Virtue, he

13. CL, TOH, 271, 530, 387, 249-50, 265.

14. Interview with Dominic Aquila, 5 January 2007; CL, MS, 295. Lasch followed William James in stressing the danger of "desiccation." In my interview with Aquila, in response to a question about Lasch's relationship to the Aristotelian tradition of virtue ethics, Aquila said: "I would say most certainly he did not have much regard for an Aristotelian sense of teleology. If anything I think he was closest to phenomenological philosophers. I think that's why a lot of people see resonance between his work and John Paul II's, when John Paul II is being most a phenomenologist. . . . Lasch would ask those questions intuitively. He knew *nothing* about phenomenology as far as I knew, as a formal discipline. . . . For example, one of the premier questions he would ask in *any* form [was] . . . 'What makes a set of ideas appealing?' So to put yourself in the subject's point of view is a peculiarly phenomenological position to take. But as far as a sense of teleology, you know, there's *nothing* in Lasch that I knew that came across that way."

stressed, was not characterized by dour subservience but rather by "superabundant vitality"; by "trust" and "wonder"; by "ardor, intensity, devotion, and imagination" (here following Emerson); by "a grateful and obedient disposition of the human will" but also "abundance, plenitude, and fullness of being" (now glossing Milton) — in short, by the spiritual vitality for which he had long been calling: narcissism's polar opposite. "The antithesis of affirmation, obedience, and submission," in turn, he described as "sin," which amounted to an "everlasting no" toward the gift of this world. "Evil" was "the absence of life, vitality, coherence, order, and creative purpose." Evil — not vice ("a pallid concept") — was the "proper antithesis of virtue," and virtue was that which, finally, made freedom possible: the "joyous submission to an order of things that we can recognize" — a joyous submission, in more guarded terms, to the reality of "limits."[15]

What this understanding lacked in ethical and metaphysical specificity it made up for in intensity and vision. Lasch's writing on the possibility of "superabundant vitality" was filled with an evangelical energy and force. The world *was* deserving of wonder: such was its nature, and wonder was the only morally fitting response to it. To not see a world deserving of wonder was to miss the world itself, with grave political and cultural consequences. Humans were knit into the very fabric of this magnificent reality. Obstinate blindness to it or indignant rebellion against it did not alter their final location within it; attempts to evade it by abstraction or divorce were mere fancy. The disposition of wonder and the practice of virtue were, in the end, the only adequate responses to life, and the only hope of true health in any form.

But if this was his answer to the problem of goodness, what of the classic problem of evil? Here Lasch turned to one of the book's heroes, Jonathan Edwards. He noted that for Edwards allowing the reality of evil to become a personal impediment to submission to God was itself the revelation of an evil heart, an indulging of the conceit that one was innocent and blameless and thus deserving of better than what the universe had on offer. "Unable to conceive of a God who did not regard human happiness as the be-all and end-all of creation," Lasch wrote of those who resisted this submission, "they could not accept the central paradox of the Christian faith, as Edwards saw it: that the secret of hap-

15. CL, TOH, 233, 530, 280, 234, 238, 239, 265.

piness lay in renouncing the right to be happy." To embrace this paradox — an embrace that was at bottom a submission to reality itself — took one out of the darkness of evil and despair and into the realm of wonder, of hope, of justice. Wonder was "an affirmation of life in the teeth of its limits." Hope reflected a "deep-seated trust in life" that did not deny "its tragic character," a courageous *yes* to "the nature of things" even in the midst of crushing loss or devastating heartbreak. Justice emerged from "a conviction that the wicked will suffer, that wrongs will be made right, that the underlying order of things will not be flouted with impunity." There could be no abiding wonder, or lasting hope, or insistent justice, apart from such fundamental submission. To reject it was to reject life itself.[16]

Lasch was careful to place this meditation within what he construed as not a narrow theological tradition but rather a more socially robust and politically consequential one: the tradition he, echoing Reinhold Niebuhr, called "Christian prophecy," with particular inspiration drawn from the Calvinist wing of it. Indeed, a good part of the book's power lay in its attempt to frame the history of this most basic of spiritual affirmations, which, he argued, had over time led necessarily to a distinct politics. It was not, in short, simply an understanding of being he was propounding, but also an approach to time; put differently, an affirmation of essence, he believed, had led ineluctably to a certain stance within the age. If being was finally good but human history reflected man's broken connection to it, this catastrophic tragedy must be confronted in a manner that both respected the existence of the brokenness and yet honored the reality — and hope — of the whole. A too easy acquiescence in the present corruption — the malign tendency to do either too little or too much — would only extend the tragedy. Either way led finally to the same end: nihilism and despair, and their attendant forms of human and ecological destruction. Wisdom lay in another direction, and its yield was a kindled vigilance against both resigned passivity and ambitious conceit: a truly radical restlessness, reflecting a deep hope.[17]

In a 1987 review essay in *Educational Theory* Lasch had suggested that the "prophetic tradition" was one of three basic "ontological strategies" that humans had developed in the face of their contingent,

16. CL, TOH, 248, 308, 81, 530, 242, 81.
17. CL, TOH, 241.

finite circumstance. While the "stoic" impulse, he wrote, reflects a resigned attempt to deny or delimit human aspiration, and the "gnostic" impulse is rooted in the desire to deny limitation, prophetic religion, he suggested, "demands that collective life be judged against the strictest moral standards," even as it exercises that judgment with the humble awareness of human complicity and failure. In *True and Only Heaven* Lasch turned to the history of Calvinism for a historical embodiment of this "prophetic tradition," as well as for his own more prescriptive vision.[18]

It was the tension the Calvinists maintained between part and whole, between the actual and the ideal, that Lasch found so worthy of emulation; in fact he maintained that of the varying cultural sources that had influenced and molded critics of progress, it was Calvinism that had in actual historical effect been most "fruitful." The Puritans, the English-speaking Calvinists, had entered into covenanted communities as an expression of their desire to live in gratitude and obedience to God in all aspects of life, seeking to respond to his grace by reflecting in every sphere the goodness of God and his creation. But they were, as the emblematic Puritan John Bunyan made evident, the very last people to believe that achieving these ideals would come easily. Hence the need for prophecy: a searching, participatory response to the community's need to keep alive its deepest ideals, to understand its failures to achieve those ideals, and, above all, to stay united through confession and practice. Puritans lived tenuously between the actual and the ideal, aiming for a fruitful tension in many dimensions: between works and grace, between the individual and the community, between church and state. They honored individuality, for instance, by making (as Lasch put it) "the inner state of one's soul" of crucial importance, while at the same time believing that health of soul required a person to be bound intimately to others. The commonweal was served as the community fostered strong, virtue-desiring individuals inclined to serve the common good. "The point," Lasch explained in discussing these varying tensions, "was not simply that Puritanism was always pulled in both directions; the point is that these tensions themselves *constituted* the Puritan tradition." And the results were impressive and enduring. "Where moral vision is alive to-

18. CL, "Review Article: Scientists of the Mind," *Educational Theory* 37:2 (Spring 1987), 203.

day" in America, he remarked to one interviewer in 1991, "it can be connected rather directly to the Puritan tradition. I believe that profoundly." It was, he suggested, "perhaps our strongest reservoir of moral idealism."[19]

In seeking to recover and perpetuate the Calvinist stream of the "prophetic tradition," Lasch parted ways with Puritans like Jonathan Edwards by devising a form of unity within the tradition that centered not on cardinal doctrines but on a more general vision of the universe and of human community. Lasch called Emerson the "central figure of the book," and this was precisely because Emerson was the first with the intellectual and spiritual acuity to discern the real heart of this "prophetic understanding of history and human nature" and separate from it the unnecessary accretions, distilling its insights in a truer, more useful way. "No more than his predecessors in the prophetic succession," Lasch underscored, "did Emerson call for a new religion." Rather, Emerson teased out and amplified that which was truly of consequence: the basic need of humans, for their own spiritual freedom and communal good, to acknowledge the fundamental goodness of life, their own dependence on a goodness beyond themselves, and the need to press for the righting of wrongs that denials of such realities perpetuated. *This* was the essence of true religion. Lasch's summary of Reinhold Niebuhr's perspective on Scripture was

---

19. CL, TOH, 227; CL, "Calvinism," in *A Companion to American Thought*, ed. Richard Wightman Fox and James Kloppenberg (Malden, Mass.: Blackwell Publishing, 1995), 99; CL, TOH, 551; Bernard Murchland, "On the Moral Vision of Democracy: A Conversation with Christopher Lasch," *Civic Arts Review* 4:4 (Fall 1991), online at http://car.owu.edu/archives.html. Lasch's admiration for the Puritans bears the mark of mid-twentieth-century Puritan scholarship, seen best in the work of Perry Miller and Edmund Morgan. In Morgan's *The Puritan Dilemma: The Story of John Winthrop*, for instance, it is precisely Winthrop's disciplined embrace of the tension between ideal and real that Morgan finds so worthy of emulation. Winthrop set out, Morgan explains, "to found a society where the perfection of God would find proper recognition among imperfect men. Those who looked for a private heaven on earth might now look in Rhode Island — and much joy to them. Those who cared not for heaven or hell could await damnation in the Old World." But the New England Puritans, more clear-headed and far-seeing, hoped to "live in the world as God required but not lose sight of the eternity that lay behind it." Edmund Morgan, *The Puritan Dilemma: The Story of John Winthrop*, 3d ed., Library of American Biography, ed. Mark C. Carnes (New York: Pearson Education, Inc., 2007), 145. The book was first published in 1958.

likely his own: "Prophetic mythology threw a powerful light on history, but it was not to be confused with the actual historical record." "Religion should be judged by its fruits — especially its capacity to bring about an underlying disposition of acceptance and affirmation": so said Jonathan Edwards and William James. And so said Lasch.[20]

Absent in this reinterpretation of the prophetic tradition was the image of prophets speaking fearfully but confidently in behalf of a personal God who was intimately engaged in the affairs of his own covenant people. On this older vision, prophets were not simply reconciling people to an ideal, or to "the nature of things," as Lasch imagined them to be doing; they were seeking to prompt a reconciliation to the One who had with fatherly intent made humans in his image. In the biblical tradition prophecy involved not simply the renewing of a covenant between people but the renewal of a covenant between people and their God — a very different conception of the universe than that which Lasch was rendering. In retaining the cosmos of the older prophetic tradition but rejecting the personal dimensions of the divine-human encounter, he had profoundly altered its cosmic and psychic frame. The kind of prophecy Lasch was defining ended up being centered on a glorious kind of submission, but one that did not retain the radically personal dimension of Calvinists such as Edwards. This was, of course, the theological direction liberal Protestants had long taken, and Lasch was following along.

At one level his was surprising, since Lasch usually had nothing but disdain for liberal Protestants, whom he tended to regard as utterly symptomatic of the worst tendencies of the self-consciously modern "progressives." So it is worth noting that in breaking with Calvinist theology proper, Lasch did maintain one very distinctive Calvinist-Augustinian emphasis: an understanding of spiritual vitality — virtue — as a gift of grace, something not achievable through human effort. Glossing Thomas Carlyle's conception of heroism (central to Carlyle's understanding of virtue), Lasch emphasized that for the heroic "creative power does not derive from the 'self.' It is a gift in the fullest sense of the word, entrusted to them for safekeeping, and their intuitive, unself-conscious understanding of this fact is what makes them heroes in the first place." Likewise, for Emerson, he empha-

20. CL, TOH, 546, 227, 261, 373, 285.

sized, it is only due to "beatitude" that we can accept the limits that we invariably confront both within and without. If the virtuous person gained new strength, in short, it was precisely because the strength came from outside the self: this was Lasch's restatement of the Calvinist teaching on human corruption and divine grace.[21]

The entire ontological framework rested on a powerful, inventive reading of an array of texts and authors, in service of a vision of the world that had moved away from satire and taken a deep, at times dark, comic turn. Lasch revealed a part of his inspiration not just for the chapter but for the book when he mentioned Raymond Williams's *Culture and Society,* which, as Williams saw it, was a "redefinition of what politics should be." Williams's redefining efforts had consisted of an "attempt to reconstruct a tradition of social criticism resistant to conventional political classifications," Lasch noted approvingly in *True and Only Heaven,* and it was obvious that in this respect he was following Williams's lead. But in another sense he veered in the opposite direction, away from Williams's confident, progressive secularity. His own experience on the left, another generation on, had left him convinced that the political hopes both he and Williams guarded needed sounder ontological and spiritual rooting than most twentieth-century radicals had understood. Oddly enough, complete secularity and true radicalism had turned out to be highly incompatible.[22]

It was in the light of this ontology, this grand spiritual-moral framework, that Lasch attempted to make sense of the dominant "left-right" ideological tendencies that had formed and forged the United States, and as in *Minimal Self* he tried to show how a third way was the morally necessary response to the bipolar tendencies of modern politics. At one pole the "conservatives" (particularly the stream of conservatism sourced in the thinking of the eighteenth-century English statesman Edmund Burke) allowed veneration of tradition and

21. CL, TOH, 243, 264. Lasch sought to make a distinction between the view he was espousing and religious liberalism in his discussion of Carlyle: "One of the many features of Carlyle's position that distinguishes it from religious liberalism . . . (and at the same time links it to an earlier Calvinism) is that he does not associate heroism with morality at all but with reverence and 'wonder' " (243).

22. CL, TOH, 241. The quotation from Williams on "politics as it should be" is in this passage. Thanks to Casey Blake for his insight on the connections between Lasch's book and Williams's.

communal unity to confine them to an ossified world of custom, habit, ritual, and tradition. The genius of this kind of conservatism lay in its appeal to the longing people feel for connection to each other, to preceding generations, and to the past. But it also tended toward a deadening passivity that made it easier for fulsome powers to triumph. In failing to move human beings out of time-encrusted patterns and toward "a deeper understanding of things," the "inner meaning of the natural world" was "lost to sight," Lasch wrote, with ramifying political and cultural consequences. Life was too fundamentally disordered and people too easily misled for any particular historical assemblage of style, taste, ideas, and habit to deliver what human communities required. The prophetic tradition, from this view, did not come to bring peace to already sleeping communities, but a reviving sword — for the sake of a truer peace, even if the cost of achieving it proved disruptive. In keeping this kind of necessary conflict at bay in the hope of an idealized stability, conservatives — including contemporary "communitarians," who grounded their hopes on this fantasy of stability and unity — actually invited the erosion of their own communities.[23]

At the other pole were the progressives, examples par excellence, in Lasch's thinking, of what Reinhold Niebuhr in his Gifford Lectures had described as "the unwillingness of man to acknowledge his creatureliness and dependence upon God and his effort to make his own life independent and secure." Their genius centered on their willingness to boldly discard past notions and forms of order, confident in their own ability to "progress" through naked human rationality. The ancient sense of inescapable limits they saw as something to conquer rather than as that to which they must submit, and the fruit of their vision was the glistening modern world itself, with its medical advances, its remarkable conveniences, its liberal political order — and its nihilism.[24]

In the course of the eighteenth and nineteenth centuries these two ideological tendencies, "conservatism" and "progressivism," had fatefully converged in at least one revolutionary way: the sanctioning of a novel, massive economic system based on the rejection of what

23. CL, TOH, 229.
24. Reinhold Niebuhr, *The Nature and Destiny of Man: A Christian Interpretation, Volume I: Human Nature* (New York: Scribner's, 1941), 137-38.

had previously been the wisdom of the ages: that life should be lived in such a way as to encourage the "limitation" rather than the "multiplication," in Lasch's words, of "needs and desires." Capitalism sought the opposite, and "conservative" resignation about human nature and "progressive" optimism about the same merged to bless it. With "insatiable appetites" redefined as the friend rather than the enemy, capitalists could count on an ever-deepening condition of dependence of those within its orbit, as marketers lured consumers with the news of their ever expanding "needs."[25]

This led to perhaps the most striking and original argument in *True and Only Heaven.* The regnant American belief in "progress," Lasch contended, far from being a misty vestige of an older, mythical, millenarian worldview that saw history moving in an upward direction, was instead mainly the mental effect of so many decades of unending improvements in the "quality of life." True, these improvements were only material in nature — which had once upon a time troubled the likes of Nathaniel Hawthorne. But the apologists for the new order had emerged quickly, having "mastered the tone and bluff of jocular dismissal, the unapologetically pristine defense of everyday comforts," and such worries were allayed with impressive dispatch. "No one could argue very long against abundance," Lasch acidly noted. Progress, "this tawdry dream of success," was here to stay. Lasch's entirely unsparing depiction of modern civilization's idolatry of convenience and dedication to the merest pleasures cast the reign of industrial capitalism not as the triumph of an ideal but as the effecting of a seduction, and the seduced were now sleeping to the steady rhythms of The Economy, shamelessly content, degradingly weak, confident in progress and lost in nostalgia, burning up the world to maintain their tenuous state of warmth.[26]

Between these polar tendencies, "progressivism" and "conservatism," lay the radical option. Recognizing humans' perennial need for the renewal of life, radicals did not give in to the life-denying forms of political and intellectual dependence — whether "traditional" or "progressive" — that characterized both right and left. Rather, radicals sought through particular practices to cultivate an independence of mind and spirit that, structured within and by the community,

25. CL, TOH, 45, 52.
26. CL, TOH, 57, 58.

could give a person the keenness to detect and strength to resist the political and economic powers that sought always to enthrone themselves as the necessary ends of human life. In short, while conservatives defaulted wearily to "tradition" and liberals ran after "progress," radicals pursued virtue — and so justice, Lasch pointed out, if at times only as a hope against hope.

In the nineteenth century this radical political sensibility came to be most fully embodied by populism, Lasch argued, but its antecedents included, along with the Puritans (and other Christian streams), the republicans of the seventeenth and eighteenth centuries, and even some species of liberal thinkers, such as Thomas Paine, who saw in incipient industrial capitalism a threat to the communal world of craftsmen and farmers they thought more desirable. In the nineteenth century these varying populist trajectories had in the crucible of the industrial economy melded oddly but powerfully to yield a "producer ethic" that was "anticapitalist but not socialist or social democratic, at once radical, even revolutionary, and deeply conservative"; it was preserved most fully in the lives of the petty-bourgeoisie — the lower middle class. Poised between the "fatuous optimism" of the scientific progressives and the "debilitating nostalgia" of Burkean conservatives, the populist sensibility held firmly to a way of life that it understood to be the foundation of the nation's promise — the old understanding of the American dream. "A whole way of life was at stake in the struggle against industrialism," Lasch concluded, following with special appreciation the argument of populist scholar Lawrence Goodwyn. "Producerism; a defense of endangered crafts (including the craft of farming); opposition to the new class of public creditors and to the whole machinery of modern finance; opposition to wage labor": all of these were the battlefronts of the great populist attempt to keep alive another America, another meaning of citizenship. But at that moment of direct confrontation at the end of the nineteenth century they had lost, steamrolled by progress — by progressives.[27]

The victors had been led by H. L. Mencken's "civilized minority," and they became the new ruling class. Their sociologists lost themselves in fruitless attempts to understand "gemeinschaft" and "gesellschaft" dynamics, typologies that only quickened their sense of disconnection from the past. Their historians (most eminently,

27. CL, TOH, 205, 170, 215, 223.

Hofstadter) told self-congratulating tales of their own righteous ascent, stories that only increased their distance from the "uneducated" masses. Blinded by their confidence in their own progressive march, they misunderstood the past and misread its inhabitants, veering sharply between sentimentality on the one hand and contempt on the other, remaining convinced all the while that, whatever its pitfalls, "modernity" made possible an undeniably superior way of life. As the twentieth century began, the populists remained in the cultural periphery, where they had usually been but now only more so, occasionally attracting the alarmed attention of the ruling class — a Father Coughlin or a Jerry Falwell inciting a periodic spate of symposia, surveys, and articles. Some latter-day Hawthornes did continue to raise questions about the direction "democracy" was taking, but the turn-of-the-twentieth-century "progressive era" turned out to be the last time, Lasch wrote, that "the assimilationist, consumerist, distributive version of democratic dogma" would elicit significant levels of "searching criticism," as the New Deal and the cold war pushed alternate voices and visions even further away and elite intellectuals persisted in the fruitless attempt to understand the modern world on its own terms.[28]

The one great moment of populist triumph Lasch saw in the twentieth century was the civil rights movement. He described Martin Luther King Jr. as populist in orientation and ethos, a shocking narrative turn that showed both the power of Lasch's historical framework but also its limits. King, due to his upbringing in the South as the child of a conservative Baptist minister, had imbibed both "prophetic religion" and more generally populist sensibilities, and his education in the Northeast, where he encountered above all the work of Reinhold Niebuhr, had attuned him to the deeper intellectual (and less orthodox) dimensions of the faith. Lasch described King as a true "liberal hero," perhaps the "last liberal hero," and the points of his appeal to Lasch were obvious: King was both a scholar and an activist, he was a theological liberal who also affirmed the fundamental reality of sin, and he committed himself to his own region even as he also sought the health of the broader nation.[29]

But it was not just King Lasch was applauding; King's followers

28. CL, TOH, 360.
29. CL, TOH, 392.

were his true heroes. Their virtuous embrace of what Niebuhr had called "the spiritual discipline against resentment" was the starkest manifestation of the sensibility and stance Lasch had throughout the book been propounding. "Their experience in the South gave little support to a belief in progress," Lasch underscored, "yet they seemed to have unlimited supplies of hope." The movement had depended on "spiritual resources — courage, tenacity, forgiveness, and hope" — that had been nurtured in their own communities. "Social theories that equate moral enlightenment with cosmopolitanism and secularization cannot begin to account for these things," he averred. The failure of the civil rights movement in the North stemmed precisely from its inability to build on the embodied, local, rooted vitality that sprang from the Southern black communities, and King's own faltering effectiveness as a leader in his last years occurred as he both departed from his own place in the south and allowed his earlier ethical ideals, centered on charity and nonviolent confrontation, to be weakened. Lasch's criticism of King's late turn away from this radical, Christian, localist vision and toward a more standard form of democratic socialism revealed the heart of Lasch's own post-socialist political economy: King "did not explain how a guaranteed income would restore self-respect or the pride of workmanship," Lasch noted. These for him needed to be at the base of any decent society; they were certainly the fruit of any decent economy. "Participation," not "distribution," he emphasized, is "the test of democracy."[30]

Americans were clearly not passing this test as Lasch's story came to a close, with the therapeutic, progressive new class and the resurgent populists still battling in the 1970s and 1980s over issues like busing and abortion. The old ideal of a nation of "self-reliant citizens" continued its steady slippage. If there was a way forward, or back, Lasch contended, it would have to come through giving serious, attentive study to the populist tradition, for it still had much to teach. In rooting its democratic vision in "proprietorship and virtue," populism had done what the progressive tradition, for all its alleged sophistication, had not: persuasively established, with actual practices, a spiritual as well as material foundation for democracy. "The populist tradition offers no panacea for all the ills that affect the modern world," Lasch granted. "And the enlightened caricature of lower-

30. CL, TOH, 377-78, 387, 404.

middle-class culture contained undeniable elements of truth; otherwise it would have been unrecognizable even as a caricature." But populism's understanding of its time and place provided the basis for the kind of distinctive vision and practices that might yet propel America out of its progressive despair. *It* was the very best of the American political tradition. The story Richard Hofstadter had so powerfully told, and of which he was still such an emblematic figure, was wrong. Corporate capitalism buttressed by liberal cosmopolitanism had no chance of leading to a satisfying end. Americans might yet discover — *re*discover — another past, another hope, and another way.[31]

*   *   *

By self-consciously addressing and resolving so many of the dominant themes and questions of his own oeuvre, and by going to such length, depth, and breadth to do so, Lasch gave *The True and Only Heaven* the character of a magnum opus, a crescendo at the end of three decades of intensive thinking and writing. It is impossible to read *True and Only Heaven,* especially at a fifteen-year remove from its publication, and not see it as a work of profound scholarship. And indeed it was not his lack of scholarship that so disturbed some readers; it was his making of scholarship a means to discover and debate how we in our times should live that unsettled them.

The book had the quality of a crescendo in another sense, and that had to do with its autobiographical quality. One section of the introductory chapter was overtly autobiographical; in it Lasch recounted his own political journey. He playfully titled the section "The Making of a Malcontent," the story of how he had come to believe that "'Middle Americans' had good reason . . . to worry about the family and about the future their children were going to inherit." But the other and equally interesting autobiography was the one he told between the lines, criticizing the assumptions that once had been his own, poking at follies that had held him captive. The "lofty position of satirical disengagement," typical of new class critics, had been his own perch. The neo-Marxist "illusion" that "the concentration of economic power had laid the foundations of a new order" he had loudly proclaimed. The sociological sentimentality that created an un-

31. CL, TOH, 366, 531, 532, 531.

bridgeable chasm between "moderns" and "premoderns" had figured into his youthful portrait of modern America. His way had been
full of misadventures and missteps, he was acknowledging, but
through them had come the discovery of a way forward, toward a more
solid, vital hope and a more coherent, defensible politics.[32]

Would others interpret his journey in this same way? Would readers be sympathetic, let alone convinced? Lasch's outrageous defiance
of the political, intellectual, and cultural conventions of his own class
— whether it be in his defense of the "petty-bourgeoisie" or his writing of a book that seemed intentionally ungainly — was practically a
dare, a challenge to most of his readers' attitudes and habits. In taking this tack he ensured, as usual, quick and harsh judgment, although the actual occasion of rejection still wounded him, perhaps
due to a slender hope that good argument just might, in the end,
break down the reigning barriers. But once again, Lasch was disappointed. Several months after its release he wrote Jean Bethke
Elshtain that "*The True and Only Heaven* has been viciously attacked,
as I knew it would be, by left and right alike — which seems to vindi-
cate my point about the exhaustion of these ideologies and the need
for a politics that defies classification in these terms."[33]

To be sure, Lasch had been treated to a robust round of reviews,
interviews, and writing opportunities. He warned readers of *Time* on
the perils of "progress," was interviewed by *U.S. News & World Report,*
and consented to be a featured guest on several television programs.
Critics who had long followed Lasch were not surprised by *True and
Only Heaven*'s argument so much as by its scope. "He takes on nothing less than 'the western human condition,'" wrote Elshtain, with
true amazement, in *First Things.* Richard Wightman Fox, this time in
the *Christian Century,* wrote that "As a thinker and writer Lasch has as-
tonishing and to my mind unique gifts"; he thought only Garry Wills
could compare to Lasch in his ability to "rove so compellingly from
history to the present and from culture to politics." Some critics took
the book's publication as a chance to review and assess Lasch's entire
trajectory; "Up from Narcissism" was the title of Mary Eberstadt's review in *Commentary.* Wilson Carey McWilliams, writing in *Commonweal,* called Lasch an "academic Orwell," who had for some three de-

32. CL, TOH, 36, 425, 65-66.
33. CL to Jean Bethke Elshtain, TL, 22 Aug 1991; 7b:9.

cades been "taking the measure of America's political soul, writing with grace and learning and relentless integrity." *The True and Only Heaven,* he wrote, was a "grand, rambling book — or even several books."[34]

The book made a larger splash than *The Minimal Self* had — including more than sixty reviews — but not the waves that *Narcissism* had generated; instead, it seemed to sink right to the bottom, a heavy stone. Although most reviewers expressed admiration for Lasch's learning and passion, many took exception to both his historical argument and his political message. The historian James Kloppenberg, while professing admiration for "Lasch's ascetic religiosity," found Lasch's populist lineage to be thinly connected at best and judged his "denunciation of liberal reformers as traitors to the populist cause" to be "overly simplified." The literary critic Mark Edmunson, writing in *Raritan,* reduced the book to "little more than a bitter screed against liberal yuppies, a highbrow version of what the popular press has been working at sporadically over the past decade." "One feels no joy in the writing," Edmundson confessed; "The only passages in this book that hum with any kind of life — even if it's a rather repugnant life — are passages of denunciation in which Lasch chains himself up on the rock and derides the objects of his current rancor." In a lengthy, smug review in the *New York Review of Books* Louis Menand scolded Lasch for ignoring the fact that "liberalism does have a moral conception of the self, which is expressed in the political doctrine of rights." And however Lasch might interpret the civil rights movement, Menand continued, white populists had certainly not distinguished themselves by prosecuting the long battle for social justice. Liberalism had. There was such a thing as "progress," Menand countered, thanks largely to the flawed but committed devotees to cardinal liberal ideals. Menand's variety of liberal defense reflected once more the very complacency that had driven Lasch to write the book. That Lasch might have been trying to make such defenses of liberalism the starting point for argument — not the end of it — was apparently unthinkable, at least in some quar-

---

34. Jean Bethke Elshtain, "A Modern Jeremiad," *First Things* 12 (April 1991), 54; Fox, "Lasching Liberalism," *Christian Century,* 11 March 1992, 277; Mary Eberstadt, "Up from Narcissism," *Commentary* (July 1991), 62-64; Wilson Carey McWilliams, "Back to the Future," *Commonweal,* 19 April 1991, 264.

ters. His hope that an overwhelmingly liberal upper-middle-class readership might be willing to consider the need of a new starting point for thinking about the state of the nation — for thinking, indeed, about what a more true, thoroughgoing form of "progress" might require — died quickly.[35]

Conservatives registered their own variety of complaint. Bruce Frohnen in the *National Review* dismissed Lasch for his contention that capitalism "is the source of all the world's ills" (though Lasch himself had attempted to head off this criticism by summarizing his stance at the book's end: "Capitalism cannot be absolved, but neither can it be made to carry the whole indictment of modern culture"). Roger Kimball, in the *New Criterion,* thought Lasch the ex-Marxist had made the petty-bourgeoisie the "modest surrogate" of the "proletariat as hero of world history." He found Lasch's analysis of the culture of the new class unpersuasive, and the virtues Lasch associated with the populists were, he claimed, not in fact their "special property." Lasch, said Kimball, was "Addicted to what the historian Herbert Butterfield described as 'the luxury and pleasing sensuousness of moral indignation.'" Far from "a triumph of hope," Lasch's worldview was merely "an unusually dour form of populist pessimism."[36]

The book, in sum, exposed as clearly as any book Lasch had written the difficulties inherent in arguing across ideological boundaries and beyond shared fundamental sympathies, however sophisticated the attempt. Two magazines in which Lasch still had a presence, *Tikkun* and *Salmagundi,* featured forums on *True and Only Heaven* that only underscored this point. In *Tikkun,* both Michael Kazin and Barbara Ehrenreich found troubling — and emblematic — Lasch's failure to make racism a central point of his narrative on populism and liberalism. Had he done so, they implied, it would have forced him to abandon his entire framework. Obviously, it was easier for him to ignore rather than admit into his narrative the simple fact that "blacks have feared close-knit white communities" for good reason,

35. James Kloppenberg, review of TOH in *Journal of American History* 78:4 (March 1992), 1402; Mark Edmundson, "Lasch's Jeremiad," *Raritan* 11:2 (Fall 1991), 139, 138, 139; Louis Menand, "Man of the People," *New York Review of Books,* 11 April 1991, 43.

36. Bruce Frohnen, "Causes without Rebels," *National Review,* 18 March 1991, 60; CL, TOH, 528; Roger Kimball, "The Disaffected Populist: Christopher Lasch on Progress," *New Criterion* 9:7 (March 1991), 13, 16.

as Kazin, a historian of populism, put it. In *Salmagundi,* Jeffrey Issac made a similar charge against Lasch but expanded it to include his failure to appreciate achievements not just in race relations but in modern civilization itself. Had Lasch not permitted his advocacy for "neo-calvinist populism" to so distort his vision, Isaac suggested, he surely would have had to grant that the gains of modernity in general discredited his insistent promotion of populism.[37]

Lasch's replies to these critics revealed an acute level of frustration and discouragement, the yield of decades of earnest, exhausting polemical warfare. Reviewing in the *Salmagundi* forum the book's reception on both the left and right, he charged that "both ideologies are now so rigid that new ideas make little impression on their adherents." Liberals, he wrote, are "single-mindedly obsessed with racism and ideological fanaticism" to the neglect of a more open, free, and probing consideration of competing emphases and concerns. Cozily ensconced behind the walls of their own upper-middle-class fortress, the "civilized minority," when confronted with perspectives such as his, was capable only of responding with an "inquisitional style of public discourse, which is designed to put opponents on the defensive — to saddle them with the burden of proving their sincere and undying abhorrence of racism." Lasch had of course opened himself up to such attacks by refusing to genuflect before such pieties. He was not trying to win allies so much as incite debate, and he hoped at least to be granted the premise that "the improvement of racial attitudes is one of the few positive developments of recent decades." These improvements, he thought, should have made it possible to begin to move beyond the categories of interpretation and areas of concern approved by the liberal consensus. But instead of good argument, he received shrill accusations and condescension (he noted that the *Progressive's* reviewer considered the book to have "insidiously 'fascistic appeal'"). Lasch was now clearly someone to keep at arm's length — a quirky and dangerous fellow who at some point along the way had taken a frightening wrong turn.[38]

37. Michael Kazin, "The People, Right and Wrong," *Tikkun* 6:5 (1991), 39; Jeffrey Isaac, "On Christopher Lasch," *Salmagundi* 93 (Winter 1992), 92.

38. CL, "A Reply to Jeffrey Isaac," *Salmagundi* 93 (Winter 1992), 98, 109; CL, "No Respect: A Reply to Michael Kazin and Barbara Ehrenreich, *Tikkun* 6:5 (1991), 43; CL, "A Reply to Jeffrey Isaac," 108.

The *New Oxford Review,* doing what it could to make up for the bi-polar negativity, featured two essays on *True and Only Heaven* in 1991. In the first, Edward R. F. Sheehan described it as "an erudite po-lemic," and after a sympathetic discussion asked whether there ex-isted "another social critic abroad today whose mind is so well-nourished, whose sight extends quite so far?" Historian Alexander O. Lian noted at the year's end that "polite indifference" had character-ized the response of most reviewers of the book. Menand, in particu-lar, "could not resist the temptation to make Lasch out to be a dis-gruntled crank, erudite but essentially wrongheaded." Lian saw things differently. "A Jeremiah," wrote Lian, "is not a loon on the street corner spitting out aspersions; he is a supreme moralist at-tempting to give people the courage to change their ways." Lasch had "striven for nothing less than a full understanding of the modern con-dition," and his achievement, over the course of thirty years, was enor-mous. "*The True and Only Heaven,* like all of Lasch's writings, is writ-ten with a hope steeled with the knowledge of the past," Lian wrote. "It is a jeremiad meant to inspire even as it condemns. It proclaims that the future is not fixed, that it is up to us."[39]

In the end, Lasch once more proved largely unable to move people (or at least professional critics) who weren't already with him. Of course, few political writers of any variety have been able to achieve such conversions in any but small numbers, and Lasch may have been as successful as any twentieth-century American political writer at making the committed think twice. But critical recalcitrance alone did not make full sense of *True and Only Heaven*'s disappointing re-ception, Lasch's arguments to the contrary notwithstanding. The book revealed tendencies long embedded in his thinking and style that had diminished the prospects of political and intellectual hopes that were nobly but painfully high.

At a literary level, Lasch's attempt to piece together a series of es-says like a string of pearls did not always end up as the stunning neck-lace he hoped it would. He had employed this form in all of his books since *Haven,* and it had worked most effectively in *Narcissism,* due to the book's concise argument and topical organization. But *True and*

39. Edward R. F. Sheehan, "Shocks of Recognition," *New Oxford Review,* May 1991, 27, 30; Alexander O. Lian, "Christopher Lasch, a Loon on the Street Cor-ner?" *New Oxford Review,* December 1991, 8, 9, 13.

Only Heaven's shape and spirit were just the opposite, and the series of vignettes seemed nearly endless (132, to be exact). If the complexity of discussion was at each turn rich, Lasch tended to indulge in discourses and debates in which he clearly delighted but which could lead the uninitiated to lose the thread of the (already complex) broader argument. His unyielding impulse to solidify his case with nit-picking argument could at times become its enemy.

The argument in *True and Only Heaven* was itself dependent on Lasch's appropriation of the neo-traditionalism that had characterized intellectual history and other work in the social sciences in the 1980s, and its power lay precisely in his ability to collect a group of thinkers and movements who bore striking resemblances and connections into a coherent group and allow them to speak. It was a far more sophisticated attempt to do what he had also done in *The New Radicalism* — use a group of writers to reveal a tendency and render a culture — but it was open to the same charge in 1991 as it was in 1965: to what extent did the coherence Lasch forged actually exist outside of his argument? Was the coherence such that it deserved to be classified as a historical "tradition"? If so, what, precisely, did "tradition" mean, and, more importantly, what was its usefulness, especially in terms of politics? The unity of Lasch's populism, if not exactly imposed, at times had a momentary, episodic feel. One could just as easily imagine most of these thinkers and activists assembled into diverging and distinct oppositional traditions — traditions, it is worth saying, that would be understood by those within them as being more definitive than the one Lasch saw. Reinhold Niebuhr would certainly have been a theological heretic to Jonathan Edwards. The mid-nineteenth-century Catholic writer and former transcendentalist Orestes Brownson, a keen presence in the book, would surely have attempted to savage the pragmatism of William James; he had already dismissed Emerson.

Instead, Lasch seemed to be wishing a convergence upon the thinkers and movements he highlighted as a way to shore up the foundations of his own worldview, which required their differences to be submerged. The fact, for instance, that in summarizing the "heart of Calvinist theology" he could lay out a series of its theological "insights" that did not include the incarnation and resurrection of Christ signaled a telling weakness in his analytic and political vision, one that led him to misrepresent, in some fashion, history itself. His interpretation of the success of the civil rights movement is worth considering in this regard, too. Convinced that it was their connection to the producer ethic, their roots in local life, and their participation in the "prophetic tradition" that had made them capable of such heroism, he neglected to consider that the actions and attitudes he was applauding may have been shaped and motivated by particular beliefs and practices he opted not to discuss — including, for example, their affirmation of a personal God who was charging them to be reconciled as equals to other persons, regardless of race, class, gender, legal status, or past offenses. "Class" and "tradition" — Lasch's two favored analytic categories at this point — needed to be understood in the light of such particular beliefs and practices, and it was emblematic of Lasch's analytical style that he considered his own broader and more general categories to be of greater significance than their own.[40]

The philosophic, theological, and political differences Lasch chose not to raise as he unfolded the populist tradition deserved amplification and debate, not merely for accuracy's sake but for the sake of his argument. Had he allowed this level of questioning, it might have forced him to answer with more clarity and force the kinds of questions his cultural criticism and prescription in *The True and Only Heaven* begged, including: What was the epistemic basis for his ontological framework? How should we — and he insisted we must — "draw a distinction between right and wrong"? Was it a God he was positing with his definition of justice ("a conviction that the wicked will suffer, that wrongs will be made right, that the underlying order of things will not be flouted with impunity")? Had he probed more deeply the philosophic questions his own argument was raising and the answers upon which his vision depended, he might have better fashioned it to meet the challenge he was assigning it.[41]

40. CL, TOH, 240. It's worth noting that in *Culture and Society* (so important as a model for Lasch in TOH), Williams expressly put his thinkers in *tension* with one another — Burke against Cobbett, Mill at odds with Coleridge — and *then* inventively and insightfully sought resolution in fashioning his own tradition of social criticism. Lasch was more intent on diffusing such tensions, which gave his "tradition" a sense of coherence, but one that did not run very deep. Given the high place he gave to tensions in discerning the nature of the good life, it seems likely that given more years Lasch would have developed a more complex and believable narrative along these lines.

41. CL, TOH, 34, 81.

Which was, by any measure, formidable. In effect, he turned to populism to recast mainstream American political and intellectual life, to supply it with more satisfying visions of morality, of citizenship, of justice, of being itself. Lasch was calling, as he had been since the start of his career, for a national renewal of what can only be understood to be religious proportions — a profound renewal of heart and mind across the nation. It is no wonder that to so many of his critics Lasch's embrace of populism was less than impressive. However these critics regarded the ideals he was advocating and attempting to embody — and many rejected them flatly — they sensed, rightly, that this "populist tradition" was inadequate to perform the enormous task Lasch was charging it to do.

Perhaps this is why *The True and Only Heaven,* beautiful, rich, nuanced study that it is, seems hopeful and hopeless at once. In his remarkably fruitful personal and intellectual explorations leading up to its publication Lasch had come to an understanding of human history that was profound and arresting, and seemed actually to have had transformative effects on his life. He knew that he was closer than he had ever been to articulating in a compelling and satisfying way a philosophic and historical basis for his long-held ideals and hopes. But the book's latent hopelessness seemed bound up in a tacit acknowledgment that what he was offering simply was not enough. It was, merely, the *best* he had to offer — the best any Americans could claim for the high and urgent end history required of them. On the one hand, his turning to an actual, substantial, historical tradition was the strength of his proposal: it did not require cultural transformation to emerge from nowhere, but rather was grounded in a realism that looked hard at history for help in the present. On the other hand, the sweeping nature of his critique of American culture and society demanded more than what the populist tradition, as he presented it, had on offer.

Lasch, to put it even more basically, needed either a university or a church, and probably both, to make possible the culture-transforming changes he was seeking. He needed, that is, a more full, complete, robust tradition than "populism," one that extended well beyond the public political sphere to touch and form mind and heart. He, strangely, had in his proposal provided fully for neither mind nor heart. Instead, with gritty, desperate intelligence, he had searched out and fashioned what amounted to merely a political tradition — one

349

touched by a powerful religious sensibility, to be sure, but one that nonetheless lacked adequate institutional embodiment for the vast political and cultural transformation for which he was calling.

But perhaps this judgment misses the mark. Perhaps, given Lasch's primary audience, his populist proposal was not void of a serious intellectual dimension but was actually an audacious attempt to *convert* the existing American intelligentsia to populism — a call to reverse, in sweeping fashion, the smug and narrow conceptions of populism that Hofstadter and other intellectuals had in the twentieth century done so much to plant, and in the process turn the university itself in a populist direction. This was, to say the least, asking a lot. It was, though, the only kind of task Lasch seemed to know how to take up.

And what of the churchly side of his hope? Lasch was certainly calling Americans back to "religion." But he was not calling them to ecclesial communities. In turning toward religion in *True and Only Heaven,* Lasch was implicitly acknowledging the deeper philosophic and communal reach of religious traditions, which could provide the epistemic and political basis necessary for redeeming the good within existing social and political frameworks while at the same time making necessary criticisms of them. But he did not go so far as to urge a renewal of actual churches, even of the liberal Protestant churches that might have been amenable to his religiously infused but quite opaque ontology. Instead, he gave more ultimacy to political rather than ecclesiastical tradition. And so Lasch's populism, absent a more comprehensive, transcending system of thought and practice, lacked both the philosophic and institutional reach that might have more successfully delivered him from a dualizing analysis that seemed unable to assimilate varying dimensions of diverging cultural and political traditions within a larger corrective framework. The polarities of his historical analysis — populists *versus* progressives — forced him, in sum, to make the new class less than it was and make populism more than it was. This was no recipe for persuasion.[42]

But this does not quite do justice to Lasch and his proposal either, for in failing to provide for the place of ecclesial communities in cultivating and maintaining the populist tradition, Lasch was not quite rejecting the place of church, any more than he had been rejecting the

42. CL, TOH, 527.

existing universities. Instead, as perhaps the archetype of a cultural Protestant in late-twentieth-century American intellectual life, he was turning not to the existing ecclesial bodies for churches, but instead turning to the nation to be the church. His America was the nation that had descended from the Puritans, they who had sought to make the sacred ethos of the church that of the state, wrapping all of life in a blanket of covenantal norms while at the same time preserving a fruitful distance between the two. Lasch himself had no church but the nation, and he stood prophetically near to it, its preaching, priestly elder, charging it to live up to the standards he was convinced were at its core, to cherish the covenant that bound it together to pursue its vision of life. He imagined a spiritually charged individuality nestled within the broader national fellowship, the one and the many held together in a bond that would make the common life potentially rich, if at the same time alertly combative. *This* was the real promise of American life.[43]

Crucially, in this book he was revealing himself to be not just a cultural Protestant but a spiritual Protestant, whose understanding of the shape of life itself was inspired by the Protestant ideals and dynamics reflected in two of his keywords, tension and limits. For Lasch, like Protestants of a similar mettle, life in this age did not permit the full, final realization of human hope and desire, the achievement of abiding, harmonic wholeness. He had earlier refused the possibility of such resolution under Freudian premises; he continued to refuse it when thinking out of a more self-consciously Calvinist frame. Still, he did not live in despair. If prophecy follows failure, failure itself can be defined only after ideals have been embraced. For Lasch, life was nothing if not a striving for these distant, defining ideals, and it required an accompanying refusal to acquiesce in denial, whether the denial of limits or the denial of despair. It was certainly no easy way to live. But it was for him the *only* way to live.

This vision of life that he so fully embraced made it hard for peo-

---

43. In a 1988 debate in *Tikkun*, Lasch defended, for instance, "the significance of the American jeremiad," which lay in its attempt "to revive the sense of lofty purpose attributed to the founders. The point of the jeremiad, which was once the dominant form of social criticism in America . . . was to remind Americans of a specific historical event, the founding covenant by which they had agreed, for all time, to submit to an unusually demanding set of ethical standards and to be judged accordingly." CL, "A Response to Fisher," *Tikkun* 3:6 (1988), 73.

ple to live with Lasch, or at least with his writing. To offer such high promise without also the promise of fulfillment — to offer it, in fact, with the promise of failure — this was a vision most Americans of his day could live without. Having embraced the painful tensions Christians believe to inhere in the present age and yet rejected the reality of a personal God who extends healing intimacy to broken humans, Lasch was left with less than his Calvinist forbears possessed to console the disappointed, let alone with which to legitimate their utopian longings. Oddly enough, Lasch's premise of a fundamental, implacable tension between the actual and the possible — so pivotal and powerful in his vision — may have been easier to accept for his readers when he had rooted it in the psychoanalytic tradition, which underwrote the necessary tension with clinical authority and whose scientism closed the door to transcendent flights of religious hope. But by redefining psychoanalysis in the 1980s as a smaller dimension of a more encompassing religious understanding of the world, and in fact rooting his own politics in that understanding, Lasch lost the authority of science and thus increased the likelihood of an easy dismissal.

By *The True and Only Heaven* Lasch, it turns out, had worked himself back to an embrace of the broad ontological and metaphysical frame that had at the dawn of the modern world called into existence the distinctly modern political ideologies that he so complexly reflected: the notions of order and fallenness that oriented the right; the paramount worth of the individual that ignited the liberals; the eschatological restlessness that called to life the left. Over the course of three fracturing decades, Lasch held these diverging yet coalescing impulses together.

But he longed for something more. The deep, necessary cultural and political changes of the kind he had for decades been calling for, Lasch declared in *True and Only Heaven,* "can come only from movements fired with religious purpose and a lofty conception of life." What he had yet to show was that his moral vision was capable of bringing such movements into being.[44]

44. CL, TOH, 80.

CHAPTER THIRTEEN

I Love Life

As for my character, whatever virtues I may possess clearly derive from the good example of my parents and my attempts, not always successful, to live up to it. I always think of you as on the run, or more precisely on a trot from one place to another, without much time to lose, and this strikes me as the best way of dealing with life that I can imagine.

Christopher Lasch to
Zora Schaupp Lasch, 7 February 1980[1]

I love life, and have tried to live with intensity, passion, and integrity; but for this very reason I am prepared to leave it if called to do so.

Christopher Lasch to Dr. Phil Rubin, 3 June 1993[2]

Zora Schaupp Lasch died in September 1982 at the age of eighty-four, after struggling with a variety of illnesses for several years. Writing to her during one of her hospital stays in 1980, Kit had quoted a passage from her old friend John Dewey: "There is sound sense in the old pagan notion that gratitude is the root of all virtue." He then expressed his own gratitude "for all the good things you have given me over the years, including whatever good health and strength of char-

1. CL to ZL, TL, 7 February 1980, 5:18.
2. CL to Phil Rubin, TLS, 3 June 1993, 7c:1.

acter I now enjoy." Zora, never failing to express gratitude of her own for letters from Kit, replied affectionately, "Your delightful letter of yesterday with its tasteful gobbles of John Dewey leavening the solid sense of C. Lasch was greatly enjoyed by your parents. Said parents, by the way, have never ceased to thank whatever powers there be for the stupendous miracle of your conception and birth."[3]

After Zora's passing, this gratitude continued to express itself in the ongoing political conversation between father and son, still going strong in its sixth decade. As Kit's thinking became more heterodox, Robert's defense of contemporary liberalism hardened. "Since he is the son of a liberal, he has a low opinion of liberalism," Robert had explained to a gathering of senior citizens in a talk he gave on *The Culture of Narcissism* soon after its publication. "My consolation is that he did not go to the right, as so many sons do, but, most satisfactorily, to the left. I also take comfort in the fact that he deals as roughly with radicals as he does with liberals." Such comfort would turn a bit cooler as Kit's moral conservatism took its religious turn. "You must be back from your vacation by now," Robert wrote in June of 1990, "the biggest question about it being: 'What in God's name were you doing at a conference on theology?'" Kit dodged that one, but the line of questioning persisted. After he had read *True and Only Heaven* his father wrote, "I am glad to hear you have not gone conservative as the *Times* reviewer suggested. I admit I wondered a bit as I read some passages." He was, he confessed, "less than entranced by the fine points of Carlyle's thought, and by Jonathan Edwards trying to punch his way out of a theological paper bag."[4]

It wasn't just Lasch's notions of morality that were shifting in the eighties — his job was too. In 1985 he agreed to become chair of Rochester's history department, just as the university was christening Eugene Genovese a "University Professor" now with only, in Lasch's words, a "tenuous connection" to the department. Lasch told a friend that "this arrangement amounts in effect to a divorce," which had left him hoping that perhaps "we can now rebuild in a serious way." For someone without a history of executive leadership or even ambition (in this sense Lasch was the anti-Genovese), his assuming of the de-

3. CL to ZL, TL, 7 February 1980, 5:18; ZL to CL, ALS, 14 February 1980, 5:18.

4. Ms. of Robert Lasch's review of *The Culture of Narcissism* for "The Forum," 13 pp, 6:17; RL to CL, TL, 16 June 1990, 7b:6; RL to CL, TL, 26 January 1991, 7b:12.

partmental leadership was an unusual move, but one motivated by his persisting reformist impulses, and more particularly by the desire to make good, after many discouraging and lonely years, on the original vision that had brought him to Rochester. "There's nothing more demoralizing than making a big move and then discovering that the new situation is worse than the one you left," Lasch wrote Jean Elshtain in 1989. "That happened to me when I came to Rochester back in 1970." He had soon discovered that his friendship with Genovese "would not survive close exposure, that his grandiose visions of building a whole new department had already come to nothing, and that I had made a big mistake, in short, in leaving a fairly congenial if somewhat dull position for this nightmare." It had been "hard going," he recalled, and "a long time" had passed "before I managed to reconcile myself to the difficulties I had brought down on myself."[5]

Lasch, the critic of the professional classes, had lived much of his life within the quintessential challenge of trying to make a home in a place where there had been none before, and where there easily could be none tomorrow. A high level of mobility had been his way of life before his arrival in Rochester in his late thirties, having divided his childhood between Omaha and Chicago, followed by stints in Massachusetts (twice), New York City, Chicago (twice), and Iowa City — not to mention summers in Vermont during the 1970s, where the Lasches owned a summer house. For their part, his parents, upon Kit's matriculation at Harvard, had moved to St. Louis and then retired in Arizona. So it is no wonder that, for one who had written so much over the years about the need for roots and a sense of place, Lasch's writing exuded little affection for any particular place, or even a connection to one. But by the 1980s Rochester had become home to the family, even if the image of Christopher Lasch as an "upstate New Yorker" does not quite fit. If Lasch was himself an upper-middle-class American through and through, defined mainly by his work, he devoted himself, as he did in any sphere that he touched, to trying to align the arena of work more closely to his sense of the necessary. In chairing the history department, he would not only direct his energies toward improving the department and the university; he would also seek to challenge

5. CL to Milton Cantor, TLS, 1 July 1985, 7:13; CL to Jean Bethke Elshtain, TL, 10 January 1989, 7c:15.

through his leadership of Rochester's history program the historical profession's conception of its identity and its purpose.

Which were, respectively, smugly self-flattering and seriously misguided, in his opinion. He had long believed historians in the United States to be ill-trained; in a 1962 review, just after receiving his Ph.D., he had criticized "the very concept of 'research'" — one of the profession's most sacred of sacred cows — as "subversive of real intellectual activity." The average card-carrying AHA historian, he wrote, worked in "slavish imitation of the natural sciences," reverently participating in the "cult of 'objectivity.'" In doing so, this average historian was complicit in the "abdication of his own obligation to make what he, like the sociologists, refers to with embarrassment as 'value judgments.'" Unsurprisingly, given this state of affairs, the historical profession was failing to attract the best students, lacking as it did any "direct and forthright appeal to the life of the mind." "What universities offer, and General Electric can't," he reminded, "is the chance to get paid for thinking."[6]

Accepting the chairmanship gave him an unprecedented opportunity to challenge the established notion of what historians considered thinking — which, of course, he had already spent two decades doing, and which was his primary point of appeal to the students drawn to study with him. In attempting now to enact a chastened version of the old vision he and Genovese had shared, Marxist history was replaced by a more modest call for a politically engaged form of "cultural history." His challenge would be to attract to the department historians with this same vocational vision — scholars with the desire not just to write for the guild but also for the wider public, and who were devoted to teaching as well.

Having been granted one new position in American history and one in European history at the beginning of his term, he went to work. "Since we'll always remain a small department and therefore can't do everything, we've decided to make a name for ourselves in cultural history," he wrote to Richard Wightman Fox in a (failed) recruitment pitch, "and also to play a part in a critical reevaluation of the historical discipline, thereby making some modest contribution to the develop-

6. CL, review of *The Education of Historians in the United States,* by Dexter Perkins, John L. Snell, and the Committee on Graduate Education of the American Historical Association," *St. Louis Post-Dispatch,* 15 May 1962, 2B.

ment of a more vocational (as opposed to careerist) definition of professionalism — on which the prospects for democracy may now largely depend." He sounded just as earnest when trying to land Jackson Lears, whose *No Place of Grace: Antimodernism and the Transformation of American Life,* published in 1981, had made a favorable impression on him, and who had recently co-edited with Fox a collection of essays called *The Culture of Consumption.* "I know perfectly well that without students I wouldn't have much of anything to write in the first place," he wrote Lears, turning his emphasis to the priority of teaching. "It's the job of having to explain things clearly to people who can't be expected to take much for granted . . . that makes it possible for us to get our ideas straightened out and makes writing, indeed, almost easy after the preliminary labor of teaching. I doubt whether there's any good substitute for this kind of activity." Lears did not come, but Lasch's vision persisted. He hoped the history faculty would see their undergraduate instruction as "a kind of embryonic form of the broader audience we hope to reach," he wrote a few years later to younger colleague.[7]

All of this was no mere sales pitch. Despite his periodic complaints about it, Lasch conceived of teaching as central to his calling. In a letter she wrote to Rochester's provost when Lasch was entertaining offers at other universities in the aftermath of *Narcissism,* history department secretary Jean M. DeGroat testified that although Lasch was a "very hard marker," his "harsh marking does not deter students from signing up for his courses for which he almost unanimously receives high praise in the History Council evaluations." The word regarding Lasch was very favorable in Christopher Shannon's circle; though he matriculated at Rochester in 1983 as an English major, among Shannon's friends "everyone was talking about this guy Lasch," he recalls. He enrolled in Lasch's survey course on recent American history, and "those lectures blew me away": "I was hooked from then on in." It was not that Lasch was a "doing-jumping-jacks kind of star professor." It was, rather, "the force of the ideas," Lasch's practice of doing "a quick historiographical essay, if you will, in speech," of the sort that would leave Shannon thinking, "Things are

7. CL to Richard Wightman Fox, TL, 30 April 1985, 7:14; CL to Jackson Lears, TLS, 23 August 1985, 7:15; CL to Celia Applegate, TL, n.d. (spring of 1988), 7:20 (this was apparently a draft).

just completely different than the way I thought they were." It was "historiography as intellectual history," he adds: *"that's* what made history come alive for me — a dramatic account of how ideas really shape our understanding of history." Shannon remained an English major but took many classes with Lasch, continued on to take several graduate courses with him after completing his bachelor's degree, and then went on to take a Ph.D. in American Studies at Yale.[8]

Lasch, Jean DeGroat wrote in 1979, sees "teaching as his profession and works hard at it." As an example of Lasch's ethic she described his practice of responding to papers, whether graduate or undergraduate, with (often) multiple pages of typewritten comments; indeed, this was Lasch's style whether he was working with a student, refereeing a manuscript for a journal, or just critiquing the work of a friend. If his criticisms could cut and his taste for quibbling could wear thin, he could also elicit unusually grateful replies. Robert Bellah's comments in response to Lasch's review of *Habits of the Heart* give some sense of this: "You have done that which an author most hopes for. You understood us better than we understood ourselves." One of his later graduate students, Catherine E. Kelly, gave witness to Lasch's teacherly engagement with his students' writing when commending him for a teaching award:

> Each paper was promptly returned with several pages of typed, single-spaced comments that confronted the questions at the heart of the paper, revealed the unarticulated assumptions upon which the paper rested, and suggested any number of possible avenues for expansion or revision. At first I was awed by the sweep of his learning. . . . Only later did I realize how carefully crafted these responses were, both in tone and detail. Critiquing the paper I had written, pointing toward the paper I might someday write, his comments testified at once to my potential, to the dedication and precision our craft demands, and to the public, political obligations of all thinkers and writers.[9]

8. Jean M. DeGroat to Richard O'Brien, TLS, 31 May 1979, 5:4; interview with Christopher Shannon, 18 August 2007.

9. Jean M. DeGroat to Richard O'Brien, TLS, 31 May 1979, 5:4; CL to Leon Fink, TL, 28 September 1976, 4:6; Robert N. Bellah to CL, TLS, 10 June 1985, 7:13; Catherine E. Kelly to David W. Beach, TLS, 17 November 1993, 7c:14.

This letter highlights the epistolary side of Lasch's relationship to his students, which he usually maintained in a careful, respectful, and even expansive way. But his personal relationships with his students were not always easy, especially for students not accustomed to what Rochelle Gurstein calls his high "sense of propriety." Lasch certainly had a disdain for what Americans of a certain class and age knew as "familiarity." Gurstein, one of his graduate students in the 1980s, recalls the slow shift toward a closer teacher-student relationship signaled by the close of his letters. At first it was "'Yours, Christopher Lasch,' and then 'Yours, C.L,' and then 'yrs, C. L.,' and then *finally* 'yrs, Kit.' And at that point, when he would say 'Kit,' you knew — or at least it seemed to me — that you had reached a new level of intimacy." But even then, as she was finishing her course work, she "didn't feel comfortable calling him 'Kit.'" "He was," as she puts it, "very formal with his students."[10]

It was for many of his students all part of the larger enigma of Lasch. "There's a way," Gurstein recalls "in which that passion in his writing made you think he'd be that kind of person when you met him, but he wasn't at all. Once you got to know him, he was urbane and spirited — but not passionate, like his writing." The warmth — sometimes fiery warmth — of Lasch the writer came out of a public silence and a private cauldron that few knew firsthand; Gurstein summarizes for many in stating that he was "very reserved in all ways." Dominic Aquila notes how this reserve affected his teaching. "When I watched him lecture undergraduates, it was riveting. He was very well prepared, all the time, and in fact I would write every word of his lectures"; the whole semester would add up to a "seamless narrative." But "the graduate seminars were a different story," he recounts. "He was so worried that his influence would be too great that he overcompensated for that, and wound up saying very little." The sharp-eyed, highly vocal social critic, it turns out, led very, very quiet seminars. "Lasch was so retiring in graduate seminars," Aquila notes, "that you really had to look hard if you were looking for cues to what he thought." Gurstein recalls that "He would ask a question, and if no one answered, we could sit there for what felt like five minutes." These periods of silence could occur in any kind of personal meeting. Whether in the seminar room, in his office, or on the telephone, "he

10. Interview with Rochelle Gurstein, 20 July 2007.

didn't care to make you comfortable. It's not that he was rude or any-thing — he was reserved."[11]

What to a group or a person might have felt like dead silence seemed in Lasch's own mind to be a more thoughtful, fruitful form of silence. "If you were with him in his office talking about your work or some idea, he really was thinking, and he obviously didn't feel like he would have to say, 'Well, let me think about that,'" Gurstein recalls, noting that he felt no need to fill the silences with commonplaces — an impulse (or lack thereof) that characterized all aspects of his life. In fact, the big, sweeping ideas of his oeuvre — "narcissism," "prog-ress," "hope" — might be understood as careful interpolations into the looming silences of American public life, emerging only after very deliberate consideration. But his reserve was also, it seems, part of a social style, a guarding of observation and wit for a certain kind of company and place. Quietly communal, he was in the right setting "gregarious," Aquila says, "just absolutely charming as a conversa-tionalist — he never put on airs." He and Aquila would range from his-tory to baseball, which Lasch followed devotedly. Casey Blake recalls that "once I was invited to his house and had a sense of his life there, it became evident to me that that that's where he was most comfortable. And it was in that setting that he was first of all personally forthcom-ing, even in an emotional way, but also more comfortable talking about ideas."[12]

What to his friends and admiring students were forgivable foibles and odd idiosyncrasies were alienating (or at least disenchanting) qualities to others. He drew many graduate students, Gurstein says, but some who had hoped to study with him switched quickly to other mentors: "He wasn't cruel to students, but he was a very tough critic." Bradley J. Gundlach, who was in Rochester from 1985 to 1995 and who began his dissertation with Lasch (he died just before Gundlach com-pleted it), recalls musing "about how as a student of cultural critics I was learning to be a dyspeptic. But," he adds, "I have to say that Lasch

11. Interview with Rochelle Gurstein, 20 July 2007; interview with Casey Nel-son Blake, 18 June 2007; interview with Dominic Aquila, 5 January 2007. Gerald Graff recalls that "Having a conversation with him could be painful because there would be these long silences on the phone . . . he wouldn't take his turn in conver-sation." Interview with Gerald Graff, 2 August 2001.

12. Interview with Rochelle Gurstein, 20 July 2007; interview with Dominic Aquila, 5 January 2007; interview with Casey Nelson Blake, 18 June 2007.

did not seem bilious at all. So I wonder how much of all of this was my own internal struggle." Lasch's unwillingness to aggressively direct his students' intellectual and professional development was easy to "misread as neglect," says Gundlach. "I think Lasch did his work, looked out for opportunities for his students, but otherwise figured that they had to make their own way."[13]

Gundlach's description of the larger graduate student scene at Rochester gives some sense of the difficulties Lasch was facing in trying to cultivate a climate more conducive for "thinking." "It seemed," Gundlach recalls, "that most of the grad students I knew (History, English, Anthropology) had a miserable attitude toward Rochester." The graduate student newsletter was called *Gradgrind,* and it reinforced precisely the wrong tendencies, Gundlach thought. "I remember thinking what ingrates these people were — getting tuition waivers and often a stipend to boot, having the privilege of advanced study, etc., but whining away in this newsletter about how unfairly they were treated." Notwithstanding this climate, or perhaps because of it, Lasch did move quickly toward the aims that had motivated him to accept the chairmanship, and he achieved some early success. The history department, he wrote his dean in 1987, two years into his tenure, had begun a graduate student publication. The department had initiated weekly talks, a colloquium series, and a revision of the undergraduate curriculum, and had made three appointments. In extending the offer of an appointment to Celia Applegate in 1988 he spelled out his vision for the department, stressing that among the faculty there would be "equality of ranks in every important respect." He was, he wrote, "eager to do everything possible to combat the atomizing effects of contemporary academic life." It was his sense that the "department will flourish only insofar as we can generate a core of common concerns that extend not only to teaching and departmental administration but finally to our scholarship as well." To order themselves by rank would certainly militate against this aim. He saw fostering "common concerns" as one of his most urgent tasks as chair.[14]

13. Interview with Rochelle Gurstein, 20 July 2007; Bradley J. Gundlach, email to author, 15 March 2002.

14. Bradley J. Gundlach, email to author, 15 March 2002; CL to Jack Kampmeir, TLS, 5 January 1987, 7:18; CL to Celia Applegate, TL, n.d. (spring of 1988), 7:20 (this was apparently a draft).

He knew, though, that to fashion a department according to his own ideals and concerns would be to stamp his students with his own reputation within the discipline — not necessarily the best way to prepare them for professional success. Casey Blake, who was working on his dissertation and teaching at Reed College in 1985, wrote Lasch with his own concerns upon hearing of the department's plans to teach students to do "historiographical and synthetic writing." "Such an emphasis may leave its graduates in a difficult position on the job market," he thought. "Some of my senior colleagues here, for example, are all too eager to inform me that they consider what Richard [Fox] and I do to be a 'sophisticated form of journalism,' as opposed to 'real' history." Acutely aware of his own imminent plunge into the market, he confessed that "I fear that University of Rochester Ph.D.s will constantly run up against this kind of idiotic prejudice against scholarship for a non-specialist public. But that's not necessarily a good reason for not pursuing such an idea."[15]

Compromises and frustration came quickly to cloud Lasch's early hopes. On the cusp of losing two senior Europeanists to Rutgers in 1989, Kit wrote in frustration to his father that "no matter how hard I work at this job, we seem to fall farther and farther behind. . . . We've made several first-rate appointments since I became chairman, but nothing seems to do any good." In the fall of 1992, his last as chair, he wrote to Richard Aslin, a dean in the College of Arts and Sciences, that he was concerned that their underfunded state would lead to "the slow death of our graduate program." "We are already doing all the things that exist elsewhere mostly in the form of endless exhortations to involve undergraduates in research, to expose them to directed study with faculty members . . . to teach them how to write, to make them feel part of the life of the discipline, etc." He had, he wrote in frustration, "spent the better part of my career in the service of the proposition that scholarship can contribute to the general conversation of a democratic society — hence my interest in teaching undergraduates as well as graduate students." Since coming to the university he had attempted "to institutionalize this ideal in our department," but it had been "an uphill fight, because it goes against the grain of massive trends toward over-specialization of scholarship." Still, he felt that they had achieved a measure of success, which had "the practical ad-

15. Casey Nelson Blake to CL, TLS, 7 May 1985, 7:13.

vantage of making our department widely recognized as unique among other departments of history. We've managed to sustain a commitment to a public conversation about ideas without any loss of scholarly rigor." To his father he was more candid. "Everyone is hot and bothered about something at all times," he wrote in the spring of 1991. "There is a permanent sense of grievance; the whole institution is built on the politics of envy. It's a poisonous atmosphere, ruinous to any serious pursuit of learning."[16]

This particular letter marked his first wave of revulsion against what would become the byword of the academy in the 1990s. "Political correctness" and all that it represented reflected a shift in climate that manifested itself in legal and structural reforms within countless colleges and universities. The university, it turns out, had become the most hospitable place for a vigorous form of post-1960s progressivism, now underpinned by a poststructuralist understanding of power and authority that sought above all a more extensive liberation of any believed to have been oppressed, whether due to race, class, ethnicity, religion, or gender.

Lasch did not welcome this long-coming surge with joy; indeed, he had been shuddering at its inevitable arrival for some time. "The worst people of all," he tried to explain to his father that spring of 1991, "are in the humanities, which have been overtaken by refugees of the New Left who are opposed on principle to any form of structure, coherence, authority, or intellectual rigor — all these things being part of the cultural imperialism long visited on the world by dead white European males." In this new climate, the old political categories and assumptions required revision. "Liberals, it seems, are no longer capable of providing a vigorous defense of liberal education; for that we have to turn to the right. This is an exaggeration, but not much of an exaggeration." "The academic left want to talk about 'race, class, and gender,'" he said. "The inclusion of class in this list, incidentally, is only a rhetorical concession to the old lefties . . . race and 'gender' exhaust the list of their interests." His conclusion: "What a mess!"[17]

He took up many of these matters that winter in an article (a later

16. CL to RL, TLS, 7 December 1989, 7b:2; CL to Richard Aslin, TLS, 21 November 1992, 7b:15; CL to RL, TLS, 25 March 1991, 7b:12.
17. CL to RL, TLS, 25 March 1991, 7b:12.

version of which was included in *The Revolt of the Elites*) in *Salmagun-di,* in which he tried to turn attention once more to the relationship of class to democracy. "While liberals and conservatives debate the revision of an allegedly 'Eurocentric' curriculum, policies designed to promote racial diversity and 'sensitivity,' and the theoretical implications of poststructuralism, the fundamental issue goes unnoticed: the abandonment of the historical mission of American education, the democratization of liberal culture." Citing studies that showed that "a liberal education (such as it is) has become the prerogative of the rich," Lasch urged academics to actually make "contact with the world outside the academy." And he also urged them to reestablish contact with their own past, for the sake of those beyond the academy. "An insidious double standard, masking as tolerance, denies those minorities the fruits of the victory they struggled so long to achieve: access to the world's culture." Far from being "oppressive," Lasch wrote, "the world's culture" had always proven to be liberating in a sense far more profound than the variety of liberation the new progressivism offered. Turning to the example of the former slave turned author, orator, and politician, Frederick Douglass, Lasch contended that Douglass's very traditional "studies did not diminish his commitment to freedom or his identification with his own people, but they enabled him to speak on their behalf, and not only to speak but to order 'interesting thoughts' that would otherwise have remained confused, incoherent, baffled, and abortive."[18]

But at just the point in his argument that Lasch seemed to be heading directly into the arms of a long-awaiting right, he veered to his more comfortable perch somewhere between, or beyond, the two sides. His traditionalist impulses ended up being softened by his own epistemological uneasiness, which kept him from embracing, for instance, the rearguard defense of foundationalism that conservative critics like Roger Kimball of the *New Criterion* were making. Lasch did not think that foundationalism, the view that knowledge rests on what philosophers call "noninferential knowledge" or "justified belief," could any longer be defended; but neither could he follow the radical skeptics who believed certainty of any kind to be automatically deserving of suspicion. Instead, he, joining legions of American historians and other academics, affirmed something of a middle ground:

18. CL, RE, 177, 182, 185, 186.

the reality of a knowable world, the knowledge of which was provisional but real and sourced in both human traditions and scientific discovery.[19]

In short, in the epistemological debates that were both elemental to and symptomatic of the culture wars, Lasch landed on "some version of pragmatism," as he put it to one of his graduate students in the summer of 1990. In the introduction to *The Revolt of the Elites* he would laud "the revival of pragmatism as an object of historical and philosophical study"; indeed, it was "one of the few bright spots in an otherwise dismal picture," a development that might provide "some hope of a way out of the academic impasse." If Lasch did indeed warm to pragmatism through the 1980s, though, he did not seize on it with a convert's enthusiasm. He was drawn, in Casey Blake's words, to pragmatism's "simultaneous critique of idealism and objectivism," as well as its preoccupation with "the civic." But Dewey, for instance, never became, senses Blake, the "kind of compelling figure who grabbed him viscerally the way that Niebuhr did, or for that matter Adorno did." In his admiring discussion of William James in *The True and Only Heaven,* Lasch seemed most drawn to pragmatism for its promise of promoting — and above all preserving — "a philosophy of wonder." Lasch's quotation of James's friend Benjamin Paul Blood captures well the point of its appeal to him: pragmatism was, per Blood, "'the only method of philosophizing' that was possible for those who had attained the understanding that 'wonder and not smirking reason is the final word for all creatures and creators alike.'"[20]

In the midst of this academic, intellectual, and spiritual turmoil Lasch as department chair was surely not becoming a middle man-

19. On foundationalism, see Richard Fumerton, "Foundationalist Theories of Epistemic Justification," *The Stanford Encyclopedia of Philosophy,* Spring 2006 edition, ed. Edward N. Zalta, at http://plato.Stanford.edu/archives/spr2006/entries/justep-foundational/, for a historical overview that brings the debates up to the present. For a book-length statement of the new consensus within the historical profession, see Joyce Appleby, Lynn Hunt, and Margaret Jacob, *Telling the Truth about History* (New York: Norton, 1995). My thanks to Robert Frazier and Keith Martel for fielding questions about foundationalism.

20. CL to Everett Akam, TLS, 1 August 1990, 7b:4; CL, RE, 14; interview with Casey Nelson Blake, 18 June 2007; CL, TOH, 286. Casey Blake notes the influence of Robert B. Westbrook, the biographer of John Dewey who joined the Rochester history faculty in 1986, on Lasch's turn toward pragmatism. See Westbrook's *John Dewey and American Life* (Ithaca: Cornell University Press, 1991).

ager; if anything, assuming the position of chair only sharpened his already harsh take on the state of the university. In a piercing 1988 review in *Academe* of former Harvard President Derek Bok's *Higher Learning,* he delivered a whole book's worth of insight in a single page. "The fair-minded reader," he wrote, "will find little to disagree with in these presidential ruminations; and that of course, is precisely the trouble." Bok "calls for 'innovation,' 'constructive change,' 'progress,' 'improvement,' 'experimentation,' and bold measures to meet the 'new challenges' facing higher education," observed Lasch, "but these phrases cannot conceal the substantive vacuum that yawns beneath this presidential rhetoric," including the "assumption that 'adequate measures' of cognitive development will somehow provide us with the secret of educational success." Still, Lasch suspected that even university presidents "must retain at least a dim memory of the experiences that drew them into the world of ideas in the first place," and proceeded to give a glimpse of how he remembered his own awakening to the pursuit of higher learning:

> The humiliating discovery that one did not measure up to one's master — the only sense in which "measurement" is relevant to a discussion of learning — coincided with the discovery of unsuspected, unused capacities within oneself. The conjunction of these jolts brought about a kind of conversion: an unnerving reassessment of what one had been content to be, a new and thrilling idea of what one might become. Henceforth one could not hope to sink back into the old comfortable world in which unexamined patterns of belief provided security. The masters had seen to that. One had no choice but to follow the road marked out by their example, even when the fallibility of their own authority became increasingly evident.[21]

This passionate world, one buzzing with ideas, friendships, and causes, was what he had wished to foster through his work from the beginning. Addressing the Rochester history department class of 1993 at the small graduation ceremony they annually held for their majors, Lasch remarked that it was common to hear faculty complain about

21. CL, review of *Higher Learning,* by Derek Bok, in *Academe* 74:1 (January-February 1988), 46.

the students' lack of interest in "the big theoretical nondebates" that were being foisted upon them — "the nonissues of structuralism and poststructuralism and deconstruction and postmodernism and Marx and Lacan and Foucault." For his own part, he had come to take this lack of interest as, in the main, a sign of health: "Much of their education in the humanities, to the extent that it is dominated by lifeless disputation of this kind, strikes them, quite properly, as irrelevant and boring." These students were not, he insisted, slackers or dullards simply interested in professional training: "It's just that they want to hear some plain words of truth. Like all students, they're looking for moral wisdom and intellectual guidance about the things that matter, which can be summarized in a single phrase as the conduct of life. They want to grow up." Instead they were being forced to ingest matter from both their professors and the broader culture that nourished them very little. "What I sense in my best students," he concluded, "is better described as a cold-eyed realism that is by no means incompatible with warm hearts." In such students he found hope.[22]

But after more than thirty years, he ended up finding little hope within the university he knew, apart from whatever good happened personally between faculty and students. The institution itself seemed utterly resistant to the nurture of the ideals, habits, and qualities he found necessary for his own life and that he believed to be necessary to the country. After failing in the fall of 1991 to arouse support in the department for a series of colloquia on the end of the cold war, he wondered to his father whether it was "their dislike of general ideas or simply the inexorable pressure of the daily grind that makes it so hard to engage academics in an intellectual discussion? Probably both. Whatever it is, the designation of the university as a place of higher learning seems increasingly inappropriate."[23]

*　　*　　*

In his writing, Lasch's immediate aim, as he absorbed the reception of *The True and Only Heaven,* was to continue to develop his thinking about the history, nature, and necessity of democracy. His next book,

---

22. CL, "The Baby Boomers: Here Today, Gone Tomorrow," *New Oxford Review,* September 1993, 8, 10.

23. CL to RL, TLS, 15 September 1991, 7b:12.

the posthumously published *The Revolt of the Elites and the Betrayal of Democracy,* would end up following *The True and Only Heaven* in the same fashion *The Minimal Self* had followed *Narcissism:* by responding more fully to the earlier book's critics and developing a corrective deepening of his earlier formulations. The very fact that this pattern was necessary is witness of both the restless originality of Lasch's thinking and his inability, or unwillingness, to engage the public in a way that would ensure a less than perplexing response.

Jeffrey Issac, in his exchange with Lasch in *Salmagundi* on *The True and Only Heaven,* had confessed to being troubled by what he called "the absence of serious attention to the problem of democracy in the book," a perception owing mainly, one suspects, to Lasch's failure to applaud enthusiastically the liberal pluralistic achievement. Such a reading of that book startled Lasch into writing a follow-up volume on democracy. "I would have thought that was its principal subject," he wrote Norton editor Edwin Barber, "but if reviewers . . . can miss it so easily, it might make sense to write a book in which democracy was more explicitly the focus." Lasch's retort to Isaac pointed toward his own apparently perplexing conception of democracy: "Tolerance is a fine thing, but it is only the beginning of democracy, not its destination. In our time, democracy is more seriously threatened by indifference rather than by intolerance or superstition." Lasch understood democracy not as a governing structure but as a form of civilization: historically contingent, sociologically complex, and distinguished by a finite nexus of spiritual, intellectual, and material qualities that must be guarded and maintained for it to prosper. Absent these qualities, democracy would devolve into something lower — or be taken over by something else.[24]

Democratic freedom, to put it differently, had a positive definition in addition to its negative one. Freedom required not simply autonomous and tolerant individuals but rather self-reliant, strong citizens who could join together in a way that would ensure protection of the weak, honor the dignity of each, and seek the preservation and conservation of the variegated gifts that make the good life possible. "If the civil rights movement was a triumph for democracy," wrote

24. Jeffrey Isaac, "On Christopher Lasch," *Salmagundi* 93 (Winter 1992), 91; CL to Edwin Barber, TLS, 17 January 1992, 7b:24; CL, "A Reply to Jeffrey Isaac," *Salmagundi* 93 (Winter 1992), 107.

Lasch in *The Revolt of the Elites,* "it was because King's leadership transformed a degraded people into active, self-respecting citizens, who achieved a new dignity in the course of defending their constitutional rights." Democracy on this view was "not an end in itself." It was in service of the higher end of helping people to live good lives. Any particular political project, whatever its constituting documents may profess, was prone, in real historical time, to fail. Serious, radical renewal was thus a constant need. Democracy, Lasch wrote, "has to be judged by its success in producing serious goods, superior works of arts and learning, a superior type of character" — this was the way nineteenth-century democrats like Whitman had seen things, he noted. Democracy, like all good things, was a tenuous achievement, in need of vigilant, jealous defense.[25]

If the winding complexity of his attempt in *The True and Only Heaven* to provide what amounted to a new intellectual history of American democracy had caused readers to miss his defense of it, then he clearly needed to take up the task of definition. As he did so, what became clearer than ever was the extent to which the common conception of Lasch as an idealistic critic in tow to unrealistic hopes missed the mark, especially in his last two decades of writing. Lasch's work possessed little of the sweetness that usually fuels such idealism. To the extent that he was a visionary, he cast his vision in a goading way, pushing readers from behind rather than drawing them from ahead. Some writers help readers to see that which they have never seen before; others help them to see the familiar in a new light. Lasch belonged to the latter class. He was most fundamentally and usefully not an architect, but a critic. His mature writing issued in a call not to the possible but to the necessary, and if Americans now judged the necessary to be unrealistic, idealistic, or undesirable, this was not the measure of the necessity of his judgments. On the moral and political matters he was compelled to confront, he could not let such responses guide his writing.

The sudden end of the cold war and the equally sudden flurry of banter and debate about the prospect, once more, of the "end of history" had reopened space for discussion of the nature and state of democracy. Much of this conversation centered on the idea of "civil society," the social sphere that comes between individuals and the state,

25. CL, RE, 83, 86.

and that includes families, schools, neighborhoods, churches, and the like — what Peter Berger and Richard John Neuhaus have termed "mediating structures." The career of one political aide in the Reagan and Bush administrations, Don E. Eberly, is poignantly reflective of this *glasnost* moment. After working in the early part of his career as a liaison between the Reagan White House and American evangelicals, Eberly embarked in the 1990s on a reforming course centered on the construction of agencies, programs, and movements designed to strengthen civil society. He gathered thinkers together across political boundaries for various endeavors (including, for example, leading liberal communitarians William Galston and Amitai Etzioni, as well as more left-conservatives like activist David Blankenhorn and Jean Bethke Elshtain), launched a think tank in Pennsylvania, founded the National Fatherhood Initiative, and wrote and edited several books on the topic, including *The Civil Society Reader* and *Building a Healthy Culture: Strategies for an American Renaissance,* both of which carried essays by thinkers and critics across the political spectrum. It was a moment when a reformer's keen instincts sensed the sudden emergence of renewed political opportunity.

Of course, the fact that both liberals and conservatives perceived the need for foundational domestic reform was itself a sign that America had not survived the cold war in an entirely healthy state. More hopefully, it was a sign that the culture wars might at some level lead to constructive collaboration. But the conversation came to a jarring halt with the September 11, 2001, attacks on the United States. Suddenly the old world order was present again, as threatening and disruptive as ever, and reformist energies were either dissipated or directed elsewhere. Eberly, after having been appointed deputy-director of George W. Bush's signature domestic program, the Office of Faith-Based and Community Initiatives, shortly after the invasion of Iraq accepted a post there, working toward the fostering of its domestic stability.[26]

26. Peter L. Berger and Richard John Neuhaus, *To Empower People: The Role of Mediating Structures in Public Policy* (Washington, D.C.: American Enterprise Institute Press, 1977). For a biographical sketch of Eberly, see http://www.media-transparency.org/personprofile.php?personID=124. His books include *The Civil Society Reader: The Classic Essays* (Lanham, Md.: Rowman & Littlefield, 2000); *America's Promise: Civil Society and the Renewal of American Culture* (Lanham, Md.: Rowman & Littlefield, 1998); *Building a Healthy Culture: Strategies for an American*

Had he lived, Lasch would hardy have been surprised by any of these developments, including the September 11 attacks — he had, ten years before, warned that the continued expansion of the global market would "generate more and more violent movements of insurrection and terrorism against the West, and bring about a deterioration of the world's political climate as threatening as the deterioration of its physical climate." If before he died he had seen the end of the cold war as an opportunity, it was along the lines of a last-ditch opportunity, an unexpected chance to clear heads before the next crisis hit, whether domestic or international. "The Gulf War provided a momentary distraction," he wrote in *Telos* in 1991, "but it ended all too quickly; and although we can look forward to further distractions of this kind, it will be impossible, in the long run, to avoid the day of reckoning." The triumph of progressive liberalism had been bound up in the denial of the authority inherent in "limits." The pervading reality of that authority would inevitably assert itself in unforgiving ways.[27]

But a populist conception of the policy was still a live historical option, he believed, and in *The Revolt of the Elites* he continued to urge it upon his readers as an alternative to the anarchy of liberal capitalist individualism. Populism, he wrote, "stands for things most Americans still believe in and are willing to defend," however submerged those beliefs might be beneath the glitter and gigantism of the market and state. What populism needed was articulate expression, and so he continued to refine his case. Against those who had argued that "populism" was merely an ideological haven for racially intolerant, ignorant provincials, Lasch began to recover and define a kind of populist cosmopolitanism — or, better, he tried to nurture a vision of what John Fea has termed "cosmopolitan rootedness": a way of participating in the republic of letters that prizes and guards first of all the actual republic. This required that he first deconstruct the self-image of those who fancied themselves the true cosmopolitans. In the lead es-

Renaissance (Grand Rapids: Eerdmans, 2001). The titles of Eberly's most recent books suggest the shifts in ethos and focus of the post-9/11 world: *The Rise of Global Civil Society: Building Nations and Communities from the Bottom Up* (New York: Encounter Books, 2008) and *Liberate and Leave: Fatal Flaws in the Early Strategy for Postwar Iraq* (Osceola, Wisc.: Zenith Press, 2009).

27. CL, TOH, 23; CL, "Liberalism and Civic Virtue," *Telos* 88 (Summer 1991), 58, 59.

say in the book and the one from which he drew his title, Lasch reversed Jose Ortega y Gasset's warning of an earlier threat to western civilization, "the revolt of the masses," and proposed that the qualities Ortega feared in "the masses" were actually, after another half-century of liberal capitalism, more likely to be those of the privileged, the winners in the rise of democracy. Whereas democracy's health required a rooted loyalty to particular places, the new elites were "international rather than regional, national, or local. They have more in common with their counterparts in Brussels or Hong Kong than with the masses of Americans not yet plugged into the network of global communications." Confident of their own unprecedented liberality of spirit and vision, the contemporary elites actually failed to meet many of the civic standards of their much-disdained predecessors, the old bourgeois, the aristocrats. "The talented retain many of the vices of aristocracy without its virtues. Their snobbery lacks any acknowledgment of reciprocal obligations between the favored few and the multitude. Although they are full of 'compassion' for the poor, they cannot be said to subscribe to a theory of noblesse oblige, which would imply a willingness to make a direct and personal contribution to the public good." Under the aegis of this peculiar combination of power and irresponsibility, particular communities, traditions, and families could not last long. Democracy was premised on a rough but real measure of economic equality, but America's elites were little troubled by its diminishing presence in their own nation. "Many of them have ceased to think of themselves as Americans in any important sense, implicated in America's destiny for better or worse. Their ties to an international culture of work and leisure — of business, entertainment, information, and 'information retrieval' — make many of them deeply indifferent to the prospect of American national decline."[28]

Such upper-middle-class cosmopolitanism was of course the true provincialism, a species more dangerous than the variety the despised lower-middle class might possess. Against this faux cosmopolitanism Lasch proposed a vision of citizenship rooted in loyalty to place and kin yet also informed, enriched, and instructed, in a dialectical man-

28. CL, "Liberalism and Civic Virtue," 67; John Fea, "The Way of Improvement Leads Home: Philip Vickers Fithian's Rural Enlightenment," *Journal of American History* 90:2 (September 2003), 490; CL, RE, 35, 44, 45.

ner, by the fruits of high culture. "Those who welcome cultural fragmentation in the name of pluralism," he wrote in 1991 in a *New Republic* review of Elizabeth Fox-Genovese's *Feminism without Illusions,* "have lost the sense of 'twoness,' as W. E. B. Du Bois called it, that formerly shaped writers attempting to navigate between the subcultures in which they had been raised and the world culture they had acquired through education. Loyal at once to their own people and to the 'republic of letters,' writers like Du Bois knew that this painful tension between the particular and the universal, between popular culture and high culture, furnished a source of creative energy." The liberationist project of the elites, premised on the need to free "the imprisoned self," he noted in a *Commonweal* review a few months later, had turned out to yield simply a "detached, formless, free-floating self — a self without prejudices, without any background at all, without a point of view of its own that is put at risk by exposure to others." *Narcissism,* clearly, was still alive. What both that book and the actual condition called for, he wrote, a decade on, was "home culture":

> Unless people start life with a culture of their own, exposure to other cultures will seldom enhance their moral or even aesthetic awareness. Without home culture, as it used to be called — a background of firmly held standards and beliefs — people will encounter the "other" merely as consumers of impressions and sensations, as cultural shoppers in pursuit of the latest novelties. It is important for people to measure their own values against others and to run the risk of changing their minds; but exposure to others will do them very little good if they have no minds to risk. New perspectives presuppose a pre-existing point of view.[29]

Here Lasch was hedging in two different directions, in ways that the nation's public language still accommodated but that left his meaning more obscure than might have been helpful. What he was referring to as "culture" in this section was on the one hand a simple and ordinary use of the anthropological meaning of the term: a presumably neutral referral to a "way of life." But in fact Lasch did not accept such a definition. No "ways of life" were neutral to him, and he contin-

29. CL, "Beyond Sentimentalism," *New Republic,* 18 February 1991, 60; "Here's Mud in Your Eye," *Commonweal,* 17 May 1991, 337, 338.

ued to follow Philip Rieff in claiming that "the heart of any culture . . . lies in its 'interdictions,'" as he in 1991 put it in *Salmagundi:* the "willingness to uphold public standards and to enforce them." In all aspects of American life he detected a shift away from this possibility of true culture, a collusion of intellectual and economic history that had turned human beings into mere individuals, and weakened individuals at that. "The 'remissive' culture of liberalism,' he noted, "cannot be expected to survive indefinitely."[30]

Lasch's attempt in these essays to preserve some sense of cultural order (or, as he put it, following Rieff, "sacred order") seemed rhetorically to push him a remove or two away from the emphasis on locating an existing historical "tradition" that had been so central in *The True and Only Heaven* and toward a more outspoken, overstated apology for, above all, public argument, argument that was not quite so absorbed in the realities of historical and philosophic difference. He was shifting his rhetorical focus, in other words, from the authority of the past to the present authority of the democratic public, in what was also perhaps a reaction against the identity politics of the nineties, when waving one's flag had become an immediate conversation-stopper. Differences among "traditions" must not stop debate, he insisted, as he sharpened his own criticism of communitarianism, working hard to distinguish it from his still-developing understanding of populism. Whereas communitarianism focused on consensus and compassion, populism, he specified, was "judgmental," standing for "plain manners and plain, straightforward speech." It was not unity that mattered most, as communitarians emphasized, but rather "mutual respect," and only the willingness to argue, to contest boldly within the public sphere, made it possible for citizens to work together toward the rebuilding of something like a culture, in Rieff's sense. If "community" denoted easy consensus and tended toward the "privatization of morality," there was little chance that looming social, political, and ecological difficulties could be confronted in anything like a truly constructive manner.[31]

As he continued to refine and deepen his case for democratic populism, Lasch emphasized all the more the pivotal role of class, property, and the family. And in doing so he continued his longstanding

---

30. CL, "The Fragility of Liberalism," *Salmagundi* 92 (Fall 1991), 16.
31. CL, "The Fragility of Liberalism," 16; CL, RE, 106, 108.

argument against post-1960s feminism. In a 1991 essay in *Women and the Common Life: Love, Marriage, and Feminism,* a posthumously published book his daughter Elisabeth edited, he judged that "The feminist movement, far from civilizing corporate capitalism, has been corrupted by it. It has adopted mercantile habits of thought as its own." "Mainstream feminism," he concluded, "is now concerned almost exclusively with a single goal — to 'empower' women to enter business and the professions on an equal footing with men." On his view, this did not bode well for democracy, much less men and women. The "real issue," he continued to insist, is "the segregation of home life and work life."[32]

Property figured centrally in this vision because it made possible "the democratic ideal of a population educated by practical experience and the exercise of citizenship." It was the *practice* of citizenship that made citizens — not a legal right conferred upon them. And such practices were premised on the qualities of mind and spirit that were nurtured through the caretaking that property demanded. This was not, though, simple agrarianism. "Populism, as I understand it, was never an exclusively agrarian ideology," he insisted. It envisioned a nation "not just of farmers but of artisans and tradesmen as well," and understood that "town and country are complementary," so long as the reality of neighborhoods and decent work remained. One of his most basic summaries was also one of his most compelling statements of his point of view: "Democracy works best when men and women do things for themselves, with the help of their friends and neighbors, instead of depending on the state."[33]

Lasch's varying influences and inclinations — republican, Tory, agrarian, progressive, Marxist, Puritan — ran though these final essays like fine thread. "Luxury is morally repugnant," he insisted, "and its incompatibility with democratic ideals . . . has been consistently recognized in the traditions that shape our political culture." It only followed that "a moral condemnation of great wealth must inform any defense of the free market, and that moral condemnation must be backed up with effective political action." Beyond this basic contention he was, in the face of the triumph of the "free market," structurally vague, for the time being. He intended to pursue a major study

32. CL, WCL, 117, 118, 119.
33. CL, RE, 74, 8, 9, 7-8.

on social class in America and had received a National Endowment for the Humanities grant to do so. But it was not to be.[34]

* * *

After a brief bout in February 1992 with a malignant tumor, which led to the removal of a kidney and the apparent elimination of the threat, Lasch turned his attention to his next book. The cancer had truly been a scare, he wrote a colleague, but "I'm beginning to feel like someone who got a lot of sympathy under a slightly false alarm."[35]

His reviews and essays continued at a steady pace, including a blast at Hillary Clinton published in *Harper's* the month before the 1992 presidential election; its sardonic title was "Hillary Clinton, Child Saver." A review of Clinton's legal career revealed her to be a leading advocate and agent of "the politicization of family life," warned Lasch; "her writings leave the unmistakable impression that it is the family that holds children back, the state that sets them free." "Her position amounts to a defense of bureaucracy disguised as a defense of individual autonomy" — making her an almost ideal type of the liberal intellectual he had been attacking for years. "I've been getting furiously indignant letters about my piece on Hillary Clinton," he wrote to his father at the end of September, "proving, if nothing else, that children's rights is not passé after all, as some of Hillary's gentler critics have argued."[36]

Despite his disdain for Hillary Clinton he was pleased that the Democrats had regained the White House. Elshtain recalled that Lasch was encouraged by Bill Clinton's talk of a "social covenant." But his hopeful assessment did not last long. When Kit wrote his father just after Clinton's inauguration he mentioned Clinton's "bumbling start," with its attempt to rifle through a policy on gays in the military and its loosening of abortion laws. The Democrats were "really the party of yuppies," and Clinton, true to form, had come "into office already obsessed with his 'place in the history books,' wanting to make a big splash, wanting to immortalize himself even before he's had a

34. CL, RE, 22.
35. CL to Richard Aslin, TLS, 18 March 1992, 7b:15.
36. CL, "Hillary Clinton, Child Saver," *Harper's*, October 1992, 75, 77, 78; CL to RL, TLS, 29 September 1992, 7b:21.

chance to compile a record of any sort. . . . As if 'history' were just a kind of protracted version of the publicity industry, and you could reserve a room just by phoning ahead with a little advance hype." "When I hear the word 'progressive,'" he wrote, "I reach, if not for my revolver, for my industrial-strength earmuffs."[37]

He mentioned in that letter that he had recently had another scare, this time linked to pain in his hips and lower back. The Lasches' family doctor had diagnosed it as cancer after looking at X-rays, but that verdict was reversed the next day by a group of specialists. Five months later the family doctor was proven right. Arriving home from Denmark, where he had given a series of lectures, Lasch, battling increasing pain in his hips and back since the previous fall, was finding sleep difficult. A return visit to the specialists ended with a diagnosis of metastatic cancer.[38]

In the face of this sudden turn, he wrote his father, he was

impressed . . . by the shallow technological optimism of the medical profession, its total lack of moral wisdom or ordinary human decency, its simple-minded obsession with the prolongation of life through any means (however degrading to the patient or expensive to the insurance companies), and its complete indifference to the traditional mission of medicine to provide comfort and relief.

He closed with a quiet, frightened admission: along with the battery of tests to which he was about to be subjected, he wrote, "My character is about to be tested too; who knows how it will stand up?"[39]

As it became apparent that his chances for recovery were low, Lasch became more and more focused on completing his book, and worked, with his daughter Elisabeth's steady aid, on fashioning many of his recently published essays and essays-in-progress into a coherent volume. Due to the cancer's rapid spread his pain was growing more and more severe, and he was receiving little relief from the drugs he was taking. He resisted the recommended chemotherapy, which, he had learned, tended not to work in metastatic cancers, and

37. Jean Bethke Elshtain, "The Life and Work of Christopher Lasch: An American Story," *Salmagundi* 106-107 (Spring-Summer 1995), 149; CL to RL, TLS, 30 January 1993, 7b:21.

38. CL to Henning Gutmann, TLS, 1 May 1993, 7b:18.

39. CL to RL, TLS, 11 May 1993, 7c:4.

which would certainly lead to the depletion of that which now mattered most to him: his strength. "My aim," he wrote to one doctor at the end of May, "is to live as normally as is possible or at least to continue as long as possible to do what I like most, which is writing and teaching (in that order)." He wondered if the doctor thought it would be possible for him to finish the book he had just begun, which he estimated he could complete in nine months. Was this an "utterly unrealistic expectation," he wished to know. His publisher, W. W. Norton, had agreed, despite his failing condition, to offer him a contract — "a big shot in the arm for me," he wrote — but he did not want to set his sights too high. The doctors reluctantly agreed to forego chemotherapy. He kept writing.[40]

Among his other writing, he wrote letters to doctors who persisted in pushing chemotherapy on him. "I despise the cowardly clinging to life, purely for the sake of life, that seems so deeply ingrained in the American temperament," he wrote to one stubborn specialist, just a little while later. He had written with biting poignancy five years earlier of the "womb-like dependence" into which moderns had descended in their aggressive efforts to resist pain, discomfort, and death — motivated, he thought, by "our long-time grudge against life." "If our aim is to make ourselves less dependent on nature and ultimately to provide ourselves with total security," he wrote, "we have no choice except to make ourselves totally dependent on machines." Nothing could be farther from his conception of a good life, even in death.[41]

By June he learned that the cancer had spread to the lymph glands and liver. "For the moment," he wrote a colleague, "my main object is to finish the book in question. Writing gives coherence and continuity to my life at a time when I am faced with serious threats to my peace of mind." He continued his heavy load of correspondence, and began to receive huge amounts of it himself as the word of his condition spread. Many friends and colleagues, spanning the course of his career, wrote words of appreciation and comfort. "Your subject is really the human condition, as you write about desire and its delusions and discontents," the historian John Patrick Diggins wrote. "But I do want to say . . . that I have always felt that you, Kit, are the Richard

40. CL to "Dr. Asbury," TLS, 29 May 1993, 7b:15.
41. CL to Phil Rubin, TLS, 3 June 1993, 7c:1; CL, "Engineering the Good Life: The Search for Perfection," *This World* 26 (Summer 1989), 16, 10, 16.

Hofstadter of our generation." "You've been most of all a moral presence," his Harvard tutor Donald Meyer wrote. "Most certainly, there are going to be intense studies over the next years of your whole trajectory that should flood the precincts with more of the fresh air and light you've already shed." A younger friend, Yale historian Jean-Christophe Agnew, voiced his "gratitude": "From the first time I read and was swept away by *The New Radicalism* to my most recent immersion in your extraordinary *True and Only Heaven,* I have never ceased to admire the originality, acuity, and honesty of your historical vision." Agnew was especially grateful for the "strong, affirmative sense of community that grows ever more visible throughout your work. This sense of alternative vision has been the most difficult, the most distressingly distant of ideals . . . and it is heartening to see that it need not be so, that it need not vanish as the price of a *critical* cultural historical perspective. For this and so many things I am grateful."[42]

After finishing the first draft of the manuscript in early October 1993, Lasch wrote Agnew that his letter had arrived "during a stint in the hospital and provided a much needed lift to my spirits. I can't begin to describe how much it meant to me." Struggling to keep up with the letters that were pouring in, Lasch had decided in August to send out a form letter to some fifty friends and acquaintances who had written, updating his situation and expressing his gratitude for their concern. When David F. Noble received his copy of it he replied that he was

> struck by the tone of surprise in your letter, at the expressions of support from your "steadfast" friends. You're only reaping what you've sown, Kit. From where I stand, you personify "steadfast" friendship. . . . Whatever help I can be to you now . . . it's only your due. If your eloquence and resolute independence of mind have been an inspiration to me, your continued support has been a great comfort. I can't see what you've gotten out of it, but it's been at times crucial and always precious to me.[43]

42. CL to Richard Aslin, TLS, 12 June 1993, 7b:15; CL to Margareta Aukin, TLS, 12 July 1993, 7b:15; John Patrick Diggins to CL, TLS, 19 July 1993, 7c:4; Donald B. Meyer to CL, TLS, 28 June 1993, 7c:4; Jean-Christophe Agnew to CL, ALS, 27 July 1993, 7b:15.

43. CL to Jean-Christophe Agnew, ALS, 4 November 1993, 7b:15; David F. Noble to CL, ALS, 29 August 1993, 7b:24.

Robert was forced to reckon with one of the most difficult lots anyone can face, the lot of a parent who has to say goodbye to a child. Remarried since 1986, he wrote four weeks before Kit's death that he and Iris were "getting to be almost regular church goers if you can call the Unitarians a church." But he was not a member, and in fact declared that he was becoming "more irreligious every year, especially when I compare your situation with mine at going on 87." A few weeks later, just days before Kit's Valentine's Day passing, Robert wrote his last letter to his son. "There is always a lot of talk at these Unitarian meetings of the purpose of life, based on the idea that there must be a purpose, a grand design, imposed by divine order." He thought this so much rubbish — people should discern their own purpose and pursue it "for its own merits rather than religious reasons," and added that Kit himself had done just that. "You have a staggering record of accomplishment in a worth-while calling, and do not need a divinely fashioned grand design to justify your life."[44]

Lasch was unable to reply, but in a sense his last book was his reply, a final reckoning with the secularist worldview of his parents and the professional class in which he had been reared, and with which he had pursued serious, consequential debate for more than four decades. Religion was the theme of the last part of *Revolt,* titled "The Dark Night of the Soul." "At its best psychoanalytic theory exposes the moral and existential dimension of mental conflict, but even then it cannot compete with religion," Lasch in one of the chapters wrote, as if concluding a long debate with himself. "Can psychoanalysis really do anything for people who suffer from an inner conviction of 'absolute unlovability'? Maybe religion is the answer after all. It is not at all clear, at any rate, that religion could do much worse." But even religion, he suggested, taking his thinking one step further in another essay, "serves only to clothe human purposes with a spurious air of sanctity" — unless "it rests on a disinterested love of being in general." His conclusion this time was strong: "God, not culture, is the only appropriate object of unconditional reverence and wonder."[45]

It was this impassioned search for a vista, this constant quest for light, that so marked his path in the end, leaving some racing after

44. RL to CL, TLS, 17 January 1994, 7b:21; RL to CL, TLS, 7 February 1994, 7b:21.

45. CL, RE, 211, 212, 228.

him and others, puzzled and tired, off to the side. Rochelle Gurstein was one who sought to keep up. She imagined, years after his passing, Lasch's life as the pursuit of "a dream," a dream of a rich and beautiful common life. As he pursued it he sought, in Gurstein's words, to "be open to things that have been forgotten, or to things that have been discredited," striving to move beyond all of the clutter and debris — "the stale debates, the commonplaces, that common wisdom that *all* of us are stuck in. That's what I took away from working with him," she says.[46]

This trail had led him toward the end of his life to write several essays on Gnosticism for the *New Oxford Review,* wading with vigor into a study of an ancient Christian heresy he thought might illumine the moment. It was an unprecedented foray for Lasch out of modern western history and into a more distant world, an attempt, as he put it, to "listen to voices from the past as participants in controversies that include our own time as well as theirs." What he heard led him to suggest that the Gnostic tendency to exalt knowledge and denounce the material world was now playing itself out in modern science's destructive reign, as it glorified human intelligence while approaching material reality in purely instrumental fashion. If this state of mind reflected the modern world's highest form of knowledge, what it badly needed, Lasch wrote, was "faith": a posture that "affirms the goodness of being, in spite of life's failure to conform to human expectations of happiness," and that makes possible "a joyful affirmation of the fitness of things." In his last essay on Gnosticism he left little doubt about the path he believed his contemporaries, whether self-consciously secular or religious, needed to take: "The only corrective to the ersatz religions of the New Age is to turn to the real thing."[47]

Had religion, then, by the end become central to Lasch's pursuit — indeed, its object — in a more creedal way? Or was he, finally, what Paul Elie calls a "secular postmodern pilgrim," one who is "not a believer himself, but a person who is attracted to belief, prone to it, often covetous of it in others, and who is brought to the threshold of belief

46. Interview with Rochelle Gurstein, 20 July 2007.
47. CL, "The Spirit of Modern Science," *New Oxford Review,* January-February 1991, 11; CL, "The New Age Movement: No Effort, No Truth, No Solutions," *New Oxford Review,* April 1991, 10, 13.

imaginatively through his reading"? No one seemed to know — perhaps not even he himself. "I certainly hadn't undergone some kind of religious conversion," he emphasized when asked in 1993 about his recent interest in religion. If Dale Vree could judge that Lasch "died a holy death," his colleague Robert Westbrook, one of Lasch's closest friends, would suggest that until the very end Lasch was, in his opinion, like Henry Adams of a century before, "deeply respectful of those possessed of religious convictions, regretful that he had none himself, and yet unable to muster the necessary faith to acquire them."[48]

"This is an outsider's perspective," Lasch had jotted down on a sheet in what appeared to be hastily written notes for a lecture on some religious theme, or perhaps for the introduction to a book he was then contemplating on religion. "Even before I took so rashly to writing about religion," he wrote on another sheet of paper, "it was an embarrassment to admit that I had none." He possessed no "institutional affiliation," and felt himself to be in a "state of suspended animation" or "suspended judgment" — an awkward and unfitting state to be in, for a person who was truly religious, he imagined, must surely have entered into an experience that was something like "falling in love."[49]

It was life itself that Lasch had come to love — life in a world that deals out disappointment and hope in uneven, unexpected ways, yet leaves the hopeful armed, as he wrote, with "a deep-seated trust in life that appears absurd to those who lack it." Reassured, through hours dark and bright, that "trust is never completely misplaced," the hopeful testify that "the underlying order of things is not flouted with impunity" — that even in the face of limits "the goodness of life" can be

---

48. Paul Elie, *The Life You Save May Be Your Own* (New York: Farrar, Straus, and Giroux, 2003), 435; Richard Wightman Fox, "An Interview with Christopher Lasch," *Intellectual Newsletter* 16 (1994), 13; Dale Vree, "Christopher Lasch: A Memoir," *New Oxford Review*, April 1994, 5; Robert Westbrook to author, 10 December 2000. Vree also claimed in this essay that Kit had once acknowledged to him that he was indeed a "believer" (4). In her *The Transformation of American Religion: The Story of a Late Twentieth Century Awakening* (New York: Oxford University Press, 2001) Amanda Porterfield terms Lasch, along with Robert Bellah, a "liberal rationalist" in the religious "awakening" at the end of the twentieth century, parallel to liberal rationalists such as the Protestant minister Charles Chauncey in the eighteenth century (229).

49. Lasch's jottings are in 41:6 (the folder is titled "'The Soul of Man under Secularism,' General") and 41:7 ("The Soul of Man under Secularism: Foreword").

confessed, celebrated, and, above all, acted on. "If progressive ideologies have dwindled down to a wistful hope against hope that things will somehow work out for the best, we need," he insisted, "to discover a more vigorous form of hope."[50]

*   *   *

When a television interviewer, shortly after *The True and Only Heaven* was published, asked Lasch to explain why he made so much of the difference between optimism and hope, Lasch answered eloquently and simply: hope requires a fundamental confidence in "the goodness of life and some kind of underlying justice in the universe, in spite of all the evidence to the contrary." Hope, he suggested, possesses a "religious quality." "Optimism" was far different, in his opinion, especially in its vapid contemporary varieties. "You mustn't confuse 'progress' with the true and only heaven," he said, gently.

His interviewer was still baffled. But his time was up and he needed to get off the air. He hurriedly put it to Lasch one last time: "Seriously — you remain hopeful, not optimistic?"

"Yes, yes," he replied, with a bemused grin. "That is my curious position."[51]

50. CL, TOH, 81, 530 529-30.
51. Lasch appeared on *Open Mind,* hosted by Richard Heffner, on 10 February 1991; the title of the week's program was "The Pursuit of Progress."

Epilogue

"**A** family's history," writes George Packer, "can be the history of an idea."

Cutting through time in strange, jagged ways, ideas of this kind exude mystery and radiate force. Packer, in quest of his own history, found himself trailing ideas that took him back into early-twentieth-century populism, through the "age of liberal decline" that was the sixties, and into the bewildering 1980s, where he as a young adult was forced to find his way. The ideas that marked this course, it became increasingly clear, had molded his life in ways that gave the lie to whatever notions of individuality his native liberalism had taught him.

Packer's recitation of these formative ideas, or "sentiments," as he calls them, has a catechetical quality. He found that he had inherited "a tendency to side with the underdog"; a belief that "society imposes mutual obligations from which no one is excused"; a confidence that "the rational mind, unconstrained by religion or tradition or authority, has the capacity to solve our problems"; a faith that "progress is possible, if not inevitable"; and last, and above all, the sense that "politics is lifeblood, an arena of moral choice, and more often than not, a place of pain." Any possibility of his achieving true freedom, Packer knew, would require a sharp, costly confrontation with this past, and with these ideas. Eventually this confrontation led him to write *Blood of the Liberals* — a memoir whose very title shows why the history of a family is never *simply* the history of an idea.[1]

---

1. George Packer, *Blood of the Liberals* (New York: Farrar, Straus, Giroux, 2000), 8, 9, 7.

Christopher Lasch and George Packer do not share a confessional style of writing, but they do share a history. Like Lasch, Packer after a childhood of liberal formation veered hard to the left, looking for transcending hope in a flattened world. Like Lasch, he sought to understand more fully the experience and possibilities of Christian faith, recognizing in it "something that can't be summoned on demand: vitality." Packer felt Lasch's visceral disgust with the conceits of the twentieth-century American upper-middle class; he acidly described "the face of American prosperity at the end of the twentieth century: racially tolerant, environmentally conscious, and determined to wall itself off from the low-paid countrymen who cut its grass and wait on its tables and look after its children." He knew that "the socialist idea" had, in real, historical time, died, but this was for him a chilling reality. "Taking that idea in its broadest sense, as a vision of human brotherhood and a just society, we are all the poorer for its death. With nothing to replace it, each of us is left alone to acquiesce in the given — or else find the will to answer in a new way the old question: What are we to do?" His generation did have the 1960s to look back to, he acknowledged. But that epoch had proven to be "more than anything else a mood: an extremely powerful mood," to be sure, "but like any mood, short-lived. It came along and changed forever the lives of those who lived through it," he wrote, his father having been a dean at Stanford during the student revolts. "But it didn't leave behind a viable worldview."[2]

Viability is the outworking of vitality — the longing for which sent Lasch, Packer, and innumerable others on long journeys into new worlds. In Lasch's quest, it was his own deeply formed love of America that was his compass, a love that was (as ever) torn between an ideal and a reality, and that left him shaking with the conviction that the two must be more perfectly joined, that past goods must be seized and safeguarded, that new goods must be turned up and tended. "Absorbing but transcending the old": with this taut political vision he tasked the left at the height of the 1960s. Few took it up, preferring either the static despair of absorbing or the vain grandiosity of transcending. Lasch, for his part, was left wondering where his companions had gone.

Many years later he would note that for Thomas Carlyle the French

2. Packer, *Blood of the Liberals,* 366, 357, 351, 387.

Revolution had not been an egregious mistake but rather a "missed opportunity to get to the bottom of things." There would be no such failure in his case, whatever his erstwhile friends might make of his course. Going back into the past and further into the present, now heading right, now shifting left, he went searching for good ground, for the point of insight, for the hint of truth that might breathe life into a desiccated world. When Robert Bellah and his team of sociologists published in 1985 their bellwether volume *Habits of the Heart: Individualism and Commitment in American Life* — a kind of sequel to *The Culture of Narcissism,* or perhaps just the next chapter of a long book that is still being written — Lasch, reviewing it, flew all of his variegated colors. "The fuller development of the individual is a legitimate social goal," he liberally stressed. Yet "the inner satisfactions associated with a more stable, rooted and orderly community life" are ineluctably bound up in this end, he more conservatively claimed. And thus, he wrote, the "implications" of the book are profoundly "radical," requiring not a compromising middle way but a renewed effort to keep in tension the two poles, seeking to forge the frame and foster the soul that might bring our hopes closer to our lives.[3]

This was not so much pastiche, this roving from left to right. It was, rather, a melding, Lasch moving deeper into learning and wisdom as the years passed, measuring what he knew against what he saw and felt. His acuity of vision and keenness of sensibility proved to be costly but illuminating. In the end it yielded a remarkable body of writing and a remarkable life. The ability to calibrate and meld history's welter of insights, dogma, and intuitions for communal ends: this is the soul of political wisdom, and it was in this most practical and necessary of activities that Lasch's great virtuosity lay. His gift to his readers and his students was his ability to help them see who they are and how, to put it simply, they might prosper.

It was his courageous willingness to give himself over to both the search for wisdom and the casting of judgment, public judgment, that made Christopher Lasch the magnetic figure he, for a time, was. Scores of students landed on his doorstep hoping to discover what he knew and how he saw, and left his care having written remarkable books, on technology and industry, on love and feminism, on race

3. CL, TOH, 227; CL, "The Search for Meaning in a Narcissistic Age," *In These Times* (June 26–July 9, 1985), 18, 19.

and democracy, on living and dying, on intimacy and reticence, on handicrafts and politics, and more. Many others were drawn along-side too, more distantly, students who never quite made it to his door-step but who found in his efforts the scent of promise, and the high hope of a better end.[4]

Of course, many never found much of this in Lasch at all — the oc-casional insight or striking phrase, perhaps, but not much more. Such is the way of the world, and especially this world, where our po-lite pluralism makes it harder and harder to listen, especially to voices emerging from a deep and thoughtful silence. But this did not keep Lasch from speaking. On this earth, he taught, we rise or fall based on what we hear and what we see. His unyielding attempt to force us to revisit our confident conclusions about our world and seize our one moment of responsibility for it surely reveals scholarship's lost prom-ise — and the promise of far, far more.

4. The following are some of the books that began as dissertations under Lasch: David F. Noble, *America by Design* (New York: Knopf, 1977); William Leach, *True Love and Perfect Union: The Feminist Reform of Sex and Society* (New York: Basic Books, 1980); Casey Nelson Blake, *Beloved Community: The Cultural Criticism of Randolph Bourne, Van Wyck Brooks, Waldo Frank, and Lewis Mumford* (Chapel Hill: University of North Carolina Press, 1990); Thomas R. Cole, *The Journey of Life: A Cultural History of Aging in America* (New York: Cambridge University Press, 1991); David L. Chappell, *Inside Agitators: White Southerners in the Civil Rights Movement* (Baltimore: Johns Hopkins University Press, 1994); Rochelle Gurstein, *The Repeal of Reticence: America's Cultural and Legal Struggles over Free Speech, Obscenity, Sex-ual Liberation, and Modern Art* (New York: Hill & Wang, 1996). Although she never technically studied with him, his daughter Elisabeth Lasch-Quinn was certainly his student in the truest sense. Her books include *Black Neighbors: Race and the Limits of Reform in the American Settlement House Movement, 1890-1945* (Chapel Hill: University of North Carolina Press, 1993); and *Race Experts: How Racial Eti-quette, Sensitivity Training, and New Age Therapy Hijacked the Civil Rights Revolu-tion* (New York: Norton, 2001).

Index